Personality and Organizations

LEA'S ORGANIZATION AND MANAGEMENT SERIES

Series Editors
Arthur P. Brief
Tulane University
James P. Walsh
University of Michigan
Associate Series Editors
P. Christopher Early
Indiana University
Sara L. Rynes
University of Iowa

Ashforth (Au.): *Role Transitions in Organizational Life: An Identity-Based Perspective.*

Bartunek (Au.): *Organizational and Educational Change: The Life and Role of a Change Agent Group.*

Beach (Ed.): *Image Theory: Theoretical and Empirical Foundations.*

Brett/Drasgow (Eds.): *The Psychology of Work: Theoretically Based Empirical Research.*

Darley/Messick/Tyler (Eds.): *Social Influences on Ethical Behavior in Organizations.*

Denison (Ed.): *Managing Organizational Change in Transition Economies.*

Earley/Gibson (Aus.): *Multinational Work Teams: A New Perspective.*

Garud/Karnoe (Eds.): *Path Dependence and Creation.*

Lant/Shapira (Eds.): *Organizational Cognition: Computation and Interpretation.*

Lord/Brown (Aus.): *Leadership Processes and Follower Self-Identity.*

Margolis/Walsh (Aus.): *People and Profits? The Search Between a Company's Social and Financial Performance.*

Pearce (Au.): *Organization and Management in the Embrace of the Government.*

Peterson/Mannix (Eds.): *Leading and Managing People in the Dynamic Organization.*

Riggio/Murphy/Pirozzolo (Eds.): *Multiple Intelligences and Leadership.*

Schneider/Smith (Eds.): *Personality and Organizations.*

Thompson/Levine/Messick (Eds.): *Shared Cognition in Organizations: The Management of Knowledge.*

For more information about LEA titles, please contact Lawrence Erlbaum Associates, Publishers, at www.erlbaum.com.

Personality and Organizations

Edited by

Benjamin Schneider
*University of Maryland and
Personnel Research Associates, Inc.*

D. Brent Smith
Rice University

LEA

LAWRENCE ERLBAUM ASSOCIATES, PUBLISHERS
2004   Mahwah, New Jersey   London

Lawrence Erlbaum Associates, Inc., Publishers
10 Industrial Avenue
Mahwah, NJ 07430
www.erlbaum.com

Cover design by Kathryn Houghtaling Lacey

Library of Congress Cataloging-in-Publication Data

Personality and organizations/edited by Benjamin Schneider, D. Brent Smith.
    p. cm.—(LEA's organization and management series)
    Includes bibliograpical references and indexes.
    ISBN 0-8058-3758-2 (paperback : alk paper)
    1. Personality and occupation.   I. Schneider, Benjamin, 1938- II. Smith, D. Brent, 1968- III. Series.

    BF698.9.O3P46 2004
    158.7–dc22   2003021746

Books published by Lawrence Erlbaum Associates are printed on acid-free paper, and their bindings are chosen for strength and durability.

Printed in the United States of America
10 9 8 7 6 5 4 3 2

For Lee and Tain, and Rhody and Sam whose personalities individually and collectively are such important lights in my life.

—Benjamin Schneider

For my wife, Shawn, and my parents, Ginger and Don, who so graciously tolerate my personality.

—Brent Smith

Contents

VI: CONCLUSIONS

Foreword

The past twenty-five years have been witness to celebration of all things organizational in organization and management research. Profound changes in both the global economy and information technology produced new organizational forms and pushed us to focus on competitiveness and wealth creation. To be sure, anyone who set foot in an organization knew that people matter, but our scholarly attention was diverted. We might even go so far as to say that individuals caught our attention only in times of failure. We are reminded of the University of Michigan hockey fans who stand up, point to the opposing goalie, and chant "It's all your fault... it's all your fault... it's all your fault!" whenever Michigan scores. People mattered most when we made person attributions for failure.

Schneider and Smith have done us all a great service. They pulled together a terrific collection of original essays to inform us about what has been happening in personality psychology over these 25 years and to show us how it all matters to life in organizations. Personality certainly plays a role in determining who is hired and fired. Moreover, we learn that personality contributes to all that happens during a person's tenure in the firm. Our understanding of work motivation, job attitudes and performance, teamwork, well-being, citizenship behavior, leadership, organizational culture, and more is all informed by personality. This book will do much to rekindle interest in a long-neglected and yet essential ingredient in understanding organizational behavior. We are privileged to publish it in our series.

James P. Walsh
University of Michigan

Arthur P. Brief
Tulane University

Preface

This book of original chapters is designed to fulfill a need for a contemporary treatment of human personality in work organizations. Currently, the study of personality, the application of personality theory, and the use of personality assessments in business and industry are experiencing a renaissance. A critical mass of knowledge related to personality in work organizations has developed over the last decade, and to our knowledge there is no book that attempts to synthesize this work across the broad domains of industrial and organizational psychology and organizational behavior.

It is only in the last decade or so that organizational scholars have begun to rediscover the usefulness of personality-based constructs for understanding phenomena central to the discipline. In recent years it is as if people who work in organizations have personalities again! Thus, while there has been continuing interest from a personnel selection vantage point in personality as a predictor of performance (Campbell, Dunnette, Lawler, & Weick, 1970; Clark & Clark, 1990; Roberts & Hogan, 2001), theory and research on the contributions of personality-related constructs to other human issues at work have been sparse. These other human issues, and the contributions a personality perspective might offer to the understanding of them, are the focus of this edited volume. We have asked scholars to address such diverse issues as teams (chap. 12), leadership (chap. 10), organizational climate and culture (chap. 13), organizational citizenship behavior (chap. 11), work motivation (chap. 9), stress (chap. 8), and job satisfaction (chap. 7) and tell us what we know about these topics from a personality perspective. In addition we present chapters on interactional psychology and work (chap. 4), personality and interests (chap. 6), some persistent measurement problems in personality assessment (chap. 5), and, of course, the relationship between personality and job performance—albeit from a person–situation perspective (chap. 3). There are also several overview chapters in the book, one providing a general survey of the landscape of personality theory and organizations (chap. 1), one presenting a view of the European perspective on contemporary issues in personality research relevant to organizations in Europe (chap. 2), and one on the origins of the title of the book (chap. 14).

This chapter, by Chris Argyris, presents his perspective on the zeitgeist existing in the middle to late 1950s with regard to the study of organizations and their human components. In 1957 he wrote a book, *Personality and Organization*, whose title we borrow for the present book. That book, along with others by McGregor (1960; *The Human Side of Enterprise*) and Likert (1961; *New Patterns of Management*) are central to the revolution that occurred at that time with regard to the study of organizations as human systems. Both Argyris' and McGregor's books focused on the adult personality, arguing that many if not most organizations treated workers as children rather than adults by ignoring their higher level (adult) needs.

In this volume we borrow the idea that personality plays out in many ways in organizations and not just as a correlate of task performance. That is, we believe and we think the chapters in the book support this belief, that personality in its many conceptualizations is a useful lens through which to shed understanding on the broadest array of contemporary topics in industrial and organizational psychology and organizational behavior.

REFERENCES

Argyris, C. (1957). *Personality and organization*. New York: Harper & Row.

Campbell, J. P., Dunnette, M. D., Lawler, E. E., III, & Weick, K. E. (1970). *Managerial behavior, performance and effectiveness*. New York: McGraw-Hill.

Clark, K. E., & Clark, M. B. (Eds.). (1990). *Measures of leadership*. West Orange, NJ: Leadership Library of America.

Likert, R. (1961). *New patterns of management*. New York: McGraw-Hill.

McGregor, D. M. (1960). *The human side of enterprise*. New York: McGraw-Hill.

Roberts, B. W., & Hogan, R. (Eds.). (2001). *Personality psychology and the workplace*. Washington, DC: American Psychological Association.

About the Authors

Chris Argyris received his Ph.D. in organizational behavior from Cornell University in 1951 and served on the Yale University faculty for the next twenty years. He then became the James Bryant Conant Professor of Education and Organizational Behavior at Harvard University and held joint appointments over time at the Business, Law, and Kennedy Schools. Argyris is the author of 33 books and monographs and over 400 articles. He has been awarded eleven honorary doctorates. Other honors include the Academy of Management's Irwin Award, the Kurt Lewin Award, the American Psychological Association's Gold Medal for Life Achievement in the Application of Psychology, and several other "lifetime achievement" awards. He has been elected a Fellow of the Academy of Management, the American Psychological Association, the National Academy of Human Resources, the Canadian School of Management, and the International Academy of Management.

Murray R. Barrick earned his Ph.D. in industrial and organizational psychology from the University of Akron. His research interests include assessing the impact individual differences in behavior and personality have on job performance, methods of measuring and predicting such differences, and organizational processes associated with developing compensation systems. His research has been published in the *Journal of Applied Psychology, Personnel Psychology, Academy of Management Journal,* and *Organizational Behavior and Human Decision Processes* among others. Along with Michael Mount, he was recognized by the Academy of Management with the "Outstanding Published Paper Award" by the Scholarly Achievement Award Committee of the Personnel/Human Resources Division. Furthermore, this paper, published in *Personnel Psychology,* was recognized as being the most frequently cited article in that journal during the past decade. In 2001, he was the recipient of the Owens Scholarly Achievement Award. This award was given to the author (co-authors include Tim Judge, Chad Higgins, and Carl Thoresen) recognized as publishing the best publication during 1999. In addition, in 1997, he was elected a Fellow of the Society for Industrial and Organizational Psychologists in the American Psychological Association. He currently serves on the editorial boards of the *Journal of Applied Psychology* and *Personnel Psychology*. Along with Ann Marie Ryan, he was a volume editor for "Personality and Work: Reconsidering the role of personality in organizations", a publication in the Society for Industrial and Organizational Psychology's Organizational Frontiers Series.

Arthur P. Brief received his Ph.D. from the University of Wisconsin-Madison in 1974 and currently is the Lawrence Martin Chair of Business at Tulane's A. B. Freeman School of Business, with a courtesy appointment in the Department of Psychology. He also is Director of the William B. and Evelyn Burkenroad Institute for the Study of Ethics and Leadership in Management. Professor Brief is a recipient of the Academic Leadership Award from the Aspen Institute's Initiative for Social Innovation through Business and the World Resources Institute for integrating social and environmental concerns into business education. His scholarship focuses on two areas—job related distress and ethical decision making in organizations. In January, 2003, Professor Brief became the editor of the *Academy of Management Review*. He is a Fellow of the Academy of Management, the American Psychological Association, and the American Psychological Society.

Adrian Furnham is a professor of psychology at the University of London and, formerly, a lecturer in psychology at Pembroke College, Oxford University. He has held visiting positions at the Hong Kong University Business School and Henley Management College. He received his Ph.D. in 1981 from Oxford and holds 2 additional doctorates. Dr. Furnham is the author of 36 books and over 500 peer-reviewed scientific papers in international journals. He is a chartered occupational psychologist, chartered health psychologist, and Fellow of the British Psychological Society. He has been cited as the most productive European psychologist in the 1990's and second most productive psychologist in the world (1985–1995).

Jennifer M. George is the Mary Gibbs Jones Professor of Management and professor of psychology in the Jones Graduate School of Management at Rice University. She received her Ph.D. in management and organizational behavior from the Stern Graduate School of Business Administration at New York University. Her research interests include affect, mood, and emotion in the workplace; creativity; personality influences; groups and teams; stress and well-being; values and work–life linkages; prosocial behavior; and customer service. She is a Fellow in the American Psychological Association, the Society for Industrial and Organizational Psychology, and the American Psychological Society and a member of the Society for Organizational Behavior. She is on the editorial review boards of the *Academy of Management Review, Organizational Behavior and Human Decision Processes, International Journal of Selection and Assessment*, and the *Journal of Managerial Issues* and is an associate editor for the *Journal of Applied Psychology*.

Robert Hogan received his Ph.D. from the University of California, Berkeley in 1967. He was professor of psychology and social relations at Johns Hopkins University in Baltimore from 1967 to 1982 and McFarlin Professor of Psychology and chair at the University of Tulsa in Oklahoma from 1982 to 2001. He was an editor of the *Journal of Personality and Social Psychology* from 1978 to 1984, and he is co-editor of the *Handbook of Personality Psychology*. He is a Fellow of the APA and SIOP. He has spent his career demonstrating the practical significance of well-validated measures of personality, especially for personnel selection and management development and has published over 250 scholarly articles, chapters, and books. Dr. Hogan is president of Hogan Assessment Systems.

Robert J. House received his Ph.D. in Management from the Ohio State University in June 1960. He was appointed the Joseph Frank Bernstein Professor Endowed Chair of Organization Studies at the Wharton School of the University of Pennsylvania in 1988. He has published 130 journal articles. In total, his articles have been reprinted in approximately 50 anthologies of readings in management and organizational behavior.

House received the Award for Distinguished Scholarly Contribution to Management, and four awards for outstanding publications. The awards were conferred by the Academy of Management and the Canadian Association of Administrative Sciences. He has also authored two papers which are Scientific Citations Classics.

He is a Fellow of the Academy of Management, American Psychological Association, and Society for Industrial and Organizational Psychology. He has served as chairperson of the Academy of Management Division of Organizational Behavior (1972–1973) and President of the Administrative Science Association of Canada (1985–1986).

House was the principle investigator of the Global Leadership and Organizational Behavior Effectiveness Research Program (GLOBE) from 1993 through 2003. In this capacity he visited universities in 38 countries.

He has been a visiting scholar or visiting professor at 14 universities, most of which are in Europe or Asia.

House's major research interests are the role of personality traits and motives as they relate to effective leadership and organizational performance, power and personality in organizations, leadership, and the implications of cross-cultural variation for effective leadership and organizational performance.

Lawrence R. James is the Pilot Oil Chair of Excellence in the Industrial and Organizational Psychology Program at the University of Kentucky Business School. Dr. James received his B.S., M.S., and Ph.D. degrees from the University of Utah in 1965, 1967, and 1970, respectively. He has been active in studying the effects of organizational environments on individual adaptation, motivation, and productivity. His statistical contributions have been designed to make possible tests of new models in areas such as personality, organizational climate, leadership, and personnel selection. He served as chairperson of the Research Methods Division of the Academy of Management and serves on the editorial boards of many leading journals. His most recent work consists of designing a new measurement system for personality. Dr. James is an American Psychological Association Fellow in Division 5 (Evaluation and Measurement) and Division 14 (Industrial and Organizational Psychology), and he is an American Psychological Society Fellow.

Timothy A. Judge is the Matherly–McKethan Eminent Scholar, Department of Management, Warrington College of Business, and University of Florida. Dr. Judge holds a Bachelor of Business Administration degree from the University of Iowa, and master's and doctoral degrees from the University of Illinois at Urbana–Champaign. Dr. Judge's previous academic appointments include Stanley M. Howe Professor of Leadership and associate professor, University of Iowa, and associate professor and assistant professor at Cornell University.

Dr. Judge's research interests are in the areas of personality, leadership and influence behaviors, staffing, and job attitudes. He has published more than 60 articles in refereed journals; 6 of which received "best paper" awards from professional societies or academies. Dr. Judge serves on the editorial review boards of six journals, including *Journal of Applied Psychology, Personnel Psychology,* and *Organizational Behavior and Human Decision Processes.* Dr. Judge is currently chair of the scientific affairs committee for the Society for Industrial and Organizational Psychology, and presently is division chair for the Human Resources Division of the Academy of Management. He is a Fellow of the American Psychological Association and the Society for Industrial and Organizational Psychology.

In 1995, he received the Ernest J. McCormick Award for Distinguished Early Career Contributions, Society for Industrial and Organizational Psychology. In 2001, Dr. Judge received the Cummings Scholar Award from the Organizational Behavior Division of the Academy of Management. In 1999, he was named to the list of Outstanding Faculty in *Business Week's Guide to the Best Business Schools*.

Amy Kristof-Brown received her Ph.D. in Organizational Behavior and Human Resource Management from the University of Maryland in 1997. She now serves as an associate professor of Management and Organizations and a Henry B. Tippie Research Fellow at the Henry B. Tippie College of Business at the University of Iowa. Her research focuses on person–environment fit, specifically on the issues of: (a) distinguishing between unique types of PE fit; (b) exploring the outcomes associated with employees' perceptions of specific types of fit; and (c) determining the antecedents and consequences of recruiters' perceptions of fit. She has published and presented several papers on these topics, including articles in *Journal of Applied Psychology, Personnel Psychology, Journal of Management, Journal of Vocational Behavior, International Journal of Selection and Assessment*, and *Human Resource Planning*. Her research has resulted in a number of awards including the Best Student Paper Award and Best Dissertation Award from the Human Resource Division of the Academy of Management.

Julie Beth McFall received her Ph.D. from the Kelley School of Business at Indiana University in Organizational Behavior and her M.A. in Labor and Industrial Relations from the University of Illinois. She was a member of the faculty at Carlson School of Management at the University of Minnesota and is currently an HR project manager for the Best Buy Corporation in Minneapolis.

Lisa Moynihan is an Assistant Professor of Organizational Behavior at London Business School. She earned her Ph.D. in Human Resource Management at Cornell University's School of Industrial and Labor Relations. Lisa's research interests include strategic human resource management, high performance work systems, teams and knowledge transfer, and personality and group processes. Her work has appeared in *Research in Organizational Behavior, Personnel Psychology, Human Resource Management*, and *Human Resource Management Journal*.

Dennis W. Organ (A.B., Ph.D., University of North Carolina) is professor of management at the Kelley School of Business, Indiana University, where he has taught since 1970. Since 1977, his research has focused largely on organizational citizenship behavior, the subject of a 1988 monograph by him that is now being updated. He edits the publication *Business Horizons*. He has taught organizational psychology, human resource management, methods of research, cross-cultural management, and undergraduate honors seminars. He is a Fellow of the American Psychological Association and the Society for Industrial and Organizational Psychology. He is a member of the editorial review board of the *Journal of Applied Psychology*.

Rita Palrecha is a doctoral candidate in the School of Management at State University of New York (SUNY), Binghamton. Her research interests include the role of personality and culture in leadership. Her research emphasis is trait–motive interactions in leadership theories; and functional, methodological and measurement issues in cross-cultural leadership research. Prior to joining the SUNY doctoral program, she worked in a corporate training center facilitating training and research for a managerial staff of 3,000 located in India. Her job responsibilities included training administration and system support, facilitating HR training programs, and research support for an-all India corporate climate and training effectiveness assessment project. She received both her MBA in Personnel Management and a B.S. in Electronics Engineering from Bombay University, India.

Randall S. Peterson is associate professor of Organizational Behavior at London Business School. His current research activities include editing and writing a book entitled *Leading and Managing People in Dynamic Organizations*. In addition to his general interest in leadership in dynamic business environments, Professor Peterson's research includes investigating how the personalities of members affect group interaction and performance, how CEOs' personalities affect top management team interaction as well as firm performance, and the effects of conflict in groups—including a recent study of the crucial role trust plays in getting the benefits of task conflict without the damage of relationship conflict in top management teams in the hotel industry. Professor Peterson holds a Ph.D. in Social and Organizational Psychology from the University of California, Berkeley.

Joan Rentsch received a B.S. degree in Psychology from Ohio State University in 1982; and M.A. and Ph.D. degrees in Industrial/Organizational Psychology from the University of Maryland in 1985 and 1988, respectively. Dr. Rentsch's research interests include team member schema similarity, cognitions in organizations, and measurement of cognitions. Her professional experience includes serving as part of the research faculty at the Air Force Research Laboratory, as a consultant on several research grants, and as an adjunct or visiting professor at several academic institutions. She is a reviewer for several major research journals and is an active member of the Society for Industrial and Organizational Psychology.

Chet Robie has staff experience in a private sector human resource department; has spent time as a senior researcher for an international consulting firm; held a staff position at a major government agency; and spent several years in tenure-track professoriates at a major public research university and a small private teaching university. Chet is currently an assistant professor at Wilfred Laurier University in Waterloo, Ontario. Chet has published in the *Journal of Applied Psychology*, *Personnel Psychology*, *Organizational Research Methods*, *Human Performance*, and *Group and Organization Management*. Chet's research interests are broad with publications in: expatriate selection and training issues; multi-source ratings; assessment centers; personality testing; leadership; business ethics; psychometrics; job satisfaction; and shift work. He received a Ph.D. in Industrial and Organizational Psychology from Bowling Green State University.

Benjamin Schneider is professor of psychology at the University of Maryland and a Senior Research Fellow with Personnel Research Associates, Inc. For 20 years he was the head of the Industrial and Organizational Psychology (I/O) program at Maryland. In addition to Maryland, Ben has taught at Michigan State University and Yale University and for shorter periods of time at Dartmouth College's Tuck School of Business Administration, Bar-Ilan University (Israel, on a Fulbright), University of Aix-Marseilles (France), and Peking University (PRC). Ben received his Ph.D. in Psychology in 1967 (University of Maryland) and his M.B.A. in 1964 (C.U.N.Y.). His academic accomplishments include more than 90 professional journal articles and book chapters, as well as seven books. Ben's interests concern service quality, organizational climate and culture, and the role of personality in organizational life. Ben is listed in *Who's Who in America* and derivative volumes, and was awarded the Year 2000 Distinguished Scientific Contributions Award by the Society for Industrial and Organizational Psychology. In addition to his academic work, he has consulted with numerous companies including Chase-Manhattan Bank, Citicorp, AT&T, Allstate, Sotheby's, the Metropolitan Opera, Prudential, the states of Alabama and Pennsylvania, GEICO, IBM, American Express, and Giant Eagle.

D. Brent Smith is an associate professor of Management and Psychology at the Jones Graduate School of Management and Department of Psychology at Rice University and is currently the managing director of the Rice Center for Organizational Effectiveness Studies. Professor Smith was formerly a member of the faculty at Cornell University where he taught in the School of Industrial and Labor Relations and the Johnson Graduate School of Management. Professor Smith's teaching interests focus primarily on leadership and management development. He received his Ph.D. in Psychology from the University of Maryland. Professor Smith's research interests focus broadly on personality issues in work organizations including response dynamics in personality measurement; the personality correlates of effective work performance; and the relationship between personality and organizational climate/culture. In addition, his current research focuses on individual differences in susceptibility to social influence, the personality correlates of justice perceptions, and integrating trait and social cognitive conceptions of personality. Professor Smith was a recipient of the 1998 Scholarly Achievement Award from the Academy of Management's Human Resources Division. His research has been published in the *Journal of Applied Psychology, Personnel Psychology, Human Performance,* and *Leadership Quarterly.* Dr. Smith is a senior consultant for Organization+Performance Group, Inc. and is a partner in the PHI Group, L.L.C.

William D. (Don) Spangler is associate professor of management in the School of Management at the State University of New York (SUNY), Binghamton. His research focuses on personality theory and leadership, particularly personality and motivation of leaders in varying organizational settings. He is also interested in methodological issues including measurement and levels of analysis. He received his Ph.D. from the University of Michigan and B.A. and M.B.A. degrees from the University of Chicago.

Barry M. Staw is the Lorraine T. Mitchell Professor of Leadership and Communication at the Haas School of Business, University of California, Berkeley. He received his Ph.D. from Northwestern University and has previously served on the faculties at the University of Illinois, Northwestern University, University of Iowa, and UCLA. He has served on the editorial boards of most major journals in the fields of organizational behavior and applied psychology. He founded the annual series, Research in Organizational Behavior, and has served as its editor or co-editor for the last 25 years. His research interests include the relationship of affect and emotion to work performance, escalation of commitment, organizational innovation, and the linkage of psychological processes to organizational strategy.

W. Bruce Walsh is currently a professor emeritus in the Counseling Psychology program at Ohio State University, where he served as program director for many years. Professor Walsh is the founder and editor of the *Journal of Career Assessment*. He has served on the editorial boards of the *Journal of Counseling Psychology*, the *Journal of Vocational Behavior*, the *Journal of College Student Development*, and the *Journal of Professional Psychology*. He co-authored *Tests and Assessment, Strategies in Counseling for Behavior Change, A Survey of Counseling Methods, Tests and Measurements*, and co-edited *Career Counseling for Women, Career Counseling, Career Decision Making, The Assessment of Interests, The Handbook of Vocational Psychology*, and *Person–Environment Psychology*. He holds Fellow status in Division 17 and is licensed as a psychologist in Ohio.

I

Introducing Personality at Work

These two chapters serve as overviews of contemporary thinking about the role of personality in the workplace. Hogan first does us a very real favor by briefly introducing his chapter by surveying the sources of contemporary personality theory. We often forget these days that there was theory and research prior to the advent of the five-factor model (FFM) of personality! Then in his typically inimitable style, Hogan surveys the landscape for personality and its relationship to such diverse topics as individual performance, team performance, and then organizational effectiveness. By considering each of these levels of analysis, Hogan serves to introduce a theme we wish to promote: Personality is useful for understanding more than individual behavior and individual performance.

In the second chapter, Furnham also provides an overview, this time of issues that are characteristic of the European perspective on personality. He too addresses issues of individual and team performance but also he addresses something not characteristic at all of American efforts,

1

consideration of the issue of employment/unemployment. Furnham's approach is salutary for Americans for it reveals national and cross-border differences in approaches to personality and organization that are less typical of American journals and American approaches. His insights can be a useful springboard for new approaches and insights.

Personality Psychology for Organizational Researchers

Robert Hogan
University of Tulsa

Personality psychology concerns the nature of human nature—the basic operating characteristics of the human machine—and it is the only academic discipline devoted to this subject. Most business leaders understand the importance of personality; witness the current popularity of Emotional Intelligence in business seminars. But inside academia, personality psychology has an uncertain status. There are probably two reasons for this. On the one hand, the majority of those involved with American psychology have adopted, in a reflexive and unconscious way, behaviorism as a model for understanding social behavior. Behaviorists believe that people's actions depend on the circumstances they are in rather than on the kinds of people they are. Behaviorists have been attacking personality psychology concepts relentlessly since the 1930s; the attack reached a crescendo in the 1970s and largely put personality psychology out of business (Funder, 2001). The discipline remained alive but on life support during the 1980s. Over the past 10 years there has been a small resurgence, but the behaviorists have not let up—see Cervone and Shoda, 1999.

On the other hand, many of the problems of personality psychology are the result of self-inflicted wounds. I might mention two. First, there is no agreement regarding an agenda for the discipline. Many personality theorists are/were psychiatrists or clinical psychologists; for them (e.g., Freud, Jung, Rogers), the agenda is to analyze the sources of psychopathology. For the humanistic psychologists (Allport, Maslow, Murray), the agenda is to capture individual uniqueness. For the factor analysts (Cattell, Eysenck, Guilford) the goal is to identify the structure of personality based on

3

psychometric assessment. For the cognitive theorists (Kelly, Rotter), the goal is to identify general laws of social perception. Nonspecialists have trouble understanding what personality psychology is about.

Second, there is no agreement regarding an agenda for personality assessment, the research method of choice in personality psychology. The agenda for cognitive assessment is to forecast training outcomes; the agenda for vocational assessment is to forecast occupational satisfaction. But personality psychologists are quite muddled about their agenda. For researchers in clinical psychology, the goal is to forecast individual differences in psychopathology. For researchers in the factor analytic tradition, the goal is to determine the degree to which the factor structures of their favorite inventories will replicate across samples. For still others, the goal is to measure traits.

In addition to the confused agendas, personality psychology suffers from an oversupply of theoretical viewpoints, a bewildering variety of technical terms, and a fine indifference to definitional issues. Nonetheless, and despite the confusion, personality psychology has enjoyed a small renaissance in industrial–organizational (I–O) psychology over the past few years (see Funder, 2001; Roberts & Hogan, 2001). This renaissance is due entirely to the "discovery" that measures of integrity—one aspect of personality—predict performance in a variety of job categories and such measures don't discriminate against women or minorities. The good news is that applied psychology has rediscovered personality; the bad news is that it has rediscovered only one aspect and one application of personality—that is, integrity measures for selection. The major claim of this chapter is that personality is an indispensable tool for understanding organizational life in general.

Why should organizational researchers know something about personality? Organizations are composed of people—as Ben Schneider says, people make the place. The core question in organizational theory ought to be (but isn't), what is the best way to organize and manage the people so as to optimize desired organizational outcomes? Behaviorists (and structural sociologists) assume that people are almost infinitely plastic and can adapt to virtually any organizational arrangement; in this model, organizational structures are determined by financial, logistic, and communications requirements. Personality psychology, on the other hand, suggests that there are limits to human flexibility, that people find certain operational arrangements and structures more congenial than others. If this is true, and I strongly believe it is, then maximizing organizational outcomes requires knowing something about people, which means knowing something about personality psychology.

This chapter concerns what there is to know, and the discussion reflects my best personal judgment on the topic. Voltaire noted that if we are to have a serious discussion, we must first define our terms. The first part of the chapter concerns definitions, including some comments on trait theory and the five-factor model. Next, I introduce a model of persons in organizations. This leads to a discussion about agendas for personality measurement and research. The chapter closes with a personality-based discussion of leadership and organizational effectiveness.

DEFINITIONS

Personality

MacKinnon (1944) suggested that the word *personality* has two definitions, and they should be kept distinct. The first definition concerns personality from the perspective of the observer—how a person is perceived by others—and is equivalent to a person's reputation. Allport (1937) argued that reputation is not part of personality; several generations of personality psychologists believed him, and they were wrong. Reputation is a crucial part of personality. People will kill to defend their reputations and that is about as serious as things can get in life. As an aspect of personality, reputation has some useful properties that are often overlooked. First, it is relatively easy to study using various forms of observer descriptions, including 360° feedback reports and assessment center exercises. Second, because the best predictor of future behavior is past behavior, and because reputation is based on past behavior, reputation is the best single clue we have as to how a person will behave in the future. Third, one of the most essential components of social skill is the ability to create and maintain a desirable reputation. And finally, the evaluations that others make of our social behavior become our reputation; these evaluations are formally identical to the appraisals that others make of our performance at work. Performance appraisal is a specific case of reputation construction.

The second definition of personality concerns personality from the perspective of the actor—how a person perceives him/herself—and is equivalent to a person's identity. As an aspect of personality, identity has some interesting properties that are often overlooked. First, our identity guides our social behavior by determining what interactions we will enter, what roles we are willing to play, and how we play them. Second, although identity—a person's view of him/herself—is the most frequently studied aspect of personality, it is actually quite hard to study accurately. It is hard to study because to do so, we must rely on a person's self-reports. Not only are these reports (e.g., "I always felt my parents loved me") often hard to verify, they are primarily reconstructions of past feelings and experiences. Identity is the story we tell about ourselves; it is part of the sense-making process in which we define who we are and what we are doing (Bruner, 1986; McAdams, 1993; Sarbin, 1986) and expect others to believe us. Third, identity—the person that we think we are—is only modestly related to reputation (the person that others think we are). The two forms of personality are conceptually quite distinct and by no means empirically equivalent. Finally, the degree to which identity and reputation are related is a function of social skill—the more, the more.

Motivation

Motivation is the key explanatory concept in virtually all theories of personality. Despite the importance of motivational terms for explaining social behavior, the concept of motivation is badly muddled. The word has three different meanings, and the failure to keep them distinct is a barrier to progress. Motivation in the first sense refers to the biological wellsprings of action; it refers to words like instinct, drive, and organic need. This is motivation as a physiological impulse. Motives, in this first sense, are biological, universal (all humans share them), unchanging, and often unconscious. Motivation in the second sense refers to goals and intentions, as in "What was the motive for the crime?" Motives in this second sense guide rather than impel action, and they are cognitive, particular (unique to each person), changeable, and usually conscious. Third, the word motive is used is to describe inner states of readiness, as in "The team is highly motivated to win." Clearly, biological impulses, cognitive intentions, and states of arousal are not the same thing, and the manner in which they are routinely confounded is puzzling and disruptive to progress.

Temperament

The word *temperament* refers to the hypothetical biological foundations of personality (see Buss & Plomin, 1984). Specifically, temperament concerns individual differences in behavior that appear early in life; these individual differences reflect a child's genetic background, and they are essentially the hand a child is dealt in life. As a person matures, the effects of temperament become harder to detect; by adulthood they will almost disappear. Developmental psychologists disagree as to how many temperaments there may be, but Buss and Plomin, using factor analyses of behavior ratings of children, make a good case for three. The first is called *emotionality*; children high on emotionality are easily startled, upset, or frightened, and hard to soothe; children low on emotionality are calm, happy, contented, and easy to soothe. The second temperament is called *sociability*; children high on sociability are bold and comfortable with strangers; children low on sociability are shy and afraid of strangers. The third temperament is called *impulsivity*; children high on impulsivity are quick to act and hard to restrain; children low on impulsivity are cautious and restrained. Please note that the concept of temperament is an inference that psychologists make about the causes of children's behavior, based on adult observers' ratings of their behavior.

Mood

The concept of mood refers to a pervasive affective state that acts like a filter, coloring our perceptions and giving a characteristic tone to our emotional life. A mood is a subdued and prolonged state-like emotion. Tellegen and his students (1985) have done the best research on mood, and it can be summarized in terms of four points. First, the research consists of factor analytic studies of self-reported mood states, and it converges quite nicely on the view that mood can be organized in terms of three general factors. These factors are positive emotionality, a generally positive and upbeat mood; negative emotionality, a generally dysphoric mood state that may include depression and anxiety; and restraint, a watchful and perhaps apprehensive mood state. Second, Tellegen's three mood factors closely resemble Buss's temperaments. Positive emotionality corresponds to sociability, negative emotionality corresponds to emotionality, and constraint corresponds to reversed impulsivity. Third, research on mood, like most factor analytic research, is more concerned with the degree to which factors replicate across samples than with what scores on mood measures actually predict. The concern is with psychometric fidelity rather than pragmatic applications—that is, what do we do with measures of mood once they are refined? And finally, the literature on mood concerns the actor's view of personality; the research is based on self-report data, which means that scores on mood measures tell us as much about a person's identity as they do about his or her state of physiological arousal.

Interests, Needs, and Values

Interests, *needs*, and *values* are motivational terms, they are all related, and they refer to the desired end states or goals of purposive action (see the previous section on motivation). The three terms differ primarily in their level of abstraction in the following way: We may value health in general, and as a result need exercise, and as a result be interested in tennis. Values concern global and abstract goals; needs concern goals that are instrumental in the pursuit of values; and interests support needs. Values, needs, and interests are assessed with self-report measures, or in the case of McClelland's (McClelland et al., 1989) system, with a projective test. Scores on measures of values, needs, and interests tend to be very stable over long periods of time; test–retest reliabilities are comparable to those for measures of cognitive ability (see J. Hogan & R. Hogan, 1996). Although I–O researchers discount measures of values, needs, and interests for selection purposes, because they seem easily faked, they actually work pretty well (see Hogan & Johnson, 1981). Most important for this discussion, values, needs, and interests concern personality from the actor's perspective, they are assessed using self-report measures, and therefore they directly express a person's identity.

Trait Theory

Gordon Allport was the most influential American in the history of personality psychology. He was also the father of trait theory; his influence is such that most people think of personality theory as trait theory, and they think personality assessment measures traits (see Hogan, DeSoto, & Solano, 1977). Trait theory argues that the consistencies in our behavior, as observed by ourselves and others, are caused by real neuropsychic structures that exist somewhere inside of us. The most important neuropsychic structures will be discovered someday by neuroscientists; in the meantime, we can measure them at a distance with standard personality questionnaires. In a nutshell, there are three parts to the trait theory argument:

1. Traits are real; they exist inside of us.
2. Our personality can be described in terms of traits.
3. Our actions can be explained in terms of traits.

This viewpoint has some real strengths. First, temperaments are almost surely under genetic control; temperaments can be measured using observer ratings, and they resemble Allportian traits. Second, some psychiatric symptoms (anxiety, depression) are almost surely under genetic control; they can be measured using self-report scales, and they resemble Allportian traits. Third, all science depends on reduction, and there must be a biological substrate to personality; consequently, Allport is correct in principle that consistencies in overt behavior have biological underpinnings. And finally, trait theory takes seriously the notion that there are observable consistencies in the behavior of individuals, a view hotly disputed by behaviorists and cognitive social learning theorists.

On the other hand, the concept of a trait is much more ambiguous than it seems. Consider first the distinction between the actor's and the observer's view of personality. As observers, we think about and describe other people using trait words; the function of trait words is to describe consistencies in the behavior of others. As actors, we think about and describe ourselves in terms of our identities—our hopes, dreams, aspirations, and agendas. Traits are for other people, not for ourselves. In addition, consistencies in behavior have different causes. For example, I have a Jack Russell terrier who is very aggressive; his aggressiveness is trait-like in Allport's sense (i.e., related to his genetic makeup). I also have a sister who is very sensitive to criticism; although her sensitivity is trait-like, it is a function of how, as a child, she was constantly criticized by our mother. My sister's trait-like behavior is more sensibly explained in terms of experience than neuropsychic structures. Moreover, to explain something in the same terms that we describe it is circular; it won't do to explain aggressiveness in terms of a trait for aggression. Finally, it isn't true that scores on personality measures necessarily reflect the strength of underlying neuropsychic structures. What happens when people endorse items on a personality scale? For trait theory, they are registering the strength of underlying traits. But think back to the distinction between the actor's and the observer's view of personality. When people tell us about themselves (using self-reports), they are telling us about their identities in a more or less conscious effort to control their reputations. The degree to which the self-report process is influenced by underlying neuropsychic structures is, in principle, unverifiable; the degree to which self-reports are influenced by identity is obvious. In short, it is a mistake to equate personality theory with trait theory and to equate personality assessment with trait measurement.

The Five-Factor Model

The development of the five-factor model (FFM; Wiggins, 1996) is an important event in the history of personality psychology because it provides a taxonomy of trait terms. It is possible now to locate virtually all trait words somewhere in a five-factor universe, which is often referred to as the *lexical hypothesis* (Goldberg, 1981). That is, the FFM concerns the structure of observer descriptions, the structure of how observers think about and describe actors, and as such it is very useful information. For example, if we want to conduct a meta-analysis of the links between personality and job performance, the FFM provides a method for classifying the personality predictors in the analysis.

However, some writers have become true believers on the subject of the FFM and make two additional claims. First, consistent with trait theory, they argue that the FFM is a taxonomy of traits that actually exist inside people, so that we can both describe and explain behavior in terms of this model. And second, they argue that the FFM is an adequate model for explaining people's behavior—that is, the FFM can account for all the stable features inside people that explain their behavior. These claims have been criticized extensively by several people (Block, 1995; Hogan, 1996;

McAdams, 1992). The bottom line is that the FFM is a taxonomy of personality from the observer's perspective; that is, it is a theory about variables and not a theory of personality.

SOCIOANALYTIC THEORY

The chapter up to this point has concerned definitions. I would now like to outline briefly a model of how personality influences organizational behavior. Socioanalytic theory is an effort to synthesize the best insights of Sigmund Freud (1955) and George Herbert Mead (1934), two of the most influential social thinkers of the last century. Although one was a Viennese psychiatrist and the other a University of Chicago social philosopher, they shared some important common interests. First, they were both ardent fans of Darwin and evolutionary theory, which means that they believed that present-day social behavior is rooted in biology and reflects ancient forms of life. To understand the behavior of turtles, we need to ask what they are adapted to do, and the same is true for humans.

Second, Freud and Mead believed that development is important and that the social behavior of adults reflects experiences in childhood. For Freud, the crucial developmental experiences concern how we adapt to the authority of our parents in early childhood; for Mead, the crucial developmental experiences concern how we adapt to the authority of our peer group in later childhood. Either way, social behavior in adulthood reflects these developmental experiences. Third, Freud and Mead both analyze the manner in which people are linked psychologically to their social groups or organizations, and this topic is at the heart of organizational psychology. For Freud, people are linked to organizations through the charismatic qualities of the organization's leadership, assuming normal developmental experiences in childhood. For Mead, people are linked to organizations through their responsiveness to the expectations of the other members of the organization, assuming normal developmental experiences in childhood.

Fourth, Freud and Mead have theories of motivation that have important implications for organizational behavior. Freud's motivational theory is more complex and can be described in terms of two points. First, he assumes that at a deep, unconscious level, people are motivated by two biological impulses—Eros and Thanatos. Eros concerns the need to develop bonds with others, some of which are overtly sexual, but some of which result in friendship, respect, and affection. Thanatos concerns the need to dominate others and bend them to one's will; sometimes this need results in hostility and overt aggression, but sometimes it results in competitiveness. The second point to note about Freud's theory is that, in his view, all human relationships are inherently ambivalent, because they are motivated by both Eros and Thanatos. Thus, for Freud, every friendship is tinged with a bit of secret resentment or competition; conversely, we are in some ways secretly drawn to our bitterest enemies.

Mead's motivational theory is more straightforward. He assumed that we are all motivated to pay attention to others' expectations, and to comply with them, once we realize what they are. In Mead's view, people are inherently social and "programmed" to try to maintain good relations with the other members of their social groups. A final point shared by Freud and Mead is that they both have a theory of why things go wrong in organizations, and this theory relates back to development. For Freud, if a child's relations with his or her parents are flawed, then the child will develop a deep resentment of all authority figures and will persistently break rules and ignore standard procedures. For Mead, if a child's relations with his or her peer group are flawed, then the child will become egocentric and will persistently violate social expectations. In a nutshell, Freud and Mead have competing but compatible theories of organizational delinquency.

Freud and Mead share a common shortcoming in their analyses of organizational behavior. They both see people as existing in one of two states, compliant or delinquent—willing to follow rules, respect authority, and attend to others' expectations, or hostile toward rules and indifferent to expectations. Campbell (1965), who introduced evolutionary theory to social psychology, makes the interesting argument that well-socialized people, people who are willing to abide by the rules of their group and attend to the expectations of their peers, often conform for perfectly selfish reasons. Their conformity has less to do with respect for authority or desire for good relations with others than it does with advancing their own careers and self interests. This situation can be seen most clearly in the behavior of politicians who argue that they are serving the interests of the public whereas they are advancing their own careers at public expense.

There are three legs to the socioanalytic stool. The first is Freud, the second is Mead, and the third is the study of free-living chimpanzees (see De Waal, 1982). Chimpanzees share 98% of the human genome, they are our closest living relatives, and it seems reasonable to think that their social behavior would resemble that of early humans. In his utterly absorbing book, De Waal shows that chimpanzee groups are organized in terms of status hierarchies and that adult chimpanzees spend their days negotiating for status by grooming, threatening, building coalitions, and destroying competing coalitions. Most important, status depends on social skill; the high-status animal is not the biggest or strongest, but is the one with the most support when a quarrel breaks out. There are, of course, real advantages to having status—choice of mates, food, nesting places, and so forth. I believe that human social behavior is dominated by precisely the same concerns. At the core of our psychological beings, we want social support—we want to be liked, we want status, and we want control of resources. We negotiate for these commodities during social interaction, and some people are clearly better at it than others. I refer to this process as getting along and getting ahead, but for the purposes of this chapter, the point is that the principle dynamic in organizational behavior is the individual search for power. There are people in every organization who do not seek power, but they have little influence on the life or culture of the organization.

Socioanalytic theory maintains that people are deeply concerned with getting along and getting ahead (or not being shunned and not losing status), and they try to attain these outcomes during social interaction. Thus personality, and organizational behavior, largely concerns social interaction. There are two necessary and sufficient conditions for an interaction: an agenda and roles to play. During informal interaction, the agendas and the roles are made up by the participants. But during interactions at work, the agendas and the roles are dictated by the organization. There is an interesting and systematic interplay between individual personality and organizational behavior (interactions at work). Our identity determines what agendas we are willing to follow, what roles we are willing to play, and how we play them (see Hogan & Roberts, 2000). For example, during a classroom lecture, all the students are in the role of student, but they all play the role differently in an effort to tell one another who they are. Once again, our identity determines what agendas we are willing to honor, what roles we are willing to play, and how we play them. Others watch our performance during interactions, evaluate them, and after many interactions, the evaluations turn into our reputation. Our reputation, in turn, is directly related to our status.

I can close this section by specifying an agenda for personality psychology. The agenda for personality theory is to explain individual differences in people's ability to get along and get ahead, because these are the crucial outcomes in life. And in a related fashion, the agenda for personality assessment is to forecast individual differences in people's potential for getting along and getting ahead.

PERSONALITY AND ORGANIZATIONAL BEHAVIOR

Motowidlo, Borman, and Schmit (1997) describe the work day as "streams of work behavior [that] are punctuated by occasions when people do something that does make a difference in relation to organizational goals and these are the behavioral episodes that make up the domain of job performance" (p. 73). The streams of work behavior are organized in episodes or interaction sequences, each has an agenda and associated roles, and performance appraisal is based on what a person does during the episode. Thus, what goes on at work is formally identical to goes on in life; any distinction between organizational behavior and social behavior in general is artificial. Finally, personality is all about social behavior; specifically, it is about trying to get along and get ahead. So in one sense, personality influences all of organizational behavior. However, that statement is too general. I can illustrate my point more specifically with three examples: occupational performance, team performance, and organizational effectiveness.

Personality and Occupational Performance

Historically, the conventional wisdom of organizational psychology has been that personality is unrelated to job performance (Guion & Gottier, 1965). However, the early reviews of this literature considered all personality measures as more or less interchangeable—measures of self-esteem were equated with measures of conscientiousness and were expected to predict the same criteria. The development of the FFM (Wiggins, 1996) provided a rational basis for classifying personality variables as predictors, which meant that, in principle, only measures of the same construct would be compared. The availability of this classification scheme led to a spate of meta-analytic studies of personality and job performance (Barrick & Mount, 1991; Tett, Jackson, & Rothstein, 1991), which are seen as establishing the reality of the link between personality and performance. In the best of these meta-analyses, J. Hogan and Holland (2003) classify both predictors and criteria; specifically they classify criteria into indices of getting along and getting ahead. Their paper is the first to align predictors with the relevant criteria. After doing so, they report the following corrected mean validities: Emotional Stability, .37; Surgency, .30; Agreeableness, .28; Conscientiousness, .31; and Intellect/Openness to Experience, .30.

Hogan and Hogan (1991) approached the question of the links between personality and occupational performance by classifying occupations using the Holland (1985) model. Holland argues that every job in the economy can be classified in terms of a combination of one of six ideal types as follows: (1) Realistic jobs involve building, operating, and maintaining equipment according to rules; (2) investigative jobs involve analyzing and solving problems, often by breaking rules; (3) artistic jobs involve entertaining people and designing or decorating things, often by ignoring rules; (4) social jobs involve helping people, often by skirting rules; (5) enterprising jobs involve persuading and manipulating others, usually in the context of rules; (6) conventional jobs involve regulating people, data, and things according to well-defined rules. Substantial data support Holland's claim that this model is an adequate and even exhaustive taxonomy of the world of work. The theory has great heuristic value for analyzing organizations as well as jobs.

Hogan and Hogan (1991) show that there is a distinct pattern of personality characteristics associated with career success for each Holland type. For example, successful investigative types (scientists) are ambitious, creative, and curious, as well as pretty mean and self-centered. The bottom line here is that there are well-established and important links between personality and occupational performance; this is a clear example of how personality influences organizational behavior.

TEAM PERFORMANCE

A team is three or more people who: (a) work toward a common goal; (b) interact and depend on one another to reach the goal; (c) perceive themselves as being part of a team; and (d) are rewarded based on the performance of the team. The empirical literature on team performance is disorderly and hard to summarize, in part because there is no reliable way to classify teams. The result is that it is hard to compare studies because we never know if the teams are comparable. Hogan, Driskell, and Salas (1989) suggest that teams can be classified using the Holland model. The Holland types are defined by coherent sets of activities, preferences, skills, and problem-solving methods. Teams can be classified in terms of their most frequent activities, and the activities can be classified in Holland's terms. Hogan et al. show that the Holland model can be used to classify team tasks with substantial reliability and that the classification system is exhaustive. This classification method allows us to examine systematically the influence of personality on team performance.

Personality influences team performance in three ways. First, some people are better team players than others. Specifically persons with high scores on the FFM dimensions of emotional stability and agreeableness are good team players—they like working as part of a team, and other people like working with them. Conversely, persons with low scores on emotional stability and agreeableness are not good team players— they tend to be moody, unpredictable, independent, and nonconforming. Second, there are two major personality dimensions running through the Holland hexagon—extraversion and conscientiousness. Enterprising and social types are extraverted, whereas realistic and investigative types are introverted. Conventional types score high on conscientiousness; artistic types score low on conscientiousness. Thus, each Holland type is a unique blend of extraversion and conscientiousness. But the important point here is that to work effectively as a member of, for example, a realistic team—virtually every work group in the military—a person should be introverted and conforming. Extraverted, nonconforming people perform poorly in military teams. Thus, there is a set of personality characteristics that enables performance on various types of teams.

The third way in which personality influences team performance concerns the personality of the team leader. I talk about this topic in more detail in the next section. Here let me illustrate my point with an example. I visited a nuclear submarine training facility a few years ago to watch the training of navigational and sonar teams. After several hours of standing around, I asked the Chief Petty Officer who was in charge what the real problems were. He said there were two kinds of problems; the first concerned the proper use of the equipment and the second concerned actually working as a team. He went on to say that the first problem really wasn't much of a problem, that in most cases the sailors were pretty proficient at operating the equipment. Most of the problems he saw concerned teamwork. I asked him what factors were the major contributors to poor teamwork, and he said the issue almost invariably was the officer in charge. Through arrogance, insecurity, or insensitivity, an officer would begin to micromanage the performance of individual team members, and the sailors would respond by doing only precisely what they were told to do. With no freedom to do their jobs, and wanting only to avoid being criticized, the sailors stopped volunteering information, searching unusual quadrants, or trying to analyze anomalies, and the performance of the team was badly degraded as a consequence.

ORGANIZATIONAL EFFECTIVENESS

From a pragmatic perspective, one might think that effectiveness would be the defining problem in organizational studies. Surprisingly, the topic rarely comes up, and when it does, the treatment is inadequate. Katz and Kahn (1966), for example, devote two chapters to the topic in their classic study of organizational psychology. But they try to define effectiveness in an ipsative way, by comparing organizations with themselves. They define effectiveness in terms of various indices of efficiency by comparing inputs with outputs, "... the extent to which all forms of energic return to the organization are maximized" (p. 165). It seems to me, however, that a crucial fact of organizational life is that every organization has competitors. Given this fact, we would be better off searching for relative, rather than absolute, indices of effectiveness. I believe that organizational effectiveness should be defined in terms of an organization's performance relative to that of its competitors. Thus, effectiveness is defined in relative rather than absolute terms.

With that relative definition in mind, let me suggest a brief and simple model of organizational effectiveness. Effectiveness is a function of how well an organization does, relative to its competition, in five areas. The first area concerns selecting, recruiting, and retaining talent; other things being equal, the team with the more talented players should win. The second area concerns motivation, the degree to which the team members are enthusiastic and filled with a sense of energy and shared purpose. Other things being equal, a less talented but more motivated team should defeat a more talented but dispirited team. The third component of organizational effectiveness concerns leadership; if teams are matched for talent and motivation, the team with the better leadership will win. The fourth component of organizational effectiveness concerns strategy; talented and motivated teams with good leadership and bad strategies—the German Army in WW II, for example—will lose to a team with a better strategy. Despite modern psychology's enthusiasm for matters cognitive, it has very little to say on the topic of strategic thinking and strategy formation. The final component of organizational effectiveness concerns having systems in place to monitor how well the organization is doing in terms of the preceding four categories: (1) attracting talented personnel, (2) motivating those personnel, (3) evaluating the competency of the organization's leadership, and (4) evaluating the appropriateness of the core business strategy.

The typical organization doesn't do very well in any of these domains. In my experience, most organizations are not very thoughtful about the process of recruiting and retaining talented personnel. As for the motivational issue, climate surveys routinely show surprisingly high levels of worker dissatisfaction in most organizations. Concerning leadership, our research suggests that 50 to 60% of the managers in most organizations are regarded by their staff as incompetent. As for strategic planning, the planning process is not taken seriously by most organizations, and there is a reason. Strategic planning, if done correctly, is based on data, on empirical comparisons of the performance of the organization with its competitors across certain categories. This means that strategic planning is, in terms of the Holland model, an investigative activity—one that would appeal to academic researchers. But organizations are managed by enterprising types, in Holland's terms. Enterprising people do not enjoy, and in fact actively dislike, investigative activities. Therefore, strategic planning is given only nominal attention in most organizations. Finally, monitoring an organization's performance across four domains is also an investigative activity and one that enterprising (managerial) types normally avoid.

Because all organizations perform at less than optimal levels across the five major components of organizational effectiveness, the organizations that make the fewest mistakes in these areas will be the most effective. Thucydides, in his *History of the Peloponnesian War*, recounts a scene in the central plaza in Athens in which the citizens debate what to do about the advancing Spartan army. The debate concerned what the Spartans' strategy might be. When Pericles rose to speak, he made my point about organizational effectiveness—that is, he remarked that he cared less about the Spartans' strategy than he did about the mistakes that the Athenian army might make in executing their own strategy. My point is that organizational effectiveness can't be defined in vacuo, and a substantial component of organizational effectiveness has to do with minimizing errors rather than meeting some ideal standard of performance.

But my major point in this discussion of the components of organizational effectiveness is that personality is central to four of the five components. The first component, talent, will include such issues as initiative, creativity, persistence, and dedication, all aspects of personality. The second component, motivation, is pure personality. The third component, leadership, is also all about personality. And the fourth component, strategy, is not well understood by psychologists, but creative problem solving, tolerance for ambiguity, and tolerance for risk—all personality variables—must be part of it. Personality underlies virtually every aspect of organizational behavior.

LEADERSHIP

Although leadership is the most extensively studied topic in the social, behavioral, and management sciences, there is nonetheless little consensus concerning the essential features of effective leadership. Part of the problem results from a lack of attention to conceptual issues, and this lack shows up in three ways. First, the term is rarely defined explicitly. Rather, it is typically defined in terms of persons who are at the top of large, bureaucratic, and hierarchical organizations—for example, CEOs and politicians. But a moment's reflection reveals that it is possible to climb a hierarchy without every demonstrating talent for leadership. Conversely, great leaders often make dreadful politicians—for example, U. S. Grant, one of the great military leaders in history, was essentially a failure as President of the United States. Because the term is so rarely defined, subsequent research uses a wide variety of ad hoc criteria to define leadership, and the resulting literature is inconclusive. There is virtually no consensus regarding the characteristics of effective leadership other than to note, limply, that it somehow depends on the situation.

A second problem with most discussions of leadership is that it is rarely linked to larger conceptions of human nature—that is, to personality. This was not true earlier on; for example, Argyris (1957), McGregor (1960), and Herzberg (1966) criticized the management practices of the 1960s on the

grounds that they were based on impoverished views of human motivation. The third problem is that academic research rarely links leadership to
the performance of the organizational units the leader is responsible for—
that is, to organizational effectiveness. For most academic discussions of
leadership, a person can be a leader even though his or her organization
fails.

People are biologically disposed toward both altruistic and selfish
behavior (Campbell, 1965). Leadership involves recruiting, motivating,
coaching, and guiding an effective team. A team is a group of people who
work toward a common goal and who feel some commitment to the other
members of the team and the team goal. Thus, when team building is
successful—when leadership is successful—the self-interested search for
power within a group is substantially, if not entirely, suppressed. And the
effectiveness of a team must be defined in terms of its performance vis-à-vis
the other teams with which it competes.

In my view, leadership must be defined in terms of the performance of
the group for which the leader is responsible. But why is that? The answer
comes from an examination of our evolutionary history. All the data indicate that humans evolved as group-living animals. The data also indicate
that, over the history of our species, human groups have been in competition with one another. They compete for territory, food, shelter, and other
vital resources, and the winning groups often perpetrate substantial atroci-
ties on the losing groups—in some cases even eating them, although social
scientists seem to want to ignore this unpleasant reality. In this context,
leadership must have been a resource in a group's ability to compete successfully. This is so because, once again, leadership involves persuading
people to set aside their selfish tendencies for a period of time and pursue
a goal that promotes the welfare of the group as a whole. But most important, in this context, the test of leadership is how well a group performs
vis-à-vis the other groups with which it is in competition—because, once
again, poor performance can, and did, lead to extinction.

This observation prompts three further comments. First, leadership is
probably as important for the survival of groups and organizations today
as it ever was—ask the suffering citizens of Serbia, Iraq, North Korea,
or Albania. Second, the fundamental dynamic in human groups is the
individual search for power, and the fundamental task of leadership is
to persuade people to stop behaving selfishly and pursue a lager group
agenda. Left to their own devices, people follow selfish agendas, and the
groups to which they belong become vulnerable to groups that are better
organized. The Celts who lived in France, Spain, and England at the time
of the Roman invasions were as aggressive and warlike as the Romans,
but they lacked the Roman genius for social organization, and they were
soon conquered. Finally, some people are better at building a team than

others; those who are better at it have some distinctive characteristics as seen by others, and at some level most people understand what those characteristics are. They are once again integrity, competence, decisiveness, and a sense of strategic direction, as identified by implicit leadership theory.

The links between personality and leadership can be summarized in terms of four points. First, it is important to distinguish between the actor's and the observer's view of personality and of leadership. Moreover, leadership can only be defined vis-à-vis a group of followers, and it is best defined in terms of a leader's reputation, based on his or her accomplishments as observed by others over time. Second, implicit leadership theory tells us (see Kouzes & Posner, 1987) that there is a specific and very well defined reputation associated with successful leadership. Namely, people look for and expect leaders to be trustworthy, competent, decisive, and visionary. Conversely, people who are seen as untrustworthy, incompetent, indecisive, or lacking vision are not seen as leaders, regardless of their nominal status in a group. Third, everyone wants acceptance and status, but some people are more successful at acquiring it than others. Leaders are, almost by definition, the well-liked, high-status people in a group. Social skill is the capacity to negotiate successfully for acceptance and status, and it is therefore essential to leadership.

The foregoing concerns the links between leadership and personality as seen from the outside. My final point concerns the links between leadership and personality from the inside—that is, the personal characteristics that enable leadership. There are two ways to approach the question—empirically and rationally. My sense is that the empirical literature on leadership effectiveness isn't very helpful because it typically consists of comparing the characteristics of persons at the top of a hierarchical organization with the people at the bottom, then repeating the study with a different organization. In my view, the people at the top of large organizations differ from those at the bottom in terms of political factors—for example, being relatives of the founder, and so forth. In any case, this research results in such nonfindings as: Leaders are somewhat taller than their followers and a little bit brighter.

The alternative way to study the personal characteristics that enable leadership is to take a rational or theory-based approach. Sigmund Freud (1955) and Max Weber (1948) described the essential features of leadership in terms of charisma; they both described charismatic leaders as having unusual interpersonal appeal and the ability to rally people to a cause based on the sheer force of their personalities. Charismatic theories of leadership are, in principle, personality-based theories of leadership. House (1977) took Weber's descriptors of charismatic leadership, translated them into a rating format, and showed that persons with high ratings on the descriptors are also seen as effective leaders. Bass (1985) also developed a theory of charismatic leadership, although drawing on Burns' (1978) influential book, he uses the terms *transactional* and *transformational* leadership.

There are several interesting points to be noted about transformational leadership theory. First, over the past 10 years, it has dominated the empirical study of leadership (see Judge & Bono, 2000). Second, there is substantial evidence now available to support the notion that the rating forms for transformational leadership (charisma) developed by Bass and Avolio (1995) predict a range of leadership and business outcomes (see Judge & Bono). Third, transformational leadership is a function of three broad personality attributes: ambition (extraversion in the Judge and Bono paper), likeability, and openness/intellectance. Finally, Hogan and Hogan (2000) show that measures of sociopolitical intelligence—the ability to read social cues and think about one's performance from the perspective of others—are reliably and substantially associated with a variety of leadership outcomes. But even more interesting is the fact that their measure of sociopolitical intelligence is composed of the same elements as Bass' measure of charisma—ambition, likeability, and intellectance.

The data are now quite clear—leadership effectiveness is a function of personality. But there is also a good bit of evidence to support the notion that incompetent leadership is also a function of personality. Hogan, Keith, & Furnham (in press) review the literature on managerial incompetence and conclude that the base rate of managerial failure is in the 50% range. They also conclude that the core cause of managerial failure is an inability to build a team. And finally, they document the many reasons why incompetent managers are unable to build a team, and the many reasons come down to fundamental flaws in the manager's personality.

SUMMARY AND CONCLUSION

This chapter argues that every aspect of organizational behavior and dynamics is related to personality, that the fundamental question in organizational theory concerns organizational effectiveness, that organizational effectiveness is a function of leadership, and that leadership is a function of personality. There are, in addition, processes at work in organizations that are independent of individuals but still the product of personality. This topic warrants extended treatment on its own; here I will give one example of the point. Let me start with the observation once again that people are capable of being both selfish and committed to larger causes in alternating order. Next, it is the case that the fundamental dynamic in every organization is the individual search for power (persons who are uninterested in power typically don't influence the history of organizations). With these two assumptions in place, one can derive a very interesting transpersonal organizational process. Max Weber (1948) characterized the life of every organization in terms of a historical trend line. Organizations are started by visionary, charismatic entrepreneurs. These people define the culture of the new organization, which will be fluid, fast-moving, and rather chaotic. Over time, the visionary leaders are replaced by bureaucrats in a process that Weber describes as rationalization. The organization becomes progressively more routinized, rational, rule bound, inflexible, and maladaptive.

It is clear that Weber described a real organizational trend. The larger question is, why does it occur? In my view, the process is straightforward. Rules are put into place in order to control the selfishness of individual incumbents who are exploiting the organization in some way—stealing stamps, abusing the phone, watching pornographic material at work. Rules accumulate—Hogan's law of nomological nonbiodegradability (Hogan & Henley, 1969)—so that, in mature organizations, there will be rules for virtually everything. This means that, to make something happen, one must literally break a rule. But the point is that organizations become progressively more regulated over time, not for rational reasons, as Weber's term *rationalization* implies, but rather to control the random selfish impulses and desires of incumbents. This is an example of a transpersonal organizational process that is driven by personality—or human nature.

REFERENCES

Allport, G. W. (1937). *Personality: A psychological interpretation.* New York: Holt, Rinehart & Winston.

Argyris, C. (1957). *Personality and organization.* New York: Harper.

Barrick, M. R. & Mount, M. K. (1991). The Big Five personality dimensions and job performance. *Personnel Psychology, 44,* 1–26.

Bass, B. M. (1985). *Leadership and performance beyond expectations.* New York: Free Press.

Bass. B. M., & Avolio, B. (1995). *The MLQ, Form 5x.* Redwood City, CA: Mind Garden.

Block, J. (1995). A contrarian view of the five-factor approach to personality description. *Psychological Bulletin, 117,* 187–215.

Bruner, J. S. (1986). *Actual minds, possible worlds.* Cambridge, MA: Harvard University Press.

Burns, J. M. (1978). *Leadership.* New York: Harper & Row.

Buss, A. H., & Plomin, R. (1984). *Temperament: Early developing personality traits.* Hillsdale, NJ: Lawrence Erlbaum Associates, Inc.

Campbell, D. T. (1965). Ethnocentric and other altruistic motives. In D. Levine (Ed.), *Nebraska Symposium on Motivation 1965* (pp. 283–311). Lincoln, Nebraska: University of Nebraska Press.

Cervone, D. & Shoda, Y. (Eds.). 1999. *The coherence of personality: Social-cognitive bases of consistency, variability, and organization.* New York: Guilford.

De Waal, F. (1982). *Chimpanzee politics: Power and sex among apes.* New York: Harper & Row.

Funder, D. C. (2001). Personality. *Annual Review of Psychology, 52,* 197–221.

Freud, S. (1955). *Group psychology and the analysis of the ego.* Standard Edition, Vol. 18. London: Hogarth Press.

Goldberg, L. R. (1981). Language and individual differences: The search for universals in personality lexicons. In L. Wheeler (Ed.), *Review of Personality and Social Psychology* (Vol. 2, pp. 141–166). Beverly Hills, CA: Sage.

Guion, R., & Gottier, R. F. (1965). Validity of personality measures in personnel selection. *Personnel Psychology, 18,* 135–164.

Herzberg, F. (1966). *Work and the nature of man.* Cleveland: World Publishing.

Hogan, J., & Hogan, R. (1996). *Motives, values, preferences inventory manual.* Tulsa, OK: Hogan Assessment Systems.

Hogan, R. (1996). A socioanalytic view of the Five-Factor Model. In J. S. Wiggins (Ed.), *The Five-Factor Model in personality: Theoretical perspectives.* New York: Guilford.

Hogan, R., DeSoto, C. B., & Solano, C. (1977). Traits, tests, and personality research. *American Psychologist, 6,* 255–264.

Hogan, R., Driskell, J. E., & Salas, E. (1989). Personality and group performance. In C. Hendrick (Ed.), *Personality and Social Psychology Review.* San Francisco: Sage.

Hogan, R., & Henley, N. (1969). Toward a science of human rule systems. *Proceedings, 77th Annual Convention, APA,* pp. 443–444.

Hogan, R., & Hogan, J. (1991). Personality and status. In D. G. Gilbert & J. J. Conley (Eds.), *Personality, social skills, and psychopathology* (pp. 137–154). New York: Plenum.

Hogan, R., & Hogan, J. (2000). Leadership and socio-political intelligence. In R. E. Riggio & S. E. Murphy (Eds.), *Multiple intelligences and leadership.* Mahwah, NJ: Lawrence Erlbaum Associates, Inc.

Hogan, J. & Holland, B. I. (2003). Using theory to evaluate personality and job-performance relations. *Journal of Applied Psychology, 88,* 100–112.

Hogan, R., & Johnson, J. A. (1981). Vocational interests, personality, and effective police performance. *Personnel Psychology, 34,* 49–53.

Hogan, R., Keith, K., & Furnham, A. (in press).

Hogan, R., & Roberts, B. W. (2000).

Holland, J. L. (1985). *Making vocational choices: A theory of personalities and work environments* (2nd ed.) Englewood Cliffs, NJ: Prentice-Hall.

House, R. J. (1977). A 1976 theory of charismatic leadership. In J. G. Hunt & L. L. Larson (Eds.), *Leadership: The cutting edge* (pp. 189–207). Carbondale, IL: Southern Illnois University Press.

Judge, T. A., & Bono, J. E. (2000). Five-Factor Model of personality and transformational leadership. *Journal of Applied Psychology, 85,* 751–765.

Katz, D., & Kahn, R. L. (1966). *The social psychology of organizations.* New York: Wiley.

Kouzes, J. M., & Posner, B. Z. (1987). *The leadership challenge.* San Francisco: Jossey-Bass.

MacKinnon, D. W. (1944). The structure of personality. In J. McV. Hunt (Ed.), *Personality and the behavior disorders* (Vol. I, pp. 4–43). New York: Ronald.

McAdams, D. P. (1992). The five-factor model in personality: A critical appraisal. *Journal of Personality, 60,* 329–361.

McAdams, D. P. (1993). *The stories we live by: Personal myths and the making of the self.* New York: Morrow.

McClelland, D. C., Koestner, R., & Weinberger, J. (1989). How do self-attributed and implicit motives differ? *Psychological Review, 96,* 690–702.

McGregor, D. (1960). *The human side of enterprise.* New York: McGraw-Hill.

Mead, G. H. (1934). *Mind, Self, and Society.* Chicago: University of Chicago Press.

Motowidlo, S. J., Borman, W. C., & Schmit, M. J. (1997). A theory of individual differences in task and contextual performance. *Human Performance, 10,* 71–83.

Roberts, B. W., & Hogan, R., (Eds.) (2001) *Applied personality psychology: The intersection of personality and I/O psychology.* Washington, DC: American Psychological Association.

Sarbin, T. R. (1986). *Narrative psychology: The storied nature of human conduct,* New York: Praeger.

Tellegen, A. (1985). Structures of mood and personality and their relevance to assessing anxiety, with an emphasis on self-report. In A. H. Tuma & J. D. Maser (Eds.), *Anxiety and anxiety disorders* (pp. 681–706). Hillsdale, NJ: Lawrence Erlbaum Associates, Inc.

Tett, R. P., Jackson, D. N. & Rothstein, M. (1991). Personality measures as predictors of job performance. *Personnel Psychology, 44*, 703–742.

Thucydides (1954). *History of the Peloponnesian War.* London: Penguin Book.

Weber, M. (1948). *From Max Weber: Essays in sociology.* H. D. Gerth & C. W. Mills, tr. New York: Oxford University Press.

Wiggins, J. S. (Ed.). (1996). *The Five-Factor Model of personality.* New York: Guilford.

2

Personality and Organization: A European Perspective on Personality Assessment in Organizations

Adrian Furnham
University College London

Just as cross-cultural psychologists are eager to describe, explain, and even exaggerate cross-cultural differences in human behavior, most personality theorists prefer to celebrate the universal nature of personality functioning. Indeed over the past 20 years there have been a number of attempts on the part of personality test constructors to demonstrate that tests, and the function and processes that they measure, are universally valid (Di Bias & Forzi, 1999; Ostendorf & Angleitner, 1992; Salgado, 1999). However what observers do acknowledge is that research on personality does vary across cultures. This chapter attempts to describe a European perspective on the use of personality and other individual difference measures in the work place very much from an Anglo-Saxon point of view.

Personality and I/O psychologists have been eager to demonstrate that traits relate to work behavior across jobs, industries, sectors, and countries and account for meaningful amounts of variance. Inevitably, however, different work-related dependent variables are important in different jobs and may vary from absenteeism, accidents, sales figures, and supervisor ratings. Furthermore, these dependent variables may be recorded in different ways, over different aggregated time periods and for different purposes. This situation naturally leads to serious problems for those doing replications, meta-analysis, and comparisons. However, to complicate matters further, there are a plethora of personality measures in the marketplace that differ in theoretical orientation and psychometric validity. Although there is often overlap between personality test constructs (traits), subtle differences in the way they are conceived and measured lead to further complications in comparing the results of different studies and understanding the mechanism or process that accounts for observed relationship. For these reasons it is impossible to talk of a unified European approach to this topic any more than one can assume North American research is homogeneous. Nevertheless there are discernable differences, which are the topic of this chapter.

Certainly within Europe the use of personality tests and psychometric testing remains a hot and continually debated topic (Barrett, 1998; Brown, 1999; Jones & Poppleton, 1998; Robertson, 1998; Warr, 1997). Some are concerned specifically with test validity (Barrett, 1998; Warr, 1997) and others with the trends of use of tests in business. Robertson has argued that European data provide clear evidence that personality is logically, consistently, and powerfully related to work behaviors. However, for practitioners he has specific advice: the unfocused (i.e., not thought-out) use of tests is not likely to be of value; only psychometrically valid instruments should be used; candidates do fake good in selection assessment testing; personality factors interact and hence one needs to look at the overall profile of individuals; work-related behavior is determined by both person(ality) and situational (contextual) factors; personality data have clear diagnostic value; but personality data alone are insufficient for most human resource decisions. Few academic researchers would disagree with these beliefs. However, how, when, and why human resource (HR) professionals use tests in Europe is quite a different matter. Use is dictated much more by comparing policy, the belief of senior managers, and the money available for selection and recruitment rather than on scientific and psychometric criteria.

This chapter aims to describe and attempt to explain why the American and European literature on personality and organization are both similar and different. It provides a flavor of salient research topics that may have particular European interests. Two issues are highlighted at the end of the chapter. The first is a particularly British interest in measuring team roles and the demonstrated efficacy of homogenous and heterogenous teams. The second is a concern with how the psychological problems of the unemployed inform the literature on the implicit and latent benefits of work.

WHENCE NATIONAL DIFFERENCES?

Most researchers interested in I/O psychology and applied psychology soon become aware of various national differences in both scientific and applied practice. These differences are not usually about how good research is done (at least within the empiricist tradition) but rather about different methodological emphases, fashions, and business concerns. Thus it is apparent that particular psychological instruments (ability and personality tests) are used extensively in one country but in few others. In addition, sociopolitical, economic, and legal issues mean that whereas it is impossible (or at least unwise) to collect certain organizational data (absenteeism, appraisal, and productivity reports) in one country these data are easily available in a second.

Thus one may find a literature of personality and organizational behavior that is very diverse even when examining a particular topic. For instance, temperament theory and research that was derived from Pavlov and his followers hardly crossed the Atlantic. Strelau and colleagues (Newberry et al., 1997) in continental Europe have spend decades developing, refining, and validating temperament measures (strength of excitation, strength of inhibition, mobility of nervous processes) that are theoretically very obviously related to work behavior. Yet the tests to measure temperament and its effect on organizational behavior have had, it seems, little impact on the Anglo-Saxon speaking world.

Many European psychologists have complained that Americans read only American academic journals. Furthermore, few speak any European language other than English. Hence articles on studies on temperament published in the *Polish Journal of Psychology* or the *European Journal of Personality* were, perhaps are, little read by American personality psychologists, let alone I/O researchers. Inevitably I/O psychologists interested in individual differences turn to their local personality specialists who seem to prefer theories and measures developed, tested, and marketed locally. Home-grown theories and specialists are equally favored over foreign imports.

Moreover, there seem to be national differences in what is the preferred outcome or dependent measure used to validate the instrument. Thus in America it seems organizations have long collected supervisor evaluations on staff, occasionally with other ratings such as self-ratings, direct report (subordinate ratings) peer ratings, all on work performance. This approach has meant the multirater (360°) feedback literature has been dominated by Americans though there are signs that the Europeans are now taking an interest (Furnham & Stringfield, 1994). However this feedback requires that organizations attempt to obtain reliable, multidimensional ratings on employees, which can prove politically difficult.

It is also apparent that some issues, and the academic literature that accompanies them, are nation specific. For instance the concern with integrity testing (honesty, integrity, conscientiousness, dependability, trustworthiness, reliability) seems almost exclusively an American obsession (Hogan & Brinkmeyer, 1997; Hough, 1996). On the other hand, the Europeans have been very concerned with employment status (De Fruyt & Mervielde, 1999).

It is not clear why integrity testing is so much more popular in America, because it is unlikely that the incidence of workplace deviance is very different in Europe and America. Cook (1998) has suggested that honesty tests have become popular in America since 1988 when the general use of the polygraph was restricted. Furthermore he suggested that the implementation of fair employment law has meant that some American organizations have stopped using tests that measure qualities like conscientiousness, which give reasonably good indexes of honesty, integrity, and morality. Hence they have felt the need to use specific tests to measure this phenomenon. It is often local employment law that affects selection procedures and which in turn, some years later, influences academic interests. Furthermore, high-profile litigation cases have a sudden and dramatic influence on companies, often dissuading them from using particular tests.

The availability of, and preference for, personality instruments differs not only over time but from one country to another. For a variety of reasons various European countries have their own preferred personality tests. The Dutch have been greatly influenced by Heyman's ideas (Vander Werff & Verster, 1987) whereas many East Europeans, as noted, look back to Pavlovian ideas about temperament (Strelau, 1983). The British were powerfully influenced by all the Eysenckian measures: Maudsley Personality Inventory (MPI), Eysenck Personality Inventory (EPI), Eysenck Personality Questionnaire (EPQ), Eysenck Personality Profiler (Jackson, Furnham, Forde, & Cotter, 2000). Indeed the Eysenckian three-factor model had considerable sway in North Europe until the establishment of the five-factor model (Costa & McCrae, 1992) in the late 1980s and early 1990s.

It is not clear if there is in Europe any one accepted personality model. There are those still faithful to the Pavlovian temperament school. However the two major models are probably the Eysenckian three-factor model and the Costa–McCrae five-factor model. The Eysenckian researchers have been concerned with developing new measures but also with testing Gray's (1987) critique of the theory (Avila & Parcet, 2000). The British-based journal *Personality and Individual Differences* has continued to ensure an outlet for researchers working within this framework for more than 50 years. However, the five-factor model is showing rapid inroads into Europe (Ferguson, Sanders, O'Hehir, & James, 2000). The advantage of the five-factor model for practitioners is that traits are measured at both the super and primary level, which I/O researchers like. That is, with the exception of the Eysenck Personality Profiler, most Eysenckian measures yielded three to four scores (extraversion, neuroticism, psychoticism, and lie) whereas right from the onset the five-factor model measures yielded as many as 30 scores per individual (i.e., 5 super factor scores and 30 facet scores).

Choice of personality instrument is often more a function of marketing science than psychometric science. There is nearly always a supply–demand function for personality tests. In Britain one consultancy/test publisher showed enormous growth in the sales of their test (the Organizational

Personality Questionnaire [OPQ]) loosely based on other tests at the time. The test has been carefully examined by psychometricians who have found it wanting (Barrett, Kline, Paltiel, & Eysenck, 1996) though it has predictable conceptual overlaps with the Big Five (Stanton, Matthews, Graham, & Brimelow, 1991). American test publishers have certainly been more active in Europe than the other way round though primarily in North Europe where English is better understood.

One important national difference is the preference for the lexical approaches to personality description and measurement. Although the approach started in America over 50 years ago and continued with the work of Goldberg, John, and others, it has been very enthusiastically adopted by the Dutch and Germans (De Raad, Mulder, Kloosterman, & Hofstee, 1988; John, Goldberg, & Angleitner, 1984). The emphasis on language, trait words, and descriptors has naturally meant that researchers in this tradition have been more interested initially with demonstrating cross-national/linguistic consistency (and inconsistency) than actually relating the results to workplace behavior. It is noteworthy that this research has been most enthusiastically embraced by Europeans who despite being bilingual are interested in the many subtle differences in language and the effects that may have on personality measurement.

Often I/O psychologists are dependent on HR specialists to provide their data, and it is the latter's rather than the former's decision about which tests to use. Certainly tests that appeal to organizations (e.g., Myers-Briggs Type Indicator [MBTI]; Fundamental Interpersonal Relations Orientation–Behavior [FIRO–B]) are often those with serious psychometric shortcomings and hence never reach the academic literature. Europeans have also taken an active part in the debate about the Big Five. Thus Eysenck (1992) has attacked the Costa & McCrae (1992) tradition, the former arguing for three super factors and the latter for five. Others have a four-dimensional model (Van Kampen, 1997). Although there seems to be more and more consensus about the parsimony of the Big Five measure, there remain in Europe many voices of dissent. This difference is particularly relevant with regard to the dimension of conscientiousness rather than extraversion and neuroticism which seem universally acknowledged. Conscientiousness appears from various meta-reviews to be an important personality correlate of work behavior, but there is still much debate as to how it is described. Thus different cultures have described this dimension/factor as dependability, prudence, self-control, the work ethic, and will to adhere as well as conscientiousness. There are clearly subtle but important differences between these different concepts.

Some of the European research has done little more than take well known and currently popular American tests, translate them into major European languages, and demonstrate their comparative psychometric qualities. Thus, according to Rolland, Parker, and Stumpf (1998), who translated it into French, the famous five-factor measure—the NEO-PI-R—has also been translated into seven other European languages (Croatian, Dutch, German, Italian, Portuguese, Spanish, Russian, plus Hebrew). Furthermore, the longer versions of the same instrument have also been translated (Silva et al., 1994).

Others have translated various well-established tests and there are major European translations (French, German, Spanish) of many established tests. The quality of translations differs. However, a more important problem revolves around the issue of normalizing the data for the particular country. Studies that have attempted to establish reasonable norms have shown important national differences that need to be taken into account when doing comparative studies (Drakeley & Kellett, 1995; Zuckerman, Eysenck, & Eysenck, 1978).

A number of European studies have compared translations of various questionnaires. Thus Ostendorf and Angleitner (1994) compared German translations of three American and one British questionnaire and concluded that the results could be most clearly defined within the NEO-PI-R scales. Similarly Perugini and Leone (1996) used an Italian translation of the Big Five to validate a shorter measure.

Historical and economic factors appear to lead to national differences in this research area. In Europe for many years there was a battle between Cattell, an Englishman living in America, and Eysenck, a German living in Britain (Cattell, 1986). The debate was predominantly over orthogonal versus oblique rotations, but both men were immensely productive. It seems Cattell was more successful at marketing his tests to the I/O community than Eysenck. However, Eysenck's ability to speak fluent French and German, his proximity to Europe, and his acceptance to speak at conferences meant many close ties were formed in the 1960s and 1970s. Indeed the personality of personality theorists, particularly those who market tests, can have a considerable impact on test development and subsequent success both in the academic and commercial world.

Within Europe it is possible to see various clear patterns. Because of dictatorships in Portugal and Spain until the 1970s, their psychology was more cut off from many other countries. The French insistence on the use of their own language meant they integrated very slowly into European psychology. The Belgians and Scandinavians have their national journals in English and the Dutch use English language textbooks. By the year 2000 there seemed to be a North/South divide in Europe with the British, Dutch, Germans, and Scandinavians being North American oriented while many psychologists in the other countries (France, Italy, Portugal, and Spain) had a more inward-looking focus. However, it is possible that those countries that resist European integration (Britain, Norway, Switzerland) may in time be different in their approach to HR issues than those big (France,

Germany, and Italy) and small (Belgium, Netherlands, Ireland) countries that embrace it so warmly. Considerably greater increase in academic contact and the hegemony of both the English language and American psychology have meant that, over time, national preferences and differences in this area have been decreasing. This decrease is, at least for those in the Anglo-Saxon empiricist tradition, good news for research.

FORCES TOWARD MORE HOMOGENEITY

Various sociopolitical and demographic factors lead to growing national differences and similarities. The first is legal. In Europe, pan-European legislation has, and will have, a homogenizing effect on selection as well as more general policies and practices. Thus in 1989 the European Commission published a Preliminary Draft Community Charter of Fundamental Social Rights (COM[89]248), which all member states will be invited to ratify. The twelve proposals concern rights to the following:

1. Freedom of movement.
2. Equitable wages.
3. Improved living and working conditions.
4. Social protection.
5. Freedom of association and collective bargaining.
6. Vocational training.
7. Equal treatment of men and women at work.
8. Information, consultation, and worker participation.
9. Health protection and safety at work.
10. Minimum working age and adequate training for adolescents.
11. Adequate income and social protection for the elderly.
12. Integration for the disabled into working life.

It is not difficult to see how such legislation creates standardized conditions and leads organizations in different countries to adopt similar practices. Europe hopes to be harmonized and hence there is much talk of the Euromanager. Managerial attitudes and behaviors are a function of various within, and between, company and national systems—assessment, compensation, recruitment, and selection.

A second homogenizing factor in Europe is similar demographics. All of the bigger countries of Europe are showing a dramatic decline in birthrates. Hence organizations have turned more to immigrants from ethnic groups as well as to older and married women. This situation has impacted on issues including sex and race discrimination, language and general skills training and upgrading, and the introduction of flexible working hours and day-care facilities.

A third factor is pan-European political movements like the Green Party who stress the relevance of environmental issues, which in turn affect working conditions as well as how products are produced and marketed. Strong political alliances in the European Parliament encourage trends that have an impact across the continent.

As well as quasi-political and legal bodies, various pan-European networks of psychologists have emerged to share resources and perspectives. The European Network of Organizational and Work Psychologists (ENOP) has produced a model for a European curriculum in work and organizational psychology, designed to serve as a common frame of reference for the training or work of organizational psychologists. The curriculum was produced through discussion with interested parties, including the European Association of Work of Organizational Psychology (EAWOP).

ENOP itself was founded in 1989, and comprises a network of university professors in work and organizational psychology from about 20 European countries. Their expectation is that the model will be used for evaluating existing educational curricula and modifying them to include a common core of work and organizational topics, and thereafter experience gained by ENOP will be important in a number of related developments, including the accreditation of European work and organizational psychologists.

The ENOP model includes three areas: personnel psychology, work psychology, and organizational psychology. Personnel psychology focuses on the realtionship between persons and the organization, in particular the establishment, development, and termination of the employment relationship (recruitment, training, and performance). Work psychology concerns the work processes and tasks people have to perform at work (workload, the work environment, error, and equipment design). Third, organizational psychology concerns how people behave collectively (leadership, working in groups, and organizational structure; Chmiel, 2000).

Although many forces remain that would seem to harmonize European activities and interests with respect to research on individual differences in the organization, there also remain various deeply ingrained national culture differences. From his extensive database collected throughout IBM, Hofstede (1980) developed four dimensions of culture—power distance, uncertainty avoidance, individualism, and masculinity/femininity—against which he was then able to plot 40 different nationalities. His study showed that within one multinational organizational culture, there can be marked differences based on national norms. Using Hofstede's dimensions, various researchers have proposed to select and carry out culturally sensitive interventions in overseas organizational development.

Hofstede's dimensions are as follows:

- Power distance (PD): The extent to which the less powerful members of institutions and organizations accept that power is distributed unequally.
- Masculinity/femininity (MF): A situation in which the dominant values in masculine society are success, money, and things, or in feminine society, caring for others and the quality of life.
- Uncertainty avoidance (UA): The extent to which people feel threatened by ambiguous situations and have created beliefs and institutions that try to avoid these.
- Individualism/collectivism (IC): A situation in which people are supposed to look after themselves and their immediate family or a situation in which people belong to ingroups or collectives that are supposed to look after them in exchange for loyalty.

More important, these national characteristics can be applied to organizations. Thus, all organizations can be described in terms of their score on four corporate cultures.

There are some interesting patterns. Germany, Great Britain, Ireland, and Switzerland show patterns similar to those of the United States (see Table 2.1). France and Belgium are surprisingly low on power-distance, and Belgium, Greece, and Portugal have very low scores on uncertainty

TABLE 2.1
The Scores on 15 European Countries and the USA as Comparison

	PD	UA	IC	MF
Belgium	20	5	8	22
Denmark	51	51	9	50
Finland	46	31	17	47
France	15	12	10	35
Germany	43	29	15	9
Great Britain	43	47	3	9
Greece	27	1	30	18
Ireland	49	47	12	7
Italy	34	23	7	4
Netherlands	40	35	4	51
Norway	47	38	13	52
Portugal	24	2	34	45
Spain	31	12	20	37
Sweden	47	49	10	53
Switzerland	45	33	14	4
USA	38	43	1	15

Note. Table derived from Hofstede (1980) Cultures' Consequences.

avoidance. Most European countries (like America) tend to be individual-istic rather than collectivistic though both Greece and Portugal show mod-erate scores. The dimension that shows most variability is masculinity/femininity with five countries (Italy, Switzerland, Ireland, Germany, and Great Britain) with high masculinity scores but the Scandinavian countries with high feminine scores.

Westwood (1992) has noted the organizational consequences of these scores. These patterns may explain why certain issues are more worthy of note in some countries rather than others (see Table 2.2). For instance, the scores of individuality in Great Britain are extremely high. These scores imply that the British would not naturally be good at teamwork; this impli-cation becomes an important and valid research topic, which is discussed later.

Two other points are worth making about personality and organiza-tion. Globalization of many forces including academic means that, in the end, most academics end up being oriented toward America. Those who speak English as an official language (those in nearly all parts of the old British Empire and new Commonwealth) or as a second unofficial language

TABLE 2.2
The Consequences of Four Cultural Difference Dimensions

Consequences Derived From the Power Distance Dimension	
High Power Distance Countries	*Low Power Distance Countries*
• Decision making highly centralised	• Decentralization of decision making
• Large pay and status differentials	• Small pay and status differentials
• Acceptance of authority and deference to the leader	• Expectations of involvement and nondeferential subordinate–superior relations
• Control of information by organisation heads/leaders	• Open information and communication systems

Consequences Derived From the Uncertainty Avoidance Dimension	
High Uncertainty Avoidance	*Low Uncertainty Avoidance*
• Greater organizational formality and formalization	• Less organizational formality and formalization formality and formalization
• Extensive use of policies, rules, and procedures	• Limited use of policies, rules, and procedures
• More use made of specialists Organizations value and strive for homogeneity	• More use made of generalists. Organizations value and encourage heterogeneity
• Managers more risk-averse in decision making	• Managers more willing to take risks in decision making
• Attention to detail emphasized	• Attention to strategy and the bigger picture

TABLE 2.2
(Continued)

Consequences Derived From the Individualism/Collectivism Dimension

Collectivist Countries	Individualist Countries
• Tendency to view the organization as a family and to expect to be looked after like a family member	• Organizations are viewed neutrally and there are limited expectations of the organization in terms of the personal life of members
• Engagement with the organization is on a moral basis	• Engagement with the organization is on a calculative basis
• Employees will reciprocate with loyalty and obedience to organizations who protect their interests	• Employees will stay with the organization only as long as the exchange relationship is relatively positive
• Holistic evaluation of persons and their performance	• Objective, criteria-driven evaluations
• Internal promotions	• Open, competitive promotions
• Personalistic relations	• Impersonal relations
• Group and team work emphasized	• Individual performance and expertise emphasized

Consequences Derived From the Masculinity/Feminity Dimension

Feminine Countries	Masculine Countries
• Acceptance of those who do not value a career—both men and women	• High expectation that men will pursue a career and will be considered as failures if they do not
• Wary of intraorganizational competition, preference for cooperation	• Encouragement and acceptance of intraorganizational competition
• Supportive and encouraging behavior is valued	• Aggressive and assertive behavior is valued
• Harmony is sought and confrontation avoided	• Conflict and confrontation are expected

Note. Adapted from Hofstede (1981).

probably get the messages and lead from America fastest. It is also true that many researchers are eager to import American theories, tests, and methodologies. It is not as if American academics are aggressive exporters, as their Europeans appear to be enthusiastic importers. Thus over time national differences are likely to decrease, though no doubt special legal or economic circumstances will lead to special interests.

There is, however, another little-known but potentially important factor to consider. That is the role of management, HR, and psychological consultancies, which have been growing at a great rate across Europe. Some are international with their home in America but many modest-sized consultancies specializing in testing have found it very difficult to break into the European market. Many are involved with personality and ability tests but often appear to be out-of-date in their knowledge of tests and are frequently unconcerned with test validity. Ability to sell a test to a client through personal validation often counts more than evidence of predictive validity. Hence consultants, some of whom are test publishers, can have a powerful and dramatic affect on which tests are used in organizations.

WITHIN-EUROPEA DIFFERENCES

Europeans, probably more so than outsiders, are highly conscious of their differences rather than similarities. With many different languages, histories, and economies, it is not by accident that organizational practices are so different (Hodgkinson & Payne, 1998). These practices inevitably impact on how organizations are structured and run, and more important for I/O psychologists, on which individual differences are measured, when, and why. The use of tests in selection provides an excellent example.

Various studies have focused on national differences in selection processes. Smith and Abrahamson (1992) looked at 10 studies done in European countries to compare their methods of selection. The authors concluded, after calculating correlations, that the results indicated far more similarities than differences. The much greater use of graphology in France and references in Great Britain are the only factors that seem to stand out (see Table 2.3).

A more recent and robust survey covered 12 Western European countries (Dany & Torchy, 1994). For Cook (1998) Table 2.4 indicates various interesting features:

- The French favour graphology but no other country does.
- Application forms are widely used everywhere except The Netherlands.
- References are widely used everywhere, but are less popular in Spain, Portugal and The Netherlands.
- Psychometric testing is most popular in Finland and Spain, and least popular in West Germany and Turkey.
- Aptitude testing is most popular in Spain and The Netherlands, and least popular in West Germany and Sweden.
- Assessment centres are not used much, but are most popular in Spain and Portugal. (p. 23)

Cook (1998) further speculates:

What the USA does today, Britain does tomorrow. "Today" and "tomorrow" are years apart—but how many? Suppose Britain is 20–30 years "behind"

TABLE 2.3
National Differences in the Use of Selection Methods

Methods of Selection	Country						
	GB	F	D	IS	N	NL	All
Interviews	92	97	95	84	93	93	93
CV/Application letter	86	89	92	72		63*	80*
Medical examination			50			71	61
Experience			40			63	52
References/recommendations	74	39	23	30		49	43
Diplomas and certificates				44		28	36
Cognitive tests	11	33	21		25	21	22
Performance evaluation			19				19
Preliminary test						19	19
Personality tests	13	38	6		16		18
Discussion groups			15				15
Trainability tests	14						14
Graphology	3	52	2	16	2	4	13
Work sample	18	16	13			5	13
Assessment centres	14	8	10		3		8
Biodata	4	1	8		1		4
Astrology	0	6		1			2

Note. Numbers refer to the percent of maximum possible usage: * indicates minimum value (GD = Great Britain, F = France, D = Germany, Is = Israel, N = Norway, NL = Netherlands).

Source. Table reproduced from Smith & Abramson, *The Psychologist, 5*, p. 206, with permission of the British Psychological Society.

the USA. The future in Britain will see mental ability tests being used very widely in all organizations at all levels. The future will see personality tests used quite widely at supervisory level and above, and Weighted Application Blanks (WABs) used quite widely below. The future will see the demise of the unstructured interview and the free-form reference, and a proliferation of rating systems.

But the future could turn out quite differently. In one important respect Britain is only 10 years "behind" the USA—equal employment legislation. British personnel managers might now be belatedly adopting methods the law will shortly force them to abandon. By 2002 mental ability tests could be virtually outlawed, personality tests suspect, and biographical methods unthinkable. Selectors might be forced back onto the classic trip, or forced out of business all together. (p. 25)

Table 2.4 shows variability in the use of psychometric (nearly all personality) and aptitude tests. Thus according to the data on which the survey are based, over half the companies in Finland, Spain, and Portugal use psychometric tests in selection whereas fewer than a third use them in

TABLE 2.4
The Price-Waterhouse-Cranfield Survey of Selection Methods in
12 Western European Countries

	AF	IV	Psy	Gph	Ref	Apt	AC	Grp
D	96	86	6	8	66	8	13	4
DK	48	99	38	2	79	17	4	8
E	87	85	60	8	54	72	18	22
F	95	92	22	57	73	28	9	10
FIN	82	99	74	2	63	42	16	8
IRL	91	87	28	1	91	41	7	8
N	59	78	11	0	92	19	5	1
NL	94	69	31	2	47	53	27	2
P	83	97	58	2	55	17	2	18
S	NA	69	24	0	96	14	5	3
T	95	64	8	0	69	33	4	23
UK	97	71	46	1	92	45	18	13

Note. Methods: AF = application form; IV = interview panel; Psy = psychometric testing; Gph = graphology; Ref = reference; Apt = aptitude test; AC = assessment centre; Grp = group selection methods. *Countries*: D = West Germany; DK = Denmark; E = Spain; F = France; FIN = Finland; IRL = Ireland; N = Norway; NL = Netherlands; P = Portugal; S = Sweden; T = Turkey; UK = Britain. NA = not applicable.

Source: From Dany, F., & Torchy, V. (1994). Recruitment and selection in Europe: Policies, practices, and methods. In C. Brewster & A. Hegewisch (Eds.), *Policy and Practices in European Human Resource Management: the Price Waterhouse Cranfield Survey*. London: Routledge.

Germany, France, Ireland, Norway, the Netherlands, Sweden, and Turkey. This may reflect either scepticism or legal restraints on the part of the latter countries. Certainly the use of tests in general (personality and aptitude) seem to be similar, though far fewer countries use assessment centers no doubt because of cost.

Another review presented an equally comprehensive cross-European study (see Table 2.5). Two features are striking from this table: first, the considerable within-Europea differences, and second, the variability between meta-analyses of the same country data by different researchers, suggesting the importance of sampling. It therefore remains difficult getting reliable and representative use of testing in organizations across Europe.

Tables 2.3 to 2.5 illustrate considerable within country variability. Enthusiasm for personality and ability tests in different countries differs widely as indeed does the use of tests of development, training, and development reasons. It is, however, probably true to say that at least in northern (Protestant) Europe (Britain, Holland, Germany, Scandinavia), there is a renewed interest in, and preference for, testing. This renewal considerably increases the database available to I/O psychologists to investigate the ever-salient issue of how individual differences impact on work-related behavior. It is no accident that British, German, Scandinavian, and Benelux psychologists

TABLE 2.5

Table of Management Selection Practices in Europe

Method	Bruchon-Schweitzer (1989: France) N = 102	Smith (1990: United Kingdom) N = 40	Beavan & Fryatt (1987: United Kingdom) N = 293	Schuler (1990: Germany) N = 88	Abramsen (1990: Norway) N = 61	Lievens (1989: Belgium) N = 89	De Witte et al. (1991: Flanders) N = 53	Mabey SHL (1989: United Kingdom) N = 300	SHE (1992: France) N = 48
Interviews	99	100	95	37	93	100	98	100	90
References	—	—	78	9	—	73	59	—	—
Vitae, application forms	—	—	91	90	—	91	—	—	86
Situational tests, work samples	7	—	32	16	—	51	37	37	8
Personality questionnaires	35	10	9	6	16	42	63	47	39
Cognitive & aptitude tests	31	5	5	15	25	71	74	66	31
Projective techniques	12	—	—	—	—	42	6	—	31
Assessment centres	—	10	—	9	3	31	6	—	6
Biodata	—	3	—	6	1	—	—	—	9
Graphology	93	2	5	6	2	36	7	3	46
Other methods*	15	0	—	—	1	2	—	—	—

Note. *Other methods include astrology and morphopsychology. Figures represent the percentage of respondents who say they use the method, and dash indicates the question was not used in the survey. Dates indicate when the survey was conducted, not published.

Source: From *Handbook of Industrial and Organizational Psychology*, Vol. 4, by Harry C. Traindis, Marvin D. Dunnette, and Leaetta M. Hough, (1994) by Consulting Psychologists Press, Inc. Modified and reproduced with permission.

seem to dominate European research doing empirical work on personality and organization.

A FLAVOR OF EUROPEAN RESEARCH

There are a number of ways to get some idea of European research into the issue of personality and organization. Perhaps the least efficient method is to search out the papers of various authors known to be working in the area (Furnham, 1996; Van de Berg & Feij, 1993). The next most efficient method would be to scan journals edited or published in Europe that were either specifically concerned with personality (e.g., *European Journal of Personality, European Journal of Psychological Assessment, Personality and Individual Differences*), work and organizational issues (e.g., *European Journal of Applied Psychology, European Journal of Work and Organizational Psychology, Journal of Occupational and Organizational Psychology, International Journal of Selection and Assessment*) as well as more general journals like *European Psychologist* or book series such as *International Review of Industrial and Organizational Psychology*. Inevitably this method would miss the many excellent journals not published in English and open only to the polyglot.

Perhaps a better method would be to examine reviews and meta-analyses done over the past five years or so. Furnham (1997) reviewed papers from 1961 to 1997 that had been inspired by Eysenckian personality measures and theory. These involved studies on personality and job fit, personality and job selection, personality and accidents, personality and training, and personality and job satisfaction. To illustrate how correlational and experimental psychology were happily "married," two areas of research will be considered. They were chosen for two reasons: first, to show how European-based personality theories have been applied to I/O research topic interests; second, to show the interest in traditionally experimentally based research still found in the European laboratories.

A second major source of information lies in meta-reviews. In perhaps the most comprehensive review, Salgado (1997) looked at the salient literature of personality and job performance in the European Community. His aim was to do a review similar to those done in North America to determine if the Big Five personality dimensions could be shown to be related to job performance. His hypotheses were that conscientiousness and neuroticism would be related to all job criteria in all organizations; extraversion and agreeableness would be related to occupational output variables where interpersonal factors are important (sales, contact with the public); and finally, openness to experience would be a valid predictor of training criteria. Overall he found very similar results to the meta-analyses done in North America, in which both conscientiousness and neuroticism were by far the most powerful and consistent predictors of all aspects of job performance. Salgado (1999) extends this review but comes to much the same conclusion.

Personality and Distraction at Work

Many people work in noisy environments—call centers, shops, open-planned offices, factories, and so forth. Whereas fewer people in Europe work in manufacturing, more work in the service sector, which is often a very distracting environment. There are many visual and verbal distractions that are often uncontrollable. Yet psychologists have been interested in using such elements as music in the workplace to improve productivity. Playing music in the workplace is a tradition dating back to at least the turn of the century, when music was used primarily in an attempt to relieve tedium and boredom. Early research into the effects of music in the workplace suggested that easy listening (which was sometimes termed *industrial music*) was most appropriate for routine activities, as it helped to relieve tension and boredom associated with these types of tasks. Smith (1961) found evidence for this result in the attitudes of keypunch operators listening to music during break periods between complex mental activities. It was shown that attitudes to the music were universally positive; all subjects wanted the music to be a permanent feature in their office and 90% said they were happier when the music was playing. However, the music had no significant effect on task performance.

There have been inconsistencies in the results of studies looking into the effects of music on task performance, as opposed to perception. In a review of the research completed in this area, Uhrbrock (1961) noted that factory workers preferred to work where music was played rather than where it was not played, but also not all workers liked music while they worked, with between 1 and 10% of them being annoyed by it. Furthermore, music can have adverse effects on the output of individual employees (Furnham & Bradley, 1997).

Early studies specifically examined how background stimulation affected the nature of the task. Others have focused on the nature of the distraction. Furnham and Allass (1999) looked at the effects of complex and simple music, as rated on factors such as tempo, repetition, melodic complexity, and instrumental layering and saw that there was no significant effect of musical complexity on performance. However, in a similar vein, Kiger (1989) found that scores in a reading comprehension test were significantly higher in a low information-load music condition than either a silent condition or a high information-load music condition, where information load was measured by tonal range, repetition, and rhythmic complexity.

Other studies have focused on individual differences and the inter-action of personality and environmental factors. Eysenck's (1967) theory of personality holds individual variation in cortical arousal as its central issue. He argued that introverted individuals have a lower optimum cor-tical arousal level than extraverted individuals, whose optimum arousal level is high. Introverts and extraverts differ in the amount of externally de-rived stimulation that they require to reach their optimum point of arousal. Because of their lower neurological threshold of arousal, introverts do not need as much external stimulation to reach their optimum level of func-tioning and so are satisfied at much lower intensities of stimulation. If they are subjected to stimulation that pushes them over their optimum func-tioning threshold, introverts experience an inhibition of excitation and be-come aversive to the overstimulating environment; their performance on a task deteriorates. Those individuals classified as extraverts need more external stimulation to reach their optimum functioning level, and this need encourages them actively to seek out stimulation in the environ-ment. Introverts are significantly more likely to choose to study in a quiet area of the library away from noise and activity, whereas extraverts con-sciously seek out busier study areas that provide the opportunity for social interaction.

Furthermore, introverts and extraverts have been shown to differ in their habits when studying to music, with extraverts choosing to listen to music while studying on more occasions than introverts (Furnham & Bradley, 1997) and extraverts reporting to study twice as much (50% of the time) as introverts (25% of the time) in the presence of music (Daoussis & McKelvie, 1986).

Furnham, Gunter, and Peterson (1994) examined the distracting effects of television on cognitive processing. The extraverts and introverts both performed better in silence, but the extraverts performed better than the in-troverts in the presence of television distraction. Their result was attributed to the television drawing on cognitive resources required for the reading comprehension.

Morgenstern, Hodgson, and Law (1974) found that extraverts tended to perform better in the presence of a distracter than in silence, whereas introverts functioned less efficiently in its presence. Subjects were required to attend to, and remember, specific words from a list read to them, either in silence or while being distracted by German or English words or distor-tions of these. The detrimental effects of distraction on short-term memory varied as a function of extraversion, where the most extraverted subjects remembered more words when distractions were present than when in silence. The most introverted individuals, however, remembered fewer words while being distracted.

Other studies have looked at music as the distracter. Furnham and Bradley (1997) found that, in the presence of pop music songs separated by a male voice, scores on a reading comprehension test and scores on a delayed recall short-term memory test were significantly reduced for introverts and significantly increased for extraverts. In an investigation into the effects of complex and simple music (as rated on factors such as instrumental layering and tonal complexity) in comparison to silence, Furnham and Allass (1999) found that there was a marked (yet nonsignificant) trend for the performance of introverts to deteriorate with music and for this performance to deteriorate further as the complexity of the music increased. Extraverts, on the other hand, showed improvement in performance as the complexity of the music increased, with the most superior performance being seen in the complex music condition. These studies provide support for Eysenck's theory of personality. However, Furnham, Trew, and Sneade (1999) did not find significant interactions as predicted, although the trend was in the predicted direction.

These and related findings lead Furnham (2001) to suggest, "It is most important to remember that personality variables act as both main-effects, but often more powerfully in *interaction* with other variables. Three quite distinct types of variables can be distinguished: *individual difference* variables (including abilities, beliefs, traits and values); *situational variables* (including corporate culture, group norms, physical context) and *work-outcome* or *task related* variables (productivity, satisfaction, supervisor ratings, absenteeism). The early literature focussed on person x situation interactions but often did not take sufficient cognizance of the possibility of three way interaction" (pp. 246–247).

Sensitivity to Reward and Punishments

All managers attempt to control and motivate their staff by a judicious mixture of stick and carrot. However one European theory asserts personality differences in sensitivity to reward and punishment. Gray's (1987; 1993) theory asserts that the extravert is motivated to gain a promised reward; the introvert is motivated to avoid a threatened punishment. The overapplication principle tends to lessen the intended effects, dampening the motivational qualities of reward and punishment. Because the extravert is motivated by opportunity to gain reward, too much rewarding reinforcement tends to create a satiating effect on the extravert's desire to achieve. Because the introvert is motivated by a need to avoid punishment, too many threats or actual enforcement of the negative reinforcement places the introvert in the position of being unable to avoid punishment, and so he or she becomes immobilized and the motivational effect of punishment is decreased, of course. The motivating effects of reward and punishment are not mutually exclusive; an extravert does not wish to be punished and will react to negative reinforcement, and all introverts want to be rewarded and are motivated by positive reinforcement.

The degree of neuroticism heightens an individual's sensitivity to reward or punishment. The introvert, sensitive to punishment, who displays high neuroticism becomes more sensitive to both reward and punishment with the greatest increase being toward punishment. That is, the neurotic introvert becomes more concerned with reward but is even more anxious about punishment than the stable introvert. As neuroticism increases, the extravert (sensitive to reward) becomes more sensitive to both reward and punishment, with high increases in reward sensitivity. Although extraverts and introverts increase in sensitivity to reward and punishment as neuroticism increases, each has the highest increase of sensitivity to that trait commonly attributed to extraversion or introversion.

Various studies have provided empirical support for the theory (Gupta, 1976; McCord & Wakefield, 1981). Boddy, Carver, and Rowley (1986) gave introverts and extraverts two tasks to do: Play a computer game involving initiation of cursor movements on a Visual Display Unit (VDU) to find a hidden target, and recode decimal numbers and letters and do calculations. Extraverts performed better under positive than negative reinforcement, whereas introverts performed better under negative than positive reinforcement. In a study looking at reactions to punishment, Patterson, Kosson, and Newman (1987) found extraverts failed to pause following punishing errors, but that longer pausing following punishment predicted better learning from punishment for both introverts and extraverts.

Furnham (1998) has considered implications of these findings:

Extravert organizations (that is, those dominated by extraverts) can motivate and shape staff by having small (but incremental and worthwhile) incentives that act as reinforcements. The more regular, consistent, and public these are, the better. "Sales-person of the month" and annual awards for efficiency, tact, customer relations, etc., are likely to be more successful with extraverts. Introverted organizations (that is, those that are dominated by introverts, and highly sensitive to potential sanctions and punishments) could be used to shape, or at least prevent, various kinds of behaviours. Thus, threats of imminent job loss, compulsory retirement, working on half time are likely to make introverts work harder than extraverts. Organizations dominated by extraverts would do well to maintain a "culture" where people give each other open, honest, and regular positive feedback for work well done, while introverted cultures would have ways to remind people regularly stepping out of line or underperforming will be punished. The obvious major implication of this work is that management systems devised to regulate the behaviour of employees should be sensitive to major individual differences. The carrot and the stick should both be available, but they will not have equal effect on all employees. (p. 484–485)

The two areas of research—musical distraction at work and the motivational force of rewards and punishments—are illustrations of the intersection between personality and I/O psychology in Europe. This research represents a tradition whereby ideas of individual difference processes by personality psychologists are seen to have applicability in the world of work.

Groups and Teams at Work

Most people work in teams and groups; they are interdependent on one another. One central concern for many managers is how best to select for and manage teams so that they are efficient and effective over time. Interestingly, intragroup and intergroup/team behavior has been a particular concern of European psychologists.

Reviewers have often pointed out a major difference in focus between American and European social psychologists, the former being less group oriented than the latter. However, over the past decade or so there has been a great deal of interest in team working in business environments where interdependence rather dependence or independence is encouraged. Often the more individualistic the culture (see Table 2.1), the more difficulty people have with teamwork and the more it becomes an issue. Although Sherif (1966), of Turkish origin, wrote about group conflict, it has mainly been Europeans who have developed theories in this area (Billig, 1976; Tajfel, 1981; Turner, 1991). For example, Social identity theory suggests that group membership provides its members with a descriptive and evaluative social identity. It is that part of the self-concept that derives from group membership and tends to involve prescriptive and proscriptive behavior. Intergroup theorists are clear that social identity is quite different from personal identity, which is linked to personality and idiosyncratic experience. In this sense social psychologists would disagree with personality psychologists as to what are the primary determinants of behavior at work.

Inevitably people have multiple social identities depending on their multiple group affiliations. Thus social identity is dynamic and is made salient by contextual features. Social identity theorists are particularly interested in group competition and hence are interested in social categorization, differentiation, and stereotyping as well as in-group favoritism. They tend to eschew theories like the authoritarian personality theory of prejudice which they see as inadequate and insufficient to explain prejudice. Indeed these social psychologists tend not to look for individual difference (personality trait) explanations for social behavior.

Social identity theory also posits that a need for positive self-esteem, which is in part derived from group membership, is a powerful motivating force. Thus one can change groups via social mobility to become a member

TABLE 2.6

The Eight Team Roles According to Belbin's Theory

Type	Symbol	Typical Features	Positive Qualities	Allowable Weakness	Observed Contributions
1. Team leaders a. Chairman	CH	Calm, self-confident, controlled	A capacity for treating and welcoming potential contributors on their merits without prejudice—a strong sense of objectives	No more than ordinary in terms of intellect, creative abilities	1. Clarifying the goals, objectives. 2. Selecting the problems on which decisions have to be made, and establishing their priorities. 3. Helping establish roles, responsibilities and work boundaries within group. 4. Summing up the feelings and achievements of the group, and articulating group verdicts.
b. Shaper	S	Highly strung, outgoing, dynamic	Drive and a readiness to challenge inertia, ineffectiveness, complacency	Proneness to provocation, irritation and impatience	1. Shaping roles, boundaries, responsibilities, tasks and objectives. 2. Seeking to find pattern in group discussion. 3. Pushing the group towards agreement on policy and action towards making decisions.
2. Creative thinker a. Plant	PL	Individualistic, serious minded, unorthodox	Genius, imagination, intellect, knowledge	Up in the clouds, inclined to disregard practical details or protocol	1. Advancing proposals 2. Making criticisms that lead up counter-suggestions. 3. Offering new insights on lines of action already agreed.
b. Monitor evaluator	ME	Sober, unemotional	Judgement, discretion, hard-headedness	Lacks inspiration or the ability to motivate to others	1. Analyzing problems or situations. 2. Interpreting complex written material and clarifying obscurities. 3. Assessing the judgements and contributions of others.

3. *Negotiators* a. Resource investigator	RI	Extroverted, enthusiastic, curious, communicative	A capacity for contacting people and exploring anything new. An ability to respond to a challenge.	Liable to lose interest once the initial fascination has passed	1. Introducing ideas and development of external origin. 2. Contacting other individuals or groups of own volition. 3. Engaging in negation-type activities.
b. Teamworker	TW	Socially oriented, rather mild	An ability to respond to people and to situations and to promote team spirit	Indecisiveness at moments of crisis	1. Emphasizing the need for task completion, meeting targets and schedules and generally promoting a sense of urgency. 2. Looking for and spotting errors, omissions and oversights. 3. Galvanizing others into activity.
4. *Company workers* a. Company workers	CW	Conservative, dutiful, predictable	Organizing ability, practical commonsense, hard-working, self-discipline.	Lack of flexibility, unresponsiveness to unproven ideas.	1. Transforming talk and ideas into practical steps. 2. Considering what is feasible. 3. Trimming suggestions to make them fit into agreed plans and established systems.
b. Completer finisher	CF	Painstaking, orderly, conscientious, anxious	A capacity for follow through, perfectionism	A tendency to worry about small things. A reluctance to let go	1. Giving personal support and help to others. 2. Building on to or seconding a member's ideas and suggestions. 3. Drawing the reticent into discussion. 4. Taking steps to avert or overcome disruption of the team.

47

of a more acceptable dominant or desirable group. Other strategies for those unable to change their group include changing the dimensions of the comparison, changing the consensual value attached to the (negative) in-group characteristic, or comparing themselves with other, lower status groups. This approach has important implications for changing jobs and the social standing of one's own social group.

Concern for behavior within and between work groups has, however, manifested itself in a concern for teamwork. Indeed there is a fairly extensive European interest in this area, certainly more so than in America. For more than 20 years people in business have been extremely concerned with team and team building. This concern resulted partly from trying to understand the success of the Japanese since the war as well as realizing that most jobs are done in groups and teams and not alone.

Nearly all psychometricians have concentrated on measures of intrapersonal, as opposed to interpersonal differences. That is, nearly all tests measure traits rather than interpersonal preferences.

There has been some interest in developing and validating team measures (Anderson & West, 1994; Kivimaki & Elovainto, 1999). A good example of a theory and instrument being very popular in one country but not traveling well is the Belbin Self Perception Inventory, which is extremely popular among consultants, trainers, and managers in Great Britain but little known outside those islands. It is particularly noteworthy that it was not until comparatively recently that this well-used measure was psychometrically evaluated. This has been a most interesting and important psychometric debate, especially the way in which issues surfaced around ipsative measures.

Over the last decade a number of British studies have examined the Belbin instrument on which the theory is based (see Table 2.6). The theory is essentially that when people work in teams, they tend to adopt certain roles. Eight are described, and it is essential for team efficacy that these roles are fulfilled.

For well over a decade Belbin (1981, 1993) attempted to answer the fundamental question of why some business teams (i.e., groups playing a week-long MBA-type business game) were successful and others were not. He contended that there are five principles of any effective team: (1) Each member contributes to achieving objectives by performing a functional role (professional/technical knowledge) and a team role; (2) an optimal balance in both functional and team roles is needed, depending on the team's goals and tasks; (3) team effectiveness depends on the extent to which members correctly recognize and adjust to the relative strengths within the team (available expertise and team roles); (4) personality and mental abilities fit members for some team roles and limit their ability to play others; (5) a team can deploy its technical resources to best advantage only when it has the range and balance of team roles to ensure sufficient teamwork. His research led him to conclude that people adopt roles in teams and that the particular roles adopted (or indeed not adopted) in a team, determine its efficiency and effectiveness. The theory is rich on description and taxonomization, but much less so on validation.

Belbin's work has had an enormous appeal in the British human resources community partly because it has few competitors. That is, of all the many personality tests available, few if any address the issue of teamwork and how to select people to work in teams.

Excellent teams, the theory goes, tend to have the following characteristics, which can be described in terms of the team member's roles in the team:

- The leader should have attributes similar to the chairman profile, described in Table 2.6. He or she should be a patient but commanding figure who generates trust and who knows how to use the spread of abilities in the team effectively.
- Excellent teams often include a person who generates creative and original solutions to problems (a plant).
- There should be a spread of mental abilities. If everyone in the team is very bright, then the team will spend most of its time arguing and won't agree on any effective solutions to problems.

Teams that excel have a wide spread of abilities, which include, in particular, one completer (to finish the work) and one company worker (to organize the team). A winning team often contains people with a wider spread of team roles than the other successful groups. To quote Belbin (1981): "A team can deploy its technical resources to best advantage only when it has the requisite range of team roles to ensure efficient teamwork" (pp. 132–133).

Belbin's (1981) self-perception inventory (BSPI) first appeared in his popular book, *Management Teams*. It outlines the theory that suggests eight quite distinct team-role types. Although norms based on a very limited number of people (78) were provided, little evidence of the psychometric properties of the test are offered. Thus, we know little of the test's reliability (test/retest, split-half, internal), validity (concurrent, content, predictive, construct), or its dimensionability. The BSPI questionnaire is unusual and problematic for several reasons (Furnham, 1998).

Various studies have examined the question most negatively (Broucek & Randall, 1996; Fisher, Hunter, & Macrossen, 1998; Furnham, Steele, & Pendleton, 1993) but some positively (Dulewicz, 1995; Senior, 1997). Broucek and Randall noted after their studies showing little support for Belbin's theory: "... it is understandable that little support has been given to team role theory in the academic literature. Nervertheless Belbin's work has attracted considerable support among trainers and consultants. Perhaps this is because the group roles themselves have more than intuitive appeal" (p. 404). It is both puzzling and annoying to academics to find that both consultants and clients seem uninterested and disinterested in validating theories and measures on which they often make enormously important decisions. Even more perplexing is the fact that once measures have been shown to be seriously wanting, the problem has little or no effect on the popular use and retaining of the measure.

Apart from the psychometric concerns about measures of team roles, there has been criticism of some of the assumptions often made about teamwork. Herriot and Pemberton (1995) have made a clearly important attack on teamrole theories, which they call myths. They outline two myths:

1. All friends together: A team cannot function effectively and complete its task until interpersonal relations are optimal.
2. Seven stages of a team: Teams have to go through a sequence of group development stages in a particular order to be successful.

Their argument is this: Work tasks determine processes, not the other way around. The organizational context sets the tasks the teams have to tackle and also impacts on the work processes. Roles, which are almost epiphenomenal, are simply the different parts people play in helping along the process. Different processes require different roles. It is therefore neither important nor productive to look at roles that do not predict team role effectiveness.

The problem lies in distinguishing real teams from experimental teams. Real teams have a well-known set of characteristics: shared leadership roles, collective work products, discussion, decisions, and so forth. Experimental teams such as those set up to play business games and those used for studies are different. They may focus on their individual roles and personalities precisely because they are unreal, whereas real groups would get on with the task. In other words, the emphasis on roles is misplaced and primarily a methodological artifact. It is a warning for researchers who prefer the laboratory in which to do their research.

European research on team roles has focused on a greatly neglected issue in the area of personality evaluation in organizations. It has posed the question of what sorts of people work together well in a team, which is an area still neglected elsewhere. It has surfaced other issues like problems associated with ipsative testing and methodological artifacts. Nevertheless it is likely to be an area of considerable interest in the future, as people become more rather than less interdependent at work.

Unemployment and Employment

One area of research that appears to have captured the attention of Europeans (and those in their ex-Dominions like Australia) much more than the Americans has been psychological research on unemployment (Feather, 1990; Fryer & Payne, 1986; Furnham, 1994; O'Brien, 1986; Warr, 1987). At first glance this field may seem quite irrelevant for I/O psychologists. However, it is clear that understanding not so much the causes as the consequences of unemployment gives one a very good insight into what psychological functions work actually fulfills. Furthermore it has implications for how individuals might cope under new working conditions like teleworking. Those interested in leisure and retirement have realized that in-work and out-of-work activities affect one another. In addition, by studying those who are not, but wish to be, in gainful employment, we can get a good idea of the psychological benefits of work. Whereas in America it is economists who have been particularly interested in unemployment and its psychological consequences, in Europe it has been I/O and social psychologists who have relied heavily on Freudian and Marxist ideas to understand the psychological functions of work.

Work on unemployment usually takes place in periods of high unemployment (e.g., 1930s, 1980s). Based on her work on the unemployed dating from the 1930s, Jahoda (1982) has developed a theory based on the idea that what produces psychological distress in the unemployed is the deprivation of the latent, as opposed to explicit, functions of work. Work structures time; it provides social contacts and a source of personal status and identity; and it provides a sense of purpose, mastery, and creativity. If a person does not work, he or she is deprived of its benefits.

Jahoda's deprivation theory has had its critics. Fryer (1986) has offered three kinds of criticism: pragmatic—the theory is very difficult to test; methodological—one cannot be sure which of, or how, the deprivations are caused by unemployment and people not deprived do not necessarily enjoy, appreciate, or acknowledge this state; empirical—the theory does not take into account changes over time and undivided difference in reaction.

In a sense, Jahoda (1982) argued that people are deprived whereas Fryer (1986) argued that institutions impose conditions on people (such as stigma). Furthermore, whereas the former underplayed individual choice on personal control, the latter tended to underplay social identity and interdependence of people at work. Jahoda's theory is essentially that work provides people with both explicit and implicit, obvious and latent, sources of satisfaction. Studies on unemployment have made apparent some of the less obvious needs that work fulfills. Although Jahoda's theory is not easy to test in its entirety, it has stimulated both research and theorizing. For instance, Warr (1987) developed a vitamin theory that suggested that work provides nonspecific beneficial opportunities. The theory is that job factors are like vitamins that can be grouped into two types. First, there are those (C and E) that improve health, but once the required dosage has been achieved, increasing amounts have no positive or negative effect. Second, there are those (A and D) that act much the same except that at high dosages they have a negative effect on health—the relationship is therefore curvilinear between these vitamins and health.

Warr has a clear concept of fit, whereby certain personality types or those with specific need profiles would presumably seek out and respond to jobs that offered more of these characteristics. To some extent these concepts are tautological, yet the basic idea is important: to the extent that certain jobs fulfill specific needs, it is likely that those with these needs will be satisfied in them. Presumably this relationship is curvilinear rather than linear, so one may use the concept of the optimal fulfillment of needs.

There are other theories in this area such as Feather's (1990) expectancy-valence theory. The search for a job is a function of the expectation of being offered one (given certain things have happened) and the value one attaches to having a job.

European studies of unemployment have examined descriptively stages and cycles of reactions to unemployment and are conceptually similar to work on the psychology of loss. Many cross-sectional and longitudinal studies have examined the relationship between unemployment and health (Feather, 1990; Warr, 1987) as there is abundant evidence that the two are related. Some have argued that unemployment leads to a deterioration in mental and physical health whereas others have associated that employees screen out the psychologically unhealthy. Longitudinal studies have shown evidence of reciprocal causation and vicious and virtuous cycles.

A few studies have looked at the personality characteristics of those particularly vulnerable to unemployment. Furnham (1992) found, as expected, that these studies tended to show neuroticism and psychoticism clearly associated with likelihood of becoming unemployed.

The study of unemployment is important because it throws light on employment: on the implicit functions of work, Jahoda's research in particular has helped elucidate on those implicit factors at work that can affect the stress and morale. Further studies on the negative consequences of unemployment have emphasized the role of individual differences from those who thrive on unemployment to those whose psychological functioning is significantly impaired. With many other changes in the world of work, particularly a movement to teleworking and self-employment, understanding individual differences in unemployment will become more important.

Furnham (2000) has examined the literature on teleworking and the virtual workplace, including those who are very positive about its benefits and those who are more skeptical. Many of the issues are the same as those mentioned previously about unemployment, social identity, and so forth.

As the nature of work changes throughout the developed world, I/O psychologists are taking a new interest in how individuals adapt to new conditions. So far personality theorists have been slow to examine individual differences in adaptation to teleworking, part-time, and unemployment but that will no doubt change, particularly given the rapid interest in the teleworking.

SUMMARY AND CONCLUSION

Over the past decade or so there has been a cautious rapprochement between personality and organizational psychology (Roberts & Hogan, 2001). Indeed it has been argued that personality theory has rejuvenated, even saved, I/O psychology (Hough, 2001). For many years personality psychologists have seemed more closely allied with abnormal/clinical psychologists and latterly health psychologists to find opportunities to test their theories in an organizational context. However, in both Europe and America there is evidence of personality psychologists taking a renewed interest in individual differences in work-related behavior (Hough, 1998; Robertson & Kinder, 1993). The initiative seems to have come much more from personality psychologists than from organizational psychologists. Nevertheless the association seems mutually beneficial.

To a large extent this closer union between two brands of psychology has been driven as by much by business as by academic considerations. Three events conspired in the 1980s—perhaps more in Europe than America—to make personality testing in industrial settings popular. First, the rapid rise of unemployment forced many to rethink valid and cost-effective selection and recruitment. Tests seemed to be cheaper and more efficient than interviews. Hence they were used much more in organizational settings and human resource staff began to appreciate the usefulness of tests not only for selection but also for development, counseling, and team building. Second, there was a sudden growth in test publishers and marketers who released the potential in the market. Sometimes well-established personality tests were simply marketed for their potential usefulness in applied settings, but also new tests were developed specifically to answer the needs of practitioners. It seemed the American market was much more developed than the European one at that stage. Third, peer publicity and benchmarking played an important role, particularly stories of company turnaround being attributed to the use of tests. Hence it became a badge of modernity to use tests and more recently to become familiar with testing theory.

However, the intention is not to suggest either that personality psychologists had little or no interest in work-related behavior or that their theories and tests had limited applicability. In fact, quite the contrary. As noted previously, work on distraction at work as well as on sensitivity to rewards and punishments shows up many areas in which personality theories are highly salient in organizational settings.

Although there remain notable national differences in the use of personality tests in the workplace, the globalization of markets, easy travel, and the Internet have meant greater similarity in research and organizational applications than ever before. Legal, historical, and deeply set culture differences do influence both pure and applied research in the field of personality and organization, but it is expected that over time the political and economic forces of globalization will reduce the current differences discussed previously.

REFERENCES

Anderson, N., & West, M. (1994). *The team climate inventory*. Windsor: NFER Nelson.

Argyle, M., Furnham, A., & Graham, J. (1981). *Social situations*. Cambridge University Press.

Avila, C., & Parcet, M. (2000). The role of Gray's impulsivity in anxiety-mediated differences in resistance to extinction. *European Journal of Personality, 14*, 185–198.

Barrett, P. (1998). Science, fundamental measurement and psychometric testing. *Selection and Development Review, 14*, 3–10.

Barrett, P., Kline, P., Paltiel, L., & Eysenck, H. (1996). An evaluation of the psychometric properties of the concept 5.2 Occupational Personality Questionnaire. *Journal of Occupational and Organizational Psychology, 69*, 1–19.

Belbin, R. (1981). *Management teams: Why they succeed or fail*. London: Heineman.

Belbin, R. (1993). *Team roles at work*. Oxford: Butterworth: Heineman.

Billig, M. (1976). *Social psychology and intergroup relations*. London: Academic.

Boddy, J., Carver, A., & Rowley, K. (1986). Effects of positive and negative verbal reinforcement on performance as a function of extraversion—introversion. *Personality and Individual Differences, 7*, 81–88.

Broucek, W., & Randall, G. (1996). An assessment of the construct validity of the Belbin Self-Perception Inventory and Observer's Assessment from the perspective of the five-factor model. *Journal of Occupational and Organizational Psychology, 69*, 389–405.

Brown, R. (1999). The use of personality tests: A survey of usage and practice in the UK. *Selection and Development Review, 15*, 3–8.

Cattell, R. (1986). The 16 PF Personality Structure and Dr Eysenck. *Journal of Social Behavior and Personality, 1*, 153–160.

Chmiel, N. (2000). *Introduction to work and organizational psychology: A European perspective*. Oxford: Blackwell.

Cook, M. (1998). *Personnel selection*. Chichester: Wiley.

Costa, P., & McCrae, R. (1992). Four ways five factors are basic. *Personality and Individual Differences, 13*, 653–665.

Dany, F., & Torchy, V. (1994). Recruitment and selection in Europe: Policies, practices and methods. In C. Brewster & A. Hegewisch (Eds.). *Policy and practice in European human resources management: The Price Waterhouse Cranfield Survey*. London: Routledge.

Daoussis, L., & McKelvie, J. (1986). Music preferences and effects of music on a reading comprehension testing for extraverts and introverts. *Perceptual and Motor Skills, 62*, 283–289.

De Fruyt, F., & Mervielde, I. (1999). RIASEC types and big five traits as predictors of employment status and nature of employment. *Personnel Psychology, 52,* 701–727.

Di Bias, L., & Forzi, M. (1999). Refining a descriptive structure of personality attributes in the Italian language. *Journal of Personality and Social Psychology, 76,* 451–481.

Drakeley, R., & Kellett, D. (1995). Criterion-related validity and personality questionnaires—A case study of a 'big five' measure. *Selection and Developmental Review, 11,* 4–6.

Dulewicz, V. (1995). A validation of Belbin's team roles from 16PF and OPQ using bosses' ratings of competence. *Journal of Occupational and Organizational Psychology, 68,* 81–99.

Eysenck, H. (1967). *The biological basis of personality.* Springfield, IC: Thomas.

Eysenck, H. (1992). Four ways five factors are *not* basic. *Personality and Individual Differences, 13,* 667–673.

Feather, N. (1990). *The psychological impact of unemployment.* New York: Springer.

Ferguson, E., Sanders, A., O'Hehir, F., & James, D. (2000). Predictive validity of personal statements and the role of the five-factor model of personality in relation to medical training. *Journal of Occupational and Organizational Psychology, 73,* 321–344.

Fisher, S., Hunter, T., & Macrosson, W. (1998). The structure of Belbin's team roles. *Journal of Occupational and Organizational Psychology, 71,* 283–288.

Fryer, D. (1986). Employment deprivation and personal agency during unemployment. *Social Behaviour, 1,* 3–22.

Fryer, D., & Payne, R. (1986). Being unemployed: A review of the literature on the psychological experience of unemployment. In C. Cooper & I. Robertson (Eds.). *International Review of Industrial and Organizational Psychology.* Chichester: Wiley.

Furnham, A. (1992). *Personality at work.* London: Routledge.

Furnham, A. (1994). The psychosocial consequences of youth unemployment. In A. Peterson and J. Mortimore (Eds.). *Youth Unemployment and Society.* Cambridge University Press.

Furnham, A. (1996). Personality and customer service. *Psychological Reports, 79,* 675–681.

Furnham, A. (1997). Eysenck's personality theory and organizational psychology. In H. Nyborg (Ed.). *The scientific study of human nature* (pp. 462 490). Oxford: Elsevier.

Furnham, A. (1998). *The psychology of behaviour at work.* Hove: Psychologist Press.

Furnham, A. (2000). Work in 2020. *Journal of Managerial Psychology, 15,* 242–254.

Furnham, A. (2001). Personality and individual differences in the work place: Person × Organization × Outcome Fit. In B. Roberts & R. Hogan. *Applied personality psychology: The intersection of personality and I/O psychology* (pp. 223–251). New York: American Psychological Association.

Furnham, A., & Allass, K. (1999). The influence of musical distraction of varying complexity on the cognitive performance of extraverts and introverts. *European Journal of Personality, 13,* 27–38.

Furnham, A., & Bradley, A. (1997). Music while you work. *Applied Cognitive Psychology, 11,* 445–455.

Furnham, A., Gunter, B., & Peterson, E. (1994). Television distraction and the performance of introverts and extraverts. *Applied Cognitive Psychology, 8,* 705–711.

Furnham, A., Steele, H., & Pendleton, D. (1993). A psychometric assessment of the Belbin Team-Role Self Perception Inventory. *Journal of Occupational and Organizational Psychology, 66,* 245–257.

Furnham, A., & Stringfield, P. (1994). Congruence of self and subordinate ratings of managerial practices as a correlate of superior evaluation. *Journal of Occupational and Organizational Psychology, 67,* 57–67.

Furnham, A., Trew, S., & Sneade, I. (1999). The distracting effect of vocal and instrumental music on the cognitive test performance of introverts and extraverts. *Personality and Individual Differences, 27,* 381–392.

Gray, J. (1987). Perspectives on anxiety and impulsivity: A commentary. *Journal of Research in Personality, 21,* 493–509.

Gray, J. (1993). Causal theories of personality and how to test them. In J. Royce (Ed.). *Multivariate analysis and psychological theory.* New York: Academic.

Gupta, B. (1976). Extraversion and reinforcement in verbal operant conditioning. *British Journal of Psychology, 67,* 47–52.

Herriot, P., & Pemberton, C. (1995). *Competitive advantage through diversity.* London: Sage.

Hodgkinson, G., & Payne, R. (1998). Graduate selection in three European countries. *Journal of Occupational and Organizational Psychology, 71,* 359–365.

Hofstede, G. (1980). *Cultures consequences.* New York: Sage.

Hofstede, G. (1981). Culture and organizations. *International Studies of Management and Organization, 4,* 15–41.

Hogan, J., & Brinkmeyer, K. (1997). Bridging the gap between overt and personality based integrity tests. *Personnel Psychology, 5,* 587–600.

Hough, L. (1996). Can integrity tests be trusted? *Employment Testing, 5,* 97–104.

Hough, L. (1998). Personality at work: Issues and evidence. In M. Hakel (Ed.) *Beyond multiple choice: Evaluating alternative to traditional testing for selection* (pp. 131–159). Mahwah, NJ: Lawrence Erlbaum Associates, Inc.

Jackson, C., Furnham, A., Forde, L., & Cotter, T. (2000). The structure of the Eysenckian Personality Profiler. *British Journal of Psychology, 91,* 223–239.

John, O., Goldberg, L., & Angleitner, A. (1984). Better than the alphabet: Taxonomies of personality—descriptive terms in English, Dutch and German. In H. Bonarius, E. van Heck, & N. Smid (Eds.). *Personality psychology in Europe* (pp. 83–100). Berwyn: Swets North America.

Jahoda, M. (1982). *Employment and unemployment: A social-psychological analysis.* Cambridge University Press.

Jones, P., & Poppleton, S. (1998). Trends in personality assessment for the millennium. *Selection and Development Review, 14,* 16–18.

Kiger, D. (1989). Effects of music information load on a reading comprehension task. *Perceptual and Motor Skills, 62,* 283–289.

Kivimaki, M., & Elovainio, M. (1999). A short version of the Team Climate Inventory. *Journal of Occupational and Organizational Psychology, 72,* 241–246.

McCord, R., & Wakefield, J. (1981). Arithmetic achievement as a function of introversion-extraversion and teacher-presented reward and punishment. *Personality and Individual Differences, 2,* 145–152.

Morgenstern, S., Hodgson, R., & Law, L. (1974). Work efficiency and personality. *Ergonomics, 17,* 211–220.

Newberry, B., Clark, W., Crawford, R., Strelau, J., Angleitner, A., Jones, J., & Eliasz, A. (1997). An American English version of the Pavlovian Temperament Survey. *Personality and Individual Differences, 22,* 105–144.

O'Brien, G. (1986). *Psychology of work and unemployment.* Chichester: Cambridge University Press.

Ostendorf, F., & Angleitner, A. (1992). On the generality and comprehensiveness of the Five Factor model of personality. In G. Caprara & G. van Heck (Eds.). *Modern Personality Psychology* (pp. 73–109). London: Harvester-Wheatsheaf.

Ostendorf, F., & Angleitner, A. (1994). A comparison of different instruments proposed to measure the big five. *European Review of Applied Psychology, 44,* 45–53.

Patterson, C., Kosson, D., & Newman, J. (1987). Reactions to punishment reflectivity, and passive avoidance learning in extraverts. *Journal of Personality and Social Psychology, 52,* 565–575.

Perugini, M., & Leone, L. (1996). Construction and validation of a short adjectives checklist to measure Big Five. *European Journal of Psychological Assessment, 12*, 33–41.

Robertson, I. (1998). Personality and organizational behaviour. *Selection and Development Review, 14*, 11–15.

Roberts, B., & Hogan, R. L. (Eds.). (2001). *Applied personality psychology: The intersection of personality and I/O psychology*. New York: American Psychological Association.

Robertson, I., & Kinder, A. (1993). Personality and job competencies: The criterion-related validity of some personality variables. *Journal of Occupational and Organizational Psychology, 66*, 225–244.

Rolland, J., Parker, W. R., & Stumpf, H. (1998). A psychometric examination of the French translation of the NEO-PI-R and NEO-FFI. *Journal of Personality Assessment, 71*, 2689–2690.

Salgado, J. (1997). The five factor model of personality and job performance in the European Community. *Journal of Applied Psychology, 82*, 30–43.

Salgado, J. (1999). Personnel selection methods. In C. Cooper & I. Robertson. *International review of industrial and organizational psychology*. Vol. 12. London: Wiley.

Senior, B. (1997). Team roles and team performance: Is there 'really' a link? *Journal of Occupational and Organizational Psychology, 70*, 241–258.

Sherif, M. (1966). *In common predicament: Social psychology of intergroup conflict and cooperation*. Boston: Houghton Miffin.

Silva, F., Avice, D., Sanz, J., Martinez-Arias, R., Grana, J., & Sanchez-Bernardos, M. L. (1994). The five factor model-1. Contibutions to the structure of the NEO-PI. *Personality and Individual Differences, 17*, 741–753.

Smith, M., & Abrahamson, M. (1992). Patterns of selection in six countries. *The Psychologist, 5*, 205–207.

Smith, P. (1997) Leadership in Europe: Euro-management or the footprint of history? *European Journal of Work and Organizational Psychology, 6*, 375–386.

Smith, W. (1961). Effects of industrial music in a work situation requiring complex mental activity. *Psychological Reports, 8*, 159–162.

Stanton, N., Matthews, G., Graham, N., & Brimelow, C. (1991). The OPQ and the big five. *Journal of Managerial Psychology, 6*, 25–27.

Strelau, J. (1983). *Temperament, personality, activity*. London: Academic.

Tajfel, H. (1981). *Human groups and social categories: Studies in social psychology*. Cambridge University Press.

Turner, J. (1991). *Social Influence*. Milton Keynes: Oxford University Press.

Uhrbrock, R. (1961). Music on the job: Its influences on worker morale and productivity. *Personnel Psychology, 14*, 9–38.

Van der Berg, P., & Feij, J. (1993). Personality traits and job characteristics as predictors of job experiences. *European Journal of Personality, 7*, 337–357.

Van der Werff, J., & Verster, J. (1987). Heyman's temperamental dimensions recompleted. *Personality and Individual Differences, 8*, 271–276.

Van Kampen, D. (1997). Orderliness as a major dimension of personality. *European Journal of Personality, 11*, 211–241.

Warr, P. (1987). *Work, unemployment and mental health*. Oxford: Clarendon.

Warr, P. (1997). The varying validity of personality scales. *Selection and Development Review, 13*, 3–7.

Westwood, R. (1992). Culture, cultural differencec, and organizational behaviour. In R. Westwood (Ed.). *Organizational behaviour: Southeast Asian perspectives*. Hong Kong: Longman.

Zuckerman, M., Eysenck, S., & Eysenck, H. (1978). Sensation seeking in England and America: Cross-cultural, age and sex comparisons. *Journal of Consulting and Clinical Psychology, 46*, 139–149.

II

Persistent Conceptual and Methodological Issues in Personality Assessment

Stewart and Barrick take on the issue of the prediction of performance at work from personality assessments. They suggest that inconsistencies and generally modest validity coefficients in that arena may be attributable to a failure to consider situational moderators as explanatory constructs, that is, that insufficient attention has been paid to the findings from interactional psychology in understanding the contribtiuons of personality in organizational situations. In a similar vein, Judge and Kristof-Brown explicitly consider the issue of person–situation interaction, specifically the different meanings the term *interaction* can have. They then proceed to identify the potential for an expanded concept of person–situation fit to contribute to our understanding of the ways persons and situations merge. Their approach complements that of Stewart and Barrick very nicely, and the two chapters provide a rich source of hypotheses for future conceptualization and research.

Other recent books on personality in work organizations (e.g., Roberts & Hogan, 2001) are concerned primarily with assessment and measurement issues—clearly an ongoing concern in personality psychology. We chose in this volume to take a road less traveled but still felt it necessary at least to address some of these issues—as Smith and Robie do by debunking traditional objections to personality assessment via structured inventories.

REFERENCES

Roberts, B. W., & Hogan, R. (Eds.). (2001). *Personality psychology and the workplace.* Washington, DC: American Psychological Association.

Four Lessons Learned From the Person–Situation Debate: A Review and Research Agenda

Greg L. Stewart
Brigham Young University

Murray R. Barrick
Michigan State University

This chapter uses four lessons learned from the person–situation debate of personality and social psychology to review research related to the role of personality traits in work organizations. These lessons include the notions that traits predict behavior only in relevant situations, that traits relate most strongly to behavior when situational cues are weak, that a person's traits can alter a situation, and that people choose situations that are congruent with their traits. As an illustration of how these lessons can guide future research, we also develop a model that builds on the first lesson. The model classifies organizational situations and describes how motivational intentions mediate the effects of personality in cooperative and competitive settings.

Prison officials once asked a psychologist to assess the personality of a convicted murderer and conclude with certainty whether the convict would commit murder again. The psychologist wisely declined. In the field of industrial and organizational psychology we normally seek to predict work-related behaviors rather than proclivity to commit murder. However, similar to the psychologist in this example, we frequently face challenges in determining the proper role of personality measurement in predicting behavior. Fortunately, research can guide us. Our objective in this chapter is to review recent research and seek some conclusions about the use of personality measures for predicting work behavior. We will also build on existing research to present a forward-looking agenda that can improve our understanding of personality–performance relationships.

The difficulty surrounding the use of a personality measure to predict murder is well understood within the context of the person–situation debate that has raged within the fields of social and personality psychology. The central question is whether behavior is the result of traits or situations. If behavior is influenced only by traits, then a conclusion that the convict would not murder again may be possible. However, if behavior is also determined by one's environment, then a definitive conclusion cannot be reached unless the convict's environment is carefully controlled (i.e., he remains in prison). Thus, most of us would agree that behavior is influenced by both traits and situations. However, the basic concept that traits and situations interact to influence behavior seems to be frequently overlooked when we conduct studies and interpret research findings. Because we believe much can be learned from viewing personality research through a person–situation lens, we adopt this perspective throughout this chapter. In particular we illustrate how lessons learned from the general person–situation debate of social and personality psychology are also being learned in employment contexts. We then provide a specific example of how lessons learned from the person–situation perspective can guide future research efforts.

FOUR LESSONS FROM THE PERSON–SITUATION DEBATE

Mischel's (1968) book, *Personality and Assessment*, set forth a number of strong arguments suggesting that traits do not really exist. Over the following decades a number of researchers set out to disprove Mischel's contention. Taken as a whole their studies suggest that traits do indeed exist, but their findings also illustrate that situations influence behavior (Kenrick & Funder, 1988). Perhaps more important, the studies conducted to test Mischel's assertion have taught us a great deal about the relationships among traits, situations, and behaviors. Kenrick and Funder (1991) summarized what can be learned from research related to the person–situation debate in four basic principles: (a) specific traits predict behavior (show up) only in relevant situations, (b) all traits are more easily expressed in some situations than others, (c) a person's traits can actually change a situation, and (d) people choose different settings to match their traits. Each of these four principles can be applied to the employment context.

Lesson 1: Specific Traits Predict Behavior Only in Relevant Situations

One lesson from the person-situation debate is that traits do not predict behavior in all situations. The social and personality psychology literature has demonstrated the lesson that traits show up in relevant settings by illustrating that traits are most easily expressed in congruent situations (Donahue, Robins, Roberts, & John, 1993; Sheldon, Ryan, Rawsthorne, & Ilardi, 1997). For instance, dominance is likely to be more frequently expressed in athletic settings, whereas intellectance is more likely to be expressed in academic settings (Kenrick, McCreath, Govern, King, & Bordin, 1990). We believe a slightly different perspective on the issue of situational relevance is more applicable in work settings. That is, we emphasize the prediction of behavior rather than simply the emergence of traits expressed across situations. Although this lesson is somewhat different than the research by others reported previously (Donahue et al.; Kenrick et al.; Sheldon et al.) and the original principle described by Kenrick and Funder (1991), we think theoretical understanding will be advanced more if we focus on which trait expressions matter (because they link with performance). We thus shift our focus away from the traits that are most likely to be expressed in specific situations and focus instead on identifying which traits are relevant for predicting behavior in specific settings.

An important element of work situations is the behaviors that are required for high performance. Because the behaviors that are required for work success vary across situations, an important element of the work situation is thus the specific behaviors that are required for high performance in that setting. This suggests that certain traits are relevant only in situations where behaviors linked to those traits constitute high work performance. If expression of the trait is not related to work performance, then the trait becomes irrelevant to the work situation. For purposes of this chapter, we therefore broaden the definition of *situation* in work contexts from being simply the individual's surrounding environment to explicitly include the behaviors that are expected of a person in that setting. In the work context the focus thus shifts from the question of which traits are expressed to the question of which traits matter.

Recent research has converged on a five-factor model (FFM) of personality. The FFM consists of extraversion, emotional stability, conscientiousness, agreeableness, and openness to experience (Barrick & Mount, 1991). Research in the work literature has underscored the relative importance of two FFM traits—conscientiousness and emotional stability—at work. For example, Dunn, Mount, Barrick, and Ones (1995) found that conscientiousness was the most important personality trait managers attend to when making hiring decisions. In this policy-capturing study, across jobs from all six Holland occupational groups (RIASEC; Holland, 1997), conscientiousness was the most important personality trait related to applicants' hirability, and it was viewed to be nearly as important as General mental ability (GMA; $\beta = .40$ for conscientiousness and $\beta = .46$ for GMA across jobs). Emotional stability was the second most important FFM trait regardless of the content of the job ($\beta = .30$ across jobs). Meta-analytic findings have confirmed the importance of these two traits by showing that conscientiousness, and to a lesser extent emotional stability, are valid predictors of job performance criteria for numerous occupations (e.g., Barrick & Mount, 1991; Hough, Eaton, Dunnette, Kamp, & McCloy, 1990; Salgado, 1997). In fact, Barrick, Mount, and Judge (2001) quantitatively summarized the results of prior meta-analytic studies investigating the relationship between the five-factor model (FFM) personality traits and job performance and found that both conscientiousness and emotional stability are valid predictors of overall work performance ($\rho = .27, k = 239, N = 48,100$ for conscientiousness; $\rho = .13, k = 2224, N = 38,817$ for emotional stability). These analyses once again illustrate that conscientiousness, and to a lesser extent emotional stability, are the traits that tend to be elicited by successful employees and are most critical for success across work settings.

Although conscientiousness and emotional stability appear to be relevant in nearly all work settings, other FFM traits are likely to relate to behavior only in specific work contexts or for specific work outcomes. For example, Barrick and Mount (1991) found extraversion to be related to overall job success when the job required extensive social interactions (e.g., managers and sales). Extraversion and openness to experience have also been found (Barrick et al., 2001) to consistently be related to training proficiency ($\rho = .28, k = 21, N = 3,484$ for extraversion; $\rho = .33, k = 21, N = 3,177$ for openness to experience). Furthermore, a meta-analysis by Mount, Barrick, and Stewart (1998) found agreeableness, an FFM trait that historically has not been linked to higher job performance, to be positively correlated to success when work is organized such that cooperation and substantial teamwork are important for accomplishing work ($\rho = .27, k = 10, N = 1,491$).

A specific example that illustrates the influence of the work situation on trait–performance relationships is a study by Stewart (1996). In this study, the organizational setting differed such that some sales representatives were rewarded for identifying and adding new members (i.e., emphasize new sales), whereas the other representatives were rewarded for contacting and renewing existing members (i.e., customer retention). The study results indicated that extraversion, which has been shown to be sensitive to the situational influence of rewards (Gray, 1973), was related to higher performance only on those dimensions that were explicitly rewarded. Changes in major dimensions of the work situation, such as reward structure, can thus be expected to elicit certain trait expressions and to affect relationships between traits and job performance.

Further evidence of traits being relevant to specific situational differences is found in a study by Tett, Jackson, Rothstein, and Reddon (1994), who concluded that studies using a confirmatory approach, where the researcher has a theoretical basis for linking the personality construct and job performance criterion, have significantly larger predictive validities than those studies that are exploratory. This study suggests that traits affect performance most strongly when they are aligned with the specific behaviors that are elicited by and that constitute high performance within the situation. However, the Tett et al. findings also demonstrated that the use of a formal job analysis did not yield significantly larger validities than those studies where researchers simply predicted a relationship between the trait and success in the job. This result coupled with the findings from Dunn et al. (1995) illustrate that many researchers and managers are likely to have an implicit theoretical understanding about how the demands of the job dictate which personality traits are likely to be relevant. Thus, implicit notions of personality establish boundary conditions that identify when personality and behavior are likely to be strongly related. In other words, managers and human resource professionals are fairly accurate judges of which traits will be predictive of success in which work situations.

Another stream of research also provides insight concerning trade-offs between broad and narrow traits for predicting performance in different work situations. Crant (1995) found a relatively specific measure of proactive personality to incrementally predict performance beyond conscientiousness, extraversion, and general mental ability. Judge, Martocchio, and Thoresen (1997) found that broad traits predicted employee absence just as well as more specific traits. In both of these cases, the criterion of interest was relatively broad. When predicting overall performance, Ones, Viswesvaran, and Schmidt (1993) found that integrity, which was a broad composite of FFM conscientiousness, agreeableness, and emotional stability, had a true score correlation of .37. These effects are larger than those found for specific facets of personality when predicting overall performance, where correlation coefficients rarely exceed .30.

Mount and Barrick (1995) found traits more narrow than the FFM to better predict some specific facets of performance, but FFM-level traits were comparable if not superior for predicting overall job performance. For example, they found dependability (a component of conscientiousness) predicted training proficiency ($\rho = .36$), employee reliability ($\rho = .47$), and quality ($\rho = .48$) better than conscientiousness ($\rho = .30, .41, .44$, respectively), while achievement predicted effort ($\rho = .58$) better than conscientiousness ($\rho = .51$). Stewart (1999) found that facets of conscientiousness predicted performance better than the broad trait when they were specifically aligned with specific aspects of job performance. However, because performance is often dynamic over time, these results also suggest that broad traits may be best when predicting performance over an extended time period.

Taken as a whole, the results of these studies suggest that the breadth of behavior appropriate for a given situation influences the appropriate level of measurement for personality traits. Narrow traits are desirable when the behavior appropriate for the situation is specifically identified. Moreover, to enhance theoretical understanding, there is considerable value in matching more specific traits with more specific performance measures. However, overall job performance is a relatively broad construct (Viswesvaran, 1993). Consequently, when making a selection decision, broader personality traits are likely to predict as well or better than specific facets of personality traits. Once again these findings illustrate that the nature of the trait, in this case its breadth, should be taken into account when determining the relevance of that trait for explaining behavior in a given situation.

Even when matched with relevant situations, critics of personality have questioned the practical usefulness of personality measures for selection purposes. Their primary concern is the relatively small relationships often reported between personality and overall performance. However, recent research that examines the nature of the relationship between specific personality traits and long-term career success has important implications for this issue. For example, Seibert, Crant, and Kraimer (1999) found that people with a proactive personality were more likely to experience both intrinsic and extrinsic career success. Similarly, Judge, Higgins, Thoresen, and Barrick (1999) found that relevant personality traits were capable of predicting multiple facets of intrinsic and extrinsic career success, even over a span of 50 years. They found that conscientiousness positively predicted intrinsic and extrinsic career success ($r = .40$ and $.41$, respectively) whereas neuroticism negatively predicted career success ($r = -.22$ and $-.34$, respectively) over very long periods of time. Thus, even if the effects of personality on job success are modest in magnitude, as critics contend, compounding these effects over a lifetime suggests that selecting employees with desirable traits will have a substantial payoff over time.

In summary, lessons regarding traits relevant to specific situations suggest that some traits—conscientiousness and to a lesser extent emotional stability—correlate with measures of job performance across work situations. Relationships with other traits are more situationally dependent. However, organizational designers can often modify situations (e.g., modify reward structures) in order to maximize trait–performance relationships. Researchers and practitioners alike will thus be wise to carefully analyze situational conditions before predicting which traits correspond with which behaviors. For instance, broad measures like the FFM are most appropriate for predicting broad sets of behavior such as overall job performance, whereas more narrow traits are best for predicting specific behaviors.

We feel that one barrier presently holding back personality research is the absence of a taxonomy for classifying both work situations and specific work behaviors that relate differentially to personality traits. We will present some ideas for overcoming this problem in the final section of this chapter. Nevertheless, returning to the basic premise of the first lesson from the person–situation debate, existing research does support the claim that work settings provide a situation where traits are at least modestly effective for predicting behavior.

Lesson 2: All Traits Are More Easily Expressed in Some Situations Than Others

A second lesson of the person–situation debate is that situations have an effect on trait expression. Some situations are so strong (i.e., they provide strong environmental cues for appropriate behavior) that everyone behaves similarly. Other situations provide weak cues, and in such settings traits greatly influence behavior. This result was demonstrated in a work context by Barrick and Mount's (1993) study finding trait–performance relationships to be strongest in situations that afforded high worker autonomy. When managers were given a great deal of discretion in selecting the way work behaviors are performed, being higher in conscientiousness, higher in extraversion, and lower in agreeableness resulted in better performance. In another study, Hochwarter, Witt, and Kacmar (2000) demonstrated that conscientiousness is more strongly related to job performance when the situation fails to provide normative guidelines for behaviors (i.e., when workers perceive moderate to high levels of workplace politics). These findings demonstrate that traits are most likely to be useful in those settings where situational pressures or demands to work in specific ways are weak (i.e., high autonomy).

One important trend at work today is that jobs are being radically restructured (Capelli, 1999; Drucker, 1999). In general, work is becoming more unstructured and shifting from physical effort to knowledge work, with less direct supervision. Although it is hard to predict how these dramatic changes in work situations will affect the relationship between personality and performance, the fact that work appears increasingly to be more autonomous (i.e., a weaker situation) implies that personality will be a more important predictor of success at work in the future.

Although perhaps not obvious, the importance of accounting for situational strength is also shown through research related to response distortion and faking on personality tests. Kenrick and Funder (1991) suggest that a job interview represents a very strong situation. Asking a job applicant to complete a personality inventory similarly creates a very strong situation. The strong situation created by interviewing and testing thus inhibit trait expression. Athough faking and response distortion are usually seen as measurement artifacts, we believe insight can be gained by viewing them with a situational lens.

Viewing personality test responses in terms of situational strength illustrates the value of trying to alter the testing situation in order to decrease the situational influence on applicant responses and thereby obtain more accurate trait measures. One example of an attempt to alter the testing situation is a study by Schmit, Ryan, Stierwalt, and Powell (1995), who found that adding tags like "at work" provides respondents with a common frame of reference and increases the criterion-related validity of the measures. Another tactic has been to focus items on behavioral patterns rather than simple adjective descriptors. The increased validity of such measures was shown by Cellar, Miller, Doverspike, and Klawsky (1996), who compared the validity of a questionnaire-based measure (NEO-PI; Costa & McCrae, 1992) and an adjective-based bipolar inventory (Goldberg, 1992). They found higher validity for the questionnaire-based measure. Similar to item tags, the behavior-based questionnaire seemed to provide a more common and behaviorally oriented frame of reference. Including measurement items that are behavioral and work focused thus appears to be one method of altering the testing setting in order to make it more congruent with the actual work setting and thereby to improve personality assessment in selection contexts.

A good deal of research has also examined whether the strong situation of applicant assessment alters applicant responses. Evidence strongly suggests that, when instructed to do so, people can distort personality scores to make themselves appear more desirable as job applicants (Hough et al., 1990). In other words, a strong situation can be created. Research also suggests that coaching applicants concerning the purposes of the test can further strengthen the situation, and in such settings faking has been found to increase even more (Cunningham, Wong, & Barbee, 1994; Zickar & Robie, 1999).

However, the question of whether job applicants actually distort their responses in typical selection settings (i.e., is the situation really that strong?), and if so, what the effect of that distortion is, has been more difficult to answer. Evidence supporting the argument that the employment application setting is a strong situation is found in studies revealing applicants to have higher mean scores than volunteer respondents or job incumbents (Barrick & Mount, 1996; Cunningham et al., 1994; Ellingson, Sackett, & Hough, 1999; Rosse, Stecher, Miller, & Levin, 1998; Stewart, 1999). Similarly, response distortion scores have been found to be higher for job applicants than for incumbents (Rosse et al.), and the variance of applicant responses has been found to increase for some measures and decrease for others (Rosse et al.; Zickar & Robie, 1999). In contrast, there is recent evidence that suggests that factor structure is consistent across volunteer, applicant, and incumbent populations (Smith, Hanges, & Dickson, 2001) and that factor structure is consistent for applicants who respond in a manner that is either high or low on social desirability (Ellingson, Smith, & Sackett, 2001). Evidence thus seems to be somewhat mixed about whether people provide different responses when they know personality measures will be used for employment evaluation.

Yet, the more critical question is how the strength of the response situation affects the usefulness of personality measures in the selection context. Across a number of studies, statistically correcting for response distortion has not been found to alter the predictive validity of personality measures (Barrick & Mount, 1996; Christiansen, Goffin, Johnston, & Rothstein, 1994; Cunningham et al., 1994; Ellingson et al., 1999; Ones, Viswesvaran, & Reiss, 1996). Moreover, R. Hogan (1991) has argued that applicant distortion captures job-relevant variance, as people who can successfully alter their responses on a personality test to make themselves appear more desirable for the job are also likely to adapt well to social expectancies at work. From this perspective, faking may not reduce the predictive validity of a personality test. In fact, successful faking may actually indicate whether someone will be successful at work.

Although the magnitude of validity coefficients is similar for studies using job applicants and incumbents, evidence suggests that some people distort their personality responses more than others and that this differential distortion can affect who gets hired (Christiansen et al., 1994; Ellingson et al., 1999; Rosse et al., 1998). In particular, when selection ratios are low, the rank order of applicants appears to change such that people with extreme distortion are ranked above others who have desirable traits but who distort less. The effect of response distortion thus seems to be an individual-level bias against people who possess relevant traits but who do not engage in extreme distortion. An interesting research question could relate to how attractive the testing and work situations are to the applicant. Differences in attractiveness may lead to differences in situational strength. These differences in turn may lead to differential applicant distortion.

In conclusion, as this principle demonstrates, researchers must consider the strength of the situation when determining the likely value of including personality measures. In very strong settings, the utility of personality scores will be reduced substantially, as the demands or pressures salient in the work setting determine behavior. Consequently, personality is likely to be more relevant in novel settings than highly familiar, routinized work environments. Furthermore, as the work setting becomes less rigid and more autonomous, this research implies that personality will be more important. The creation of a strong situation during applicant assessment also suggests a need to find methods for altering the testing situation. In particular, gains seem possible when (a) the assessment situation more closely resembles the work situation and (b) the strength of the assessment situation is reduced so that traits are easily expressed and observed.

Lesson 3: A Person's Traits Can Actually Change a Situation

A third lesson from the person–situation debate is that an individual with a certain set of traits can alter a situation. This effect is demonstrated in many university classes. The presence of a single disagreeable student can vastly affect the cooperation and learning of a class. The effect of individuals on situations at work has been demonstrated by research linking traits to team-level performance.

Barry and Stewart (1997) found that highly extraverted team members were generally seen by their peers as the strongest contributors to team success. However, teams with approximately half of their members scoring high on extraversion performed better than teams with either too few or too many extraverts. This suggests that in team settings the desirability of an individual's traits may depend on the traits of other team members. Simply hiring people based on desirable individual traits such as extraversion may be counterproductive. The potential contribution of any individual is largely dependent on how that individual affects the situation created for others.

Barrick, Stewart, Neubert, and Mount (1998) also examined personality in a team context. They found that higher aggregate levels of team-member conscientiousness, agreeableness, and emotional stability enhance team performance. They also found that team performance can suffer by the inclusion of a single member who scores low on conscientiousness, agreeableness, or extraversion. Neuman and Wright (1999) similarly found team performance to suffer when individuals low in agreeableness and conscientiousness were included in teams. Thus, whereas someone's traits may have only a limited impact on his or her individual behavior, they have the potential to either help or harm the performance of the team as a whole. Again, these results suggest that a single individual can alter the environment of coworkers and thereby influence their behavior.

Recognition that a person can change a situation has important implications for selection. Typically, we encourage practitioners to hire the highest scoring candidate, irrespective of other employees. However, as team-focused research suggests, there may be some settings where the decision about whom to hire depends on who is already employed. Whether you should hire an extraverted applicant may depend on whether the present workforce is composed of other extraverts or introverts. Although the selection decision becomes more complex, the potential payoff for making a good selection decision increases as the performance of many, rather than only one, can be improved.

Lesson 4: People Choose Different Settings to Match Their Traits

Another lesson from the person-situation debate is that people choose settings congruent with their traits. For instance, extraverts seek out parties whereas introverts seek out places of solitude. The influence of traits on situational choice has been nicely demonstrated recently in research related to work contexts.

DeFruyt and Mervielde (1999) found Holland's (1997) measure of career interest to be an optimal predictor of career choice. However, they also found that FFM traits could help explain vocational choices. Individuals scoring high on extraversion chose more social and enterprising positions ($r = .26$ and $.44$, respectively). People scoring high on openness chose more artistic and social jobs ($R = .54$ and $.42$, respectively), and people scoring high on emotional stability were more apt to choose enterprising and conventional jobs ($R = .32$ and $.26$, respectively). Conscientiousness was positively correlated with choosing enterprising and conventional occupations ($r = .33$ and $.44$, respectively), and was negatively correlated with artistic positions ($r = -.20$). Finally, people scoring high on agreeableness were less apt to choose enterprising jobs but were more likely to choose social occupations ($r = -.25$ and $.20$, respectively). Judge et al. (1999) also found evidence that people with certain FFM trait patterns gravitate toward certain types of jobs, supporting the notion that FFM traits can help explain why people choose certain careers. Ackerman and Heggestad (1997), in a review of this literature, conclude that agreeableness and emotional stability are not related to any of the six Holland vocational choices, but conscientiousness is correlated with conventional jobs, extraversion is associated with both enterprising and social jobs, and openness to experience is linked to investigative, artistic, and social occupations. Thus, while this research is not conclusive, it is more than suggestive that certain personality traits not only determine the probability of success in a particular job, but also influence one's motivation to choose the occupation (situation).

Personality traits also link to perceived fit with certain organizational cultures (Judge & Cable, 1997). Job seekers scoring high on neuroticism were less attracted to innovative and decisive organizations. Those scoring high on extraversion were attracted to aggressive and team-oriented organizations, but not to supportive organizations. Individuals open to experience preferred innovative and detail-oriented organizations. Agreeable people preferred team-oriented and supportive organizational cultures, but shunned aggressive, outcome-oriented, and decisive cultures. Highly conscientious job seekers preferred detail-oriented and outcome-oriented organizations, but not innovative organizations.

Fit between traits and organizational cultures is confirmed by Schneider, Smith, Taylor, and Fleenor (1998) and Schaubroeck, Ganster, and Jones (1998) who found organizations to be homogeneous in terms of the personality characteristics of their managers. In particular, Schneider et al. found organizations were most likely to differ with respect to the fit (variation) of agreeableness (thinking–feeling), openness to experience (sensing–intuition), and extraversion (extraversion–introversion) of their managers. This suggests that firms can actively manage the modal personality attributes of their managers and that benefits can potentially derive from creating the desired environment by focusing on niche personality traits such as agreeableness, extraversion, and openness to experience. These traits are labeled *niche traits* because their relative importance depends on the specific work situation, whereas conscientiousness and emotional stability are likely to be important across jobs. Organizations can therefore create a competitive advantage by emphasizing the contextual factors that create a unique organizational environment, one that is desired by people with certain traits. Specifically, variation in agreeableness, openness, or extraversion is likely to be influential in determining which people choose to join and remain with the firm.

The fourth lesson thus suggests that considering fit issues during selection should enable firms to identify those applicants who are more likely to remain with the firm. However, one caution to this research is that Schneider (1987) has predicted that greater homogeneity will not be beneficial to long-term organizational effectiveness, as homogeneous firms will not be as adaptive or flexible in dealing with difficult tasks involving demands for creativity and innovation. At the individual level there is also cause for concern, particularly in regard to person–job fit. For example, research illustrates that those individuals who are sensitive to negative affect (neurotics) tend to avoid threatening situations. Thus, emotionally stable employees are more likely to volunteer for stressful settings. To the extent that such experiences enhance one's career, there may well be severe negative consequences to the long-term success of individuals who avoid challenging work experiences because of their personality traits. Nevertheless, these speculations about the cost of these choices must be labeled as such—speculations. In contrast, recent research has begun to underscore the influence one's traits have on career choices, and the evidence suggests greater fit will result in greater career satisfaction and tenure in organizations.

MODELING THE EFFECTS OF SITUATIONAL DEMANDS

In the past decade or so, personality research has made significant strides in understanding the nature of the relationship of personality to job performance. This progress appears to be largely due to the use of the FFM personality taxonomy and meta-analytic methods to summarize results quantitatively across studies. As illustrated in the previous discussion, much has been learned from this body of research; however, much more can be learned. Our review of findings in social psychology, personality psychology, and industrial/organizational psychology suggests that future research in personality and performance is most likely to make meaningful contributions when situational influences are taken into account. Thus, future research should consider four important principles: (a) personality predicts behavior only in relevant work settings, (b) personality–performance relationships increase as situational strength decreases, (c) an individual's traits can change a setting, and (d) employees are attracted to, selected by, and remain with organizations and jobs that match their traits.

Because space limitations prevent us from discussing research applications for each of the four principles, we will focus specifically on the first lesson associated with the relevance of situations. In particular, we propose an initial method for classifying work situations. This classification enables us to categorize situations broadly and thereby begin a theoretical explanation of the effects of situational differences. We then link this classification method to our recent research examining the motivational intentions that underlie personality–performance relationships. Combining situational classification with motivational intentions results in the development of a model that describes how specific situational characteristics influence relationships between personality traits and work performance.

Identifying Fundamental Characteristics of Work Settings

Much effort has been directed toward understanding situational characteristics of the immediate work situation (e.g., the job analytic literature). However, efforts to specify and assess situational characteristics that systematically affect relationships between personality and work performance, as well as motivation, have been relatively rare (Murtha, Kanfer, & Ackerman, 1996; Peters & O'Connor, 1980). To fully describe or theoretically justify a consensual, replicable taxonomy of psychologically meaningful situations is beyond the scope of this chapter. Rather, our intent here is to begin to develop a model that focuses on situations likely to be encountered at work that have substantial effects on employee behavior, yet describe relatively broad situational characteristics. Hierarchically, these situations would be second-order factors that consist of a number of lower level situations that elicit responses that when aggregated do not markedly change the nature of the relationship between the personality trait and response (Murtha et al.). This kind of taxonomy should improve prediction with personality traits and enhance our understanding of how traits and situations interact to influence behavior at work.

The open systems perspective presents one avenue for exploring the effect of situational characteristics. From this perspective, organizations are seen as having dynamic interaction with their environments. Moreover, an organization is seen as an entity that is composed of many partially nested open subsystems (Katz & Kahn, 1978). Given this framework, each individual within an organization is seen as an embedded subsystem that interacts with elements of the larger environment created by the organization. As pointed out by Argote and McGrath (1993), each subsystem (person) staves off entropy (the tendency toward energy depletion) by seeking to achieve net gain from its environmental interactions. The organization is thus in a state of competition with its subsystems (people), which often results in conflicts of interest between individuals and the organization as a collective entity. What is best for an individual may often be different than what is best for the collective. This inherent conflict between individuals and the collective creates competing needs for coordination and individual success (Argote & McGrath).

This conflict underscores the importance of how tasks are coordinated and controlled within an organization. Successful organizations (and employees) must properly manage lateral relationships with peers and coworkers as well as properly manage vertical relationships with subordinates and supervisors. Recognizing the importance and universality of these work situations suggests that how an organization manages its cooperative and competitive social demands can serve as fundamental situational characteristics to all work settings.

Additional support for the fundamental importance of cooperative and competitive situations is also provided by examining research findings derived from the work design literature. Research regarding work design has progressed from both an organizational and an individual perspective. From the organizational perspective, several dimensions of work design have been identified, but empirical evidence suggests that the critical dimensions can be summarized by two parameters: structuring of activities (e.g., determining who does which tasks) and concentration of authority (Pugh & Hickson, 1997; Pugh, Hickson, & Turner, 1968). Organizations must therefore resolve two problems: issues associated with coordination and issues associated with control. From the individual perspective, Hackman and Oldham's (1980) widely recognized model proposes critical issues surrounding both the determination of who does what (e.g., skill variety, task identity, and task significance) and the identification of how an individual's work tasks relate to the tasks of others (e.g., autonomy, feedback). Thus, from both perspectives, work design research highlights the importance of determining how work tasks are coordinated and controlled. These findings buttress the claim derived from open systems theory that situational differences may be represented by considering variance among cooperative and competitive demands at work.

A fundamental difference in organizations is thus the extent to which a situation (the larger system) requires cooperation rather than competition among individuals (subsystems). Some organizations requiring high levels of cooperation are structured with substantial hierarchical controls and extensive integration. Other organizations place more emphasis on the unique contributions of individuals and are thus structured with high levels of autonomy and extensive differentiation, thereby increasing competition among individuals. Different approaches to structure for work organizations thus result in settings that differ extensively from situation to situation in terms of cooperative and competitive demands.

The social aspects associated with cooperation and competition at work are likely to be psychologically important to individuals, as there is considerable evidence that individual self-perceptions are substantially influenced by how a person is defined as separate from versus connected to others (Markus & Kitayama, 1991). More specifically, R. Hogan and Shelton (1998) argue from a socioanalytic perspective that getting along with others (cooperation) and getting ahead of others (competition) are fundamental features of the evolutionary history of people. This suggests that people are predisposed to meaningfully distinguish work settings according to the cooperative and competitive social aspects. Because we expect the tension between cooperation and competition to be ubiquitous across work settings, we thus propose that differences in expectations for cooperation and competition will systematically affect the strength of relationships between personality traits and work performance.

Although each worker's setting is influenced somewhat by both cooperative and competitive pressures, each organization and position is expected to emphasize these characteristics to a different extent. Differentiating work settings using these two characteristics differs from many current classification systems, as jobs that have the same title are often differentiated in terms of cooperation and competition. For instance, in some organizations the job of computer programmer may involve team participation that requires extensive interdependence with coworkers. The main focus in this environment thus is cooperation. In other organizations the programmer job may include management of several subordinates, as well as opportunity for advancement into positions that afford increased social status. In this environment the focus moves more toward competition and advancement within the social structure. Situational differences may therefore be represented by variance among cooperative and competitive demands, which provides a fresh perspective for broadly distinguishing variation in work settings.

Mapping the Process Through Which Traits Influence Performance

Several scholars theorize that proximal motivational constructs represent the mechanisms through which distal personality traits link to performance (Kanfer, 1991; McCrae & Costa, 1996). Although a number of different theories have been developed to identify these motivational constructs, a common theme among most motivation research is an emphasis on cognitive processes. Mitchell (1997) captures this emphasis in his definition of motivation as "those psychological processes involved with the arousal, direction, intensity, and persistence of voluntary actions that are goal directed" (p. 60). Consistent with this definition, the cognitive processes associated with motivation include choice of the goal (i.e., direction) and choice of the amount of effort (i.e., arousal, intensity, persistence) to expend toward achieving the goal. Therefore, to understand the motivational processes linking traits to performance, we must first determine the basic goals associated with traits, and then determine the arousal, intensity, and persistence associated with those goals.

Although the number of specific goals an individual may choose is virtually unlimited, we believe that progress is most likely to occur by identifying generally broad categories for goals at work. This belief is based on our experience with understanding personality relations, where the greatest gains emerged after traits were classified into meaningful yet relatively broad categories (i.e., the FFM). Once broad motivational categories have been identified, they can then be linked to traits and situations in order to gain a deeper understanding of personality–performance relationships.

Recent research has identified two broad motivational goals or intentions that people pursue during social interactions (Digman, 1997; R. Hogan, 1996; Wiggins & Trapnell, 1996). Building on research from biology, anthropology, and sociology, these theorists argue that individuals have basic goals directed toward either communion striving, which encompasses the broad goal of obtaining acceptance in personal relationships and getting along with others, or status striving, which encompasses the broad goal of obtaining power and dominance within a status hierarchy.

Although communion striving and status striving represent two broad goals associated with social interactions, work tasks are often completed without social interaction. Communion and status may therefore not completely capture an individual's motivational goals at work. We thus add a third goal category designed to capture achievement that is independent and fulfills one's need for competence. Accomplishment striving thus encompasses the broad goal of independently completing tasks.

Our original expectation for the three motivational orientations was that each would relate uniquely to performance. However, our empirical research has led us to reassess how the three orientations relate to each other, and thereby how they relate to performance. Specifically, a study that we recently conducted (Barrick, Stewart, & Piotrowski, 2000) assessed the three motivational orientations for a group of sales representatives. In this study we found no relationship between communion striving and performance, but a relatively strong relationship between status striving and performance. We also found that accomplishment striving was linked to performance, but not in a direct relationship. Instead, the effect of accomplishment striving on performance was mediated by status striving.

Consistent with the work of R. Hogan (1996) and Wiggins and Trapnell (1996), communion striving and status striving may thus be the two most fundamental motivational orientations, with accomplishment striving affecting performance through these other strivings. The results of the study with sales representatives also reinforce the first lesson of the person–situation debate, as only status striving—the basic motivation most relevant for a competitive sales setting—was related to performance. Consistent with our description of cooperative and competitive demands, we expect communion striving to have similar relationships in other settings where success is more dependent on cooperation.

Based on existing theory, as well as early empirical findings, we thus propose communion striving and status striving as two fundamental goals that people pursue in organizations. We also propose that people strive for accomplishment as a means for achieving either status or communion. In short, people are motivated to accomplish tasks in order to achieve either communion or status, depending on the situational context. These broad goals thus represent proximal motivational variables that can be used to explain why personality traits relate to job performance. Moreover, because they correspond to the basic situational elements of cooperation and competition, motivational orientations are helpful for demonstrating how research can advance to elaborate more fully on the effect of situational influences on personality–performance relationships.

A Model Explaining Situational Demands and Mediating Motivational Influences

As previously noted, the first principle of the person–situation debate suggests that personality traits predict performance only in relevant settings. Using the situational demands of cooperation and competition derived from work design, along with the motivational orientations of communion

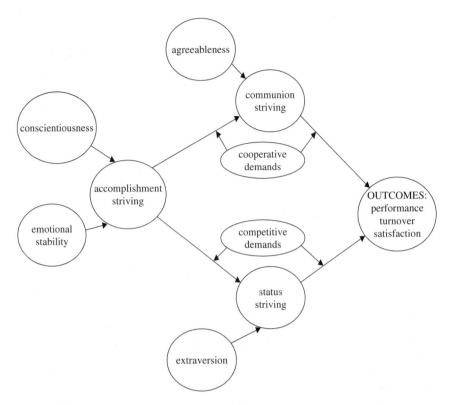

FIG. 3.1 A model of the relationship between FFM personality traits, situational demands, cognitive motivational orientations, and work outcomes.

striving and agency striving, we can begin to not only predict which traits relate to performance in which settings but also why these differential relationships exist. A basic model portraying our expectations is shown in Figure 3.1.

As shown in the figure, organizationally relevant outcomes such as job performance, turnover, and employee satisfaction are directly affected by communion and status strivings. Communion striving has its strongest influence on these outcomes when the situation emphasizes cooperative demands. In contrast, status striving has its strongest influence when the situation emphasizes competitive demands. People striving for high accomplishment will contribute to the organization through either communion striving or status striving. In cooperative settings, high accomplishment will link with communion striving, whereas high accomplishment will link with status striving in competitive settings.

Having established the foundation of situational demands and motivational strivings, we can now illustrate how FFM traits are expected to link to outcomes such as job performance. In a setting that emphasizes cooperation and coordination with coworkers, traits linking to the motivational orientation of communion striving should predict performance. Because work success is dependent on an individual's proclivity to help others and build personal relationships, the FFM trait most closely associated with this orientation is agreeableness. People who are agreeable tend to be compliant, trusting, considerate, and cooperative (Costa & McCrae, 1992; Goldberg, 1992). Agreeableness is thus expected to be linked to performance only when the work setting involves a high degree of teamwork and cooperation with coworkers. This expectation is supported by research that has linked agreeableness to success in team settings (Mount et al., 1998). Based on the fourth lesson of the person–situation debate (people choose environments congruent with their traits), agreeable employees are also expected to have higher satisfaction and less organizational withdrawal when the situation has primarily cooperative demands.

In a setting that emphasizes competition and advancement through a hierarchy, traits linking to the motivational orientation of status striving should predict performance. In these situations, work performance depends on assertiveness and accomplishing goals that focus on getting ahead of others. The FFM trait most closely associated with this orientation is extraversion. People who are extraverted tend to be assertive, active, and dominant (Costa & McCrae, 1992; Goldberg, 1992). Extraversion is thus expected to predict performance when the work setting emphasizes competition, such as advancing through an organizational hierarchy. This expectation is supported by research that has linked extraversion to sales success (Barrick & Mount, 1991; Stewart, 1996), as well as research that has found extraversion to predict performance in environments that emphasize competition or opportunities for promotion (J. Hogan, Rybicki, Motowidlo, & Borman, 1998). The benefits of extraversion are also expected to link with greater employee satisfaction and decreased turnover, as extraverts are predicted to enjoy working in competitive situations.

The FFM trait most closely associated with accomplishment striving is conscientiousness. People who are conscientious tend to be self-disciplined, organized, and efficient at carrying out tasks (Costa & McCrae, 1992; Goldberg, 1992). They also have higher levels of generalized self-efficacy (Colquitt & Simmering, 1998; Martocchio & Judge, 1997). These characteristics suggest that conscientious employees should be more effective at getting things done. Consistent with our model of motivational orientations, conscientious people should thus accomplish a lot of work, which aids them in striving for either communion or status. Conscientiousness is therefore expected to relate to higher work performance regardless of whether the setting calls for cooperation or competition. This expectation is consistent with research that has found conscientiousness to correspond with higher performance across work settings (Barrick & Mount, 1991; Salgado, 1997). The current model, however, provides an explanation of why this robust relationship exists. In cooperative situations the effect of conscientiousness is through increased communion, whereas the effect in competitive situations is through increased status.

The importance of accounting for motivational orientations as a mediator of the personality–performance relationship is also illustrated by considering emotional stability. As previously noted, prior meta-analytic research (Barrick et al., 2000; Salgado, 1997) shows that individuals high on emotional stability perform better on the job, although the magnitude of this effect is not as strong as for conscientiousness. This finding makes sense if one considers how emotional stability affects performance. Viewed from the negative pole, neurotic individuals are stress-prone, nervous, emotional, irritable worriers who lack self-confidence, are insecure, and can be depressed. Such nonoptimal human functioning tends to result in less interest, energy, and confidence (i.e., lowered motivation), which in turn is manifested by reduced achievement striving. Thus, people who spend time worrying about their performance, doubting their capabilities, requiring reassurance from others, and being depressed and lethargic will have lower accomplishment striving goals, which in turn reduces their motivational orientation toward communion striving or status striving. In short, low emotional stability leads to poor performance because the individual is not as motivated toward accomplishment as is an emotionally stable person.

Although both conscientiousness and emotional stability are linked to accomplishment striving, we expect the magnitude of these links to differ significantly. To illustrate this effect, it is helpful to think about the two-part definition of motivation provided earlier. That is, the motivational process involves both the choice of the goal and the amount of effort to be expended toward goal attainment. In the case of conscientiousness, we expect that it is significantly related to both aspects of accomplishment striving (i.e., conscientious people set more ambitious goals and also work harder to attain those goals). In the case of emotional stability, however, it seems less likely that it is substantially related to the choice of goals per se. Rather, neurotic individuals lack confidence, optimism, and self-efficacy and so expend less effort to achieve their goals. Thus, we believe it is important to differentiate the magnitude of the expected effects between these two dimensions and accomplishment striving by recognizing that conscientiousness is likely to have a larger effect than emotional stability.

Our model does not predict relationships with the final FFM factor, openness to experience. In general, openness is the least well-defined factor in the five-factor model (Mount & Barrick, 1995). With the exception of training proficiency (Barrick & Mount, 1991), research has also been unable to identify clear links between openness and organizational performance. Perhaps one reason for this failure is that openness does not link to any of the fundamental motivational strivings.

SUMMARY AND CONCLUSION

The four lessons from the person–situation debate thus help summarize many of our current findings related to personality in work settings. They also provide direction for identifying promising avenues for future research. One such avenue related to the first lesson is the identification of specific situational influences. Our review of the work design literature, coupled with our identification of basic motivational goals, suggests cooperative and competitive demands as fundamentally different situational influences. By developing a model that incorporates these demands as moderators of personality–performance relationships, we can begin to establish theoretical predictions about which traits relate to desired outcomes in which situations. Moreover, by including motivational strivings, we begin an exploration of why such differential relationships exist.

Of course, our model should be seen more as a launching point than as a final destination. Future research is needed to examine relationships between personality, motivational orientation, and outcomes across a variety of settings that differ in their cooperative and competitive demands. We expect that the model will need further development and refinement as additional studies provide greater insight. Nevertheless, the development of such a model does provide a theoretically meaningful method for classifying work situations and thereby incorporating the first lesson from the person–situation debate.

Other lines of research can similarly be developed around the other three person–situation lessons. For instance, the second lesson suggests that traits are more easily manifest in settings with weak situational cues. This finding leads to the question of whether removing cues for desired cooperation or competition from the testing environment will improve the accuracy of personality measures for predicting work performance. The third lesson suggests that people will alter situations. Given this lesson, is it possible that including a highly extraverted individual in a team will increase the likelihood that the emphasis of team members shifts from cooperation to competition? The final lesson suggests that people with different traits will choose different situations. Based on this lesson, it seems plausible that assessments of fit to organizational cultures may be meaningfully described in terms of the firm's emphasis on cooperation and competition.

In the end, an increased acknowledgment of situational influences thus seems to be helpful for advancing research related to the effects of personality traits in work organizations. As differences in situational demands are recognized and identified, a more clear understanding of the proper use of personality testing in work settings can be developed. In particular, progress will be made as we develop situational boundaries and theoretical explanations for relationships with personality. These boundaries and explanations will allow us to delineate conditions when certain traits will predict performance, as well as improve our understanding of the relationship between personality and performance constructs.

REFERENCES

Ackerman, P. L., & Heggestad, E. D. (1997). Intelligence, personality, and interests: Evidence for overlapping traits. *Psychological Bulletin, 121,* 219–245.

Argote, L., & McGrath, J. E. (1993). Group processes in organizations: Continuity and change. *International Review of Industrial and Organizational Psychology, 8,* 333–389.

Barrick, M. R., & Mount, M. K. (1991). The Big Five personality dimensions and job performance: A meta-analysis. *Personnel Psychology, 44,* 1–26.

Barrick, M. R., & Mount, M. K. (1996). Effects of impression management and self-deception on the predictive validity of personality constructs. *Journal of Applied Psychology, 81,* 261–272.

Barrick, M. R., Mount, M. K., & Judge, T. A. (2001). The FFM personality dimensions and job performance: Meta-analysis of meta-analyses. *International Journal of Selection and Assessment, 9,* 9–30.

Barrick, M. R., Stewart, G. L., Neubert, M. J., & Mount, M. K. (1998). Relating member ability and personality to work-team processes and team effectiveness. *Journal of Applied Psychology, 83,* 377–391.

Barrick, M. R., Stewart, G. L., & Piotrowski, M. (2000). Personality and sales performance: Test of the mediating effects of motivation. Manuscript submitted for publication.

Barry, B., & Stewart, G. L. (1997). Composition, process, and performance in self-managed groups: The role of personality. *Journal of Applied Psychology, 82,* 62–78.

Capelli, P. (1999). *The new deal at work: Managing the market-driven workforce.* Boston: Harvard Business School Press.

Cellar, D. F., Miller, M. L., Doverspike, D. D., & Klawsky, J. D. (1996). Comparison of factor structures and criterion-related validity coefficients for two measures of personality based on the five factor model. *Journal of Applied Psychology, 81,* 694–704.

Christiansen, N. D., Goffin, R. D., Johnston, N. G., & Rothstein, M. G. (1994). Correcting the 16PF for faking: Effects on criterion-related validity and individual hiring decisions. *Personnel Psychology, 47,* 847–860.

Colquitt, J. A., & Simmering, M. J. (1998). Conscientiousness, goal orientation, and motivation to learn during the learning process: A longitudinal study. *Journal of Applied Psychology, 83,* 654–665.

Costa, P. T., Jr., & McCrae, R. R. (1992). *Revised NEO personality inventory (NEO PI-R) and NEO five-factor inventory (NEO FFI) professional manual.* Odessa, FL: Psychological Assessment Resources.

Crant, J. M. (1995). The proactive personality scale and objective job performance among real estate agents. *Journal of Applied Psychology, 80*, 532–537.

Cunningham, M. R., Wong, D. T., & Barbee, A. P. (1994). Self-presentation dynamics on overt integrity tests: Experimental studies of the Reid report. *Journal of Applied Psychology, 79*, 643–658.

De Fruyt, F., & Mervielde, I. (1999). RIASAC types and big five traits as predictors of employment status and nature of employment. *Personnel Psychology, 52*, 701–727.

Digman, J. M. (1997). Higher-order factors of the big five. *Journal of Personality and Social Psychology, 73*, 1246–1256.

Donahue, E. M., Robins, R. W., Roberts, B. W., & John, O. P. (1993). The divided self: Concurrent and longitudinal effects of psychological adjustment and social roles on self-concept differentiation. *Journal of Personality and Social Psychology, 64*, 834–846.

Drucker, P. F. (1999). *Management challenges for the 21st Century*. New York: Harper Business.

Dunn, W. S., Mount, M. K., Barrick, M. R., & Ones, D. S. (1995). Relative importance of personality and general mental ability in managers' judgments of applicant qualifications. *Journal of Applied Psychology, 80*, 500–509.

Ellingson, J. E., Sackett, P. R., & Hough, L. M. (1999). Social desirability corrections in personality measurement: Issues of applicant comparison and construct validity. *Journal of Applied Psychology, 84*, 155–166.

Ellingson, J. E., Smith, D. B., & Sackett, P. R. (2001). Investigating the influence of social desirablity on personality factor structure. *Journal of Applied Psychology, 86*, 122–133.

Goldberg, L. R. (1992). The development of markers of the big-five factor structure. *Psychological Assessment, 4*, 26–42.

Gray, J. A. (1973). Causal theories of personality and how to test them. In J. R. Royce (Ed.), *Multivariate analysis and psychological theory* (pp. 409–464). New York: Academic.

Hackman, J. R., & Oldham, G. R. (1980). *Work redesign*. Reading, MA: Addison-Wesley.

Hochwarter, W. A., Witt, L. A., & Kacmar, K. M. (2000). Perceptions of organizational politics as a moderator of the relationship between conscientiousness and job performance. *Journal of Applied Psychology, 85*, 472–478.

Hogan, J., Rybicki, S. L., Motowidlo, S. J., & Borman, W. C. (1998). Relations between contextual performance, personality, and occupational advancement. *Human Performance, 11*, 189–207.

Hogan, R. (1991). Personality and personality measurement. In M. D. Dunnette and L. M. Hough (Eds.), *Handbook of industrial and organizational psychology, Vol. 1* (2nd ed.). Palo Alto, CA: Consulting Psychologists.

Hogan, R. (1996). A socioanalytic perspective on the five-factor model. In J. S. Wiggins (Ed.), *The five-factor model of personality* (pp. 163–179). New York: Guilford.

Hogan, R., & Shelton, D. (1998). A socioanalytic perspective on job performance. *Human Performance, 11*, 129–144.

Holland, J. L. (1997). *Making vocational choices: A theory of vocational personalities and work environments*. Odessa, FL: Psychological Assessment Resources.

Hough, L. M., Eaton, N. K., Dunnette, M. D., Kamp, J. D., & McCloy, R. A. (1990). Criterion-related validities of personality constructs and the effect of response distortion on those validities. *Journal of Applied Psychology, 75*, 581–595.

Judge, T. A., & Cable, D. M. (1997). Applicant personality, organizational culture, and organization attraction. *Personnel Psychology, 50*, 359–394.

Judge, T. A., Higgins, C. A., Thoresen, C. J., & Barrick, M. R. (1999). The big five personality traits, general mental ability, and career success across the life span. *Personnel Psychology, 52*, 621–652.

Judge, T. A., Martocchio, J. J., & Thoresen, C. J. (1997). Five-factor model of personality and employee absence. *Journal of Applied Psychology, 82*, 745–755.

Kanfer, R. (1991). Motivation theory and industrial and organizational psychology. In M. D. Dunnette & L. M. Hough (Eds.), *Handbook of Industrial and Organizational Psychology*, (pp. 75–170). Palo Alto, CA: Consulting Psychologists Press.

Katz, D., & Kahn, R. L. (1978). *The social psychology of organizations* (2nd ed.). New York: Wiley.

Kenrick, D. T., & Funder, D. C. (1988). Profiting from controversy: Lessons from the person-situation controversy. *American Psychologist, 43*, 23–34.

Kenrick, D. T., & Funder D. C. (1991). The person-situation debate: Do personality traits really exist? In V. J. Derlaga, B. A. Winstead, & W. H. Jones (Eds.), *Personality: Contemporary theory and research*. Chicago: Nelson-Hall.

Kenrick, D. T., McCreath, H. E., Govern, J., King, R., & Bordin, J. (1990). Person-environment intersections: Everyday settings and common trait dimensions. *Journal of Personality and Social Psychology, 58*, 685–698.

Markus, H. R., & Kitayama, S. (1991). Culture and self: Implications for cognition, emotion, and motivation. *Psychological Review, 98*, 224–253.

Martocchio, J. J., & Judge, T. A. (1997). Relationship between conscientiousness and learning in employee training: Mediating influences of self-deception and self-efficacy. *Journal of Applied Psychology, 82*, 764–773.

McCrae, R. R., & Costa, P. T., Jr. (1996). Toward a new generation of personality theories: Theoretical contexts for the five-factor model. In J. S. Wiggins (Ed.), *The five-factor model of personality* (pp. 51–87). New York: Guilford.

Mischel. W. (1968). *Personality and assessment*. New York: Wiley.

Mitchell, T. R. (1997). Matching motivational strategies with organizational contexts. *Research in Organizational Behavior, 19*, 57–149.

Mount, M. K., & Barrick, M. R. (1995). The Big Five personality dimensions: Implications for research and practice in human resource management. *Research in Personnel and Human Resources Management, 13*, 153–200.

Mount, M. K., Barrick, M. R., & Stewart, G. L. (1998). Five-factor model of personality and performance in jobs involving interpersonal interactions. *Human Performance, 11*, 145–165.

Murtha, T. C., Kanfer, R., & Ackerman, P. L. (1996). Toward an interactionist taxonomy of personality and situations: An integrative situational-dispositional representation of personality traits. *Journal of Personality and Social Psychology, 71*, 193–207.

Neuman, G. A., & Wright, J. (1999). Team effectiveness: Beyond skill and cognitive ability. *Journal of Applied Psychology, 84*, 376–389.

Ones, D. S., Viswesvaran, C., & Reiss, A. D. (1996). Role of social desirability in personality testing for personnel selection: The red herring. *Journal of Applied Psychology, 81*, 660–679.

Ones, D. S., Viswesvaran, C., & Schmidt, F. L. (1993). Comprehensive meta-analysis of integrity test validities: Findings and implications for personnel selection and theories of job performance. *Journal of Applied Psychology, 78*, 679–703.

Peters, L. H., & O'Connor, E. J. (1980). Situational constraints and work outcomes: The influences of a frequently overlooked construct. *Academy of Management Review, 5*, 391–397.

Pugh, D. S., & Hickson, D. J. (1997). *Writers on organizations* (5th ed.). Newbury Park, CA: Sage.

Pugh, D. S., Hickson, D. J., & Turner, C. (1968). Dimensions of organizational structure. *Administrative Science Quarterly, 13*, 289–315.

Rosse, J. G., Stecher, M. D., Miller, J. L., & Levin, R. A. (1998). The impact of response distortion on preemployment personality testing and hiring decisions. *Journal of Applied Psychology, 83*, 634–644.

Salgado, J. F. (1997). The five factor model of personality and job performance in the European Community. *Journal of Applied Psychology, 82*, 30–43.

Schaubroeck, J., Ganster, D. C., & Jones, J. R. (1998). Organization and occupation influences in the attraction-selection-attrition process. *Journal of Applied Psychology, 83*, 869–891.

Schmit, M. J., Ryan, A. M., Stierwalt, S. L., & Powell, A. B. (1995). Frame-of-reference effects on personality scale scores and criterion-related validity. *Journal of Applied Psychology, 80,* 607–620.

Schneider, B. (1987). The people make the place. *Personnel Psychology, 40,* 437–453.

Schneider, B., Smith, D. B., Taylor, S., & Fleenor, J. (1998). Personality and organizations: A test of the homogeneity of personality hypothesis. *Journal of Applied Psychology, 83,* 462–470.

Seibert, S. E., Crant, J. M., & Kraimer, M. L. (1999). Proactive personality and career success. *Journal of Applied Psychology, 84,* 416–427.

Sheldon, K. M., Ryan, R. M., Rawsthorne, L. J., & Ilardi, B. (1997). Trait self and true self: Cross-role variation in the Big Five personality traits and its relations with psychological authenticity and subjective well-being. *Journal of Personality and Social Psychology, 73,* 1380–1393.

Smith, D. B., Hanges, P. J., & Dickson, M. W. (2001). Personnel selection and the five factor model: Reexamining the effects of applicants' frame of reference. *Journal of Applied Psychology, 86,* 304–315.

Stewart, G. L. (1996). Reward structure as a moderator of the relationship between extraversion and sales performance. *Journal of Applied Psychology, 81,* 619–627.

Stewart, G. L. (1999). Trait bandwidth and stages of job performance: Assessing differential effects for conscientiousness and its subtraits. *Journal of Applied Psychology, 84,* 959–968.

Tett, R. P., Jackson, D. N., Rothstein, M., & Reddon, J. R. (1994). Meta-analysis of personality-job performance relations: A reply to Ones, Mount, Barrick, and Hunter (1994). *Personnel Psychology, 47,* 147–156.

Viswesvaran, C. (1993). Modeling job performance: Is there a general factor? Unpublished doctoral dissertation, University of Iowa, Iowa City.

Wiggins, J. S., & Trapnell, P. D. (1996). A dyadic-interactional perspective on the Five-Factor Model. In J. S. Wiggins (Ed.), *The Five-Factor Model of Personality: Theoretical Perspectives* (pp. 88–162). New York: Guilford.

Zickar, M. J., & Robie, C. (1999). Modeling faking good on personality items: An item-level analysis. *Journal of Applied Psychology, 84,* 551–563.

Personality, Interactional Psychology, and Person–Organization Fit

Timothy A. Judge
University of Florida

Amy Kristof-Brown
University of Iowa

Personality psychology is concerned with the nature of individuals. The study of the nature of individuals rests on the philosophy (implicit or explicit) that individuals are the basic agents or causes of their behavior. This individualistic philosophy contrasts with other social sciences, which may focus on the society (sociology) or the culture (anthropology), and other areas of psychology, which may focus on the relationships among individuals (social psychology). Of course, other issues besides individualism distinguish personality psychology from other social sciences such as economics and from other areas of psychology such as cognitive or developmental psychology, but these issues are not relevant to our discussion here. The point is that if personality psychology is concerned with the nature of individuals, why do we need to be concerned with situations? Why not leave such issues to the sociologists, the anthropologists, or even the social psychologists?

The answer is because we cannot. It is impossible to be a personality psychologist who is interested in understanding how personality affects behavior without being an interactionist. Humans are social animals and social interactions are perhaps the most basic manifestations of personality (Hogan, 1996). These social interactions provide the context through which personality effects can be understood. As Winter and Barenbaum (1999) noted, "Personality psychology will need to pay increased attention to context. Whatever the evolutionary origins, genetic basis, or physiological substrate of any aspect of personality, both its *level* and *channels of expression* will be strongly affected, in complex ways, by the multiple dimensions of social context" (p. 19).

Let us be clear—we do not argue and indeed do not believe that personality is best understood through statistical interactions. Clearly, there are main effects of personality on practically any meaningful attitude or behavior. In writing on behalf of the merits of interactional psychology for personality psychology, we take a broader view of interactions. At its most basic level, interactional psychology merely argues for study of the "relationship between the individual and the environment" (Magnusson, 1990, p. 196). This relationship can take many forms and need not be (and generally is not) confined to the assumed statistical moderation effect. As we will note, mediation, reciprocal causation, and dynamic interactionism are other person–environment (P–E) processes consistent with interactional psychology. In short, we will discuss the role of personality in context: how personality, in relation to the situational environment in which the individual finds him/herself, relates to his or her attitudes and behaviors. Within this general concern with personality and interactional psychology, we are more specifically concerned with the concept of P–E fit and, most specifically, with person–organization (P–O) fit.

To us, P–O fit is a type of P–E fit in that the organization is one of many contexts or situations in which people may fit or misfit. At the same time, it is hard to imagine a single context more central to one's identity than the organization in which one works because to many, we are defined by the work we do (Hulin & Judge, 2003). Because we see P–E fit and P–O fit as being differentiated only by the breadth of their focus (P–O fit on work, P–E fit on any situation), the lines of demarcation in what follows will not be satisfying to those who make cleaner distinctions between these constructs. Thus, we discuss both P–E and P–O fit concepts somewhat interchangeably in the chapter, depending on the purpose for which we use them.

Often, those of us interested in the role of personality in applied psychology have been remiss in ignoring the environment and the interaction between the person and the environment. In part, this omission may be due to the desire to show main effects when, as little as a decade ago, the view among many was that personality was of little practical importance (Davis-Blake & Pfeffer, 1989). In part, this omission also may be due to the fragmentation of psychology (Staats, 1981), where one is a personality psychologist or a social psychologist but rarely both. In applied psychology, now that main effects of personality are widely accepted, the time has come to turn our attention to how these main effects operate and what aspects of the situation may enhance or suppress expression of these effects.

This chapter is organized as follows. Because the literatures are rarely integrated, and because many theoretical issues underlie them, we first discuss various conceptual issues. Specifically, we provide a working definition of personality and briefly discuss how it fits within the framework of interactional psychology. We then discuss several important issues in the area of interactional psychology. Second, we provide a review of past research on P–E fit and personality, organizing our discussion around Pervin and Lewis's (1978) and Terborg's (1981) forms of interaction. Finally, we provide a research agenda that seeks to advance research on personality, P–O fit, and interactional psychology.

CONCEPTUAL ISSUES

Personality

Perhaps the most often used definition of personality was supplied by Gordon Allport. He defined *personality* as follows: "Personality is the dynamic organization with the individual of those psychophysical systems that determine his unique adjustments to his environment" (Allport, 1937, p. 48). It is telling that Allport explicitly factored person–situation interactionism into his definition. In Allportian personality theory, traits are not situationally specific, but neither do they function independent of the situation. He explicitly noted that it was crucial for a trait to remain adaptive and plastic, or it would lose its usefulness. Henry Murray (1938), similarly, viewed personality as necessarily interacting with the environment, proposing, "Since at every moment an organism is within an environment, the organism and its milieu must be considered together" (p. 43). Although these conceptualizations of personality are still widely accepted in personality psychology, it strikes us that many in the fields of industrial–organizational psychology (I–O), organizational behavior (OB), and human resource (HR) management have either not accepted or understood these systems perspectives. In much of our research, we study personality as if it were (a) not part of an organized system and (b) a fixed set of traits wholly independent of the environment. Such views do not comport with traditional and even contemporary views of personality ("We are all pretty much interactionists at this point," Pervin, 1990, p. 14); therein lies an opportunity for future research.

Interactional Psychology

A number of personality models have existed over the years, including the trait, situational, and finally the interactional model. Whereas trait theorists emphasized personality characteristics as the primary determinants of behavior (e.g., Cowley, 1931), situational theorists regarded environmental factors as the key determinants of individual behavior (e.g., Bandura, 1971; Mead, 1934; Skinner, 1953). The concept of interactionism, which suggests that behavior is a function of both person and situation, offered a resolution between the antithetical positions previously described and necessitated a more complicated view of personality.

With the introduction of Lewin's (1935) field theory, represented by the now famous equation $B = f(P, E)$—behavior is a function of the person and the environment—interactionism took on its most popularized form. His ideas, however, had roots in earlier works such as Murray's (1938) need-press theory, which proposed that parallel dimensions of individuals' needs and environmental stimuli were the best predictor of individual behavior. Another influence can be found in writings by Kantor (1924), who suggested that the proper unit of study for psychology was the "individual as he interacts with all of the various types of situation which constitute his behavior circumstances" (p. 24). Interest in interactionism became further solidified when the first international conference on person-by-situation interactions took place in Stockholm, Sweden, in June 1975. Since that time, numerous books, articles, and conferences on the topic have furthered our understanding of this concept.

Endler and Magnussen (1976) summarize four key tenets of the interactional model. The first and most basic principle is that an individual's behavior is determined by an ongoing feedback process between the person and the situation. The second component is that the individual plays an intentional, active role in creating this interaction by interpreting the situation and assigning it meaning. Because of this role, the third tenet emphasizes the importance of cognitive factors such as encoding strategies, self-regulation, and expectancies in determining the outcome of an interaction. Finally, Endler and Magnussen emphasize the importance of the psychological environment (i.e., the meaning that it holds for an individual) in the $B = f(P, E)$ equation. Thus, most interactional psychologists emphasize the perceived rather than the actual situation when predicting outcomes.

One area of research that has drawn heavily on these tenets of interactionism is that of P–E fit. The concept of fit is that for each individual there are particular environments that are most compatible with his or her personal characteristics. If a person works in those environments, he or she will experience positive consequences, such as improved work attitudes, better performance, and reduced stress (Downey, Hellriegel, & Slocum, 1975; French, Rogers, & Cobb, 1974; Jahoda, 1961; Pervin, 1968). Although the basic concept of fit appears logical and straightforward, what exactly is meant by a good-fitting environment is often difficult to define (and even harder to study). Fit is sometimes conceptualized as the similarity between person and environment (*supplementary fit*; Muchinsky & Monahan, 1987). Other times it is said to exist when the person and environment are dissimilar, such that one completes the other (*complementary fit*; Muchinsky & Monahan). One of the unfortunate consequences of this paradox is that fit is often judged after the fact by the existence of positive consequences. That is, if a person is satisfied and productive and does not experience stress, good fit is inferred.

To better assess the existence of fit and its consequences, researchers have devised a number of different strategies. Each of these strategies conceptualizes and operationalizes fit in a slightly different way, although they all share the underlying premise of considering the impact of both the person and the situation on individual behavior. Because comparing research using different operationalizations of a construct is difficult, we organize our discussion of P–E fit into the five types of interactions discussed by Pervin and Lewis (1978) and Terborg (1981). We also add a sixth type not discussed by Terborg that has characterized much of the recent research on fit. Given the focus of this book and our chapter, we place particular emphasis on personality fit in our discussion.

PAST RESEARCH ON P–E FIT AND PERSONALITY

Type 1: Nonadditive Interactions

This type of interaction is how most researchers conceptualize an interactive effect, whereby the effect of one variable on another depends on a third (moderating) variable. Most typically, when considering fit, the interaction is such that the effect of the situation depends on the personality of the individual. However, sometimes it is the other way around, where the effect of personality depends on the situation (see the Mount, Harter, Barrick, & Colbert, 2000, study described later). Most studies that explicitly identify themselves as testing personality × situation models fall into the nonadditive interaction category, regardless of which variable exerts the moderating effect.

In the I–O psychology literature, many of the personality × situation studies have been carried out in job choice contexts. Burke and Deszca (1982), for example, found that individuals with type A personalities preferred organizations with climates that were thought to be compatible with their personalities (e.g., high performance standards, ambiguity, toughness). Turban and Keon (1993) found that the attractiveness of organizational characteristics such as centralization, size, and reward structure depended on job seekers' self-esteem and need for achievement. Bretz and Judge (1994a) investigated whether the effect of various human resource systems on applicant attraction depended on applicant personality. They found, for example, that applicants with an internal locus of control were more attracted to hypothetical organizations with competitive, merit-based promotion systems than were applicants with an external locus of control. Bretz, Ash, and Dreher (1989) discovered that certain personality traits (e.g., locus of control, risk aversion) predicted the attractiveness of organizations with various types of compensation systems. For example, individuals with a high need for achievement preferred organizations offering individually based reward systems. Similarly, Cable and Judge (1994) found interactions between personality and compensation system attributes in predicting job choice. For example, materialism moderated the effect of pay level on job choice such that materialistic job seekers were more attracted to organizations offering high levels of pay. Thus, job choice research seems to clearly support this form of interaction—the effect of the situation (in terms of job attributes or organizational characteristics) on applicant attraction depends on applicants' personalities.

Additional research on nonadditive personality × situation interactions has occurred outside of the job choice domain. Barrick, Mount, and Strauss (1993), for example, found that conscientiousness moderated the effect of autonomy on job performance, such that conscientiousness was more strongly related to job performance in jobs with high degrees of autonomy than in jobs with limited autonomy. Similarly, Mount et al. (2000) found that job satisfaction moderated the effect of conscientiousness on performance such that the job satisfaction–job performance relationship was stronger for individuals low in conscientiousness than for individuals high in conscientiousness. Judge, Locke, and Durham (1997) hypothesized that core self-evaluations would moderate the effect of intrinsic job characteristics on job satisfaction such that individuals with positive core evaluations (high self-esteem, internal locus of control, etc.) would be more satisfied by jobs high in intrinsic job characteristics than would individuals with negative core evaluations. In an empirical test, however, Judge, Locke, Durham, and Kluger (1998) did not find support for this hypothesis. More studies have tested the moderating effect of growth need strength (GNS) on the job characteristics–job satisfaction relationship, with generally positive results. Specifically, evidence indicates that the relationship of intrinsic job characteristics with job satisfaction is stronger for high GNS employees ($\rho = .57$) than for low GNS employees ($\rho = .32$; Loher, Noe, Moeller, & Fitzgerald, 1985). Taken as a whole, results generally support the usefulness of nonadditive personality × situation interactions for predicting job choices, as well as for attitudes and performance in several studies.

Type 2: Mediating Effects

A second form of interaction discussed by Terborg (1981) is a mediating mechanism whereby the effect of a personality trait on an outcome is expressed through a situational attribute. This is not the typical form of interaction considered by researchers and clearly is in no way a statistical interaction. However, if one's definition of an interaction is that person and situation variables must be jointly considered to understand how each affects a criterion, then the mediating effects model is an interactive model.

One example of a mediating effects model including personality and situation factors is Judge et al.'s (1997, 1998) model, whereby intrinsic job characteristics mediated the relationship between core self-evaluations and job satisfaction. House, Spangler, and Woycke (1991), in a study of U.S. Presidents, also found that various personal and contextual factors helped explain the relationship between power motivation and presidential performance. Similarly, Barry and Stewart (1997) found that various group processes mediated the relationship of member personality on group performance. Thus, there is some evidence for the predictive power of the mediating effects model of interactionism.

Type 3: Noninteractive Additive Effects

In this type of interaction, both person and situation variables have independent (but noninteractive) influences on a criterion. As noted by Terborg (1981), this form also is not typically considered an interaction. However, like Type 2 models, noninteractive additive effects might be considered interactive because, in order to best explain attitudes or behavior, both person and situation variables are required. In contrast to Type 2 models, though, in Type 3 models the person and situation variables exert independent (rather than mediated) influences on a criterion. Most I–O psychologists would probably argue that such models are appropriate, yet studies in which personality and situational variables are included in an additive manner are not particularly common in the literature.

There are a few exceptions. O'Reilly and Roberts (1975) showed that situational variables explained variance in job satisfaction controlling for personality traits, but the reverse was not true. Ostroff (1993) found that personal orientations and organizational climate each contributed independently to work outcomes, yet the interactions between these two factors were not significant. More recently, Judge et al. (1998) showed that personality and intrinsic job characteristics explained unique, additive variance in job satisfaction (though, as noted in describing Type 2 models, a significant part of the influence of core self-evaluations on job satisfaction was mediated through intrinsic job characteristics). There is little doubt that including both person and situation predictors increases the amount of variance explained in outcomes, versus including either one alone. However, studies reporting these types of noninteractive additive effects rarely are considered in the realm of interactionism.

Type 4: Reciprocal Effects

According to Terborg (1981), a fourth type of interaction occurs when people, situations, and behaviors are mutually interdependent. As he notes, the sine qua non of testing for reciprocal interactionism is a longitudinal design, which would allow examination of how the person changed the situation and vice versa. One example of such a study was conducted by Kohn and Schooler (1982). They investigated the reciprocal relationship between purported personality characteristics (e.g., ideational flexibility, sense of distress) and job characteristics. Although it is not clear that the personality characteristics were truly traits, the authors found that structural job conditions influenced personality over a ten-year period (e.g., self-directed work conditions lead to ideational flexibility), and personality also influenced job characteristics (e.g., ideational flexibility lead to more responsible jobs with greater latitude for self-direction).

Clearly, Schneider's (1987a) attraction–selection–attrition (ASA) model deserves mention in discussions of reciprocal effects, as it posits that situations are defined by the behavior of the people who create them. The ASA model proposes that individuals are attracted to, selected by, and likely to remain in organizations that help them achieve their personal goals. Fundamental to this model is the notion that goal achievement is most likely to be maximized when the individual's personality matches the modal personality of the organization. As Schneider's (1987b) review makes clear, Holland's (1985) RIASEC model also hypothesizes a type of reciprocal interaction, whereby "... people select themselves into and out of situations (career environments) that they fit and that situations are defined in terms of the attributes of the persons there" (Schneider, 1987b, p. 355). In Holland's model the focus is on people and occupations rather than organizations, but the underlying processes are similar. Occupations are differentiated into six basic types (realistic, investigative, artistic, social, enterprising, and conventional), based on the personalities of the people typically employed in them. People are expected to be most successful in occupations that are congruent with their personalities (i.e., a realistic person will flourish in a realistic career). This concept assumes, of course, that vocational interests are dispositional in nature—an assumption with support with respect to the RIASEC (Tokar & Swanson, 1995) and MBTI (McCrae & Costa, 1989) attributes. Although the ASA and RIASEC models involve dynamic relations between the person and situation, they clearly favor the effect of the person on the situations (arguing that people define the situation). Thus, implicit in these models is the argument that situations shape behavior (in the ASA model, for example, by leading people who do not fit in an organization to leave), but only inasmuch as the situations are a function of the people.

Both the ASA and RIASEC models have been extremely influential. Schneider (1987a), for example, has been cited more than 260 times by researchers. Although there is much evidence indirectly supporting the ASA model (see Schneider, Goldstein, & Smith, 1995, for a review), direct tests of the model are lacking. There are a few exceptions. Schneider, Smith, Taylor, and Fleenor (1998) found support for the homogenization premise of the ASA model. Specifically, these authors found, in a sample of 13,000 managers from 142 organizations, that organizations were similar with respect to the personality traits of their managers. These results replicated those of an earlier study (Jordon, Herriott, & Chalmers, 1991) based on a much smaller sample (344 managers in four British organizations). Similarly, Schaubroeck, Ganster, and Jones (1998) found partial support for ASA predictions in a complex array of analyses (multiple interactions tested across multiple dependent variables, with variables being entered in eight blocks). Despite this supporting evidence in favor of the homogenization hypothesis of the ASA model, most research has not examined it longitudinally. Furthermore, with few exceptions (such as Schneider et al., 1998), most of the research has not been at the organizational level of analysis, a prerequisite to direct tests of the model (Schneider et al., 1995).

The RIASEC model has been more extensively reviewed (Assouline & Meir, 1987; Spokane, 1985; Tranberg, Slane, & Ekeberg, 1993). Results generally support its main constructs and the positive relationship between individual–occupation match and satisfaction, career path stability, and performance. However, many of the studies are correlational in nature (Spokane, 1985), and a meta-analysis by Tranberg et al. suggests that the relationship is moderated by strength of study design, with stronger support being found in methodologically weak studies. The RIASEC model explicitly recognizes the role of personality by delineating specific traits associated with each of the six types (e.g., a realistic person is characterized as asocial, conforming, practical, uninsightful, and inflexible). Empirical investigations have generally supported the trait characterizations proposed by Holland, using numerous personality inventories, including the 16PF, the MBTI, the NEO Personality Inventory, and the Personality Research Form. However, the evidence is not always consistent and some of the relationships are modest (De Fruyt & Mervielde, 1997; Tokar & Swanson, 1995). In sum, there is strong evidence supporting homogenization of personality in organizations and occupations. However, research rarely investigates the effects of this homogenization over time, a necessary component of reciprocal effects models of interaction.

Type 5: Perceptual Interaction

The final form of interaction discussed by Terborg (1981) is perceptual, in that "different people may perceive similar situations in different ways and similar people may perceive different situations in the same way" (p. 572). Perceptual interaction appears to deal with the relationship between the situation and individuals' perceptions of it. Terborg, for example, points to the literature on climate as an example of perceptual interaction. Specifically, why are there high levels of within-organization agreement in perceptions of climate in some organizations but not in others? In short, why do some people see the situation in one light and others view the same situation differently? Although research on perceptions such as job satisfaction (Ostroff, 1992) at the organizational level of analysis has been fast accumulating, little research has sought to understand sources of agreement (or disagreement) among individuals or aspects of the person or situation that influence this level of agreement. A recent exception is a study by Klein, Conn, Smith, and Sorra (2001) that identified characteristics of groups that promote agreement. Also, research in the leadership area has shown that level of agreement on leadership ratings is both important and predictable (Atwater, Ostroff, Yammarino, & Fleenor, 1998). Clearly, more research is needed on how personality influences the degree to which individuals form similar perceptions of situations.

Type 6: Congruence

There is a sixth type of interaction in the fit literature that is not easily classified into any of Terborg's five types. It is the interaction that occurs when individual and environmental characteristics are congruent and their similarity (rather than either aspect independently) is what best predicts outcomes. The most obvious example is research using the Organizational Culture Profile (OCP), an instrument developed by O'Reilly, Chatman, and Caldwell (1991) to assess the fit between individuals and organizations (as well as Ravlin & Meglino's [1989] research on the Comparative Emphasis Scale, a measure of work values). Although the OCP is primarily as an instrument of value congruence, its authors describe its factor structure as "easily interpretable patterns of personality and cultural preferences" (O'Reilly et al., p. 502). Supporting this conclusion, Judge and Cable (1997) found that the Big Five personality traits could be used to predict an individual's culture preferences. Their findings include a positive relationship between (a) extraversion with aggressiveness and team orientation, (b) openness with innovation and detail orientation, (c) agreeableness with supportiveness and team orientation, and (d) conscientiousness with detail orientation and outcome orientation.

Research using the OCP has generally supported the importance of P–O congruence in the hiring process and for posthire employee attitudes and behavior. Two studies by Cable and Judge (Cable & Judge, 1996; Judge & Cable, 1997) reported that congruence between individuals' cultural preferences and organizational cultures was positively related to ratings of organizational attractiveness. Similarly, congruence between recruiters' perceptions of applicant values and their perceptions of their organizations' values predicted the recruiters' judgments of fit, which in turn predicted hiring recommendations (Cable & Judge, 1997). Additional research by Chatman and colleagues (Chatman, 1991; O'Reilly et al., 1991) found that congruence between employees' and organizational values (as reported by top managers) was related to a number of outcomes including job satisfaction, organizational commitment, intentions to quit, and turnover.

Although the support is strong that congruence between individual and organizational characteristics has numerous benefits, when congruence is assessed between individuals' personalities and the modal personality of people in the organization, the results are less clear. In a study of three of the Big Five dimensions in a hospital setting, Day and Bedeian (1995) reported a positive relationship between similarity on agreeableness and job performance, a negative relationship between conscientiousness congruence and organizational tenure, and no relationship between extraversion similarity and any work-related outcome. Moreover, the strength of all the congruence relationships in this study were modest when the mediating variables of psychological climate and role stress were also considered. Similarly, Tischler (1996) found no evidence of a significant relationship between individuals' similarity to the modal organizational personality type on the MBTI with either salary increases or number of promotions over time. Finally, in a study of training performance, Ferris, Youngblood, and Yates (1985) found no support for a relationship between newcomer-incumbent personality congruence, assessed using the 16PF, and absenteeism and turnover. Thus, it appears that congruence has a stronger impact on work outcomes when it is determined as the similarity between individuals' characteristics and the organization's culture (as reported by top managers), than as the similarity between individuals' and typical employees' personality scores.

FUTURE RESEARCH DIRECTIONS IN P–O FIT AND PERSONALITY PSYCHOLOGY

Even this brief review of the literature makes it clear that careful thought should be put into designing future research on the topic of personality fit. In the following paragraphs we articulate some of our ideas regarding the future of research in this area. We believe future fit research would benefit from drawing more explicitly from each of Terborg's interaction types and from recent advances in personality psychology. Specifically, we focus on three areas of research that we think are promising in terms of their implications for fit research. These areas include the self-concordance model, situation selection research, and meso-level research. We review these areas and their implications for future fit research in the sections that follow.

Self-Concordance Model

The self-concordance model, formulated by Sheldon and Elliot (1998, 1999) and influenced by earlier work on intrinsic motivation (Deci & Ryan, 1985), seeks to explain the cognitive processes underlying goal-directed behavior. The model is a good exemplar for person–organization fit research because it describes how the choice of goals (with the accompanying reasons for pursuit of these goals) leads to congruence, which in turn leads to outcomes such as well-being and stress. For various reasons we explain shortly, we believe this model is one that suggests new avenues for future fit research.

The self-concordance model argues that individuals may pursue a goal for one of four types of reasons (Sheldon & Elliot, 1998): (1) external—pursuing a goal because of others' wishes or to attain rewards that indirectly satisfy needs or interests (e.g., money, praise), (2) introjected—pursuing a goal to avoid feelings of shame, guilt, or anxiety, (3) identified—pursuing a goal out of a belief that it is an intrinsically important goal to have, and (4) intrinsic—pursuing a goal because of the fun and enjoyment it provides. The model further stipulates that identified and intrinsic goals are self-concordant because they better fulfill an individual's enduring needs, interests, and values. There are several points worth noting with respect to the self-concordance model. First, these reasons are not argued to be mutually exclusive; individuals may pursue a goal for several reasons. Second, the reasons can be classified as approach (identified and intrinsic) versus avoidance (external and introjected). Third, in self-concordance research, goals are not objectively classifiable. Rather, two individuals may pursue the same goal for different reasons. Thus, in order to measure self-concordance, one must ask people about their reasons for pursuing various goals rather than assuming certain goals per se are self-concordant or not self-concordant.

Research on the self-concordance model has been supportive. Elliot, Sheldon, and Church (1997) showed that the pursuit of avoidance goals leads to lower subjective well-being, partly because avoidance goals are associated with diminished perceptions of goal progress. Elliot and Sheldon (1998) demonstrated that avoidance goals were positively related to health symptoms. Sheldon and Elliot (1999) found that self-concordant motives are more likely to lead to well-being across three studies. Although self-concordance is mostly concerned with well-being, goal attainment is another outcome. Research clearly demonstrates that autonomous goals are more likely to be attained than were controlled goals (Sheldon & Elliot, 1998, 1999). Related pursuit of avoidance goals leads to low perceptions of progress, and low perceptions of progress are negatively related to subjective well-being (Elliot, Sheldon, & Church).

Although the self-concordance model has yet to be studied in organizational contexts, there are several ways in which the model is relevant to future P–O fit research. First, the model is relevant because it avoids the statistical and methodological problems when fit has to be assessed by a statistical combination of person and environment measures. Statistical procedures to test the effects of P–O fit are hotly debated. Edwards (1994), for example, argues that single index measures of congruence (e.g., difference scores or profile similarity indices) cannot accurately assess fit because of limitations such as conceptual ambiguity, discarded information, and unrealistically restrictive constraints. Edwards offers an alternative approach to assessing fit that involves a complex series of polynomial regressions with quadratics and interactions of main effects. Others argue that such an approach is not always the best strategy. Meglino and Ravlin (1998) argue that single index measures using ipsative scales have a number of important theoretical and methodological advantages. Our approach here is not to take sides on this issue. Rather, our point is that theories that can be tested without reliance on complex statistical procedures (on the principle of parsimony) on the one hand, and without the limitations of difference scores on the other hand, are advantageous. Because self-concordance is measured directly, it avoids the statistical conundrums that have plagued recent fit research.

A second advantage of the self-concordance model is that it moves P–O fit research beyond its predominant focus on job search and choice. We believe fit research has become somewhat moribund in its focus on job choice. Though job choice clearly is an important outcome, it is only one of many outcomes of fit. More research needs to consider other outcomes, and the self-concordance's focus on well-being, which easily could be recast in terms of work attitudes such as stress and job satisfaction (see Roberson, 1990), clearly does this. One might ask what this model has to do with personality. Research shows that avoidance goals are negatively related to self-esteem (Elliot & Sheldon, 1997) and neuroticism (Elliot & Sheldon, 1998; Elliot, Sheldon, & Church, 1997). Similarly, neuroticism has been found to be negatively correlated with perceived autonomy and positively correlated with perceived controlledness (Elliot & Sheldon, 1998). Thus, self-concordance may explain why certain personality traits are related to work attitudes. Recently, Judge, Heller, and Mount (2001) showed that four of the five traits from the five-factor model were related to job satisfaction. These traits' effects on job satisfaction may be explained, in part, by self-concordance. For example, neurotic individuals may be more likely to pursue goals for introjected reasons and agreeable or conscientious individuals may be more likely to pursue goals for identified reasons.

In the context of the fit literature, the self-concordance model can be used to address many important research questions. For example, are individuals who pursue work goals for self-concordant reasons happier in their jobs? Does self-concordance mediate the relationship between personality and affective outcomes such as job satisfaction? Do organizations and occupations differ in the degree to which they facilitate self-concordance (i.e., is it easier to attain self-concordance in certain organizations or vocations)? Finally, what is the nature of the relationship between self-concordance and P–O fit perceptions? Integrating several of these questions, we could envision a model in which personality leads to self-concordant goal pursuit, which leads to goal attainment and fit perceptions, which in turn lead to job satisfaction and other positive outcomes.

Situation Selection

Another research stream from personality and social psychology that is directly relevant to the P–O fit literature is research on situation selection. There is a great deal of research in the vocational psychology literature that considers how personality influences choice of jobs (e.g., Tokar, Fischer, & Subich, 1998) and choice of occupations (e.g., Holland's [1985] RIASEC model). However, a hodgepodge of traits have been considered in the job choice literature, including self-esteem, locus of control, need for achievement, Type A personality, risk aversion, materialism, and many others. This variety has made assimilation of the research findings difficult. In the vocational choice literature, the status of the RIASEC traits is unclear. Some research suggests that these vocational interests are related to the Big Five personality traits, but the relationships are not strong (De Fruyt & Mervielde, 1997). Our purpose here is not to criticize these studies. Rather, it is to point out that the P–O fit literature may benefit from more thematic investigations.

Emmons and Diener (1986) argued that individuals seek out situations that allow them to achieve certain goals. These goals satisfy certain needs. Need satisfaction, in turn, leads to positive affective reactions. According to Emmons and Diener, goal motivation leads people to (a) spend more time in situations in which they have important goals and believe they are making progress toward these goals and (b) to choose situations in which they feel positive affect and avoid those in which they feel negative affect. Emmons and Diener found that having important goals was strongly associated with positive affect, irrespective of goal attainment. Consistent with our discussions under self-concordance, this evidence supports the hypothesis that positive people are more likely to choose goals that will put them in intrinsically rewarding situations. Emmons and Diener noted, "Choice of ... situations may be best explained not in terms of anticipated goal attainment but rather in terms of affect arising from direct involvement with the ... activity" (p. 324).

Increasing our understanding of situation selection is a critical first step in exploring Terborg's idea of reciprocal interaction. This research is explicitly interactional when one takes into account that choice of situations, and goal-directed behavior more generally, are dispositionally based. For example, Diener, Larsen, and Emmons (1984) revealed the following associations between personality and choice of situations: (a) individuals with high need for achievement spent more time in work situations and less time in novel situations, (b) individuals with a high need for order spent less time in novel situations, and (c) extraverts spent more time in social recreational activities. Furthermore, Diener et al. found that individuals were happiest when they were in situations that fit their personalities. For example, extraverts and individuals with high need for affiliation were happiest in social and recreational situations. Finally, the time spent in situations across individuals had some relationship with affect (though because of the small sample size these associations did not reach statistical significance). Irrespective of personality, individuals who spent time in work situations reported somewhat less positive affect whereas those who spent time in recreational and social activities reported more positive affect and less negative affect.

Several conclusions regarding interactions can be drawn from this type of research. First, individuals select situations based on their personalities (a first step in reciprocal effects interactions). Second, there are nonadditive interactions in which individuals are happier when their personality is a good fit with their situation. Performance also may be an outcome of this type of fit (Pervin, 1968). There is also support for a third type of interaction by which personality affects outcomes like satisfaction through situational choices—that is, people choose situations based on their personality, and these situational choices influence outcomes directly. This interaction is akin to the mediating effects model of interaction described by Terborg (1981). As a general example, conscientious individuals live longer (Friedman et al., 1995). It is not that conscientiousness carries with it properties that have direct physiological effects. Rather, conscientious individuals live longer through an interactive process—they pursue different goals, make different decisions, and choose different lives than less conscientious individuals. These interactions with the environment are manifested in life-relevant outcomes such as less risky smoking behavior (Hampson, Andrews, Barckley, Lichtenstein, & Lee, 2000), safer driving behavior (Arthur & Graziano, 1996), and a greater degree of rule-abiding behavior and social competence (Shriner, 2000). Thus, one can observe that conscientiousness is related to longevity without considering the environment, but one cannot possibly understand the process without considering the interaction of the trait within the person's environment.

The implications of this line of research for fit research are direct. A few suggested areas follow:

- How is personality related to goal-setting behavior? Here, we are not only referring to the effect of personality on goal difficulty (see Judge & Ilies, 2001, for a review), but also to the effects of personality on whether individuals self-set goals, the reasons for pursuing these goals, and whether the goals are concrete or abstract (see Emmons, 1992). Because goals are one of the most important correlates of well-being and performance, more research is needed on how personality traits play on interactive role in this process. Recent research suggests, for example, that achievement goals can be considered as one of four types, along two dimensions—positive/approach vs. negative/avoidance and absolute/intrapersonal (mastery) vs. normative (performance) (Elliot & McGregor, 2001)—and both of these dimensions are important in well-being, learning, and performance (Dweck, 1999; Emmons). What role does personality play when these goals are studied in a work context?
- How does personality affect the choice of situations at work? For example, though we know that conscientious employees perform better, in part, because they set more ambitious goals (Gellatly, 1996), goal orientation is not explicitly a choice of a situation. How does conscientiousness, extraversion, or other traits influence how people spend their time at work, and how are these choices important for job performance, job satisfaction, and other outcomes? For example, do conscientious employees spend more time on tasks and are introverted employees more likely to isolate themselves socially at work?
- How are job satisfaction and other affective reactions affected by personality and choice of situations? Are conscientious employees happier and more productive when performing core job responsibilities, are agreeable or affiliative individuals happier when helping others and performing citizenship duties, are extroverts happier and more productive in social situations? Similarly, are open individuals more creative (Feist, 1998) because of choices they make at work?

Meso-Level Research

Meso-level theory and research, which concerns the simultaneous study of at least two levels of analysis (e.g., individual and team, individual and organization, group and organization), has the potential for answering interesting questions regarding P–E interactions. Research on person–group and P–O fit can be considered meso-level, because it typically involves the nonadditive interaction or congruence between an individual and higher-level aspects of their work environments. These higher-level aspects can be assessed objectively, but the interactionist perspective suggests that it is individuals' perceptions of their work groups and organizations that will be most predictive of outcomes. When individual personality and perceptions of the environment are used to assess fit, it is less clear whether the research is truly meso-level, given that all predictors and outcomes are assessed at the individual level of analysis.

Despite these questions, it is clear that the full potential of fit research as meso-level has not been explored. House, Rousseau, and Thomas-Hunt (1995) defined a variety of meso-level processes, including isomorphisms, discontinuities, and interlevel relationships. Current fit research has not explored the processes by which fit influences outcomes across levels; therefore, we offer some suggestions for what these processes might be and how they might be explored:

- Isomorphisms refer to processes that are similar across multiple levels of system. That is, if a positive relationship holds between personality congruence and individual outcomes, a similar relationship will hold between personality congruence and team or organizational outcomes.
- Discontinuities describe the processes by which the same variables produce one outcome at one level of analysis and a distinctly different outcome at another level of analysis. For example, personality congruence may have benefits for individuals but result in negative outcomes for their teams or organizations.
- Interlevel relationships occur when variables or relationships at one level of analysis affect or moderate outcomes at another level. Such might be the case if personality congruence changed the relationship between a team characteristic (e.g., size) and a team outcome (e.g., cohesion) or between an organizational characteristic (e.g., structure) and an organizational-level outcome (e.g., flexibility).

Currently, the evidence supports the benefits of personality congruence for individuals, such as improved work attitudes and reduced stress and intentions to quit. These effects may be isomorphic to the extent that reducing individuals' intentions to quit will result in decreased turnover for their team or organization. However, the potential for discontinuities also exists. For example, Bretz and Judge (1994b) demonstrated the positive effects of fit on individual career success, suggesting a positive relationship between fit and individual performance; on the other hand many researchers have suggested that high levels of employee fit could result in reduced organizational performance. Schneider et al. (1995) describe the dark side of fit, which includes excessive homogenization of a company's workforce, strategic myopia, and inability to adapt to a changing environment. In addition, concerns have been raised that hiring for fit may limit demographic diversity in organizations (Powell, 1998). This, in turn, may reduce a company's ability to meet the needs of a diverse customer base and engage in creative problem solving. These examples highlight potential discontinuities between the consequences of personality fit for individuals versus broader work units.

To examine which of these processes holds, researchers should assess individual personality traits, modal personality in their teams and organizations, and organizational climate or personality (as perceived by top managers), and use these to predict various individual, team, and organizational level outcomes. It is likely that both isomorphic and discontinuous processes exist, but it is an empirical question as to which type of processes influence particular outcomes.

Numerous possibilities for interlevel relationships exist. For example, House et al. (1995) suggest the tight versus loose coupling of organizational units can have an important impact on relationships within the organization. It is possible that the degree of coupling between units may change the strength or even direction of the relationship between fit and individual outcomes. In a loosely coupled organization, the influence of P–O fit on individual attitudes may be less important than in a tightly coupled organization where company culture is highly visible and widely shared. In cases such as these, the predictive power of person–group fit should exceed that of P–O fit, because individuals are likely to be more influenced by the culture or personalities in their immediate work group than in the organization at large. Conducting this type of research implies that researchers incorporate multiple types of interactionism in their investigations. In the example just presented, personality fit could be assessed as a congruence relationship, and organizational coupling would be included as a nonadditive interaction in the personality fit–attitudes relationship.

Finally, we note that there is a continuing need for research on the classification of situations. Personality will best predict relevant outcomes when personality and situations are assessed in commensurate terms. But what does *commensurate* mean? O'Reilly, Chatman, and colleagues (e.g., O'Reilly et al., 1991) have achieved person–situation correspondence through the study of values, where organizational contexts reflect the values of the individual (e.g., tolerance, working long hours). At first blush, it would appear that such an approach might be generalized to traits, whereby certain situations (organizational cultures) reflect the traits of the individuals in those situations. Such an approach might appear compatible with Schneider's (1987a) ASA model, by considering situations to be defined by the individual behavior within that context. On the other hand, despite some noteworthy attempts to describe college student situations in personological terms (e.g., Murtha, Kanfer, & Ackerman, 1996), accurately labeling organizational cultures as neurotic or extraverted is more difficult than describing them as team-oriented or supportive. Thus, it seems likely that the classification of situations must do more than classify situations according to the five-factor model or some other personality typology.

SUMMARY AND CONCLUSION

Our purpose in this chapter was to organize the existing literature on personality and interactional psychology, specifically with regard to P–E and P–O fit, and present ideas for future research on these issues. Although personality researchers often emphasize the importance of traits in determining attitudes and behaviors, our review makes it clear that personality studied in the absence of situation is a limitation in the literature. Using Terborg's (1981) five types of interactions, and adding a sixth that is reflected in much of the current P–O fit research, we describe a wide variety of ways in which personality and situation can be jointly considered as predictors of outcomes. Building on these types of interactions and emerging areas of research in I–O psychology and OB, we outline three distinct future research agendas. We hope that these ideas spark new areas of interest for readers and advance research on personality, fit, and interactional psychology.

REFERENCES

Allport, G. W. (1937). *Personality: A psychological interpretation.* New York: Holt, Rinehart & Winston.

Arthur, W., Jr., & Graziano, W. G. (1996). The five-factor model, conscientiousness, and driving accident involvement. *Journal of Personality, 64,* 593–618.

Assouline, M., & Meir, E. I. (1987). Meta-analysis of the relationship between congruence and well-being measures. *Journal of Vocational Behavior, 31,* 319–332.

Atwater, L. E., Ostroff, C., Yammarino, F. J., & Fleenor, J. W. (1998). Self-other agreement: Does it really matter? *Personnel Psychology, 51,* 577–598.

Bandura, A. (1971). *Social learning theory.* New York: General Learning Press.

Barrick, M. R., Mount, M. K., & Strauss, J. P. (1993). Conscientiousness and performance of sales representatives: Test of the mediating effects of goal setting. *Journal of Applied Psychology, 78,* 715–722.

Barry, B., & Stewart, G. L. (1997). Composition, process, and performance in self-managed groups: The role of personality. *Journal of Applied Psychology, 82,* 62–78.

Bretz, R. D., Ash, R. A., & Dreher, G. F. (1989). Do the people make the place?: An examination of the attraction-selection-attrition hypothesis. *Personnel Psychology, 42*, 561–581.

Bretz, R. D., & Judge, T. A. (1994a). The role of human resource systems in job applicant decision processes. *Journal of Management, 20*, 531–551.

Bretz, R. D., & Judge, T. A. (1994b). Person-organization fit and the theory of work adjustment: Implications for satisfaction, tenure, and career success. *Journal of Vocational Behavior, 44*, 32–54.

Burke, R. J., & Deszca, E. (1982). Preferred organizational climates of Type A individuals. *Journal of Vocational Behavior, 21*, 50–59.

Cable, D. M., & Judge, T. A. (1994). Pay preferences and job search decisions: A person-organization fit perspective. *Personnel Psychology, 47*, 317–348.

Cable, D. M., & Judge, T. A. (1996). Person-organization fit, job choice decisions, and organizational entry. *Organizational Behavior and Human Decision Processes, 67*, 294–311.

Cable, D. M., & Judge, T. A. (1997). Interviewers' perceptions of person-organization fit and organizational selection decisions. *Journal of Applied Psychology, 82*, 546–561.

Chatman, J. A. (1991). Matching people and organizations: Selection and socialization in public accounting firms. *Administrative Science Quarterly, 36*, 459–484.

Cowley, W. H. (1931). Three distinctions in the study of leaders. *Journal of Abnormal and Social Psychology, 26*, 304–313.

Davis-Blake, A., & Pfeffer, J. (1989). Just a mirage: The search for dispositional effects in organizational research. *Academy of Management Review, 14*, 385–400.

Day, D. V., & Bedeian, A. G. (1995). Personality similarity and work-related outcomes among African-American nursing personnel: A test of the supplementary model of P-E congruence. *Journal of Vocational Behavior, 46*, 55–70.

Deci, E. L., & Ryan, R. M. (1985). *Intrinsic motivation and self-determination in human behavior.* New York: Plenum.

De Fruyt, F., & Mervielde, I. (1997). The five-factor model of personality and Holland's RIASEC interest types. *Personality and Individual Differences, 23*, 87–103.

Diener, E., Larsen, R. J., & Emmons, R. A. (1984). Person × situation interactions: Choice of situations and congruence response models. *Journal of Personality and Social Psychology, 47*, 580–592.

Downey, H. K., Hellriegel, D., & Slocum, J. W. (1975). Congruence between individual needs, organizational climate, job satisfaction and performance. *Academy of Management Journal, 18*, 149–155.

Dweck, C. (1999). *Self-theories: Their role in motivation, personality, and development.* Philadelphia: Psychology Press.

Edwards, J. R. (1994). The study of congruence in organizational behavior research: Critique and a proposed alternative. *Organizational Behavior and Human Decision Processes, 58*, 51–100.

Elliot, A. J., & McGregor, H. A. (2001). A 2 × 2 achievement goal framework. *Journal of Personality and Social Psychology, 80*, 501–519.

Elliot, A. J., & Sheldon, K. M. (1997). Avoidance achievement motivation: A personal goals analysis, *Journal of Personality and Social Psychology, 73*, 171–185.

Elliot, A. J., & Sheldon, K. M. (1998). Avoidance personal goals and the personality-illness relationship. *Journal of Personality and Social Psychology, 75*, 1282–1299.

Elliot, A. J., Sheldon, K. M., & Church, M. A. (1997). Avoidance personal goals and subjective well-being. *Personality and Social Psychology Bulletin, 23*, 915–927.

Emmons, R. A. (1992). Abstract versus concrete goals: Personal striving level, physical illness, and psychological well-being. *Journal of Personality and Social Psychology, 62*, 292–300.

Emmons, R. A., & Diener, E. (1986). A goal-affect analysis of everyday situational choices. *Journal of Research in Personality, 20*, 309–326.

Endler, N. S., & Magnussen, D. (1976). *Interactional psychology and personality*. Washington, DC: Hemisphere.

Feist, G. J. (1998). A meta-analysis of personality in scientific and artistic creativity. *Personality and Social Psychology Bulletin, 2*, 290–309.

Ferris, G. R., Youngblood, S. A., & Yates, V. L. (1985). Personality, training performance, and withdrawal: A test of the person-group fit hypothesis for organizational newcomers. *Journal of Vocational Behavior, 27*, 377–388.

French, J. R. P., Jr., Rogers, W., & Cobb, S. (1974). Adjustment as person-environment fit. In G. V. Coelho, D. A. Hamburg, & J. E. Adams (Eds.), *Coping and adaptation* (pp. 316–333). New York: Basic Books.

Friedman, H. S., Tucker, J. S., Schwartz, J. E., Martin, L. R., Tomlinson-Keasey, C., Wingard, D. L., & Criqui, M. H. (1995). Childhood conscientiousness and longevity: Health behaviors and cause of death. *Journal of Personality and Social Psychology, 68*, 696–703.

Gellatly, I. R. (1996). Conscientiousness and task performance: Test of cognitive process model. *Journal of Applied Psychology, 81*, 474–482.

Hampson, S. E., Andrews, J. A., Barckley, M., Lichtenstein, E., & Lee, M. E. (2000). Conscientiousness, perceived risk, and risk-reduction behaviors: A preliminary study. *Health Psychology, 19*, 496–500.

Hogan, R. (1996). A socioanalytic perspective on the five-factor model. In J. S. Wiggins (Ed.), *The five-factor model of personality: Theoretical perspectives* (pp. 163–179). New York: Guilford.

Holland, J. E. (1985). *Making vocational choices: A theory of careers*. Englewood Cliffs, NJ: Prentice Hall.

House, R. J., Rousseau, D. M., & Thomas-Hunt, M. (1995). The meso paradigm: A framework for the integration of micro and macro organizational behavior. *Research in Organizational Behavior, 17*, 71–114.

House, R. J., Spangler, W. D., & Woycke, J. (1991). Personality and charisma in the U.S. presidency: A psychological theory of leader effectiveness. *Administrative Science Quarterly, 36*, 364–396.

Hulin, C. L., & Judge, T. A. (2003). Job attitudes: A theoretical and empirical review. In W. Borman, R. Klimoski, & D. Ilgen (Eds.), *Comprehensive Handbook of Psychology* (pp. 255–276). Hoboken, NJ:Wiley.

Jahoda, M. (1961). A social-psychological approach to the study of culture. *Human Relations, 14*, 23–30.

Jordan, M., Herriott, P., & Chalmers, C. (1991). Testing Schneider's ASA theory. *Applied Psychology: An International Review, 40*, 47–54.

Judge, T. A., & Cable, D. M. (1997). Applicant personality, organizational culture, and organization attraction. *Personnel Psychology, 50*, 359–394.

Judge, T. A., Heller, D., & Mount, M. K. (2001, April). *Personality and job satisfaction: A meta-analysis*. Paper presented at the 16th annual conference of the Society for Industrial and Organizational Psychology, San Diego, CA.

Judge, T. A., & Ilies, R. (2001). *Relationship of personality and to task and work motivation: A review*. Manuscript submitted for publication.

Judge, T. A., Locke, E. A., & Durham, C. C. (1997). The dispositional causes of job satisfaction: A core evaluations approach. *Research in Organizational Behavior, 19*, 151–188.

Judge, T. A., Locke, E. A., Durham, C. C., & Kluger, A. N. (1998). Dispositional effects on job and life satisfaction: The role of core evaluations. *Journal of Applied Psychology, 83*, 17–34.

Kantor, J. R. (1924). *Principles of psychology* (Vol. 1). Bloomington, IL: Principia.

Klein, K., J., Conn, A. B., Smith, D.B., & Sorra, J. S. (2001). Is everyone in agreement? An exploration of within-group agreement in employee perceptions of the work environment. *Journal of Applied Psychology, 86*, 3–16.

Kohn, M. L., & Schooler, C. (1982). Job conditions and personality: A longitudinal assessment of their reciprocal effects. *American Journal of Sociology, 87*, 1257–1286.

Lewin, K. (1935). *A dynamic theory of personality.* New York: McGraw-Hill.

Loher, B. T., Noe, R. A., Moeller, N. L., & Fitzgerald, M. P. (1985). A meta-analysis of the relation of job characteristics to job satisfaction. *Journal of Applied Psychology, 70*, 280–289.

Magnusson, D. (1990). Personality development from an interactional perspective. In L. A. Pervin (Ed.), *Handbook of personality: Theory and research* (pp. 193–222). New York: Guilford.

McCrae, R. R., & Costa, P. T., Jr. (1989). Reinterpreting the Myers-Briggs Type Indicator from the perspective of the five-factor model of personality. *Journal of Personality, 57*, 17–40.

Mead, G. H. (1934). *Mind, self, and society.* University of Chicago Press.

Meglino, B. M., & Ravlin, E. C. (1998). Individual values in organizations: Concepts, controversies, and research. *Journal of Management, 24*, 351–389.

Mount, M. K., Harter, J. K., Barrick, M. R., & Colbert, A. (2000, August). *Does job satisfaction moderate the relationship between conscientiousness and job performance?* Paper presented at the Academy of Management Annual Meeting, Toronto, Canada.

Muchinsky, P. M., & Monahan, C. J. (1987). What is person-environment congruence? Supplementary versus complementary models of fit. *Journal of Vocational Behavior, 31*, 268–277.

Murray, H. A. (1938). *Explorations in personality.* New York: Oxford University Press.

Murtha, T. C., Kanfer, R., & Ackerman, P. L. (1996). Toward an interactionist taxonomy of personality and situations: An integrative situational—dispositional representation of personality traits. *Journal of Personality and Social Psychology, 71*, 193–207.

O'Reilly, C. A., Chatman, J., & Caldwell, D. F. (1991). People and organizational culture: A profile comparison approach to assessing person-organization fit. *Academy of Management Journal, 34*, 487–516.

O'Reilly, C. A., & Roberts, K. H. (1975). Individual differences in personality, position in the organization, and job satisfaction. *Organizational Behavior and Human Performance, 14*, 144–150.

Ostroff, C. (1992). The relationship between satisfaction, attitudes, and performance: An organizational level analysis. *Journal of Applied Psychology, 77*, 963–974.

Ostroff, C. (1993). The effects of climate and personal influences on individual behavior and attitudes in organizations. *Organizational Behavior and Human Decision Processes, 56*, 56–90.

Pervin, L. A. (1968). Performance and satisfaction as a function of individual-environment fit. *Psychological Bulletin, 69*, 56–68.

Pervin, L. A. (1990). A brief history of modern personality theory. In L. A. Pervin (Ed.), *Handbook of personality: Theory and research* (pp. 3–18). New York: Guilford.

Pervin, L. A., & Lewis, M. (1978). *Perspectives in interactional psychology.* New York: Plenum.

Powell, G. N. (1998). Reinforcing and extending today's organizations: The simultaneous pursuit of person-organization fit and diversity. *Organizational Dynamics, 26*, 50–61.

Ravlin, E. C., & Meglino, B. M. (1989). The transitivity of work values: Hierarchical preference ordering of socially desirable stimuli. *Organizational Behavior and Human Decision Processes, 44*, 494–508.

Roberson, L. (1990). Prediction of job satisfaction from characteristics of personal work goals. *Journal of Organizational Behavior, 11*, 29–41.

Schaubroeck, J., Ganster, D. C., & Jones, J. R. (1998). Organization and occupation influences in the attraction-selection-attrition process. *Journal of Applied Psychology, 83*, 869–891.

Schneider, B. (1987a). The people make the place. *Personnel Psychology, 40*, 437–453.

Schneider, B. (1987b). $E = f(P, B)$: The road to a radical approach to P-E fit. *Journal of Vocational Behavior, 31*, 353–361.

Schneider, B., Goldstein, H. W., & Smith, D. B. (1995). The ASA framework: An update. *Personnel Psychology, 48*, 747–773.

Schneider, B., Smith, D. B., Taylor, S., & Fleenor, J. (1998). Personality and organizations: A te of the homogeneity of personality hypothesis. *Journal of Applied Psychology, 83,* 462–470.

Sheldon, K. M., & Elliot, A. J. (1998). Not all personal goals are personal: Comparing autonomous and controlled reasons for goals as predictors of effort and attainment. *Personality and Social Psychology Bulletin, 24,* 546–557.

Sheldon, K. M., & Elliot, A. J. (1999). Goal striving, need satisfaction, and longitudinal well-being: The self-concordance model. *Journal of Personality and Social Psychology, 76,* 482–497.

Shriner, R. L. (2000). Linking childhood personality with adaptation: Evidence for continuity and change across time into late adolescence. *Journal of Personality and Social Psychology, 78,* 310–325.

Skinner, B. F. (1953). *Science and human behavior.* New York: Macmillan.

Spokane, A. R. (1985). A review of research on P-E congruence in Holland's theory of careers. *Journal of Vocational Behavior, 26,* 306–343.

Staats, A. W. (1981). Paradigmatic behaviorism, unified theory construction, methods and the zeitgeist of separatism. *American Psychologist, 36,* 239–256.

Terborg, J. R. (1981). Interactional psychology and research on human behavior in organizations. *Academy of Management Review, 6,* 569–576.

Tischler, L. (1996). Comparing P-O personality fit to work success. *Journal of Psychological Type, 38,* 34–43.

Tokar, D. M., Fischer, A. R., & Subich, L. M. (1998). Personality and vocational behavior: A selective review of the literature, 1993–1997. *Journal of Vocational Behavior, 53,* 115–153.

Tokar, D. M., & Swanson, J. L. (1995). Evaluation of the correspondence between Holland's vocational personality typology and the five-factor model of personality. *Journal of Vocational Behavior, 46,* 89–108.

Tranberg, M., Slane, S., & Ekeberg, S. E. (1993). The relation between interest congruence and satisfaction: A meta-analysis. *Journal of Vocational Behavior, 42,* 253–264.

Turban, D. B., & Keon, T. L. (1993). Organizational attractiveness: An interactionist perspective. *Journal of Applied Psychology, 78,* 184–193.

Winter, D. G., & Barenbaum, N. B. (1999). History of modern personality theory and research. In L. A. Pervin & O. P. John (Eds.), *Handbook of personality: Theory and research* (2nd ed., pp. 3–27). New York: Guilford.

5

The Implications of Impression Management for Personality Research in Organizations

Brent Smith
Rice University

Chet Robie
Wilfred Laurier University

The study of individual differences in personality has a long history in the fields of industrial–organizational psychology and organizational behavior. However, this history can best be described as somewhat peculiar. Although personality has been implicated as a factor in employee motivation, absenteeism, leadership, job performance variability, goal setting, and organizational climate (see Hogan, 1991), persistent critics over the past several decades have questioned the importance, meaning, and measurement of personality constructs (e.g., Davis-Blake & Pfeffer, 1989; Mischel, 1968). Many of these criticisms now appear resolved as demonstrated by the proliferation of research on the dispositional antecedents of various work-related behaviors. However, one particularly pernicious critique has remained and experienced some reinvigoration following the renewed interest in personality applications. Unlike other concerns, this particular critique does not question the importance of personality constructs per se; rather, it is a denunciation of the methods of measurement we employ to identify a person's traits, primarily self-report questionnaires, and casts doubt on the basic assumption that responses to self-report personality questionnaires are veridical. Rather, these critics suggest that self-report measures of personality are infused with distortions based on a person's perception of the desirability of various response options. In short, rather than being veridical reports, some (currently unknown) percentage of respondents may actively attempt to manage impressions and misrepresent their true personalities.

As noted, this concern is not new. Response distortion on personality and other noncognitive measures has been a significant concern for well over 60 years (with the earliest published study, to our knowledge, being Kelley, Miles, and Terman, 1936). Sadly, as in many areas of social science research, our understanding of the issues and processes surrounding response distortion and impression management does not reflect the amount of time spent or the number of studies conducted on the topic. We would be extremely optimistic if we were to suggest that this exposition will break significant new ground in the decades-old social desirability debate. Fortunately, we have no such aspirations. Rather, we would like to review, in brief, some of the more recent research that addresses impression and attempt to place this research in a slightly broader context. As we will note, much of the recent research on response distortion arose from the application of personality measures to an applicant selection context. Although selection is clearly an important application for personality assessment, it has limited the scope of questions asked regarding the nature and meaning of impression management. We hope to frame the current status of impression management research in the broader context of theoretical frameworks for personality assessment (see Hogan & Hogan, 1998)—that is, what exactly does a response to a personality questionnaire item really indicate and what implications does this finding have for impression management as a response style?

Before proceeding, we would like to make a few observations about the current status of research on impression management (not that these will be our last!). First, most recent research on impression management was initiated by researchers focusing on the applied use of personality measures in applicant selection contexts. Although it seems natural to question the verity of responses to personality questionnaires in these settings, it is certainly not the only domain in which questions of impression management are germane. The implications of impression management as a personality response style are equally relevant to anyone conducting research in organizational settings using self-report personality questionnaires. In fact, this application has been the subject of extensive discussion and study (e.g., Arnold & Feldman, 1981; Ganster, Hennessey, & Luthans, 1983; Howard, 1994; Moorman & Podsakoff, 1992; Schmitt, 1994; Spector, 1994; Zerbe & Paulhus, 1987). Although much of the recent research we will review in this chapter originates from research on applicant selection, we want to remind the reader that the concern is much broader and has implications for all research conducted in organizational settings using self-report questionnaires.

Second, our review of the literature on impression management and socially desirable responding suggests to us that there is a great, expansive divide separating those who appear fundamentally to believe that personality responses are prone to impression management (and this is a key indictment of self-report questionnaires) from those who believe that impression management does not significantly affect people's responses. We do not wish to imply that researchers consciously frame their investigations of impression management to prove or disprove its deleterious effects on the validity of personality assessments; rather, we wish to suggest simply that the tenor of some of the recent discussions of impression management might lead a casual observer to this conclusion. It is our hope that framing this issue in the larger context of theoretical perspectives on assessment will help to bridge this divide and refocus our attention on the science and practice of personality assessment.

Third, we propose that researchers interested in impression management look beyond the stream of research on applicant selection and review the broader literature on social desirability in personality psychology and, more important, the broader theoretical perspectives on impression management from the sociological and social psychological traditions. We believe this latter literature has significant implications for the current debates on response distortion effects, in particular, and suggests an important and sometimes overlooked perspective on what item responses actually mean.

Finally, we offer a brief note on terminology. Throughout this chapter we will use the term *impression management* to refer to any conscious attempt to alter one's scores on a personality questionnaire. As such, we consider the term to be interchangeable with faking, malingering, claiming unlikely virtues, socially desirable responding, gaming, and so forth. Although we do recognize that many authors have argued that there are important distinctions among these terms, we prefer to use the term impression management because, we believe, it best represents the underlying characteristic of all of these terms and is consistent with the broader literature and theoretical perspectives on social interaction (that we believe are relevant for this discussion of response distortion). We also focus on impression management as it is distinct from the component of socially desirable responding referred to commonly as self-deception (Paulhus, 1984). Self-deception represents the unconscious tendency to evaluate oneself positively and appears to be a culturally instilled ego-defense mechanism—in other words, self-deception is nonintentional distortion. We also will make no distinction between impression management that is motivated by societal pressure (i.e., social desirability) versus impression management that is more specifically motivated (i.e., employee or job desirability). We will address this last issue in more detail later.

We have organized our review of the literature in terms of three questions. First, do people manage impressions when they respond to personality questionnaires? Second, what are the effects of impression management? Third, how can you reduce impression management (assuming for the moment that you should)? We will offer some additional research on some of these topics, and as a conclusion to the chapter, we will attempt to place the research we have reviewed in the broader context of theoretical perspectives on item responses. In our review, we will focus more attention on recent research in this area.

RESEARCH ON IMPRESSION MANAGEMENT

Research of Limited Value

Before commenting on the literature we believe to be of use in furthering our understanding of impression management, we would first like to provide a justification for not focusing on research that we believe is of limited utility in advancing our understanding of the processes that underlie (and the effects of) impression management. Specifically, we believe that laboratory research on impression management (including directed faking studies, whether conducted in the lab or not) provide little insight into impression management beyond the fact that when instructed to do so people can alter their scores on a personality assessment. Although laboratory research can provide internally and externally valid results for many areas of the social sciences (Locke, 1986), we believe the research evidence suggests that laboratory research (as it is typically conducted using a directed faking approach) is probably an inappropriate vehicle for studying impression management issues.

First, there is a theoretical rationale for considering laboratory studies to be inappropriate. Hogan (1991) suggests that impression management has two subcomponents: the desire to impression manage (i.e., distort) and the ability to do so. Two recent studies provide evidence that individual differences in the ability to impression manage do exist (McFarland & Ryan, 2000; Mersman & Shultz, 1998). Although research to date has provided no convincing evidence that individuals differ in the desire to distort, Hogan's two-part model of impression management (or faking) provides a compelling rationale for not considering laboratory impression management processes to be commensurate with real-world response processes. Specifically, in the laboratory, the desire to impression manage is presumably held constant because respondents are instructed whether or not to distort their responses and in which direction. Only ability to manage impressions is free to vary in laboratory experiments. However, in applicant settings, both desire and ability to impression manage are free to vary and they may interact with one another in as yet not understood ways. It is unlikely therefore that studying one factor in isolation (i.e., ability) will lead to any generalizable conclusions regarding impression management processes in general.

Second, the use of student samples in laboratory impression management studies presents unique obstacles to interpreting findings properly. Specifically, in laboratory settings, impression management ability may be confounded by the ability to follow directions and stay on task. It is not uncommon to encounter situations in laboratory studies in which participants are overtly engaging in subterfuge activities such as talking to other participants or are hurriedly completing the research materials so they can make their next class. It is unlikely that monetary incentives eradicate this issue. This begs the question—how much of the variance in impression management ability identified by McFarland and Ryan (2000) and Mersman and Shultz (1998) is true variance and how much is unrelated variance caused by a lack of real-world motivation?

Third, and probably most important, empirical research findings from the laboratory do not tend to converge with empirical research findings from the field. Hough (1998a) provides an excellent overview of laboratory and field studies that show that: (a) effect sizes in studies comparing applicant and incumbent mean scores are smaller than effect sizes in studies comparing fake good and honest mean scores, but tend to vary more across constructs for applicant–incumbent comparisons (see Hough, 1998a; Viswesvaran & Ones, 1999), and (b) the criterion-related validity of personality scales for incumbent and applicant samples tends to be much higher than that for directed faking study samples (see Barrick & Mount, 1996; Douglas, McDaniel, & Snell, 1996). Most recently, two studies employing item response theory (IRT) methods, one using a directed faking design (Zickar & Robie, 1999) and one using an applicant–incumbent design (Robie, Zickar, & Schmit, 2001), reached different conclusions. Zickar and Robie found that two of the three scales evidenced differential test functioning (DTF), and for one of the two scales that evidenced DTF, one half of the items evidence differential item functioning (DIF). On the other hand, Robie et al. (2001) did not find any DTF and only two items that evidenced DIF from one of the five scales analyzed. Hough (1998a, p. 211) cited the following quote from Schwab and Packard (1973, p. 374) as being appropriate today: [the data] "strongly suggest that the conclusions obtained from distortion research on students . . . tell us little about what to expect in employee selection and predictive validation studies." We agree and strongly urge other researchers to abandon this technology in favor of other methodologies. The only caveat we give to this rather strongly worded urging is that directed faking studies can be useful when combined with field studies such that valid comparisons can be made across the methods. In this way, we can investigate not whether the results will diverge across methods, but by how much and in what ways. Ideally, a combination of directed faking, quasi-experimental, and computational modeling (see Deshon, 2000; Zickar, 2000; Zickar, Rosse, & Levin, 1996) methodologies could best help us in approximating a true score for how impression management operates under realistic conditions.

DOES IMPRESSION MANAGEMENT OCCUR?

The obvious origin for research on impression management is to determine whether or not it actually occurs. Although the research is clear regarding the ability of respondents to alter their scores on a personality assessment when instructed to do so (Hogan, 1991), there is much greater ambiguity regarding the nature and extent of impression management in real-world settings (Smith, Hanges, & Dickson, 2001). A review of the published literature on impression management reveals an impressive amount of research supporting both the conclusion that it does and that it does not occur to a substantial degree. Traditionally, researchers interested in determining the extent of impression management in real-world settings have used three evidentiary sources: (1) the degree to which mean personality scale scores for job applicants differ from those of other populations, (2) the degree to which criterion-related validity is affected by impression management, and (3) the degree to which people endorse clearly falsifiable items.

Mean differences

The first line of research, discussed briefly earlier, relates to the consistent differences found between applicant and incumbents on mean scale scores (see Hough, 1998a; Rosse, Stecher, Miller, & Levin, 1998). The investigation of mean differences as a source of information regarding response distortion rests on the assumption that applicants will attempt to portray themselves positively (or in a manner suggested by the profile of the job they are seeking). Applicants, therefore, should score higher on scales measuring conscientiousness and agreeableness and lower on scales designed to measure neuroticism (and, for instance, higher on extroversion if they are applying for a sales job). As noted, the research supporting mean differences is inconsistent. Rosse et al., Bass (1957), Kirchner, Dunnette, and Mousley (1960), Michaelis and Eysenck (1971) and others have found evidence of mean differences between applicants and incumbents, whereas Hough et al. (1990), McClelland and Rhodes (1969), Orpen (1971), and Schwab and Packard (1973) found evidence of insignificant mean differences. Based on these findings Mount and Barrick (1995b) concluded that "it is not possible to draw definitive conclusions about the incidence of response distortion on personality inventories in real-applicant settings" (p. 182). However, it is troubling that there are several studies reporting consistently higher mean scale scores for job applicants. This finding would tend to suggest the existence of some impression management.

We believe this area of research could potentially provide quite valuable insights into the nature of response distortion in real-world contexts. Unfortunately, many previous studies have been criticized for their reliance on small, localized samples. To augment previous research on mean differences, we present the results of recent analyses of mean differences between organizational samples (promotion or selection and development) and normative (general population) samples. These analyses extend prior research by comparing a selection context with a development context and are based on substantially larger sample sizes.[1]

Recently, Personnel Decisions International (RDI) transitioned from the use of the California Psychological Inventory (CPI), an empirically developed measure (see Gough, 1987, for more information regarding the CPI), to the Global Personality Inventory (GPI) (for more information regarding the GPI see Schmit, Kihm, & Robie, 2000), a content-based and normatively-developed measure. The items in the GPI were designed to be both more transparent and more job related than those in the CPI. One of the primary concerns raised by the transparency of the items was the possibility that they might be significantly susceptible to impression management. Research by Kluger and Colella (1993) and others (see Meehl & Hathaway, 1946; Schrader & Osburn, 1977) suggest that subtle items may be less susceptible to impression management than transparent items. If transparent items are more susceptible to impression management, this fact would limit the usefulness of the GPI to contexts that do not provide an incentive or motivation to distort responses.

To demonstrate the utility of the GPI and assuage the concerns regarding the transparency of the items, analyses were conducted comparing the scale scores (both means and variances) for samples of respondents who took the measure for promotion or selection purposes versus respondents who took the measure for developmental purposes. Both mean and variance differences were examined because impression management at the extreme could potentially result in a large proportion of individuals increasing their observed scores beyond their true score, which would result in both elevation and restriction. To date, research has typically examined the mean differences between applicants and incumbents (see Hough, 1998a) with the assumption being that incumbents have a lower motivation

---

[1] These analyses are based on research conducted by Chet Robie, the second author, during his tenure at Personnel Decisions International. We would like to thank PDI for graciously allowing us to publish these results.

to fake good. The present analyses improve on these prior studies because the samples in the comparisons we are making are much similar in terms of demographic variables (e.g., managerial status, gender, age) than the applicant–incumbent comparisons done in the past. Thus, third-variable interpretations are less likely for the results in the present analyses. We also included a comparison of scale means and variances for individuals taking the measures for promotion or selection with normative samples to illustrate how large differences can be with samples of a markedly different demographic makeup.

We used data from six samples. Four samples (referred to as organizational samples) represented data from client organizations of PDI's assessment business (235 client organizations for the GPI and 666 client organizations for the CPI). As part of every assessment, respondents were asked to fill out either the CPI (we used data from the years 1995 to 1999) or the GPI (data available only from the year 2000, when it began being administered). In two of the organizational samples, hereafter referred to as the promotion/selection samples ($N = 1069$ for the GPI and $N = 7929$ for the CPI), respondents were given the GPI or CPI for the purposes of promotion (for internal candidates; $n = 394$ for the GPI and $n = 3850$ for the CPI) or selection (for external candidates; $n = 675$ for the GPI and $n = 4079$ for the CPI). In the other organizational samples, hereafter referred to as the development samples ($N = 946$ for the GPI and $N = 5096$ for the CPI), respondents were given the GPI or CPI for the purpose of managerial development. All of the individuals in the development samples were currently employed in the client organizations. Approximately 65% and 85% of client organizations were common across the two organizational samples for the GPI and CPI, respectively.

Two normative samples were used, one for the GPI and one for the CPI. For the GPI normative sample, a proportionate, random sample of individuals from listed telephone households was used. The random sample of 9,927 contained name, address, and phone number of individuals from the 48 contiguous United States. Once individuals were contacted by phone and an agreement to participate obtained, a packet containing a personally signed cover letter, PDI survey instrument, response sheet, and postage-paid return envelope was mailed to each potential respondent. Of the total 9,927 individuals in the initial phone sample, 1,980 agreed over the phone to participate in the study. Including only those individuals who could be reached and were eligible to participate in the study, just over 50% agreed to participate. Of the 1,980 individuals who agreed to participate over the phone, a total of 1,006 respondents completed and returned the inventory. The final participation rate for the mailing portion of the study was 50.8 percent ($1006/1980 = .508$). Eighteen of the questionnaires contained substantial amounts of missing data; we decided to remove those

TABLE 5.1
Characteristics of Organizational and Normative Samples
for the GPI and the CPI

	Organizational						Normative		
	Promotion/Selection			Development			Normative		
	GPI								
Age	M		SD	M		SD	M		SD
	39.47		8.44	41.06		7.01	52.79		15.19
Gender	%Male			%Male			%Male		
	71.5			72.2			56.0		
Job	%Mgr	%Prof	%Cler	%Mgr	%Prof	%Cler	%Mgr	%Prof	%Cler
	63.8	33.7	2.4	84.5	15.3	.2	34.7	48.3	16.9
	CPI								
Age	M		SD	M		SD	M		SD
	40.52		7.93	41.58		7.25	NA		NA
Gender	%Male			%Male			%Male		
	76.2			76.3			50.0		
Job	%Mgr	%Prof	%Cler	%Mgr	%Prof	%Cler	%Mgr	%Prof	%Cler
	69.2	29.2	1.6	78.7	21.1	.2	NA	NA	NA

Note. **GPI**—Promotion/Selection ($N = 1069$). Development ($N = 946$). Normative ($N = 988$). **CPI**—Promotion/Selection ($N = 7947$). Development ($N = 5096$). Normative ($N = 2000$). %mgr = percentage of sample who hold managerial jobs. %prof = percentage of sample who hold professional/technical jobs. %cler = percentage of sample who hold clerical/administrative jobs. NA = data not available.

questionnaires from analysis (final $N = 988$). The CPI normative sample data was taken from the 2nd edition test manual (Gough, 1987).

Only three demographic variables (age, gender, and job) were common across five of the samples (with the exception of the CPI normative sample that listed only gender). Table 5.1 displays the distributions of these variables across the samples. The organizational samples appeared to be much more similar to one another than the normative samples were to either of the organizational samples. The distribution of age across the organizational samples was similar in both mean level and dispersion (promotion/selection $M = 39.47$ and $SD = 8.44$; development $M = 41.06$ and $SD = 7.01$). The GPI normative sample was both older ($M = 52.79$) and approximately twice as diverse in age ($SD = 15.19$) than either of the GPI organizational samples. All of the organizational samples were composed of approximately 70 to 75% males whereas both of the normative samples were composed of approximately 50 to 55% males. The distributions of the type of job held were similar across all of the organizational samples with the development samples having higher numbers of managers than the promotion/selection samples. In contrast, the GPI normative sample's distribution of type of job held was much more uniform than either of the organizational samples with a much lower percentage of managerial jobs held (34.7%) and a higher percentage of professional/technical (48.3%) and clerical/administrative (16.9%) jobs held. Although not listed per se, the CPI normative sample appeared to have a low percentage of managerial jobs as well.

TABLE 5.2
Effect Sizes and Standard Deviation Ratios for GPI Scale Scores in
Comparisons of Organizational and Normative Samples

Scale	Effect Size[a]	SD Ratio[a]	Effect Size[b]	SD Ratio[b]
Agreeableness	**.28**	**.94**	**.72**	**.80**
Consideration	.34	.88	.21	.76
Empathy	.30	.90	.44	.82
Interdependence	.13	1.03	1.05	.90
Openness	.43	1.00	.88	.85
Thought agility	.29	.95	.74	.79
Trust	.16	.91	.99	.68
Conscientiousness	**.26**	**1.00**	**.33**	**.90**
Attention to detail	.26	1.00	−.33	1.04
Dutifulness	.15	1.06	.31	.87
Responsibility	.31	.97	.72	.80
Work focus	.31	.95	.61	.88
Extroversion	**.01**	**.96**	**.95**	**.82**
Adaptability	.07	.98	.98	.81
Competitive	−.23	.99	.67	.96
Desire for achievement	.01	.97	1.18	.76
Desire for advancement	−.11	.91	.64	.88
Energy level	.05	.96	1.25	.80
Influence	.02	1.01	1.01	.84
Initiative	.12	.99	.98	.81
Risk-taking	.01	.97	.95	.87
Sociability	.35	.81	.87	.76
Taking charge	−.15	1.06	.96	.71
Neuroticism	**.32**	**.91**	**1.06**	**.76**
Emotional control	.42	.81	1.05	.72
Negative affectivity*	−.26	.96	−1.29	.75
Optimism	.25	.93	.96	.75
Self-confidence	.18	.95	.91	.76
Stress tolerance	.50	.88	1.08	.82
Openness to experience	**.03**	**.97**	**.39**	**.83**
Independence	−.27	.98	−.93	.74
Innovativeness/creativity	.20	.90	.72	.82
Social astuteness	.06	.99	.56	.91
Thought focus	.09	1.03	.87	.86
Vision	.09	.94	.72	.83

(Continued)

TABLE 5.2
(Continued)

Scale	Effect Size[a]	SD Ratio[a]	Effect Size[b]	SD Ratio[b]
Trait composites	**.18**	**.96**	**.66**	**.81**
Ego-centered*	.01	.99	−.20	.81
Intimidating*	−.23	.91	−.63	.82
Manipulating*	−.20	.95	−.45	.82
Micro-managing*	−.11	.96	−1.16	.84
Passive-aggressive*	−.26	.94	−1.14	.81
Self-awareness/Self-Insight	.27	1.02	.77	.76
Average across all scales	**.16**	**.96**	**.73**	**.82**

Note. Promotion/selection ($N = 1069$). Development ($N = 946$). Normative ($N = 988$).

*High scores on these scales are undesirable. Effect size is the standardized mean difference between the two groups' scores (i.e., $\overline{X}_1 - \overline{X}_2 \div SD_{pooled}$). SD ratio is the ratio of the standard deviations for the scale scores between comparison groups (i.e., $SD_1 \div SD_2$).

[a]Effect size or SD ratio for the comparison of promotion/selection versus development.

[b]Effect size or SD ratio for the comparison of promotion/selection versus normative. Numbers in bold represent averages across scales. Positive effect sizes for each comparison denote higher mean scores for the promotion/selection sample. Effect sizes for scales in which high scores were considered undesirable were first multiplied by −1 before computing averages. Numbers below 1.00 for each comparison denote lower variance in the scale scores for the promotion/selection sample.

We computed effect sizes for the mean scale score differences and standard deviation ratios for the comparisons of the promotion/selection samples ($N = 1069$ for the GPI and $N = 7947$ for the CPI) to both the development samples ($N = 946$ for the GPI and $N = 5096$ for the CPI) and the normative samples ($N = 988$ for the GPI and $N = 2000$ for the CPI). As noted earlier, we computed both indices because impression management could result in both elevation and restriction of variability in personality scale scores.

Results of these analyses are presented in Table 5.2 for the GPI and Table 5.3 for the CPI. As noted in the tables: (a) positive effect sizes for each comparison denote higher mean scores for the promotion/selection samples, (b) effect sizes for scales in which high scores were considered undesirable were first multiplied by −1 before computing averages, and (c) numbers below 1.00 for each comparison denote lower variance in the scale scores for the promotion/selection samples. Overall, the average effect sizes were smaller (.16 vs. .73 for the GPI and .16 vs. 1.03 for the CPI) and the SD ratio was larger (.96 vs. .82 for the GPI and .95 vs. .65 for the CPI) for the comparison of selection/promotion to development than the comparison of promotion/selection to normative. Results varied by scale for both comparisons for both the GPI and CPI.

TABLE 5.3
Effect Sizes and Standard Deviation Ratios for CPI Folk Concept Scale
Scores in Comparisons of Organizational and Normative Samples

Scale	Effect Size[a]	SD Ratio[a]	Effect Size[b]	SD Ratio[b]
Dominance	**.14**	**.92**	**2.06**	**.73**
Capacity for Status	.22	.93	1.24	.64
Sociability	.26	.87	.83	.65
Social Presence	.14	.92	.79	.88
Self-Acceptance	.05	.91	1.03	.70
Independence	.08	.93	1.43	.54
Empathy	.28	.96	1.12	.76
Responsibility	**.20**	**.97**	**.76**	**.60**
Socialization	.12	.93	.73	.58
Self-Control	.22	.97	.91	.73
Communality	.07	.99	.91	.47
Well-being	**.23**	**.89**	**1.22**	**.43**
Tolerance	.15	.99	1.00	.55
Achievement via Conformance	.26	.92	1.43	.48
Achievement via Independence	.12	1.01	1.15	.57
Intellectual Efficiency	.21	.97	.80	.56
Psychological-Mindedness	.19	.94	1.12	.61
Flexibility	−.01	1.01	.08	.90
Femininity/Masculinity*	−.06	.98	−.88	1.07
Average across all scales	**.16**	**.95**	**1.03**	**.65**

Note. Promotion/Selection ($N = 7947$). Development ($N = 5096$). Normative ($N = 2000$).

*High scores on this scale are undesirable. Effect size is the standardized mean difference between the two groups' scores (i.e., $\overline{X}_1 - \overline{X}_2 \div SD_{pooled}$). SD ratio is the ratio of the standard deviations for the scale scores between comparison groups (i.e., $SD_1 \div SD_2$).

[a] Effect size or SD ratio for the comparison of promotion/selection versus development.

[b] Effect size or SD ratio for the comparison of promotion/selection versus normative. Numbers in bold represent averages across scales. Positive effect sizes for each comparison denote higher mean scores for the promotion/selection sample. Effect sizes for the scale in which high scores were considered undesirable were first multiplied by −1 before computing averages. Numbers below 1.00 for each comparison denote lower variance in the scale scores for the promotion/selection sample.

First, we will discuss the specific results for the promotion/selection versus development comparisons. At the scale level, the minimum effect size values were −.27 for the GPI Independence scale and −.01 for the CPI Flexibility scale and the maximum effect size values were .50 for the GPI Stress Tolerance scale and .28 for the CPI Empathy scale. The corresponding minimum and maximum values for the standard deviation ratio at this level were .81 for the GPI (GPI Sociability and Emotional Control were tied) and .89 for the CPI Sociability scale and 1.06 (GPI Dutifulness and Taking Charge were tied) and 1.01 (CPI Achievement via Independence and Flexibility were tied), respectively. At the GPI Big Five factor and trait composite averages level, the minimum effect size value was .01 for the Extroversion factor and the maximum effect size value was .32 for the Neuroticism factor. The corresponding minimum and maximum values for the standard deviation ratio at this level were .91 (Neuroticism) and 1.00 (Conscientiousness), respectively.

Next, we will discuss the specific results for the promotion/selection versus normative comparisons. At the scale level, the minimum effect size values were −.93 for the GPI Independence scale and .08 for the CPI Flexibility scale and the maximum effect size values were −1.29 for the GPI Negative Affectivity scale (note that negative effect size values for scales in which high scores are undesirable should be interpreted similarly to positive effect size values for scales in which high scores are desirable) and 2.06 for the CPI Dominance scale. The corresponding minimum and maximum values for the standard deviation ratio at this level were .68 (GPI Trust) and .47 (CPI Communality) and 1.04 (GPI Attention to Detail) and 1.07 (CPI Femininity/Masculinity), respectively. At the GPI Big Five factor and trait composite averages level, the minimum effect size value was .33 for the Conscientiousness factor and the maximum effect size value was 1.06 for the Neuroticism factor. The corresponding minimum and maximum values for the standard deviation ratio at this level were .76 (Neuroticism) and .90 (Conscientiousness), respectively.

Some interesting findings to note relate to the GPI Impressing scale and the GPI Good Impression scale, which both purport to tap into overt impression management. For the GPI, in both comparisons, the mean effect size values for the Impressing scale were smaller (.11 for Promotion/ Selection vs. Development and −.18 for Promotion/Selection vs. Normative) than the average mean effect size value across the scales (.16 for Promotion/Selection vs. Development and .73 for Promotion/Selection vs. Normative). For the CPI, however, in both comparisons, the mean effect size values were larger (.32 for Promotion/Selection vs. Development and 1.23 for Promotion/Selection vs. Normative) than the average mean effect size value across the scales (.16 for Promotion/Selection vs. Development and 1.03 for Promotion/Selection vs. Normative).

The selection/promotion versus development analyses for both the GPI and CPI suggest that, although some impression management is likely occurring, it does not result in extreme elevation or restriction of range in personality scale scores. Furthermore, although some studies have shown transparent items to be more susceptible to impression management (e.g., Kluger & Colella, 1993), the present results suggest that inventories with more transparent items (assuming for the moment that the CPI items are more transparent) are not necessarily less prone to response distortion.

The results of this study also suggest that constructs saturated with neuroticism themes may be the most likely to be affected by impression management. For the GPI, the scales that loaded into the Neuroticism Big Five factor had the highest average mean difference and most restriction between promotion/selection and the development samples. Correspondingly, the CPI Well-being scale (arguably saturated with neuroticism) had one of the largest mean differences and highest restriction in this comparison. An alternative explanation for these large mean difference on constructs saturated with neuroticism could be true differences in the samples. For example, individuals in PDI assessments who are experiencing derailment problems at work are many times given the opportunity to participate in formal developmental experiences (M. Schmit, personal communication, October 31, 2000). These individuals may, on average, be less tolerant to stress, less optimistic, and lower in well-being than individuals who do not participate in formal developmental experiences.

The larger differences in scale score means and variances for selection/promotion versus normative samples are sensible. The normative samples are composed of a higher proportion of women and nonmanagers; evidence is consistent that substantial differences exist between these groups on personality variables (Hough, 1998b; Mount & Barrick, 1995a).

One class of analyses that may be interesting to conduct in future studies is to control for various demographic variables to examine whether that reduces the differences in means and variances for promotion/selection versus normative samples. Unfortunately, in the present study, many of the demographic comparisons were crude because the variables across samples were not identical nor could they be easily transformed. For example, in the GPI normative sample, various levels of management were distinguishable; however, in the GPI organizational samples, only a general class of managers was distinguishable.

The results of the present analyses are consistent with a very similar in-progress study using the CPI and comparing scale scores for selection versus development contexts (Ellingson & Sackett, 2000). In this study, individuals were identified who took the CPI twice: (a) a group of 30 individuals who responded for development purposes both times, (b) a group of 50 individuals who responded for development purposes the first time and selection purposes the second time, (c) a group of 68 individuals who responded for selection purposes the first time and development purposes the second time, and (d) a group of 162 individuals who responded for selection purposes both times. Analyses showed no systematic differences between scale scores based on context. This study was a natural experiment in which individual differences between motivational contexts are controlled by using the same people. Thus, this study suggests that the aforementioned analyses controlling for demographic differences may not need to be done.

Validity Differences

The second line of research focuses on identifying anticipated effects of impression management as evidence of its occurrence. Specifically, researchers have focused on the differences between validity coefficients between predictive and concurrent validity designs. This analysis presumes that, if impression management contaminates personality scale scores (obscuring true scores), then validity coefficients from predictive designs (based on job applicant responses) should be lower than validity coefficients from concurrent designs (based on incumbent responses). Hough (1998b) meta-analyzed the criterion-related validities of personality scales for a variety of job performance measures (job proficiency, training success, educational success, and counterproductive behavior) separately for concurrent and predictive validity studies. She found that both study designs yielded useful validity coefficients but that the average validity coefficient was .07 lower for predictive designs in comparison to concurrent designs. However, the interpretation of this comparison is made difficult by the fact that corrections for range restriction were not made. Whether the correlations for predictive or current designs are increased more by corrections for range restriction is not immediately ascertainable because there are many different types of predictive and concurrent designs and they vary in the degree to which they suffer from range restriction (Guion & Cranny, 1982).

Falsifiable Information

Finally, research (in other domains) has examined the degree to which applicants provide information that is clearly false. For example, Anderson, Warner, and Spencer (1984) conducted a study in which self-assessment examinations were administered to 351 job applicants for 13 occupational classes. The self-assessments were composed of lists of tasks that were either job-related as determined by job analysis or bogus but superficially resembling the job-related tasks. Applicants were asked to rate the extent of their training and experience on each task. Analyses found that inflation bias was prevalent. It should be noted, however, that there is a substantial leap of inference in moving from impression management on task inventory self-assessments to impression management on a personality inventory.

None of the three lines of research provides definitive proof that impression management does occur. For instance, research conducted by Schmit, Ryan, Stierwalt, and Powell (1995) and Robie, Schmit, Ryan, and Zickar (2000) suggests that the observed mean differences across incumbent and applicant samples may be partially a function of actual differences in how individuals perceive how they typically behave in general versus how they typically behave at work. Specifically, it is possible that incumbents fill out a personality measure with their frame of reference being how they typically behave across a range of life contexts, whereas applicants may fill out the measure using a frame of reference more geared to how they typically behave at work. As might be expected, personality scales that are composed of items contextualized to a work environment consistently evidence statistically and practically significant higher means than for those scales that are composed of items that are context free (Robie, Schmit, et al., 2000; Schmit et al., 1995). However, the weight of the evidence suggests to us that some degree of impression manage does likely occur in natural contexts, although the research suggests that the degree is miminal (Hough & Furnham, 2003). What, then, are the impacts of impression management on personality measures and decisions made based on personality data?

EFFECTS OF IMPRESSION MANAGEMENT

The study of the effects of impression management on personality measures and inferences drawn from personality data has focused on three primary areas: (1) criterion-related validity, (2) the utility of selection decisions made on the basis of personality data, and (3) measurement properties or the factorial validity of personality measures.

Criterion-Related Validity

We have touched on this topic already to some extent. As described earlier, Hough's (1998b) meta-analysis found correlations to be slightly lower for predictive versus concurrent criterion-related validity designs. However, the criterion-related validities of predictive studies remained at useful levels for selection purposes. Hough (1998a, pp. 210–212) provides an excellent overview of studies that have examined criterion-related validity using both designs.

Other researchers have used scales designed to capture impression management (usually general social desirability, which confounds self-deception and impression management) from the correlation between personality and performance criteria. Ones, Viswesvaran, and Reiss (1996) conducted the largest meta-analysis to date on the impact of partialling social desirability from the correlation between the Big Five factors and overall job performance criteria. Their results suggest that social desirability does not act as a moderator of the validities of self-report personality measures and likely is a substantive personality characteristic related to neuroticism, agreeableness, and conscientiousness. If social desirability scales are capturing valid personality variance (this has also been suggested by McCrae & Costa, 1983; Smith & Ellingson, 2002; and Smith et al., 2001), it would be inappropriate to control for social desirability in the personality-to-performance relationship. It is important to note that this research has been criticized for its reliance on general social desirability scales.

Selection Utility

In response to the finding that social desirability does not moderate criterion-related validity, several authors have suggested that the correlation coefficient is an inappropriate indicator of the possible effects of impression management (Christiansen, Goffin, Johnston, & Rothstein, 1994; Rosse et al., 1998; Zickar et al., 1996). These authors argue that impression management may occur at different points along the bivariate predictor-criterion distribution, and the correlation is not sensitive to differential predictability at different points on the regression line (i.e., heterogeneity of variance). This is an interesting and quite valid supposition. Two of these studies found that the rank order of applicants to be hired changed following the adjustment of scores to control for response distortion, using self-report measures of such (Christiansen et al., 1994; Rosse et al.). These findings have come to be interpreted as evidence that impression management changes the rank order of applicants. However, if personality scores were adjusted with a variable computed using a random number generator, rank order would also likely change. Given that many have questioned the validity of self-report measures of intentional response distortion, we believe it is premature to use these measures to aid in making an inference that impression management affects hiring decisions. Furthermore, if measures of intentional distortion do include valid variance related to substantive personality characteristics, it would be inappropriate to make corrections based on these scales. For instance, Rosse et al. examined the number of applicants who would be hired based on scores on the NEO-PI Conscientiousness scale (at various selection ratios for the applicant population) and then examined their impression management scores. This comparison makes sense if it is assumed that impression management scores are orthogonal to self-deception scores and, thus, capture variance attributable only to response distortion. However, our experience suggests that particularly in organizational settings, impression management and self-deception scores are substantially correlated. Given that Ones, Viswesvaran, and Reiss (1996) and Smith et al. (2001) have demonstrated that social desirability scales overlap with conscientiousness, it is not surprising that people with high conscientiousness scores also have high impression management scores.

It is interesting that a computational modeling study that did not rely on self-report measures of response distortion conducted by Zickar et al. (1996) found that although even the most extreme impression management conditions produce little or no change in validity correlations, modest amounts of impression management can result in lower than expected predicted performance from hires who are engaging in impression management. However, this study assumes that impression management affects only the predictor. We will return to this point in the conclusion. These three studies suggest that impression management may affect the validity of inferences made from personality scores more than one would suspect from examination of correlations. However, more research using actual field data and methodologies that do not rely on self-report measures of response distortion should be conducted to more adequately ensure that these findings generalize to real-world settings.

Measurement Properties

Much of the recent research on the impact of impression management has focused on its effects on the measurement properties of personality assessments, particularly their factor structure. For instance, Douglas et al. (1996) suggest that impression management causes the construct validity of measures of the Big Five to decay. Their research (based on the directed-faking paradigm) demonstrated that when respondents were instructed to fake a personality measure, the factor structure collapsed—a large desirability factor emerged. Similarly, Schmit and Ryan (1993) compared the factor structure from a sample of job applicants to a sample of students and found that an additional factor emerged representing an ideal employee. These are only two representative studies in this domain; however, it is interesting to note that their results appear to be at odds. We would expect that if the impression management hypothesis were true, then factor structure should become less complex, not more so. Ellingson, Smith, and Sackett (2001), Smith and Ellingson (2002), and Smith et al. (2001) investigated this issue in detail and determined that when (1) real-world samples are used and (2) appropriate statistical techniques are employed, personality factor structures remain robust to impression management effects. Similarly, Costa (1996) and Ones and Viswesvaran (1998), after reviewing research on factor structure differences, concluded that the effects of (assumed) impression management on factor structure are modest and definitely do not destroy the measurement properties of personality instruments. Robie et al.'s (2001) recent IRT study showing little to no differential item or test functioning in an applicant–incumbent comparison would tend to support this conclusion.

WHAT CAN WE DO TO REDUCE FAKING?

Two approaches have generally been advanced to reduce faking. One general approach to reducing impression management is based on scale construction. The two major methods of scale construction that have been utilized to reduce impression management are: (a) forced-choice inventories in which statements are paired according to their similarity in social desirability (e.g., the Edwards Personal Preference Schedule, Edwards, 1954), and (b) empirically keyed instruments that result in more subtle items in terms of their measurement of the underlying construct (e.g., the California Psychological Inventory, Gough, 1987). Research has shown that individuals can distort their scores successfully on forced-choice and empirically keyed instruments when instructed to do so (see Waters, 1965, for forced-choice inventories; see Hough, 1998a, p. 213, for a full listing of such studies in regard to empirically keyed instruments). Several studies have found that, although not fake resistant, subtle items (Kluger & Colella, 1993) and forced-choice items (Christiansen, Edelstein, & Fleming, 1998; Jackson, Wroblewski, & Ashton, 2000) may be more difficult to fake in comparison to face-valid, transparent items when subjects are instructed to fake. More important, however, Hough and Paullin (1994) meta-analyzed the cross-validities of scales constructed using empirical, internal, and rational strategies and concluded that empirical and rational strategies yield highly similar results. No similar meta-analysis has been conducted comparing the validities of forced-choice and rationally based personality scales. (We "cheated" by including a discussion of validity in a section talking about how to reduce impression management a priori, but believed it important lest the reader be led to believe that findings from the lab showing a reduction in impression management leads to reduction of validity in field settings).

The other general approach that has been examined in its effect on reducing impression management has been warning respondents about consequences of distorting their responses and saying that detection methods and verification procedures exist. Hough (1998a, p. 214) provides a listing of these studies and generally concludes in her review of those studies that warnings do reduce the amount of intentional distortion in self-report instruments. These studies have generally inferred a reduction of impression management in elevated scale scores in the no-warning groups in comparison to the warned groups. The effect of warnings on criterion-related validity has not been examined to date. One study has found the measurement properties of the no-warning group to degrade in comparison to the warned group (Griffith, Frei, Snell, Hamill, & Wheeler, 1998). The main problem with this general approach to reducing impression management is that it may not take too long for respondents to realize that the emperor has no clothes (i.e., we actually do not have acceptable ways to identify fakers—see next section) and, thus, this approach may be only a temporary solution.

WHAT CAN WE DO TO REDUCE THE EFFECTS OF FAKING?

What can we do once somebody has already distorted their responses on a personality measure? Major efforts in this area can be categorized into three areas: self-report measures of response distortion, appropriateness measurement, and response latencies. None of the efforts has resulted in a widespread solution to the impression management problem. We shall briefly review the research relevant to each in turn.

Typically, the research using self-report measures of response distortion involves developing prediction equations involving those measures to discriminate between fake good and honest individuals (Lanning, 1989). These prediction equations can achieve adequate levels of accuracy in discriminating between the aforementioned groups. However, these equations tend to have high false-positive rates, which dilute their usefulness (see Zickar & Drasgow, 1996, for a discussion of this topic). Also, as has been discussed, directed impression management protocols probably share little resemblance to how impression management actually occurs in real life. For example, in several large applicant samples, Hough (1998a) used a self-report measure of intentional distortion (i.e., an unlikely virtues or UV scale) to either (a) correct individuals' personality scale content scores based on the individuals' UV scale, or (b) remove individuals from the applicant pool because their score on the UV scale suggested they were presenting themselves in an overly favorable way. Neither strategy affected criterion-related validity. Another study using multiple large field samples found that the measurement properties of several popular personality measures did not degrade when tested for groups identified via self-report distortion scales as honest versus responding in highly socially desirable manners (Ellingson, Smith, & Sackett, 2001).

Appropriateness measurement, another potential method of identifying fakers, has not even been particularly successful in a directed impression management setting. For example, Zickar and Drasgow (1996) found that the optimal appropriateness measurement approach classified a higher number of impression management respondents at low rates of misclassification of honest respondents (false-positives) than did a social desirability scale. At higher false-positive rates, the social desirability approach did slightly better. However, the authors stated that their results suggested that both social desirability scales and appropriateness measurement approaches to detecting fakers using this experimental induction were not sensitive enough to justify operational use. In addition, a recent study using a student sample found that misfit via appropriateness measurement techniques was associated with decreased validity (using GPA as a criterion) for a cognitive ability test but increased validity for conscientiousness (Schmitt, Chan, Sacco, McFarland, & Jennings, 1999). Finally, in the only study employing appropriateness measurement methods with in-use personality data that we are aware of, levels of misfit did not differ between a sample of applicants and a sample of incumbents that either were applying to or worked in the same service organization (Robie et al., 2001).

The use of response latencies, or the time it takes to answer a personality item, has shown promising results using a directed impression management paradigm. Individuals told to fake good on personality measures typically take longer to respond to schema-incongruent responses than individuals told to answer the personality measure honestly (Holden, 1995, 1998). However, no research has investigated the impact of the use of response latencies in field settings; this lack probably is due to the typical need for an honest sample to calibrate the response latencies for the fake good sample. Moreover, one study has found that coaching eliminates the usefulness of response latencies in identifying fakers (Robie, Curtin, et al., 2000).

One promising method of reducing the effects of impression management once it has already occurred is the use of observer ratings of personality. Mount, Barrick, and Strauss (1994) found that supervisor, coworker, and customer ratings of personality incremented the validity of self-ratings in predicting performance ratings. Piedmont, MacRae, Riemann, and Angleitner (2000) suggested that the use of personality ratings from well-informed observers in conjunction with profile agreement statistics (McCrae, 1993) should be used in lieu of self-report validity scales. More research needs to be conducted on this potentially useful method of reducing faking. However, this particular method is probably tenable only for situations in which the personality measure is being used for promotion decisions because well-informed others may be difficult to locate for external selection contexts.

A BROADER CONTEXT FOR IMPRESSION
MANAGEMENT RESEARCH

We noted at the beginning of this chapter that it was our intent to attempt to provide a broader context for the research on impression management, particularly that research originating from the application of personality measures to applicant selection contexts. Our hope is that providing a richer theoretical context for impression management research will advance our understanding of this basic phenomenon and direct research towards potentially more fruitful avenues. Again, what we have to say is not new; rather, we believe it is a neglected perspective on impression management and helps explain why impression management may not yield the presumed deleterious effects for criterion-related validity and selection utility. In fact, we propose, as have others before us (Hogan, 1983, 1991; Hogan & Hogan, 1998), that impression management is a valid and useful general theory explaining responses to personality questionnaires.

Much of the current debate regarding response distortion is grounded in the belief that responses to personality measures reflect underlying traits or neuropsychic structures that cause people to behave in a particular manner. Personality assessments attempt to quantify a person's neuropsychic structures, and impression management obscures attempts to assess these traits accurately. This model follows the Allportian tradition in personality psychology and has a long history. Alternatively, Hogan (1983; Hogan & Hogan, 1998) suggests that responses to a personality questionnaire represent self-presentations (not self-reports) and do not differ fundamentally from any form of social interaction. He argues that during unstructured social interaction (in which roles are not clearly defined), people negotiate their identities with other parties in the interaction. In other words, I behave in the way I want you to perceive me. The practice of personality assessment is identical to social interaction—I respond to the questionnaire in the manner in which I want to be perceived.

This perspective is grounded in the social interactionist tradition in sociology and social psychology and is based on the work of Goffman (1959) and Mead (1934). Our call for impression management researchers to look beyond the stream of research focusing on applicant context is a recognition of the wealth of information that has been collected in countless studies from this tradition (see Schlenker & Weigold, 1992, for an excellent overview). This interactionist position takes as a given that impression management and impression regulation are basic human activities that guide not only our responses to questionnaires but also our behavior in any context. So, what are the implications of a self-presentation view of item responses to the debate over impression management in applicant contexts?

A broader view of impression management (as the basis for general social interaction) suggests that it is, at best, myopic to focus attention exclusively on the predictor–personality measures and presume that impression management does not equally affect or explain variance in criterion measures. Research into the affect of impression management on selection outcomes fails to examine the impact of impression management on performance criteria. It is presumed that if I exaggerate my conscientiousness when completing a personality measure because I recognize it to be an important component of a job, I will ignore this recognition when I perform my job and behave in a way that reflects my true level of conscientiousness (whatever that may be). The research on impression management and regulation would suggest that it is more likely that I would attempt to maintain the image that I have presented by behaving in a more conscientious manner. In other words, if I recognize the characteristics important for the role I am playing I am likely to engage in those behaviors when in that role, not just when completing a personality inventory. Thus, we would expect a consistency between scores on a personality questionnaire taken in an applicant context and behavior on the job.

Some may now be concerned that we are suggesting that personality is inconsistent across situation and that we adapt infinitely to the roles we play. This is not our suggestion. We believe people tend to choose roles (jobs, occupations, organizations) on the basis of their personalities. There is a wealth of literature from personality, vocational, and organizational psychology suggesting this belief to be true (for a review see Schneider, Goldstein, & Smith, 1995). So, it is unlikely that we will require extensive impression management to adapt to a role. How many introverts do you know who dream of becoming a salesperson?

Schmit et al.'s (1995) study provides empirical evidence to support the notion that respondents to personality measures engage more in self-presentation than overt faking. Specifically, criterion-related validity was highest in the condition that used context-specific items in the applicant situation; conversely, validity was essentially zero when general context items were used in the applicant condition. As Johnson (1981) has hypothesized, making self-presentation easier by using work-specific items appeared to increase validity.

This self-presentation hypothesis has implications for the decision of whether to use personality measures that use subtle versus transparent (i.e., obvious) items. If respondents to personality questionnaires are attempting to present themselves such that they believe they can pull it off in an interview or job setting, perhaps we should be using obvious items to ensure that the respondent is able to present him/herself in an accurate manner. Given that the results of this study suggested no overall difference in the scale score means for tests composed of subtle versus obvious items, and previous research has provided evidence to suggest lower validity for subtle items (Duff, 1965; McCall, 1958; Wiener, 1948), perhaps we should be using more obvious items in our personality scales when used for occupational assessment.

SUMMARY AND CONCLUSION

Based on the review of the literature and the results of the PDI data, it should be clear that there is no magic bullet for dealing with impression managment. Impression management probably does occur, but its prevalence will probably always be unknowable and its effects are certainly not catastrophic. It is unlikely in our view that a good fix to the impression management problem will ever occur or should occur, although we wholeheartedly promote its continued study in the hopes that an innovation in this area is developed. However, we tend to agree with Piedmont et al. (2000, pp. 590–591) who suggest that "Perhaps attention should shift from detecting invalidity toward improving the quality of assessment. Every effort should be made to motivate the respondent and ensure that the instructions are understood. Although immensely useful, questionnaires are not an infallible method of assessing personality, and validity scales will not make them so. Instead of blind faith in validity scales, clinicians and researchers must rely on the use of well-validated instruments, the development of rapport with the respondent, and the judicious comparison of multiple sources of data in interpreting results."

ACKNOWLEDGMENTS

Thanks are extended to Mark Schmit and Michael Zickar for their helpful comments on a previous version of this chapter and to Jill Ellingson and Eric Heggestad for many conversations regarding social desirability.

REFERENCES

Anderson, C. D., Warner, J. L., & Spencer, C. C. (1984). Inflation bias in self-assessment examinations: Implications for valid employee selection. *Journal of Applied Psychology, 69,* 574–580.

Arnold, H. J., & Feldman, D. C. (1981). Social desirability response bias in self-report choice situations. *Academy of Management Journal, 24,* 377–385.

Barrick, M. R., & Mount, M. K. (1996). Effects of impression management and self-deception on the predictive validity of personality constructs. *Journal of Applied Psychology, 81,* 261–272.

Bass, B. M. (1957). Faking by sales applicants of a forced choice personality inventory, *Journal of Applied Psychology, 41,* 403–404.

Christiansen, N. D., Edelstein, S., & Fleming, B. (1998, April). *Reconsidering forced-choice formats for applicant personality assessment.* Paper presented at the 13th annual conference of the Society for Industrial and Organizational Psychology, Dallas, TX.

Christiansen, N. D., Goffin, R. D., Johnston, N. G., & Rothstein, M. G. (1994). Correcting the 16PF for faking: Effects on criterion-related validity and individual hiring decisions. *Personnel Psychology, 47,* 847–860.

Costa, P. T. (1996). Work and personality: Use of the NEO-PI-R in industrial/organizational psychology. *Applied Psychology: An International Review, 45,* 225–241.

Davis-Blake, A., & Pfeffer, J. (1989). Just a mirage: The search for dispositional effects in organizational research. *Academy of Management Review, 14,* 385–400.

Deshon, R. P. (2000). Computational models of personality and faking. In D. Ilgen & C. L. Hulin (Eds.), *Computational modeling of behavior in organizations* (pp. 109–113). Washington, DC: American Psychological Association.

Douglas, E. F., McDaniel, M. A., & Snell, A. F. (1996). The validity of non-cognitive measures decays when applicants fake. In J. B. Keyes & L. N. Dosier (Eds.), *Proceedings of the Academy of Management* (pp. 127–131). Madison, WI: Omnipress.

Duff, F. L. (1965). Item subtlety in personality inventory scales. *Journal of Consulting Psychology, 29*, 565–570.

Edwards, A. L. (1954). *Edwards Personal Preference Schedule*. New York: Psychological Corporation.

Ellingson, J. E., & Sackett, P. R. (2000). *Consistency of personality scale scores across selection and development contexts*. Manuscript in preparation.

Ellingson, J. E., Smith, D. B., & Sackett, P. R. (2001). Investigating influence of social desirability on personality factor structure. *Journal of Applied Psychology, 86*, 122–133.

Ganster, D. C., Hennessey, H. W., & Luthans, F. (1983). Social desirability response effects: Three alternative models. *Academy of Management Journal, 26*, 321–331.

Goffman, E. (1959). The presentation of self in everyday life. Garden City, NY: Doubleday Anchor.

Gough, H. G. (1987). *Manual: The California Psychological Inventory* (2nd ed.). Palo Alto, CA: Consulting Psychologists Press.

Griffith, R. L., Frei, R. L., Snell, A. F., Hamill, L. S., & Wheeler, J. K. (1998). *Warnings versus no-warnings: Differential effect of method bias*. Unpublished manuscript.

Guion, R. M., & Cranny, C. J. (1982). A note on concurrent and predictive validity designs: A critical reanalysis. *Journal of Applied Psychology, 67*, 239–244.

Hogan, R. (1983). A socioanalytic theory of personality. In M. M. Page & R. Dienstbier (Eds.), *1982 Nebraska Symposium on Motivation* (pp. 58–89). Lincoln: University of Nebraska Press.

Hogan, R. (1991). Personality and personality measurement. In M. D. Dunnette & L. M. Hough (Eds.), *Handbook of industrial and organizational psychology* (Vol. 2, pp. 873–919). Palo Alto, CA: Consulting Psychologists Press.

Hogan, R., & Hogan, J. (1998). Theoretical frameworks for assessment. In R. Jeanneret & R. Silzer (Eds.), *Individual psychological assessment: Predicting behavior in organizational settings* (pp. 27–53). San Francisco, CA: Jossey-Bass.

Holden, R. R. (1995). Response latency detection of fakers on personnel tests. *Canadian Journal of Behavioural Science, 27*, 343–355.

Holden, R. R. (1998). Detecting fakers on a personnel test: Response latencies versus a standard validity scale. *Journal of Social Behavior and Personality, 13*, 387–398.

Hough, L. M. (1998a). Effects of intentional distortion in personality measurement and evaluation of suggested palliatives. *Human Performance, 11*, 209–244.

Hough, L. M. (1998b). Personality at work: Issues and evidence. In M. Hakel (Ed.), *Beyond multiple choice: Evaluating alternatives to traditional testing for selection* (pp. 131–166). Mahwah, NJ: Lawrence Erlbaum Associates, Inc.

Hough, L. M., & Furnham, A. (2003). Importance and use of personality variables in work settings. In W. C. Borman, D. R. Illgen, & R. J. Klinoski (Eds.), *Comprehensive Handbook of Psychology* (Vol. 12, pp. 131–169). Industrial/Organizational Psychology. New York: Wiley.

Hough, L. M., Eaton, N. K., Dunnette, M. D., Kamp, J. D., McCloy, R. (1990). Criterion-related validities of personality constructs and the effect of response distortion on those validities. *Journal of Applied Psychology, 75*, 581–595.

Hough, L. M., & Paulin, C. (1994). Construct-oriented scale construction: The rational approach. In G. S. Stokes, M. D. Mumford, & W. A. Owens (Eds.), *The biodata handbook: Theory, research, and use of biographical information in selection and performance prediction* (pp. 109–145). Palo Alto, CA: Consulting Psychologists Press.

Howard, G. S. (1994). Why do people say nasty things about self-reports? *Journal of Organizational Behavior, 15*, 399–404.

Jackson, D. N., Wroblewski, V. R., & Ashton, M. C. (2000). The impact of impression management on employment tests: Does forced choice offer a solution? *Human Performance, 13*, 371–388.

Johnson, J. A. (1981). The "self-disclosure" and "self-presentation" views of item response dynamics and personality scale validity. *Journal of Personality and Social Psychology, 40*, 761–769.

Kelley, E. L., Miles, C. C., & Terman, L. M. (1936). Ability to influence one's score on a typical pencil-and-paper test of personality. *Character and Personality, 4*, 206–215.

Kirchner, W. K., Dunnette, M. S., Mousley, N. (1960). Use of the Edwards Personal Preference Schedule in the selection of salesman. *Personnel Psychology, 13*, 421–424.

Kluger, A. N., & Colella, A. (1993). Beyond the mean bias: The effect of warning against faking on biodata item variances. *Personnel Psychology, 46*, 763–780.

Lanning, K. (1989). Detection of invalid response patterns in the California Psychological Inventory. *Applied Psychological Measurement, 13*, 45–56.

Locke, E. A. (Ed.) (1986). *Generalizing from laboratory to field settings.* Lexington, MA: Lexington.

McCall, R. J. (1958). Face validity in the D scale of the MMPI. *Journal of Clinical Psychology, 14*, 77–80.

McClelland, J. N., & Rhodes, F. (1969). Prediction of job success for hospital aides and orderlies from MMPI scores and personal history data. *Journal of Applied Psychology, 53*, 49–54.

McCrae, R. R. (1993). Agreement of personality profiles across observers. *Multivariate Behavioral Research, 28*, 25–40.

McCrae, R. R., & Costa, P. T. (1983). Social desirability scales: More substance than style. *Journal of Consulting & Clinical Psychology, 51*, 882–888.

McFarland, L. A., & Ryan, A. M. (2000). Variance in faking across noncognitive measures. *Journal of Applied Psychology, 85*, 812–821.

Mead, G. H. (1934). *Mind, self, and society.* Chicago: University of Chicago Press.

Meehl, P. E., & Hathaway, S. R. (1946). The K factor as a suppressor variable in the MMPI. *Journal of Applied Psychology, 30*, 525–564.

Mersman, J. L., & Shultz, K. S. (1998). Individual differences in the ability to fake on personality measures. *Personality and Individual Differences, 24*, 217–227.

Michaelis, W., & Eysenck, H. J. (1971). The determination of personality inventory factor patterns and intercorrelations by changes in real-life motivation. *Journal of Genetic Psychology, 118*, 223–234.

Mischel, W. J. (1968). *Personality and assessment.* New York: Wiley.

Moorman, R. H., & Podsakoff, P. M. (1992). A meta-analytic review and empirical test of the potential confounding effects of social desirability response sets in organizational behaviour research. *Journal of Occupational & Organizational Psychology, 65*, 131–149.

Mount, M. K., & Barrick, M. R. (1995a). *Manual for the Personal Characteristics Inventory.* Iowa City, IA. Unpublished Technical Report.

Mount, M. K., & Barrick, M. R. (1995b). The Big Five personality dimensions: Implications for research and practice in human resource management. *Research in Personnel and Human Resources Management, 13*, 153–200.

Mount, M. K., Barrick, M. R., & Strauss, J. P. (1994). Validity of observer ratings of the big five personality factors. *Journal of Applied Psychology, 79*, 272–280.

Ones, D. S., & Viswesvaran, C. (1998). The effects of social desirability and faking on personality and integrity assessment for personnel selection. *Human Performance, 11*, 245–269.

Ones, D. S., Viswesvaran, C., & Reiss, A. D. (1996). Role of social desirability in personality testing for personnel selection: The red herring. *Journal of Applied Psychology, 81*, 660–679.

Orpen, C. (1971). The susceptibility of the EPPS to faking in simulated and actual employment situations. *Journal of Personality Assessment, 35*, 480–485.

Paulhus, D. L. (1984). Two-component models of socially desirable responding. *Journal of Personality & Social Psychology, 46*, 598–609.

Piedmont, R. L., McCrae, R. R., Riemann, R., & Angleitner, A. (2000). On the invalidity of validity scales: Evidence from self-reports and observer ratings in volunteer samples. *Journal of Personality and Social Psychology, 78*, 582–593.

Robie, C., Curtin, P. J., Foster, T. C., Phillips, H. L., Zbylut, M., & Tetrick, L. E. (2000). The effect of coaching on the utility of response latencies in detecting fakers on a personality measure. *Canadian Journal of Behavioural Science, 32*, 226–233.

Robie, C., Schmit, M. J., Ryan, A. M., & Zickar, M. J. (2000). Effects of item context specificity on the measurement equivalence of a personality inventory. *Organizational Research Methods, 3*, 348–365.

Robie, C., Zickar, M. J., & Schmit, M. J. (2001). Measurement equivalence between applicant and incumbent groups: An IRT analysis of personality scales. *Human Performance, 14*, 184–207.

Rosse, J. G., Stecher, M. D., Miller, J. L., & Levin, R. A. (1998). The impact of response distortion on preemployment personality testing and hiring decisions. *Journal of Applied Psychology, 83*, 634–644.

Schlenker, B. R., & Weigold, M. F. (1992). Interpersonal processes involving impression regulation and management. *Annual Review of Psychology, 43*, 133–168.

Schmit, M. J., Kihm, J. A., & Robie, C. (2000). Development of a global measure of personality. *Personnel Psychology, 53*, 153–193.

Schmit, M. J., & Ryan, A. M. (1993). The Big Five in personnel selection: Factor structure in applicant and nonapplicant populations. *Journal of Applied Psychology, 78*, 966–974.

Schmit, M. J., Ryan, A. M., Stierwalt, S. L., & Powell, A. B. (1995). Frame-of-reference effects on personality scale scores and criterion-related validity. *Journal of Applied Psychology, 80*, 607–620.

Schmitt, N. (1994). Method bias: The importance of theory and measurement. *Journal of Organizational Behavior, 15*, 393–398.

Schmitt, N., Chan, D., Sacco, J. M., McFarland, L. A., & Jennings, D. (1999). Correlates of person fit and effect of person fit on test validity. *Applied Psychological Measurement, 23*, 41–53.

Schneider, B., Goldstein, H. W., & Smith, D. B. (1995). The ASA framework: An update. *Personnel Psychology, 48*, 747–773.

Schrader, A. D., & Osburn, H. G. (1977). Biodata faking: Effects of induced subtlety and position specificity. *Personnel Psychology, 30*, 395–404.

Schwab, D. P., & Packard, G. L. (1973). Response distortion on the "Gordon Personal Inventory" and the "Gordon Personal Profile" in a selection context: Some implications for predicting employee tenure. *Journal of Applied Psychology, 58*, 372–374.

Smith, D. B., & Ellingson, J. E. (2002). Substance vs. style: A new look at social desirability in motivating contexts. *Journal of Applied Psychology, 87*, 211–219.

Smith, D. B., Hanges, P. J., & Dickson, M. W. (2001). Personnel selection and the five factor model: A reexamination of frame of reference effects. *Journal of Applied Psychology, 86*, 304–315.

Spector, P. E. (1994). Using self-report questionnaires in OB research: A comment on the use of a controversial method. *Journal of Organizational Behavior, 15*, 385–392.

Viswesvaran, C., & Ones, D. S. (1999). Meta-analyses of fakability estimates: Implications for personality measurement. *Educational and Psychological Measurement, 59*, 197–210.

Waters, L. K. (1965). A note on the "fakability" of forced-choice scales. *Personnel Psychology, 18*, 187–191.

Wiener, D. N. (1948). Subtle and obvious keys for the Minnesota Multiphasic Personality Inventory. *Journal of Consulting Psychology, 12*, 164–170.

Zerbe, W. J., & Paulhus, D. L. (1987). Socially desirable responding in organizational behavior: A reconception. *Academy of Management Review, 12*, 250–264.

Zickar, M. J. (2000). Modeling faking on personality tests. In D. Ilgen & C. L. Hulin (Eds.), *Computational modeling of behavioral processes in organizations* (pp. 95–108). Washington, DC: American Psychological Association.

Zickar, M. J., & Drasgow, F. (1996). Detecting faking on a personality instrument using appropriateness measurement. *Applied Psychological Measurement, 20*, 71–87.

Zickar, M. J., & Robie, C. (1999). Modeling faking good on personality items: An item-level analysis. *Journal of Applied Psychology, 84*, 551–563.

Zickar, M. J., Rosse, J. G., & Levin, R. A. (1996, April). Modeling faking in a selection context. In C. L. Hulin (Chair), *The third scientific discipline: Computational modeling in organizational research*. Paper presented as part of symposium conducted at the annual meeting of the Society for Industrial and Organizational Psychology, San Diego, CA.

III

The Role of Personality in Work and Well-Being

The three chapters in this section, as the section title suggests, all deal with one or more facets of well-being. Walsh presents an overview of the good evidence showing the relationship between personality and vocational choice and also the influence of appropriate choice on vocational satisfaction. He then introduces an overarching personality attribute, self-efficacy, as a way of suggesting the pervasive role personality may play in vocational success. This discussion is followed by a thorough consideration of the role of personality in vocational satisfaction.

Staw's chapter picks up on the satisfaction theme. His chapter does an excellent job of summarizing the burgeoning literature on what has come to be called the dispositional approach to job satisfaction. Staw then considers alternative explanations for job satisfaction—like attributes of the situation and cognitive processes—and concludes that although these may have an effect, the dispositional attributes (e.g., positive and negative affectivity) people bring with them to the workplace are not easily if ever overcome.

George and Brief also pay considerable attention to positive and negative affectivity in their exploration of personal correlates of job distress. Brief and George present an unfolding model of the relationship between personality and distress at work: choice of job, creation of the work setting, reactions to the workplace, and coping with the distress that can be associated with working. The unfolding model suggests many opportunities for further research.

These three chapters portray a very rich picture of the many ways personality is played out at work, ways that frequently yield positive subjective well-being but in many cases also the outcome is negative subjective well-being. The conclusion here is that a failure to consider personality as a key (not the key but a key) to understanding people's reactions to work and the workplace and resultant subjective well-being is nonsense.

6

Vocational Psychology and Personality

W. Bruce Walsh
The Ohio State University

The notion that personality relates in meaningful ways to the kinds of careers people select and their performance and satisfaction in those careers has a long and significant history in vocational psychology. There is a substantial database indicating that people tend to move toward, enter, and remain in occupational environments congruent with their personality traits. Stated differently, individuals in a given occupational environment tend to have similar personality traits. In addition, a large database demonstrates that personality is predictive of career choice behaviors, work values, vocational interests, and career satisfaction.

The goal here is first to present a selective review of the literature on vocational psychology and personality. This task has been for the most part recently accomplished by Tokar, Fischer, and Subich (1998) in their article entitled "Personality and vocational behavior: A selective review of the literature, 1993–1997" that appeared in the *Journal of Vocational Behavior* in 1998. A second goal considering new directions in the field of vocational psychology and personality focuses on the concept of self-efficacy. Evidence indicates that self-efficacy is an influential variable in the process of career choice and development. Finally, a third goal in the new directions context explores vocational psychology and subjective well-being. The focus here is to investigate personality as a determinant of individual reports of subjective well-being and of vocational satisfaction.

PERSONALITY AND VOCATIONAL BEHAVIOR

The links among personality and other domains have received significant attention recently, most notably in the areas of interests, abilities, and self-efficacy. To some extent this attention is motivated by the emergence of the five-factor model of personality (Digman, 1990).

The Five-Factor Model

The five-factor model represents a widely recognized system for describing the basic dimensions of normal personality most often labeled *extraversion, agreeableness, conscientiousness, neuroticism,* and *openness to experience.* There are also lower-order personality descriptors associated with each of the five broad dimensions as follows: extraversion (reclusive–sociable; submissive–dominant), agreeableness (irritable–good natured; cold–warm), conscientiousness (undependable–responsible; lackadaisical–persistent), neuroticism (calm–anxious; emotionally stable–unstable), and openness to experience (conventional–original; inflexible–flexible). Based on a substantial amount of research (Costa & McCrae, 1992; Digman; Wiggins & Trapnell, 1997) it is reasonable to conclude that the five-factor model provides a useful and meaningful structure in which other personality systems may be interpreted and organized.

Holland's Theory

A second driving force behind the attention focused on personality and other domains is the Holland (1997) personality model. Holland's model reports that there are six personality types (realistic, investigative, artistic, social, enterprising, and conventional) and that people enter occupations because of their personalities. The relationship between Holland's model and personality variables has been substantiated in a number of empirical studies relating scores on measures of Holland's types to a wide range of personality inventories (Holland).

There are rather consistent results linking aspects of the five-factor model of personality to Holland's model. These findings indicate that investigative and artistic personality types are related to openness to experience, and social and enterprising personality types are related to extraversion. Agreeableness also differentiated the social and enterprising personality types. These findings have been documented by a number of researchers (Costa, McCrae, & Holland, 1984; Gottfredson, Jones, & Holland, 1993; Tokar et al., 1998). Also of significance is a study by Tokar and Swanson (1995) that tested the ability of the Big Five factors to discriminate among groups of employed adults assigned to their highest personality Holland type. The evidence indicates that scores on the measures of the five-factor model can effectively predict membership in Holland's vocational environments.

Linking the FFM and Holland's Approach

It is in this context that Tokar et al. (1998) carried out a selective review of the literature focusing on personality and vocational behavior using the five-factor model as a framework for summarizing and integrating this knowledge base. The authors framed the personality aspects of the research in terms of the five-factor model of personality when this approach seemed reasonable in order to enhance and facilitate a synthesis across the literature. The literature reviewed included the connections of personality to choice-related processes, general career processes, occupational satisfaction and well-being, and organizational outcomes. This is from all indications the most recent and comprehensive review of the literature in this area and in this context deserves some attention in this chapter.

A number of themes emerged from the empirical literature reviewed by Tokar et al. (1998). In general, the authors concluded that neuroticism, extraversion, and conscientiousness emerged most frequently in associations with vocational behavior. More specifically, the authors identify a number of additional themes. First, the authors note that considerable personality and job satisfaction research has focused on the personality variables of neuroticism and extraversion. For example, a number of researchers (Necowitz & Roznowski, 1994; Parkes, Mendham, & von Rabenau, 1994) found that negative affectivity (neuroticism) predicted some aspects of lower job satisfaction. Overall, Tokar et al. conclude that greater job satisfaction is related to lower neuroticism, as well as to higher extraversion and related traits.

Second, in the domain of occupational stress and strain, a considerable portion of this research has focused on the role of workers' negative affectivity (or neuroticism). Several studies have investigated the relations of occupational stress and strain with type A personality tendency, neuroticism, and locus of control. The authors conclude that personality dimensions reflecting neuroticism, type A traits, and external locus of control tend to predict more negative perceptions of occupational stress and strain.

A third theme in general suggested by the authors is that some Big Five dimensions are more important than others in the prediction of job performance. In this context, conscientiousness appears to be a valid predictor of job performance criteria for most occupations. In addition, extraversion appears to be a valid predictor for jobs involving an interpersonal performance component. The authors further note that the findings of these studies suggest that personality performance relations depend to some extent on job type, trait taxonomy, and performance criteria.

A fourth theme emerging focuses on desirable and undesirable occupational behaviors in the context of job performance. For example, desirable occupational behaviors investigated include social desirability, goal commitment, integrity, and mentoring. Undesirable occupational outcomes studied include employee absenteeism, accident proneness, involuntary turnover, outplacement, theft, and employee deviance or criminality. Tokar et al. (1998) concluded that better job performance and more desirable occupational behaviors tend to be consistently related to higher conscientiousness and to emergent integrity.

Fifth, in the domain of career processes Brown (1996) carried out a meta-analysis of the job involvement literature and found that a stronger work ethic endorsement (conscientiousness) and higher self-esteem (low neuroticism and high extraversion and conscientiousness) correlated positively with measures of job involvement. On the variable of career indecision, consistent findings indicate that chronically undecided, or indecisive, individuals experience greater levels of neuroticism than do developmentally undecided persons. For example, Chartrand, Rose, Elliott, Marmarosh, and Caldwell (1993) using a sample of college students found that neuroticism was associated with problem-solving deficits, a dependent decision-making style, and antecedents of career indecision. In the person–environment fit domain, limited findings suggest that congruent choices may to some extent be a function of personality. Findings here suggest that incongruent male and female ministers tend to score higher on scales conceptually related to neuroticism than did the congruent male and female ministers (Celeste & Walsh, 1997; Celeste, Walsh, & Raote, 1995). In general, Tokar et al. (1998) concluded that greater neuroticism tends to be related to lower frequency and quality of job-search activities, less congruence, and greater career indecision. Furthermore, they conclude that greater extraversion is linked to higher frequency in quality of job-search activities.

In summary, this selected review of the literature by Tokar et al. (1998) does indicate that the Big Five taxonomy may be used as a framework for integrating research findings linking personality and vocational psychology. As previously noted, neuroticism, extraversion, and conscientiousness emerged most frequently in associations with vocational behavior. One could argue that Holland's (1997) six personality types might also effectively be used as a framework for organizing and integrating results of the empirical studies linking personality and vocational psychology. The recent work of DeFruyt and Mervielde (1999) tends to support this proposal. These authors investigated the validity of the five-factor model of personality and Holland's model in predicting employment status and the nature of employment in a sample of graduating college seniors as they entered the job market. The senior college graduates ($N = 934$) completed Costa and McCrae's NEO-PI-R (1992) and Holland's Self-Directed Search (1979). One year after graduation, they were requested to describe their labor market positions and jobs, using the Position Classification Inventory (Gottfredson and Holland, 1991). Of those responding the second time, 335 were employed and 66 were unemployed. The results showed that extraversion and conscientiousness were the only valid predictors of employment status and that Holland vocational type did not show incremental validity over and above these factors. However, the Holland types were clearly superior in explaining the nature of employment. The authors conclude that the Holland model is more employee driven and more effective at predicting the nature of employment. The five-factor model is more employer oriented with greater validity in evaluating the employability and employment status of applicants. The five-factor model permits the mapping of personality traits and requirements for different jobs. But Holland's model is superior in explaining the nature of employment.

Personal Styles and the Strong Interest Inventory

One could further argue that the personal styles of the 1994 revision of the Strong Interest Inventory might also effectively be used as a framework for organizing results of empirical studies linking personality and vocational psychology. The personal styles represent four measures of interests and personality. As noted in the Strong Interest Inventory manual (Harmon, Hansen, Borgen, & Hammer, 1994), the four scales are as follows:

1. Work style differentiates individuals who prefer to work with people from those who have a preference for working with data, ideas, or things.
2. Learning environment differentiates people who prefer academic learning environments from those who prefer a practical, hands on learning environment.
3. Leadership style distinguishes people who enjoy leading, persuading, meeting, and directing others from those preferring not to take charge or be responsible for others.
4. The risk-taking adventure style differentiates among those tending to take risks and act spontaneously from people who avoid risks and tend to be more cautious (Harmon et al.).

Recently, Lindley, and Borgen (2000) explored the relationships of the personal style scales to the Big Five personality dimensions using two samples of college students (Ns of 740 and 321). The Big Five dimensions were assessed with the John (1990) scales for the Adjective Check List (Gough & Heilbrun, 1983). The strongest relationships as anticipated were between leadership style and extraversion ($r = .48$ and $.55$ for men in the two samples and $r = .48$ and $.59$ for women in the two samples). In addition, learning environment was found to be consistently related to openness ($r = .34$ and $.44$ for men in the two samples and $r = .35$ and $.42$ for women in the two samples). The hypothesized relationships with Big Five factors agreeableness and conscientiousness for the personal style scales were not consistently obtained. In summary, the Lindley and Borgen (2000) findings demonstrate that the personal style scales are linked to relevant dimensions of personality and in particular to extraversion and openness.

Summary

In any event, Tokar et al. (1998) concluded with several recommendations, a few of which are mentioned here. They noted limited research on career processes (e.g., search intentions and behaviors, career progression, career processes stemming from welfare reform in the United States) relative to vocational outcomes (e.g., satisfaction, choice, performance). They suggested a need for additional work in this area. Similarly, the authors noted a relatively small amount of research with clear consideration of cultural issues. They recommended that researchers attend to issues of culture, ethnicity and race, sexual orientation, age, class, disability status, religion and spirituality, and related variables. Researchers are also encouraged to investigate personality in relation to supportive employee behaviors such as organizational citizenship, mentoring effectiveness, and team-building skills. Positive attitudes such as confidence and motivation for training and sensitivity to diversity issues may, in addition, be productively studied in relation to personality. Finally, longitudinal work is needed to clarify the meaning of the relation between negative affect and job satisfaction, positive affect and job satisfaction, and the influence of work environments (positive and negative) on affectivity.

PERSONALITY, INTERESTS, SELF-EFFICACY, AND WORKING

Fred Borgen (1999) noted that two salient current topics are the overlap between interests and personality and the overlap between interests and self-efficacy. However, the overlap between personality and self-efficacy has remained a rather neglected area. In this context, I here discuss the concept of self-efficacy, the overlap between interests and self-efficacy, the need to independently assess vocational interests and vocational self-efficacy, and finally the relations between personality and self-efficacy.

A contemporary trend in career assessment is the integrated use of vocational self-efficacy and vocational interests. This trend is founded on substantial empirical evidence that vocational self-efficacy is a significant predictor of career choice and vocational behavior (Betz & Hackett, 1981; Hackett & Betz, 1981; Lent, Brown, & Hackett, 1994). The applicability of self-efficacy theory to vocational behavior was first suggested by Hackett and Betz (1981; Betz & Hackett, 1981). Self-efficacy theory as introduced by Bandura (1977, 1997) is discussed in the paragraphs that follow.

Self-Efficacy

The concept of self-efficacy was initially proposed by Bandura (1977, 1997) to describe a person's beliefs concerning his or her ability to successfully perform a given behavior. Thus, self-efficacy expectations are theorized to pertain to a specific domain of behavior such as teaching, breeding animals, mathematics, repairing computers, or repairing trucks. Bandura's self-efficacy theory predicts that beliefs regarding abilities in a particular domain influence choice, performance, and persistence. Stated differently, self-efficacy beliefs are concerned not with skills but with judgments of what one can do with those skills.

According to Bandura (1977, 1997) efficacy beliefs are relevant to behavior in at least three ways: First, self-efficacy beliefs influence whether a person will exhibit approach or avoidance behavior. For example, a person will tend to avoid behaviors perceived to be beyond his or her capabilities and will approach behaviors about which he or she feels some sense of confidence. Second, perceived self-efficacy effects the quality of a person's performance. Is the task performed successfully? Third, self-efficacy beliefs influence persistence and whether or not a person will pursue a given behavior in the presence of obstacles. Greater self-efficacy tends to be related to the likelihood that an individual will persist at a given task.

The implications of self-efficacy theory for career development are clear as noted by Hackett and Betz (1981; Betz & Hackett, 1981). For an individual to consider a particular vocational alternative, he or she needs to have some confidence in the ability to successfully perform the educational and occupational requirements of the program or vocation. Individuals with high self-efficacy beliefs in a wide range of vocational categories will perceive more alternatives available to them for career choice. Low self-efficacy beliefs result in avoidance and fear of a particular domain of behavior. Thus, an individual will avoid experiences that would facilitate the development of skills and improve confidence and interests in a vocational area. On the other hand, high self-efficacy beliefs tend to stimulate approach behavior and facilitate the development of skills and interests.

Finally, Bandura (1977, 1997) asserted that self-efficacy beliefs for a particular domain of behavior develop through and are modified by four sources of information and reinforcement: performance accomplishments or past successes in completing the behavior; vicarious learning or observing others performing the behavior; lower levels of emotional arousal (anxiety); and verbal persuasion or encouragement from others. Of these sources of self-efficacy information, performance accomplishments or past successes are believed to exert the greatest influence on the development of self-efficacy beliefs (Bandura, 1977, 1997).

Early Self-Efficacy and Career Research

A review of relevant research indicates that the first study investigating the applicability of self-efficacy theory to career development was carried out by Hackett and Betz in 1981. They used a 20-item occupational self-efficacy scale that they developed to measure student's perceptions of self-efficacy with respect to the educational requirements and job duties of 20 well-known occupations. The authors hypothesized that low self-efficacy expectations about traditionally male-dominated career areas would tend to act as a barrier to women's career development. Findings showed significant gender differences in occupational self-efficacy expectations when traditionality of the occupation was taken into account. Stated differently, the women's self-efficacy was higher in traditional female occupations and lower in nontraditional occupations. Male occupational self-efficacy was essentially equivalent for traditional male-dominated and traditional female-dominated occupations. The assessment of general occupational self-efficacy as pioneered by Hackett and Betz (1981; Betz & Hackett, 1981) has been used in many additional studies and most have found gender differences in occupational self-efficacy. In a discussion of interest and ability measures with women, Betz (1992) suggested that at least a moderate level of perceived self-efficacy is needed for interest to develop in a particular career domain. In addition, the research of Lent and his colleagues (Hackett & Lent, 1992; Lent et al., 1994; Lent, Brown, & Larkin, 1984, 1986) found that perceived self-efficacy was related to performance and persistence among students who had made a career choice. Thus, the literature tends to support the role of perceived self-efficacy as a factor in performance and persistence in career choice behaviors.

SELF-EFFICACY AND VOCATIONAL INTERESTS

A number of theorists (Bordin, 1943; Holland, 1997; Strong, 1943) have suggested that new interests may develop with new experiences. Research

(Campbell & Hackett, 1986; Korman, 1968, 1969; Osipow & Scheid, 1971) suggests that task success may tend to increase interest and/or past liking. Strong initially suggested that past success was rewarding and generated task liking and ultimately an interest.

More recently, Lapan and his colleagues (Lapan, Boggs, & Morrill, 1989; Lapan, Shaughnessy, & Boggs, 1996) have been investigating the hypothesis that increased self-efficacy may be associated with increased interests. In the 1989 study the authors found evidence that lower self-efficacy with respect to the Holland realistic and investigative areas may offer an explanation of women's lower realistic and investigative interests. In the 1996 study they found that math self-efficacy and math interests were important in predicting entry into math and science majors.

A social cognitive model developed by Lent et al. (1994) relates self-efficacy theory and vocational interest development. This approach to career behavior focuses on self-efficacy, outcome expectations, and goals. Efficacy and outcome expectations are hypothesized to influence the development both of interests and career goals. Lent, Lopez, and Bieschke (1993) tested the social cognitive model and found that self-efficacy facilitates the effects of prior performance on interests and that interests facilitate the effect of self-efficacy on choice intentions. A more comprehensive study of the social cognitive model by Lopez, Lent, Brown, and Gore (1997) used a sample of 296 students enrolled in math courses in high school. This study focused on predicting math-related interests and performance. The findings showed that both self-efficacy and outcome expectations predicted subject matter interests.

It is in this context and background that Betz, Borgen, and Harmon (1996) developed the Skills Confidence Inventory as a companion to the traditional Strong Interest Inventory. The Skills Confidence Inventory measures level of perceived confidence with respect to the six Holland themes. Betz (1999) argues that interests and confidence (self-efficacy) tend to overlap, but that sufficient independence exists to warrant joint interpretation. Stated differently, Betz argues that interests and confidence are both necessary before a client will pursue a given career option.

Validity work on the Skills Confidence Inventory (Betz et al., 1996) produced a substantial relationship between vocational self-efficacy for the Holland themes and vocational interests. Betz and her colleagues concluded that confidence for and interest in a theme were moderately correlated (Betz et al.).

A meta-analytic review by Lent et al. (1994) found an average weighted correlation of .53 between vocational self-efficacy and vocational interests across 13 studies. Interpreted this finding means that approximately 27% of the variance in vocational interests appears to be accounted for by self-efficacy. Lent et al. (1994) further found that both vocational self-efficacy and vocational interests are positively related to career choice with correlations of .40 and .60, respectively.

In summary, additional empirical verification is clearly needed, but at this time there is some evidence indicating that increases in self-efficacy beliefs may facilitate the development of new interests and assist individuals in acting on their interests.

COMBINING INTERESTS AND SELF-EFFICACY
TO PREDICT OCCUPATION

In an effort to examine interests, self-efficacy, and occupation, Donnay and Borgen (1999) investigated the relative role of vocational self-efficacy and vocational interests in explaining tenured and satisfied membership in an occupational group. For this research Donnay and Borgen were able to match up 1,105 individuals who had taken the Strong Interest Inventory in 1992–1993 and the Skills Confidence Inventory in 1993–1994. The sample contained 537 adult women and 568 adult men. Men and women represented 21 different occupations that were distributed across the six Holland occupational themes. Thus, the six general occupational themes of the 1994 Strong Interest Inventory assessed participant's patterns of vocational interests and the Skills Confidence Inventory assessed participant's level of confidence in the six general occupational theme areas. In summary, the findings demonstrated that the Holland theme scales from the Strong Interest Inventory and the Skills Confidence Inventory contribute significantly to the understanding of occupational groups. Donnay and Borgen found that interests and self-efficacy (on the six Holland themes) each solidly predicted membership in the 21 occupations. Furthermore, the combined effect indicated that interests and self-efficacy each contributed important independent variance. The authors note that interests accounted for 79% of the variance and self-efficacy accounted for 82% of the variance, and together they accounted for 91% of the variance. Donnay and Borgen conclude that both counseling and theory will be improved if we integrate interests and self-efficacy in our models.

A similar study by Isaacs, Borgen, Donnay, and Hansen (1997) and discussed in Borgen (1999) investigated interests, self-efficacy, and college major choice rather than adult occupation. The sample consisted of 760 college students. The study asked the question whether interests and self-efficacy as measured by the six general occupational themes of the Strong Interest Inventory and the six general confidence themes could predict college major within one of the six Holland themes (Borgen). Isaacs et al. found that interests and self-efficacy on the six Holland themes each substantially predicted membership in the six Holland major fields. The hit rates for predicting major were 42% for interests, 47% for confidence, and 49% for interest and confidence combined (Borgen). The authors found that interests accounted for 47% of the variance, self-efficacy accounted for 48.5% of the variance, and interests and confidence combined accounted for 57% of the variance. Again, the findings indicate that theory and practice will benefit from combining interests and self-efficacy in our models.

PERSONALITY, SELF-EFFICACY, AND CAREER GOALS (WORKING)

In discussing personality, interests, and self-efficacy I have in earlier sections of this chapter acknowledged the overlap between interests and personality and the overlap between interests and self-efficacy. However, the intriguing connection that for the most part has been neglected (Borgen, 1999) is the overlap between personality and self-efficacy. For a brief glimpse at this connection we return to the work of Donnay (1998) and Borgen. Donnay (1998) and Borgen explore relations between, personality, self-efficacy, and work using the 1,105 working adults in 21 occupations drawn from the national norm groups for the 1994 Strong Interest Inventory and the 1996 Skills Confidence Inventory. These authors present data for 48 life insurance agents and 27 physicists on the work style scale of the Strong Interest Inventory and the investigative confidence scale of the Skills Confidence Inventory. The work style scale distinguishes individuals who prefer to work with people from those who prefer working with ideas, data, or things (Harmon et al., 1994). Lower scores on this scale suggest a preference for working alone; liking ideas, data, and/or things; a preference for scientific and technical activities; a preference for the realistic and investigative themes; and enjoyment in learning about the physical sciences, machine trades, engineering, biological sciences, computer and information sciences, and math. Higher scores on this scale suggest a preference for working with people; a preference for helping others; liking smoothing disagreements between people; a preference for the enterprising and social themes; and enjoyment in learning about education, journalism, business, and the social sciences.

Borgen (1999) and Donnay (1998) pointed out that based on the interest assessment literature, life insurance agents and physicists live on different psychological planets. The physicists very much like science and the life insurance agents detest it. The life insurance agents very much enjoy selling and persuading and the physicists have no interest in that activity. Borgen and Donnay suggest that these two groups are also very different people in terms of self-efficacy and personality. The evidence tends to support this inference. In general, the physicists tend to score high on the investigative confidence scale and low on the work style scale. The life insurance agents in general as a group tend to score rather high on the work style scale and low on the investigative confidence scale. Given this sample fact exploring personality and self-efficacy, Borgen suspects that the Skills Confidence Inventory may reflect personality dimensions (Borgen). Borgen further notes that as we explore the links between personality, interests, and self-efficacy, we may be tapping into personality dimensions such as human resilience, which evidence suggests is a component of subjective well-being (see the next section of this chapter). Lightsey (1996), similar to Borgen, suggested that generalized self-efficacy may be useful in understanding subjective well-being because it has been found to facilitate coping and behavioral responses and to relate to decreased depression (Davis-Berman, 1990). According to Bandura (1989) generalized and domain-specific self-efficacy refers to either broad or situation-specific beliefs that certain actions can be taken and successfully accomplished. However, Lightsey and Robbins (1985) further indicate that the relationship between generalized and domain-specific self-efficacy remains an empirical question. Thus, at this time it seems possible and very limited evidence suggests that the links between personality, interests, self-efficacy, and career goals may interact to facilitate human strength and subjective well-being.

In this section I have attempted to define vocational self-efficacy. The work of Betz and her colleagues has been reviewed showing that on the Holland dimensions there are moderate relations between interests and self-efficacy. Next, the work of Donnay and Borgen (1999) and Isaac et al. (1997) has shown that interests and self-efficacy each have valid independent variance. The Holland theme scales from the Strong Interest Inventory and the Skills Confidence Inventory contributed substantially and significantly to the understanding of occupational groups (Donnay and Borgen, 1999). Stated differently, the vocational self-efficacy measures may be used to predict occupational choice. Finally, a brief glimpse of the links between personality, interests, self-efficacy and career goals suggests that these dimensions may interact to facilitate human strength and subjective well-being.

PERSONALITY, GOALS, AND SUBJECTIVE WELL-BEING

Career Relevant Personality Dimensions

Rodney Lowman (1991) in his book *The Clinical Practice of Career Assessment: Interests, Abilities, and Personality* suggested a number of career-relevant personality dimensions. Lowman defined a career-relevant personality variable as one with demonstrated theoretical and empirical relevance for various occupational groups. Those people scoring in the desired direction will be more likely to perform successfully in a given career path. Those individuals scoring in the opposite direction will tend to perform less effectively in the same occupation. Lowman listed the following career-relevant personality dimensions: achievement orientation, introversion–extraversion, ascendance–dominance and need for power, emotional stability–neuroticism, and masculinity–feminity. Lowman further cited other personality variables that have shown promise for use in career assessment but have been less extensively researched. These include conscientiousness, agreeableness, need for affiliation, energy, general activity level, field dependence–independence, openness, sensitivity versus tough mindedness, intuiting versus sensing, thinking versus feeling, and judging versus perceiving. Lowman concluded citing the need for research on the clinical applicability of personality assessment in the career assessment process. Thus, his discussion tended to focus on personality and the quality and goals of work and leisure experiences. According to Csikszentmihalyi (1999) and Diener (2000) these (personality and the quality and goals of work and leisure activities) tend to be clues informative of subjective well-being.

Goals and Subjective Well-Being

Recent research from the life satisfaction and subjective well-being literature suggests other relevant goal and work properties. In terms of a functional definition the goal constructs tend to assume a purposefulness in behavior and are operationalized differently depending on the theoretical perspective (Hogan & Roberts, 2000; Little, 2000; Pervin, 1992; Swindle & Moos, 1992) being used and researched. For example, Cantor and Sanderson (1999) and Emmons (1986) have found that making progress toward goals and work objectives is related to subjective well-being. Brunstein, Schultheiss, and Grässmann (1998) have shown that progress toward need-congruent goals is positively related to subjective well-being, whereas commitment to incongruent goals was found to be negatively related to reports of well-being. Diener and Fujita (1995) found that having resources (e.g., money, physical attractiveness, or social skills) in areas related to one's goals is a more accurate predictor of satisfaction and well-being than having fewer resources related to one's important goals. Robbins and Kliewer (2000) further note that personal goals (i.e., life tasks, personal projects, and personal strivings) tend to serve as central organizers of affect, cognition, and behavior. In general, research has shown a significant and strong relationship between different goal constructs and subjective well-being estimates. The findings suggest that goal and work properties including achieved goals, unachieved goals, goal conflict, and goal congruence are related to life satisfaction and subjective well-being estimates.

However, as reported by Robbins and Kliewer (2000), the relationship of goals and subjective well-being is more complex than simply assuming that a purposeful behavior (goal attainment) contributes to increased subjective well-being. For example, community participation and affiliation have been found to be more related to subjective well-being than financial goals are (Kasser & Ryan, 1993, 1996). Diener (2000) further noted that the environmental context within which one pursues goal attainment facilitates the processes by which goals influence subjective well-being. Similarly, culture is a relevant dimension. According to Robbins and Kliewer, culture may influence the type of goals or behaviors that are valued, the resources available to obtain these goals, and the context in which subjective well-being is understood.

The previous paragraphs have discussed in the Lowman context desirable characteristics of career-relevant personality dimensions. Stated differently, we have looked at personality traits and the quality of work goals. The second theme discussed previously has focused on life satisfaction, subjective well-being, and important goal and work properties. This literature suggests that defined goals and making progress toward goals is related to subjective well-being. Thus, I have attempted to link personality and occupational goals, and occupational goals and subjective well-being. The next link to be discussed focuses on how personality might influence subjective well-being and occupational goals. As we move ahead, keep in mind the overarching theme noted by Csikszentmihalyi (1999) and Diener (2000) that personality traits, quality of work, and sense of well-being tend to be interrelated and informative about one another.

Personality and Subjective Well-Being

Diener (2000) noted that there are a number of components of subjective well-being that include life satisfaction, satisfaction with important domains such as work, positive affect, and low levels of negative affect. Diener and DeNeve (1999) suggest that since 1970 psychologists have moved from investigating demographic factors to focusing on personality as the primary determinant of individual reports of life quality or subjective well-being. These authors and others indicate that the two most commonly cited personality traits when predicting subjective well-being are extraversion (defined by high levels of energy and enthusiasm) and neuroticism (defined with high levels of negative mood and self-concept). Thus, it has been hypothesized that extraversion predicts the presence of subjective well-being, whereas neuroticism predicts its absence (DeNeve).

In order to shed some light on the conceptual issues, DeNeve and Cooper (1998) conducted a meta-analysis of 137 personality traits as correlates of subjective well-being. They found 1,538 correlations between personality and well-being representing 197 distinct samples of individuals, for a total of 42,171 adult respondents. Results of the meta-analysis showed that personality is strongly related with subjective well-being and that only subjective ratings of health is more strongly correlated with well-being estimates. More specifically, findings revealed that neuroticism was one of the strongest negative correlates of subjective well-being. However, a surprising finding was that extraversion was not the primary factor associated with increased well-being. The most important personality trait was repressive defensiveness (a tendency to avoid threatening information). Additional personality correlates of subjective well-being were trust, emotional stability, desire for control, hardiness, positive affectivity, locus of control–chance, and tension. Of the seven variables, the first five were positive correlates and the final two were negative correlates.

DeNeve and Cooper (1998) and DeNeve (1999) noted that subjective well-being cannot be explained only in terms of extraversion and neuroticism. First, they pointed out that positive emotionality relates strongly to well-being (emotional stability and positive affectivity). Second, personality traits that facilitate the fostering of relationships are important for well-being. Affiliation, trust, and sociability are relationship-enhancing traits that facilitate well-being. Third, people reporting subjective well-being tend to explain their life events in optimistic and adaptive ways. Stated differently, they are resilient. They are better able to bounce back from emotional and physical stress than others.

In summary, DeNeve and Cooper (1998) and DeNeve (1999) speculated that personality plays an important role in influencing such psychological factors as social activity, social support, coping style, goal striving, daily events, and resources. They further suggested that these factors subsequently directly effect the various aspects of subjective well-being. Diener (2000) and Diener, Suh, Lucas, and Smith (1999) tended to suggest similar conclusions. These authors together suggested that subjective well-being itself has some of the qualities of a personality trait. An important theme to be noted here for our purposes is that people and work experiences are embedded in a social context. According to these authors, personality plays an important role in influencing the social context and subjective well-being.

Diener (2000) asked the basic question, if subjective well-being is really a good thing? He notes that people high in well-being tend to have a number of desirable qualities. For example, evidence indicates that happy people participate more in community organizations, are more liked by others, are less likely to get divorced, tend to live slightly longer, perform better at work, have meaningful goals, and earn higher incomes. In other words, according to Diener happy individuals seem on average to be more productive and more sociable. Happy people tend to select goals congruent with available resources, and successful goal attainment tends to reinforce happiness (Diener & Fujita, 1995).

In summary, over the past 30 years, as noted by Diener (2000) and DeNeve (1999) psychologists have moved from exploring demographic variables to focusing on personality as the major determinant of individual reports of life quality and subjective well-being. A recent review by Robbins and Kliewer (2000) reported that, although we know more about what does and does not influence subjective well-being than we did 30 years ago, a number of questions remain. These questions involve the stability of subjective well-being over the life span, how to effectively measure subjective well-being, contributing factors to subjective well-being, and the process of subjective well-being (Robbins and Kliewer). Much has been done, but there is much that needs to be done to solve the riddle of subjective well-being.

SUMMARY AND CONCLUSION

Similar to Tokar et al. (1998), I see an urgent need for research on career processes relative to vocational outcomes. In addition, there is an urgent need for research with clear consideration of cultural issues. We need to attend to issues of culture, ethnicity and race, sexual orientation, age, class, disability status, religion and spirituality, and related variables. We also need to investigate personality in relation to supportive employee behaviors such as organizational citizenship, mentoring effectiveness, and team-building skills. Positive attitudes such as confidence and motivation for training and sensitivity to diversity issues in the work environment need to be explored. There is also a very important need for longitudinal work to clarify the meaning of the interactions between negative affect, positive affect, job satisfaction, and the work environment (positive and negative). We really need longitudinal work of all kinds to study the dynamic developmental interaction between personality and the environment. People in environments are in constant transaction, and any assessment of the person is incomplete without some assessment of the environment (Walsh and Betz, 2000). We cannot take the person out of personality (Mischel, 1977), but at the same time, we cannot ignore the fact that environments, like people, have personalities and influence behavior. People change and environments change, and only longitudinal research can explore this developmental process and dynamic interaction. We also need better and more effective measures of the environment. As noted by Tinsley (2000a, 2000b), some work environments are more broadly appealing to individuals than other environments. Tinsley noted that enriched environments produce higher satisfaction, whereas environments devoid of this richness produce lower levels of satisfaction. Tinsley suggested that environmental quality in and of itself plays an influential role in determining work attitudes and work behaviors, regardless of the personality of the individual in the environment. In sum, the fact remains that the concept of environment is not well defined in any existing psychologically based theoretical framework. There is no question that we need better (more reliable and valid) assessments of the environment (Chartrand & Walsh, 1999). This improvement alone could contribute substantially to our understanding of work attitudes, work behavior, work satisfaction, and, in general, the dynamic interaction between personality and environment.

In the section on personality, interests, self-efficacy, and working, I discussed the concept of self-efficacy, the overlap between interests and self-efficacy, the need to independently assess vocational interests and vocational self-efficacy, and finally the intriguing relationship between personality and self-efficacy. The evidence here does indicate that self-efficacy beliefs facilitate the development of new interests and assist individuals in acting on those interests. Furthermore, the evidence indicates that theory and practice will benefit from combining interests and self-efficacy in our models. Also, some limited initial evidence suggests that as we explore the links between personality, interests, and self-efficacy, we may be tapping into personality dimensions such as human resilience. Thus, stated differently, it seems possible that the links between personality, interests, self-efficacy, and career goals may interact to facilitate human strength and subjective well-being.

Finally, I discuss personality, goals, and subjective well-being. DeNeve and Cooper (1998) speculate that personality facilitates the development of subjective well-being through the psychological factors of social activity, social support, coping style, goal striving, daily events, and resources. Diener (2000) notes that people high in subjective well-being tend to have a number of desirable qualities. For example, evidence indicates that happy people participate more in community organizations, are more liked by others, are less likely to get divorced, tend to live slightly longer, perform better at work, have meaningful goals, and earn higher incomes. In other words, happy individuals reporting subjective well-being tend to be more productive and more sociable.

REFERENCES

Bandura, A. (1977). Self-efficacy: Toward a unifying theory of behavioral change. *Psychological Review, 84*, 191–215.
Bandura, A. (1989). Human agency in social cognitive theory. *American Psychologist, 44*, 1175–1184.

Bandura, A. (1997). *Self-efficacy: The exercise of control.* New York: Freeman.

Betz, N. E. (1992). Counseling uses of career self-efficacy theory. *Career Development Quarterly, 41,* 22–26.

Betz, N. E. (1999). Getting clients to act on their interests: Self-efficacy as a moderator of the implementation of vocational interests. In M. L. Savickas & A. R. Spokane (Eds.), *Occupational interests: Their meaning, measurement and use in counseling* (pp. 327–344). Palo Alto: Davies-Black.

Betz, N. E., Borgen, F. H., & Harmon, L. W. (1996). *Skills Confidence Inventory: Applications and technical guide.* Palo alto, CA: Consulting Psychologists Press.

Betz, N. E., & Hackett, G. (1981). The relationship of career-related self-efficacy expectations to perceived career options in college women and men. *Journal of Counseling Psychology, 28,* 399–410.

Bordin, E. S. (1943). A theory of vocational interests as dynamic phenomena. *Educational and Psychological Measurement, 3,* 49–65.

Borgen, F. H. (1999). New horizons in interest theory and measurement. In M. L. Savickas & A. R. Spokane (Eds.), *Vocational interests: Meaning, measurement, and counseling use* (pp. 383–412). Palo Alto, CA: Davies-Black.

Brown, S. P. (1996). A meta-analysis and review of organizational research on job involvement. *Psychological Bulletin, 120,* 235–255.

Brunstein, J. C., Schultheiss, O. C., & Grässmann, R. (1998). Personal goals and emotional well-being: The moderating role of motive dispositions. *Journal of Personality and Social Psychology, 75,* 494–508.

Campbell, N. K., & Hackett, G. (1986). The effects of mathematics task performance on math self-efficacy and task interest. *Journal of Vocational Behavior, 28,* 149–162.

Cantor, N., & Sanderson, C. A. (1999). Life task participation and well-being: The importance of taking part in daily life. In D. Kahneman, E. Diener, & N. Schwarz (Eds.), *Well-being: The foundation of hedonic psychology.* New York: Russell Sage Foundation.

Celeste, B. L., & Walsh, W. B. (1997). Congruence and psychological adjustment for practicing female ministers. *Journal of Mental Health Counseling, 19,* 277–285.

Celeste, B. L., Walsh, W. B., & Roate, R. G. (1995). Congruence and psychological adjustment for practicing male ministers. *Career Development Quarterly, 43,* 374–384.

Chartrand, J. M., Rose, M. L., Elliott, J. R., Marmarosh, C., & Caldwell, S. (1993). Peeling back the onion: Personality, problem solving, and career decision making style correlater of career indecision. *Journal of Career Assessment, 1,* 66–82.

Chartrand, J., & Walsh, W. B. (1999). What should we expect from congruence? *Journal of Vocational Behavior, 55,* 136–146.

Costa, P. T., & McCrae, R. R. (1992). *NEO-PI-R manual.* Odessa, FL: Psychological Assessment Resources.

Csikszentmihalyi, M. (1999). If we are so rich, why aren't we happy? *American Psychologist, 54,* 821–827.

Davis-Berman, J. (1990). Physical self-efficacy, perceived physical status, and depressive symptomatology in older adults. *Journal of Psychology, 124,* 207–215.

De Fruyt, F., & Mervielde, I. (1999). RIASEC types of big five traits as predictors of employment status and nature of employment. *Personnel Psychology, 52,* 701–727.

DeNeve, K. M. (1999). Happy as an extraverted clam? The role of personality for subjective well-being. *Current Directions in Psychological Science, 8,* 141–144.

DeNeve, K. M., & Cooper, H. (1998). The happy personality: A meta-analysis of 137 personality traits and subjective well-being. *Psychological Bulletin, 124,* 197–229.

Diener, E. (2000). Subjective well-being: The science of happiness and a proposal for a national index. *American Psychologist, 55,* 34–43.

Diener, E., & Fujita, F. (1995). Resources, personal strivings, and subjective well-being: Anomothetic and idiographic approach. *Journal of Personality and Social Psychology, 68,* 926–935.

Diener, E., Suh, E., Lucas, R. E., & Smith, H. C. (1999). Subjective well-being: Three decades of progress. *Psychological Bulletin, 125,* 276–302.

Digman, J. M. (1990). Personality structure: Emergency of the five-factor model. *Annual Review of Psychology, 41,* 417–440.

Donnay, D. A. C. (1998). Assessing careers: Vocational interest and vocational self-efficacy. Unpublished doctoral dissertation, Iowa State University, Ames, Iowa.

Donnay, D. A. C., & Borgen, F. H. (1999). The incremental validity of vocational self-efficacy: An examination of interest, self-efficacy, and occupation. *Journal of Counseling Psychology, 46,* 432–447.

Emmons, R. A. (1986). Personal strivings: An approach to personality and subjective well-being. *Journal of Personality and Social Psychology, 51,* 1058–1068.

Gottfredson, G. D., & Holland, J. L. (1991). *The Position Classification Inventory.* Odessa, FL: Psychological Assessment Resources.

Gottfredson, G. D., Jones, E. M., & Holland, J. L. (1993). Personality and vocational interests: The relation of Holland's six interest dimensions to the five robust dimensions of personality. *Journal of Counseling Psychology, 40,* 518–524.

Gough, H. G., & Heilbrun, A. B., Jr. (1983). *The Adjective Check List manual.* Palo Alto, CA: Consulting Psychologists Press.

Hackett, G., & Betz, N. E. (1981). A self-efficacy approach to the career development of women. *Journal of Vocational Behavior, 18,* 326–339.

Hackett, G., & Lent, R. W. (1992). Theoretical advances and current inquiry in counseling psychology. In S. D. Brown & R. W. Lent, Jr. (Eds.), *Handbook of counseling psychology* (2nd ed., pp. 419–452). New York: Wiley.

Harmon, L. W., Hansen, J. C., Borgen, F. H., & Hammer, A. C. (1994). *Strong Interest Inventory: Applications and technical guide.* Stanford, CA: Stanford University Press.

Hogan, R., & Roberts, B. W. (2000). A socioanalytic perspective on person-environment interaction. In W. B. Walsh, K. H. Craik, & R. H. Pierce (Eds.), *Person-environment psychology* (2nd ed.). Mahwah, NJ: Lawrence Erlbaum Associates, Inc.

Holland, J. L. (1979). *The Self-Directed Search professional manual.* Palo Alto, CA: Consulting Psychologists Press.

Holland J. L. (1997). *Making vocational choices: A theory of vocational personalities and work environments* (3rd ed.). Odessa, FL: Psychological Assessment Resources.

Isaacs, J., Borgen, F. H., Donnay, D. A. C., & Hansen, J. A. (1997). Self-efficacy and interests: Relationships of Holland themes to college major. Poster session at the 105th annual Convention of the American Psychological Association.

John, O. P. (1990). The Big Five factor taxonomy: Dimensions of personality in the natural language and in questionnaires. In L. A. Pervin (Ed.), *Handbook of personality: Theory and research* (pp. 66–100). New York: Guilford.

Kasser, J., & Ryan, R. M. (1993). A dark side of the American dream: Correlates of financial success as a central life aspiration. *Journal of Personality and Social Psychology, 65,* 410–422.

Kasser, J., & Ryan, R. M. (1996). Further examination of the American dream: Differential correlates of intrinsic and extrinsic goals. *Personality and Social Psychology Bulletin, 22,* 280–287.

Korman, A. K. (1968). Task success, task popularity, and self-esteem influences on task liking. *Journal of Applied Psychology, 52,* 484–490.

Korman, A. K. (1969). Self-esteem as a moderator in vocational choice: Replications and extensions. *Journal of Applied Psychology, 53,* 180–192.

Lapan, B. T., Boggs, K. R., & Morrill, W. H. (1989). Self-efficacy as a mediator of Investigative and Realistic General Occupational Themes on the Strong Interest Inventory. *Journal of Counseling Psychology, 36,* 176–182.

Lapan, B. T., Shaughnessy, P., & Boggs, K. R. (1996). Efficacy expectations and vocational interests as mediators between sex and choice of math/science college majors: A longitudinal study. *Journal of Vocational Behavior, 49,* 277–291.

Lent, R. W., Brown, S. D., & Hackett, G. (1994). Toward a unifying social cognitive theory of career and academic interest, choice and performance. *Journal of Vocational Behavior, 45*, 79–122.

Lent, R. W., Brown, S. D., & Larkin, K. C. (1984). Relation of self-efficacy expectations to academic achievement and persistence. *Journal of Counseling Psychology, 31*, 356–362.

Lent, R. W., Brown, S. D., & Larkin, K. C. (1986). Self-efficacy in the prediction of academic success and perceived career options. *Journal of Counseling Psychology, 33*, 265–269.

Lent, R. W., Lopez, F. G., & Bieschke, K. J. (1993). Predicting mathematics-related choice and success behaviors: Test of an expanded social cognitive model. *Journal of Vocational Behavior, 42*, 223–236.

Lightsey, O. R., Jr. (1996). What leads to wellness? The role of psychological resources in well-being. *Counseling Psychologist, 24*, 589–759.

Lindley, L. D., & Borgen, F. H. (2000). Personal styles of the Strong Interest Inventory: Linking personality and interests. *Journal of Vocational Behavior, 56*, 22–41.

Little, B. R. (2000). Free traits and personal contexts: Expanding a social ecological model of well-being. In W. B. Walsh, K. H. Craik, & R. H. Price (Eds.), *Person-environment psychology* (2nd edition). Mahwah, NJ: Lawrence Erlbaum Associates, Inc.

Lopez, F. G., Lent, R. W., Brown, S. D., & Gore, P. A., Jr. (1997). Role of social-cognitive expectations in high school students' mathematics related interest and performance. *Journal of Counseling Psychology, 44*, 44–52.

Lowman, R. L. (1991). *The clinical practice of career assessment: Interests, abilities and personality.* Washington, DC: American Psychological Association.

Mischel, W. (1977). On the future of personality measurement. *American Psychologist, 32*, 246–255.

Necowitz, L. B., & Roznowski, M. (1994). Negative affectivity and job satisfaction: Cognitive processes underlying the relationship and effects on employee behaviors. *Journal of Vocational Behavior, 45*, 270–294.

Osipow, S. H., & Scheid, A. B. (1971). The effect of manipulated success ratios on task preference. *Journal of Vocational Behavior, 1*, 93–98.

Parkes, K. R., Mendham, C. A., & von Rabenau, C. (1994). Social support and the demand-discretion model of job stress: Tests of additive and interactive effects in two samples. *Journal of Vocational Behavior, 44*, 91–113.

Pervin, L. A. (1992). Transversing the individual-environment landscape: A personal odyssey. In W. B. Walsh, K. H. Craik, & R. H. Price (Eds.), *Person-environment psychology*. Hillsdale, NJ: Lawrence Erlbaum Associates, Inc.

Robbins, S. B. (1985). Validity estimates for the Career Decision Making Self-Efficacy Scale. *Measurement and Evaluation in Counseling and Development, 18*, 64–71.

Robbins, S. B., & Kliewer, W. L. (2000). Advances in theory and research on subjective well-being. In S. D. Brown & R. L. Lent (Eds.), *Handbook of counseling psychology* (3rd ed.). New York: Wiley.

Strong, E. K., Jr. (1943). *Vocational interests of men and women.* Stanford, CA: Stanford University Press.

Swindle, R. W., & Moos, R. H. (1992). Life domains in stressors, coping, and adjustment. In W. B. Walsh, K. H. Craik, & R. H. Price (Eds.), *Person-environment psychology*. Hillside, NJ: Lawrence Erlbaum Associates, Inc.

Tinsley, H. E. A. (2000a). The congruence myth: An analysis of the efficacy of the person-environment fit model. *Journal of Vocational Behavior, 56*, 147–179.

Tinsley, H. E. A. (2000b). The congruence myth revisited. *Journal of Vocational Behavior, 56*, 405–423.

Tokar, D. M., Fischer, A. R., & Subich, L. M. (1998). Personality and vocational behavior: A selective review of the literature. *Journal of Vocational Behavior, 53*, 115–153.

Tokar, D. M., & Swanson, J. L. (1995). Evaluation of the correspondence between Holland's vocational personality typology and the five-factor model of personality. *Journal of Vocational Behavior, 46,* 89–108.

Walsh, W. B., & Betz, N. E. (2000). *Tests and assessment* (4th ed.). Upper Saddle River, NJ: Prentice Hall.

Wiggins, J. S., & Trapnell, P. D. (1997). Personality structure: The return of the Big Five. In R. Hogan, J. Johnson, & S. Briggs (Eds.), *Handbook of personality psychology* (pp. 737–765). San Diego: Academic.

7

The Dispositional Approach to Job Attitudes: An Empirical and Conceptual Review

Barry M. Staw
University of California, Berkeley

Many scholars now believe that job satisfaction is as much a product of the person as the situation. Yet this was not always the case. Like many areas of the behavioral sciences, the study of job attitudes has undergone several shifts in emphasis regarding dispositional versus situational causes. I will outline some of these shifts in thinking over the past three decades, showing how dispositional approaches to satisfaction moved from relative obscurity to widespread acceptance. I will also outline some of the current weaknesses with the dispositional approach, showing how contemporary formulations can be limited theoretically. Finally, I will propose a new model for understanding the mechanisms underlying dispositional influence, illustrating how individual differences in affect translate into differing levels of job satisfaction.

But first some background is necessary. In order to appreciate the impact of individual characteristics on job attitudes, one must look at more than a simple inventory of results. Like other behavioral theories, the dispositional approach to job satisfaction is the product of a longer-term evolution of ideas, one that has been punctuated by theoretical as well as empirical developments. Thus, let us begin our study of the dispositional perspective by turning back the clock about 30 years.

SOME BACKGROUND

During much of the 1960s and 1970s, the dominant perspective on personality, at least within organizational psychology, was Maslow's (1954, 1970) need theory. It was commonly assumed that people could be characterized by their profiles of safety, social, esteem, and actualization needs. Efforts to validate a specific hierarchy of needs, where people move through a prescribed, ladder-like sequence of desires, had not been terribly successful (e.g., Hall & Nougaim, 1968; Lawler & Suttle, 1972). Nor had been Herzberg's (1966) analogous claim that job satisfaction and motivation come primarily from intrinsic rather than extrinsic aspects of the work situation (House & Wigdor, 1967; Schneider & Locke, 1971). Yet, both Maslow's and Herzberg's theories helped gain acceptance for the idea that people work for reasons other than money or financial security, so that factors like challenge, recognition, and achievement could be taken into account when explaining work motivation.

Against this conceptual backdrop, Hackman and Oldham (1975) proposed their job characteristics theory. They argued that a series of core job dimensions (skill variety, task identity, task significance, autonomy, and feedback) generally lead people to be motivated and satisfied at work. Their model implicitly incorporated prior thinking of Maslow and Herzberg by assuming that people derive pleasure from enriched jobs, the kind of work that would satisfy higher-order needs. However, they were also careful to incorporate individual differences into their model, noting that the overall effects of job characteristics would be moderated by employee growth needs:

> Many workers with high growth needs will turn on eagerly when they have jobs that are high in the core dimensions. Workers whose growth need are not so strong may respond less eagerly—or, at first, even balk at being "pushed" or "stretched" too far (Hackman, Oldham, Janson, and Purdy, 1975, p. 61).

Shortly after the publication of Hackman and Oldham's (1975) theory of job enrichment, there also appeared an influential review of the job satisfaction literature by Edwin Locke. Locke (1976) argued that information about the attributes of a job would not be sufficient for predicting a person's level of satisfaction. Whether (and to what degree) features like job challenge, independence, and pay were rewarding to an individual would depend on his or her value structure. For example, the slope of the relationship between money and satisfaction might generally be positive, but the steepness of the curve would depend on a person's value of material goods. Likewise, the slope of features such as job challenge and autonomy might reverse direction for people who view difficult work or independence as aversive states.

Both Hackman and Oldham's (1975) job characteristics theory and Locke's (1976) value model of satisfaction were typical of organizational psychology in the 1960s and 70s. In both models the process of job satisfaction was prompted by a set of objective conditions at work. But, in both models, the appraisal of working conditions was considered to be a function of the person's values or needs, thus embracing a limited form of interactionalism.

THE MOVEMENT TOWARD SITUATIONALISM

Although the job characteristics and value models of work attitudes reflected decades of research on people in organizations, these perspectives did not incorporate contrary developments in the field of psychology. Throughout much of the 1970s, personality psychology was very much on the defensive. Critics of personality theory (e.g., Mischel, 1968) trumpeted the low predictive power of individual differences, arguing that personality could not explain behavior across situations. Meanwhile, a cognitive revolution was taking hold in several areas of psychology. Newfound emphasis on information processing and perceptual biasing meant that attitudes and beliefs were no longer seen as a function of the objective situation, but as something largely attributed to oneself and others.

Salancik and Pfeffer (1972, 1978) brought these two psychological trends—the movement away from personality and the emphasis on social cognition—home to organizational research. First, they organized a broad argument against need satisfaction models in organizational studies (Salancik & Pfeffer, 1977). They outlined theoretical inconsistencies with Maslow's theory and stressed many of the difficulties empirical researchers had faced trying to confirm the theory. Then, in a highly influential essay, Salancik and Pfeffer (1978) proposed a social information processing theory (SIP) to replace need-based theories of job satisfaction and motivation. They argued that attitudes are socially constructed by job holders, and, as such, are highly subject to external influence. They posited that work attitudes are rather fluid assessments, easily colored by the opinions of others, information about why one is performing the task, and even prior responses to questions from researchers. According to the SIP approach, job attitudes are only loosely connected to the objective features of the job and/or characteristics of the individual worker.

Empirical tests of the SIP perspective mainly consisted of laboratory manipulations of social information. In one experiment, subjects were told that a task had been either liked or disliked by people with previous experience with the work (O'Reilly & Caldwell, 1979). In two other studies, a confederate who worked alongside the subject noted positive or negative features of the activity (Weiss & Shaw, 1979; White & Mitchell, 1979). Finally, a field study was conducted in which factory foremen were trained to provide cues about the job to their workers (Griffen, 1983). In each of these studies, the positively described jobs were found to be more satisfying than those negatively portrayed.

Because of the popularity of the SIP approach, the field of organizational behavior took on a deeply situational cast by the early 1980s. Maslow's (1954, 1970) need theory had been vanquished, and along with it any interest in individual differences as an explanatory variable. Faith in the power of job characteristics was likewise weakened. With the growing popularity of the SIP model, job satisfaction was seen to be a product of the external situation, and that situation could potentially be manipulated by subtle social influences from coworkers, supervisors, and leaders of the organization.

PERSONALITY THEORISTS FIGHT BACK

Just as things looked most bleak for advocates of personality and individual differences, some psychologists started to rebuild the case for dispositional influence. A few noted that the interaction of individuals and social contexts might be more complicated than the mechanical interactions tested in previous research (Magnusson & Endler, 1977; Schneider, 1983). Others noted that one should not expect personality to be influential in situations where role demands are strong, that effects of personality would be more likely to be manifested under ambiguous circumstances (Monson, Hesley, & Chernick, 1982). Still others argued that personality constructs would be more predictive of multiple instances of behavior than behavior in a single situation (Aries, Gold, & Weigel, 1983). Finally, it was argued that in-depth assessments of personality by trained specialists would be much more predictive than paper-and-pencil measures that typify most trait research (Block, 1977).

Weiss and Adler (1984) brought these and other arguments for personality to the forefront of debate in organizational psychology. They noted that most organizational research had been designed to test situational theories of influence, either through the careful orchestration of the experimental context or the choice of an organizational situation to highlight situational forces. They argued that the significance and meaning of personality variables would be much greater if organizational research were actually designed to assess or evoke the effects of personality.

THE STABILITY OF JOB ATTITUDES

Like Weiss and Adler (1984), I also believed that organizational research had moved too far in the situational direction by the early 1980s. Therefore, to demonstrate the power of the dispositional perspective I began some research on attitudinal consistency over time and place (Staw & Ross, 1985). Epstein (1979) had earlier found strong consistency in emotions such as happiness when a large number of measures were aggregated. And, Schneider and Dachler (1978) found strong temporal consistency in job-satisfaction scores over a 16-month period. However, Mischel and Peake (1982) had noted that consistency within a single situation did not constitute evidence for individual dispositions—that cross-situational consistency would be needed to substantiate any claim for dispositional influence.

Fortunately, Jerry Ross and I located a data set that enabled a test for consistency of job attitudes within and between organizational contexts. The Longitudinal Survey of Mature Men, originally collected by the Center for Human Resource Research at Ohio State University, was administered to a national random sample of over 5,000 men aged 45 to 59. Data were collected over multiple waves, with the majority of the sample assessed on job satisfaction during 1966, 1969, and 1971. For our purposes, the important feature of this database was that it documented major changes in a respondent's work situation over time. Thus, while many workers remained in their jobs over the course of the study, some changed their employers, their occupations, or both. A change of employer could be conceived as a major situational change, because it usually brings a new supervisor, different physical surroundings, and a new set of working conditions. Such situational changes are probably larger than those reported by most job redesign experiments, because small, noncontroversial changes are the ones that tend to be implemented in workplaces (Oldham & Hackman, 1980). A change in occupation could likewise be expected to bring major situational changes. Although it is possible for one to continue performing a similar task for a new employer, a change in occupation usually involves an entirely different set of work tasks. The Longitudinal Survey of Mature Men therefore provided several degrees of situational change: little change (the same employer and occupation), moderate change (a new employer or new occupation), and substantial environmental change (new employer and new occupation).

The measurement of job attitudes was not as well documented by the longitudinal survey as changes in people's work situation. Although the survey contained relatively sophisticated measures of labor market behavior, it contained only a one-item global satisfaction measure, with four levels of possible response ranging from highly satisfied to highly dissatisfied. Nonetheless, even with measurement that was far from ideal, re-analyses of the longitudinal data proved quite interesting.

As shown in Table 7.1, the correlation in job satisfaction over time was reasonably high (.47 over a 2-year period) when people remained in the same occupation and with the same employer. And, as expected, when

TABLE 7.1
Correlations of Job Satisfaction Over Time When
Employer and Occupation Are Changed

	Occupation	
Employer	Same	Changed
Same	.47	.31
N	2156	171
Changed	.36	.33
N	891	735

Note. All correlations are significant at $p < .001$.
Adapted from Staw & Ross (1985), Stability in the midst of
change: A dispositional approach to job attitudes. *Journal
of Applied Psychology, 70,* 469–480. Table 2, p. 474.

people changed occupations or employers, there was some decrease in
the correlations over time. Nevertheless, when people changed both their
jobs and occupations, the longitudinal relationship did not drop to a nonsignificant level, as might have been expected by those arguing against the
dispositional perspective (e.g., Mischel, 1968; Davis-Blake & Pfeffer, 1989).
Some additional regression analyses also examined whether 1971 job satisfaction could be predicted by changes in pay, changes in job status, and
prior job attitudes from 1966. Although change in pay was a significant
determinant, the person's earlier level of job satisfaction was by far the
most important predictor of subsequent job attitudes.

The results of the Staw and Ross (1985) study were very controversial.
Gerhart (1987), for example, argued that the results might have been a function of the age of those assessed by the longitudinal survey. The sampled
group might have been too old to have experienced major alterations in
employment and subsequent attitudinal changes. Therefore, Gerhart examined the young male sample of the national longitudinal survey, along
with additional controls for changes in job complexity. His results turned
out to be fairly similar to the pattern of data shown in Table 7.1, upholding
the finding of cross-situational stability. More recently, Steel and Rentsch
(1997) examined the stability of job attitudes for military employees over
a ten-year period. As in the Staw and Ross study, there was again a strong
correlation between previous and current job satisfaction for employees
performing similar work ($r = .46$), although the stability of job satisfaction
was lower (but still significant) among those performing different work
over time ($r = .23$).

In a study seldom cited by organizational researchers, Costa, McCrae,
and Zonderman (1987) also examined the temporal consistency of well-
being for a national sample of nearly 5,000 people. They looked at reports

of positive and negative affect from people whose employment status (employed vs. unemployed) had changed or stayed the same during the course of the study. They also noted whether respondent's marital status or state of residence had changed between the waves of data collection. The results were surprising. On measures of positive and negative affect, Costa and his colleagues found retest correlations of .43 and .45 for those who had undergone no changes in employment, whereas the correlations were .43 and .40 for those who changed employment status. Very similar results were found for marital status and state of residence. These data showed that even major life changes did not reduce the consistency of attitudinal responses over time.

PERSON VERSUS ENVIRONMENT

Although consistency studies have been quite supportive of the dispositional perspective, none has specifically addressed the question of the strength of situational versus dispositional forces. Investigations of the role of genetics in personality suggest some answers to this question, however. By examining the degree to which personality traits are shared by identical twins compared to that shared by fraternal twins, it is possible to estimate the heritability of a particular trait. Using this approach, Tellegen et al. (1988) estimated that about 40 percent of the variability in positive emotionality and 55 percent of the variability in negative emotionality is explained by genetics. Their research also has shown little reduction in heritability when examining identical twins separated at birth and raised by different sets of parents (Bouchard, Lykken, McGue, Segal, & Tellegen, 1990).

If one assumes that personality is (at least in part) genetically determined, this still does not mean that job satisfaction is inherited. It is possible that genetic effects become so diluted by strong work situations that they ultimately have little influence on job satisfaction. Arvy, Bouchard, Segal, and Abraham (1989) therefore examined the job satisfaction of a small sample of monozygotic (identical) twins separated and reared apart since early childhood. They found a significant genetic influence on job satisfaction, though the effect was stronger for intrinsic than extrinsic satisfaction. Cropanzano and James (1990) criticized this finding on the grounds that there could have been some similarity in the jobs held by twins. Nonetheless, Plomin and Neiderhiser (1992) have argued that, because of self-selection, people's genes can actually be a source of situational properties, such that individual differences help shape the nature of the person's environment.

An alternative way of assessing dispositional versus environmental effects could involve the comparison of how person and situational changes influence job satisfaction. A relatively obscure technical report by Goiten (1977) took such an approach. As part of a longitudinal study (Quinn, 1977) conducted at Michigan's Institute for Social Research, Goiten examined two waves of questionnaire responses, administered approximately 20 months apart. Two hundred seventy-two people (from two automobile parts manufacturers and a hospital) were divided into three groups: (1) 163 cases where workers were employed in the same job for Phases 1 and 2 of the study; (2) 73 cases where workers changed jobs between the two phases of the study; and (3) 36 cases where different workers were employed in exactly the same job during Phases 1 and 2 of the study. The first two groups of this study correspond to the usual separation of respondents, such as those used by Staw and Ross (1985) in examining consistency under high and low job changes. The third group in this study was rather unusual, however. It measured the consistency of attitudes across different people within the same work role.

Table 7.2 displays autocorrelations under the three conditions of job change, person change, and no change (in either person or job conditions). Consistency in response was measured on several indices of job satisfaction as well as subjective ratings of the quality of employment. As one might expect, consistency was generally high when the person did not change jobs and responded to questions about his or her work at two points in time. Logically, one might have expected the autocorrelations to decline, however, when people took new jobs over the course of the study. Surprisingly,

TABLE 7.2

Correlations Over Time of Work-Related Variables in Conditions of Job Change, Person Change, and No Change

Variable	Job Change ($n = 73$)	Person Change ($n = 36$)	No Change ($n = 163$)
Global job satisfaction	.51	.22	.51
Satisfaction with			
Coworkers	.47	.17	.16
Challenge	.63	.21	.57
Comfort	.57	.48	.45
Resource adequacy	.42	.36	.51
Financial rewards	.56	−.02	.54
Total of quality of employment	.65	.31	.66

Note. Adapted from Goiten (1977), Identifying sources of instability in measures of working conditions and work-related attitudes and behaviors. In R. P. Quinn, *Effectiveness in work roles: Employee responses to work environments.* Ann Arbor: University of Michigan, table 18, p. 352.

the ratings of the job were just as highly correlated under job changes as when the respondent stayed in the same work role. Even more surprising was the disparity in autocorrelations between the job change and person change conditions. In every case, the autocorrelations for the person change condition were lower than their counterparts in the job change condition, often by a substantial margin. Because the sample sizes were rather small (especially in the person change condition), I conducted a statistical check on the differences between the correlation coefficients for the broadest attitudinal measures. Using the formula for differences between independent samples (Guilford, 1965), the total quality of employment index was found to differ significantly ($p < .02$) between the job and person change groups, whereas a marginally significant difference ($p < .06$) was found between the groups on global satisfaction.

The correlations reported in Table 7.2 could have been due, in part, to idiosyncratic differences between the three participant groups. The changes in working conditions in the job change condition might have been relatively minor, and those comprising this group might be individuals who were especially ambitious or good at overcoming situational obstacles (i.e., strong personalities), thereby contributing to a high autocorrelation in attitudes. It is also possible that the sampled organizations intentionally replaced people in the person change condition with those exhibiting different personalities, thereby contributing to a low autocorrelation in attitudes. However, even with these caveats, the Goiten (1977) results are provocative. Though these data were collected many years before the publication of other consistency studies of job satisfaction (and were unknown to the authors of these later studies), they still offer one of the few comparisons of the relative power of dispositional versus situational changes on job attitudes.

LINGERING DOUBTS

While many studies have shown attitudinal consistency across time and situation, some scholars remain to be convinced of the dispositional case. In their critique of personality research, Davis-Blake and Pfeffer (1989), for example, argued that what has been identified as dispositional sources of variance may be the product of unspecified situational differences. For instance, people who changed jobs may continue in low paid or low power positions if they lack requisite skills or proper placement in social networks. Although this is a plausible critique, I would argue that it is not a reasonable one. First, many studies have included controls for situational variables such as job complexity, status, and pay, yet these controls have not eliminated the consistency effects. Second, Davis-Blake and Pfeffer's insistence that all situational variables be controlled when examining dispositional sources of stability is methodologically unfeasible. There will always be uncontrolled variables in nonexperimental research, and professional ethics prohibit most attempts to conduct true experiments on personality, such as through long-term socialization or genetic engineering.

Throughout their critique, Davis-Blake and Pfeffer (1989) argued that organizations comprise strong situations that obviate individual differences. Yet many of the situational effects they cited as being more powerful than dispositions are not themselves controlled for individual differences. Schein (1983) noted that the structure and culture of an organization may be a reflection of the founder's personality. Schneider (1987) argued that personality can shape organizations through the sequence of attraction, selection, and attrition. Bell and Staw (1989) have described ways people can build their work roles around their own personalities. Thus, dispositionalists might logically reverse Davis-Blake and Pfeffer's claim by arguing that all tests of situational effects should account for individual differences masquerading as environmental influences.

In my view, the findings of cross-situational consistency have been robust enough to conclude that Davis-Blake and Pfeffer (1989) were simply wrong in calling them a statistical artifact. Nonetheless, I would not dismiss all of Davis-Blake and Pfeffer's critical points. They correctly noted that consistency findings do not tell us what individual differences may be underlying the maintenance of job attitudes. From the consistency results alone, it is impossible to discern exactly what feature of the person constitutes a dispositional source of job satisfaction. Nor is it possible to know how dispositions actually influence a person's attitudes and behavior. To answer these questions, it is necessary to move from autocorrelations to more specific predictions based on personality and individual characteristics.

STEPS TOWARD A DISPOSITIONAL THEORY

Personality-based investigations of job satisfaction generally require the assessment of individual differences and job attitudes over time. And, the longer the temporal separation between the measurement of personality and job attitudes, the stronger will be the dispositional inference. Thus, an ideal data source for dispositional research would be a longitudinal study with measures of personality and job attitudes separated by significant periods of time.

Just such a data source has been documented and housed at Berkeley's Institute of Human Development. Begun in the late 1920s and 1930s, three longitudinal studies (the Berkeley Growth Study, the Oakland Growth

Study, and the Guidance Study) were started with different principal investigators, samples, and research goals. However, as the samples of these three studies experienced shrinkage over time, they were aggregated into a single database called the Intergenerational Study. Block (1971) devised an ingenious procedure for combining the individual studies. Although the materials available from each of the studies were not the same during any particular time period, there was enough information for clinicians to appraise a participant's personality through individual Q-sorts. Q-sorts were done separately for five time periods: early adolescence (ages 12–14), late adolescence (ages 15–18), first adult period (ages 30–38), second adult period (ages 40–48), and third adult period (ages 54–62). At least three judges rated each adolescent and at least two rated each adult for the various time periods. Though combinations of judges were systematically varied so that no judge rated the same individual at more than one time period, the Q-sort ratings were quite reliable for participants within any particular time period.

Staw, Bell, and Clausen (1986) examined each of the personality Q-sort ratings for their affective meaning. Many appeared to capture intrapersonal aspects of affect such as cheerful, irritable, and feels lack of personal meaning, and some appeared to capture interpersonal aspects of affect such as behaves in a giving way, feels victimized, and has hostility toward others. After a series of factor analyses, a single scale of 17 items was contructed to tap the affective disposition of individuals. This measure of disposition was then correlated with questionnaire measures of job attitudes completed by the Intergenerational sample during the Adult 2 and 3 time periods.

Table 7.3 shows the relationship between dispositional affect and two broad measures of job attitudes. The attitude scale for the Adult 2 period consisted of an average of self-ratings of career satisfaction and a facet measure of job satisfaction (which included 18 specific job dimensions). The Adult 3 attitude scale was an average of an index of facet satisfaction, a measure of overall satisfaction, as well as one-item measures of career satisfaction, participant's feelings about work, and whether the person would take the job again. To compensate for possible differences in job content, the Adult 2 results were controlled for the socioeconomic status (SES) of the person's job. The Adult 3 results were controlled for the complexity of the individual's job.

Given the time lag between the assessments of personality and job attitudes, the results shown in Table 7.3 were surprisingly strong. Of particular note were the significant relationships between affective disposition during adolescence and overall job attitudes during the Adult 3 period—relationships linking observer ratings of personality with self-ratings of job satisfaction across nearly 50 years in time. Also surprising was the

TABLE 7.3
Correlations Between Affective Disposition and Subsequent Job Attitudes

Measurement of Affective Disposition	Job Attitudes	
	Adult 2	Adult 3
Early Adolescence	.20*	.37***
	(n = 59)	(n = 46)
Late Adolescence	.26**	.39***
	(n = 52)	(n = 40)
Adult 1	.30***	.48***
	(n = 70)	(n = 67)
Adult 2	.40***	.12
	(n = 76)	(n = 63)
Adult 3		.23**
		(n = 81)

Note. $^*p < .10$; $^{**}p < .05$, $^{***}p < .01$; one-tailed tests. Adapted from Staw, Bell, & Clausen (1986), The dispositional approach to job satisfaction: A lifetime longitudinal test. *Administrative Science Quarterly, 31,* 56–77. Tables 2 and 3, pp. 67–68.

fact that adolescent measures of affect predicted adult job attitudes better than some measures of affect taken at a later time. Such a pattern might mean that adults tend to revert back to characteristics of a much earlier age. It may also mean that personality assessments taken from adolescent years were more valid indicators of personal tendencies than those taken from later life. As Clausen (1985) noted, adolescents may not yet have learned to camouflage their true personalities with socially desirable or culturally approved responses.

POSITIVE AND NEGATIVE AFFECT

Not long after the publication of the Staw, Bell, and Clausen (1986) study, more sophisticated measures of affect appeared in the literature.[1] Watson, Clark, and Tellegen (1988) composed scales of positive and negative affect (PA and NA) designed to tap individual mood states. They also proposed that these scales, with small changes in the time frame, could measure long-term affective states, thus operationalizing the concept of affective disposition or temperament (Watson, 1988; Watson & Clark, 1992).

---

[1] Both Judge (1992) and Davis-Blake and Pfeffer (1989) questioned the conceptual meaning of the affective disposition scale used by Staw, Bell, and Clausen (1986). Although this scale (actually a selection of Block's Q-sort items) was internally consistent and appeared to be face valid in terms of content, it had not been previously used in research studies on affect.

Watson's positive and negative affect scales (PANAS) have been widely used by organizational researchers. For example, George (1989) found measures of PA and NA to be significantly associated with positive and negative mood at work. Levin and Stokes (1989) found that NA was inversely related to job satisfaction, and that this relationship held after controlling for several characteristics of the job such as autonomy and skill variety. In a longitudinal study, Watson and Slack (1993) also found that PA was positively related to overall job satisfaction at two periods of time. More recently, Thoresen and Judge (1997) reviewed 29 studies exploring the PA–job satisfaction link and 41 in which the NA–job satisfaction link was examined, finding overall true score correlations of .52 and −.40, respectively.

Though research has strongly supported the relationship between affect and job satisfaction, some questions about this linkage can be raised. One concern is common method bias, because both the PANAS and measures of job satisfaction contain evaluative overtones and are usually measured on a single questionnaire. A second problem concerns the theoretical meaning of the PANAS. When most people think of affect, adjectives such as happy, sad, cheerful, or pleased are brought to mind. Yet none of these pleasantness items are included in PANAS. Included instead are items that are higher in activation as well as positive/negative evaluative tone. For example, the adjectives for positive affect (the PA scale) include items such as interested, excited, enthusiastic, and attentive. The adjectives for negative affect (the NA scale) contain items such as upset, distressed, nervous, and scared. Thus, as Larsen and Diener (1992) and Russell and Barrett (1999) noted, what Watson and his colleagues have termed positive and negative affect are rather stylized (or complex) representations of emotion rather than a direct scaling of pleasant and unpleasant states.[2]

A third and perhaps more fundamental issue raised by research on positive and negative affect concerns the dimensionality of emotion itself. Watson and his colleagues have argued for a bivariate model of affect in which PA and NA are relatively independent dimensions rather than two ends of a single bipolar scale. Their position has been supported by a number of empirical studies using questionnaire measures such as PANAS (Watson & Tellegen, 1985; Watson & Tellegen, 1999). Also bolstering the bivariate position are neuropsychological studies showing that positive (appetitive) and negative (aversive) processing take place in different locations of the brain, thereby consisting of physiologically separable processes (e.g., Gray, 1994).

---

[2]For a simple solution to this problem, it is possible to add pleasantness items as an addendum to the PANAS items or use other questionnaire scales such as Tellegen's well-being scale.

Two arguments have been leveled against the bivariate model of affect. First, with respect to studies using questionnaire data, Green, Salovey and Truax (1999) have noted that much of the empirical evidence supporting the independence of positive and negative affect is likely the result of measurement error and scaling artifacts. With regard to neurological research on affect, Cacioppo and his colleagues have noted that there may be important differences between physiological and psychological sources of affect (Cacioppo & Berntson, 1999; Cacioppo, Gardner, & Berntson, 1999). Just because positive and negative stimuli may be processed by different physiological systems does not mean that they cannot be cognitively integrated into a single evaluative process. They argue that all combinations of positive and negative activation are cognitively combined into a net predisposition toward a particular object, and that there may be evolutionary importance for people to aggregate preferences and organize action toward (and away from) external objects.

MORE DISTAL PREDICTORS

While there has been substantial debate over the best way to represent the construct of affect, less consideration has been given to whether affect should itself remain the focus of dispositional research. On the one hand, it can be argued that affective disposition is so close conceptually to job satisfaction as to make theoretical predictions uninteresting, if not somewhat tautological (Staw, 1985). On the other hand, the emphasis on affect may have been appropriate given the defensive position in which dispositional researchers have been placed. After being dismissed as largely irrelevant to the prediction of individual attitudes and behavior, dispositional researchers have had little incentive to set an extremely high hurdle for demonstrating effects. Now that dispositional effects have become more widely accepted, however, the time may be right for making more distal predictions.

One possibility for moving research in a more distal direction might entail joining the recent trend toward broader personality constructs such as the Big Five (e.g., Barrick & Mount, 1991; McCrae & John, 1992). Because neuroticism has generally been found to predict negative emotional states, and extraversion has been predictive of positive emotions (Costa & McCrae, 1980), one could logically rely on components of the Big Five as dispositional predictors of job satisfaction. Such a strategy may still not bring much separation between independent and dependent variables, however. Any empirical data resulting from this approach would again demonstrate interrelationships of closely related constructs—emotional reaction toward general stimuli (be it measured by PA, NA, neuroticism, or extraversion) and an emotional reaction toward a more specific stimulus such as satisfaction with one's job. Thus, the Big Five solution may beg the theoretical question of what really underlies the dispositional approach to job satisfaction.

An alternative path toward a distal yet dispositional explanation of job satisfaction is suggested by research on human happiness. If predictors of happiness can be found, then it might be assumed that these same determinants influence job satisfaction via their impact on a person's affective disposition. It might also be assumed that predictors of happiness influence job satisfaction directly if they tap processes that generally enhance or diminish affective states.

Judge and Locke (1993) took this approach in examining the effects of dysfunctional thought processes on subjective well-being. Drawing on Beck's (1987) cognitive theory of depression, Judge and Locke argued that dysfunctional thoughts make people vulnerable to depression because they undermine self-worth. To tap dysfunctional thought processes, they administered the Dysfunctional Attitude Survey (Weissman & Beck, 1978) to a sample of university clerical workers. The survey measures tendencies for perfectionism (e.g., "A person should do well on everything he or she undertakes"), overgeneralization (e.g., "If I do a bad thing, it means I am a bad person"), dependence on others (e.g., "If whom I care about do not care for me, it is awful"), and desire for social approval (e.g., "I often do things to please others rather than myself"). Judge and Locke also measured dysfunctional thought processes about one's job by posing a series of work scenarios portraying dysfunctional thinking, asking employees how descriptive these scenarios were of them.

The results of the Judge and Locke (1993) study showed dysfunctional thought processes to be negatively related to subjective well-being as well as having an adverse impact on job satisfaction. A major strength of this study was the researchers' efforts to minimize common method variance (i.e., assessments of dysfunctional thought processes were obtained from significant others such as a spouse, close friend, or sibling). However, Judge and Locke's efforts to separate dysfunctional thought processes concerning job and life events can be questioned. If dysfunctional thought processes are really a fundamental cause of human unhappiness and are dispositional in nature, it is unlikely that thoughts about work would differ (stylistically) from those about other aspects of life. Only if dysfunctional thinking is situationally determined would such a division be theoretically useful.

Because dysfunctional thought processes were found to foster negative affect, perhaps it is also possible to isolate mental processes that induce happiness. Taylor and Brown (1988) pointed to the functional nature of self-illusions in their summary of mental health determinants. Whereas most people engage in a wide array of self-protective or ego-defensive biases (Greenwald, 1980; Kunda, 1990), this tendency tends to be diminished in those suffering from depression (e.g., Alloy & Abramson, 1982). In fact, Sackeim and Gur (1979) found negative correlations between measures of self-deception and psychopathology (e.g., depression, neuroticism), while Paulhus (1986) found positive relations between self-deception and variables such as self-esteem, need for achievement, and internal locus of control. Thus, it appears that people who are adept at self-serving biases are able to enhance life satisfaction by either blocking threatening information or reconstructing this feedback so that it is less damaging to the self.

Erez and Judge (1994) tested the self-deception hypothesis in the context of work roles. They administered both general and job-related measures of self-deception (Paulhus, 1984) to a sample of nonacademic employees. Self-deception was posited to be directly related to subjective well-being, whereas job self-deception was predicted to be a significant determinant of job satisfaction. Both hypotheses were upheld by Erez and Judge's analyses.

More recently, Judge, Locke, and Durham (1997) moved beyond self-deception and dysfunctional thought processes to argue that some core self-evaluations influence people's appraisal of job conditions. Included in this core are notions of self-esteem, generalized self-efficacy, neuroticism, and locus of control. So far, several studies have supported relationships between these four variables and job satisfaction (Judge & Bono, 2001; Judge, Bono, & Locke, 2000; Judge, Locke, Durham, & Kluger, 1998). However, one must ask why these four particular variables should be given priority over other psychological constructs. Are there special advantages in pursuing these core variables rather than the personality dimensions posed by other authors or those already summarized by the Big Five? One must also question whether these core dimensions are themselves independent, because there would seem to be much conceptual overlap among self-esteem, self-efficacy, locus of control, and neuroticism. These and other questions await further research.

STATUS OF EXTANT RESEARCH

As can be seen from this overview, many approaches have been taken toward a dispositional theory of job satisfaction. The initial approach was to demonstrate consistency in attitudes over time and situation, without specifying exactly what might be behind such consistency. Subsequent research attempted to fill in the "black box" of dispositionalism by categorizing people on the basis of their general emotional tendencies. PANAS descriptors were used to depict the person's emotional state over long as well as short periods of time. Broader categories of personality, be they aspects of the Big Five or core evaluations, have also been used as dispositional predictors of satisfaction. Although each of these approaches has furthered our knowledge of the dispositional causes of job satisfaction, none can yet claim victory in this pursuit. What is still missing is a mapping of the processes underlying dispositional influence—that is, how properties or tendencies of the person get translated into the experiences and evaluations comprising job satisfaction.

DISPOSITIONAL PROCESSES OF JOB SATISFACTION

Motowidlo (1996) provided a valuable starting point for specifying dispositional processes underlying job satisfaction. He described job satisfaction as a series of information processing steps, noting how individual differences influence the assessment, recall, and reporting of job attitudes. Judge and Larsen (2001) also described a process model of job satisfaction. They outlined how personality variables both moderate and mediate the relationship between environmental stimuli and affective responses such as job satisfaction. I will draw heavily on both the Motowidlo and Judge–Larsen models in illustrating how individual differences can influence job satisfaction, though my formulation (Figure 7.1) is a bit different than either of these prior presentations.

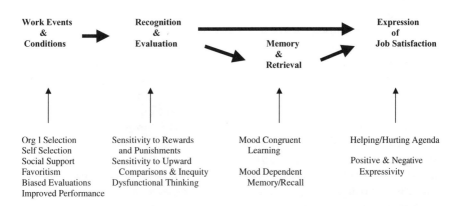

FIG. 7.1   The experience and expression of job satisfaction.

The Nature of the Situation

Since its inception, dispositional research has been subjected to criticism over whether situational variables have been adequately controlled or held constant (e.g., Davis-Blake & Pfeffer, 1989). As a result, most dispositional studies have either assumed sampled jobs to be approximately equal on variables such as scope, responsibility, status, and pay, or some attempt has been made to statistically control for such differences.

In the effort to compensate for situational differences, what is often overlooked is the fact that effects of personality may be largely expressed through alteration of the organizational environment (Schneider, 1987). Organizations consciously (and unconsciously) select individuals on the basis of individual differences, be they demographic or psychological in nature (Judge, 1992). Corporations try to achieve fit (Chatman, 1991) or replicate themselves in terms of background and personality (Kanter, 1977), while applicants often self-select themselves into organizations on the basis of similarity.

Previous work in organizational psychology suggests several ways in which affective disposition might influence the work situation. First, research has shown that positive people are more likely to get selected for desirable jobs. In several experimental studies, subjects were shown videotapes of simulated job interviews in which an applicant displayed varying levels of emotion such as smiling, hand gesturing, and eye contact. Results showed that interviewees displaying positive emotion were more likely to be rated as desirable future employees (e.g., Imada & Hakel, 1977; McGovern & Tinsley, 1978; Rasmussen, 1984). Similar experimental studies have found that a person's work performance was rated higher if he or she displayed positive affect, satisfaction, and was likeable (Cardy & Dobbins, 1986; Krzystofiak, Cardy, & Newman, 1988; Smither, Collins, & Buda, 1989).

Not all the benefits going to positive individuals may be due to systematic bias or favoritism, however. Several studies have shown that those with more positive affect may actually perform better in organizations. Staw, Sutton, and Pelled (1994) found significant effects of positive affect on changes in supervisory ratings and pay over time. Wright and Staw (1999) also showed that dispositional affect could predict changes in performance in a longitudinal study with four measurement periods. Finally, a laboratory study by Staw and Barsade (1993) demonstrated advantages for those with positive affect in terms of decision skills and interpersonal performance. Thus, at least some of the benefits going to positive individuals may be merited.

From the research outlined here, one can conclude that the work environment is a decidedly different place for those with positive and negative affect. Positive individuals are not only likely to be given preference in the job selection process, but also provided with a more munificent environment once they are on the job. Positive individuals may actually perform better—yet even if they do not, they are generally given the benefit of the doubt. Such advantages may not be optimal from either an efficiency or fairness point of view, but they are more than an alternative explanation or methodological artifact to be controlled by researchers. They are a principal means by which individual dispositions get expressed in organizations.

Recognition and Evaluation of the Situation

Though the work situation can be quite different for those with positive and negative affect, there may remain dispositional effects even after the context has been controlled. One reason is that people vary in their sensitivity to positive and negative events in their environment. For example, Larsen and his colleagues (Larsen & Ketlear, 1989, 1991; Rusting & Larsen, 1997; Zelenski & Larsen, 1999) found that individual differences in extraversion relate to differential susceptibility to positive mood inductions, and neuroticism relates to sensitivity to negative mood inductions (via false performance feedback). In a field experiment, Brief, Butcher, and Roberson (1995) also found that people with negative affect were less sensitive to a positive event at work, that their mood was not as easily elevated following a positive experience as those who were more dispositionally positive.

The role of dispositional affect in people's reactions to work environments is also being tested in a longitudinal field study. Jennifer Chatman, Ariel Malka, and I asked MBA students about the ideal jobs they would like to have following graduation, using relatively neutral descriptors such as the amount of travel, social interaction, speed of decision making, and the overlap between the job and personal life. Several years after graduation, we again surveyed these former students about the nature of the jobs they actually held, using the same set of job descriptors. It is predicted that there will be significant effects of the work environment on reported job satisfaction, such that jobs are rated more positively when they are closer to one's ideal. It is also predicted that there will be significant effects of positive affect (reported during MBA years) on job satisfaction, supporting a dispositional effect. Finally, we expect to find an interaction of disposition and environment on job satisfaction. For those who are low in positive affect, the nature of the job (how close it is to one's ideal) may be strongly related to satisfaction, whereas for those who are high in positive affect the nature of the job may be less influential. A positive disposition may serve to insulate the person from the slings and arrows of organizational life.

Why exactly do individuals differ in their reactions to organizational events and conditions? Some clues may be provided by the literature on depression. Such research shows that on-going negative affect is associated with tendencies to blame oneself for failures and to generalize from failure experiences (e.g., Peterson & Seligman, 1984), whereas more positive affect is facilitated by self-deception, ego-enhancement, and optimism (Taylor & Brown, 1988). Social comparisons may also be integrally involved with dispositional affect. In several experiments, Lyubomirsky and Ross (1997) found that unhappy people were more sensitive to social comparison information. These researchers found that the moods of unhappy people were substantially altered by whether they performed better or worse than a peer. In contrast, happy individuals seemed to heed social comparisons only when they could be used in a self-protective manner—that is, when negative performance could be buffered by the knowledge that a peer had done even worse.

Other researchers have turned to physiological processes for an explanation of why people respond the way they do to life events. Gray (1981, 1994) hypothesized that two separate neural systems are responsible for reactions to positive and negative stimuli. He argued that extraverts are differentially sensitive to cues of reward, while those classified as high in neuroticism are especially sensitive to punishment cues. Research has generally upheld these affective distinctions (Judge & Larsen, 2001). Using EEG measures of brain activity, it has been shown that positive affect is associated with left prefrontal activation, whereas negative affect is associated with right prefrontal activation (Davidson & Tomarken, 1989). Frontal cerebral asymmetry tends to reflect both current emotional states and one's predisposition to experience positive versus negative emotional states. That is, people with greater left side activation (at rest) generally report more intense emotional reactions to positive stimuli, whereas people with greater right side activation (at rest) generally display greater emotional reactions to negative stimuli (Tomarken, Davidson, & Henriques, 1990). It has also been shown that depressives tend to have heightened right hemispheric activation (compared to controls), and that people with brain damage to a particular hemisphere have excessive emotion of a corresponding (positive or negative) nature (Leventhal & Tomarken, 1986; Tomarken & Keener, 1998). Taken together, these findings provide a physiological basis for people's emotional reactions to positive and negative conditions in their environment.

MEMORY AND RETRIEVAL

Because inquiries about job satisfaction usually probe one's past as well as present reactions to a job, it is important to consider the interplay of emotion and memory in shaping job attitudes over time. Fortunately, prior research points to several systematic influences of emotion on memory. The first line of research pertains to the encoding of information or what Bower (1981) and his associates have termed *mood congruent learning*. Positive material may be better learned by people who are experiencing a positive emotional state and negative material learned better by those who are in a more negative state (e.g., Gilligan & Bower, 1984). Isen and Baron (1991) questioned whether this effect may be limited to the mood induction procedure used by Bower and his associates (hypnosis), and Leventhal and Tomarken (1986) have noted that the effects for positive emotion have been more consistent than for negative emotional states (depression seems to impede memory in general). Less controversial have been studies showing the influence of affect on information retrieval. As noted by Isen and Baron, several studies have shown that when positive affect has been induced at the time of recall, people are better able to remember positively valenced material.

If we make the simple assumption that people who differ on dispositional affect have varying tendencies to experience positive and negative emotional states, then it is likely that there will be overall effects of disposition on both encoding and retrieval. Positive individuals are more likely to remember good things about their jobs (e.g., their positive experiences in performing tasks and interacting with others), whereas negative individuals may tend to remember unpleasant or disturbing events in the workplace. We might also expect that the more ambiguous or conflicting the stimuli at work, the greater would be the influence of one's affective disposition on encoding and retrieval. Likewise, the more faint is the memory of prior work experiences, the greater might a person's current affective state influence his or her recall. Finally, because most people are somewhat positive in affective tone, one might expect to find a generally positive bias for memory over time. The longer time passes, the more positively people may tend to view the work experience. Such a prediction fits with the long-standing finding that tenure is positively correlated with job satisfaction (Price, 1977). It also fits Mitchell, Thompson, Peterson, and Cronk's (1997) recent finding that vacations are remembered more positively than they were actually experienced.

THE EXPRESSION OF JOB SATISFACTION

To this point I have assumed that inquiries about job satisfaction, be they written, verbal or observational in nature, are valid representations of the person's emotional state. Although there are numerous and well-known sources of error in attitudinal measurement (e.g., Selltiz, Wrightsman, & Cook, 1976), a seldom discussed issue is whether individuals choose to disclose their psychological state.

Motowidlo (1966) called attention to the question of volition in reports of job satisfaction. He noted that when surveys are not anonymous, job satisfaction could be inflated out of fear of retaliation from management. He also noted that reports of job satisfaction could be used to aid or punish supervisors, especially if they are viewed by higher management. Thus, the presumed purpose of a satisfaction survey and its sponsorship (e.g., by management vs. union) might substantially influence what is reported. Moreover, because affect and helping behavior are empirically linked (George & Brief, 1992), it is likely that affective disposition will contribute to the voluntary disclosure of job satisfaction.

Gross and John (1997, 1998) demonstrated that people differ systematically in their expression of emotion. Given the same positive or negative stimuli (such as films designed to evoke amusement or sadness), differences in expressivity were found to predict the display of sadness and happiness. Personality differences in extraversion were also found to be strongly related to positive expressivity, whereas neuroticism was strongly related to negative expressivity (Gross & John, 1998). Thus, it is likely that individual differences in affect not only color the person's experience of particular emotional states but also their expression.

Because of cultural norms about emotion (or feeling rules), one cannot expect all emotions to be expressed equally. In American culture, for example, it is often easier to express positive than negative emotions, and this may be one of the reasons why reported job satisfaction is generally high in the United States. However, given the tendency to express positive rather than negative emotions, we might also expect individual differences in expressivity to be more of a factor when people face negative rather than positive circumstances. Gross, John, and Richards (2000) found exactly such a pattern. Although there was some effect of expressivity on displays of amusement following exposure to a comedy film, they found much greater effects of expressivity on displays of sadness following exposure to a film with tragic content.

In a now classic study, Hochschild (1983) noted that service workers are often required to express positive emotion, even when such an expression is not a reflection of their true emotional state. Moreover, she argued that differences between felt and expressed emotion constitute an aversive state, which she labeled *emotional dissonance*. Other scholars have taken a more sanguine view of the management of emotions, however. Richards and Gross (2000) hypothesized that the management of emotion is less costly to the individual if it comes before a negative experience (through reappraisal) rather than after it is experienced (through suppression). Others have recognized self-regulation of emotion as a key component of emotional intelligence (Mayer & Salovoy, 1993), positive mental health (Taylor & Brown, 1988), and effective social behavior (Eisenberg, Fabes, Guthrie, & Reiser, 2000; Goffman, 1969). Thus, it may not be accurate to describe the match between felt and expressed emotion as a uniformly positive or negative condition.

THE PROCESS OF JOB SATISFACTION

As I have described it, the process of job satisfaction may comprise several informational steps. First, there is exposure to various events and conditions, be they interpersonal or task related. Then there is recognition and evaluation of these events and conditions. These steps are followed by the storage of affectively laden materials as well as the recall of prior positive and negative experiences. Finally, satisfaction is reported or expressed to others, either in the form of quantitative surveys or qualitative observations.

This description of the process of job attitudes may, of course, be an oversimplification. Not every step illustrated in the causal model may be undertaken when one expresses job satisfaction, and the sequencing of informational steps may not always follow such a precise or chronological order. What one sees in the work world could, for example, be influenced by what is remembered from the past, and the events with which one must cope may be a product of the emotions displayed in a previous encounter. Thus, the causal paths I have specified in this paper should be taken as typical rather than exclusive routes toward job satisfaction. The sequence of cognitive events shown in Fig. 7.1 should be considered a rough guide to the process of job satisfaction rather than a definitive statement on how satisfaction arises and develops over time. As future research accumulates on this attitudinal process, a more precise theoretical mapping should emerge.

SUMMARY AND CONCLUSION

Much of this essay has been devoted to a chronology of thinking about job attitudes. I noted that the fields of organizational psychology and organizational behavior had long portrayed both the person and the work environment as important determinants of job attitudes. This dual perspective, as well as the interactionalism inherent in theories by scholars like Maslow, Locke, and Hackman and Oldham, gave way to a more extreme form of situationalism once the cognitive revolution took hold in psychology. Led by Salancik and Pfeffer, organizational researchers systematically replaced individuals and working conditions as principal determinants of job attitudes. People and places were, in a sense, overwritten by a social construction of reality in which external social agents (such as coworkers, leaders, and even the organization's culture) became the primary determinants of attitudes.

In the last decade, there has been a resurrection of the person in organizational research. From conceptual arguments put forth by theorists such as Weiss and Adler as well as Schneider, to empirical contributions by researchers such as Arvey, Brief, George, and Staw, dispositional research is once again flourishing. All of this activity has failed to silence confirmed critics such as Davis-Blake and Pfeffer, however. They still maintain that dispositional research is flawed because of its inability to hold all situational variables constant, and they caution against sinister implications of this research on decisions concerning personnel selection and resource allocation. As noted throughout this paper (and by House, Shane, & Herold, 1996), dispositional researchers have already addressed many aspects of these (inherently contradictory) hurdles. Still, it should be recognized that control of all exogenous variables can never be achieved in field research. Likewise, the achievement of a fully ethical organization will always depend more on a firm's set of values than the use of particular criteria in selection and resource allocation decisions. Therefore, rather than working from a defensive posture in which real and/or imaginary critics are served, it is time for dispositional researchers to set their own agenda for understanding the role of personality in organizational settings.

With luck, this paper can help shape the agenda for future research on at least one aspect of dispositional research. By reviewing the available literature and formulating a summary model, I have tried to show how dispositional affect can be a theoretically and empirically robust explanation of job attitudes. Although a person's affective disposition may not be the only individual difference relevant to job attitudes, it is, in my view, one of the key determinants. What is experienced in the workplace, how one evaluates it, how it is remembered over time, and how it is expressed, can all depend on one's affective disposition. In these and other ways, people really do make the place.

REFERENCES

Alloy, L. G., & Abramson, L. Y. (1982). Learned helplessness, depression, and the illusion of control. *Journal of Personality and Social Psychology, 42,* 1114–1126.

Aries, E. J., Gold, C., & Weigel, R. H. (1983). Disposition and situational influences on dominance behavior in small groups. *Journal of Personality and Social Psychology, 44,* 770–786.

Arvey, R. D., Bouchard, T. J., Segal, N. L., & Abraham, L. M. (1989). Job satisfaction: Environmental and genetic components. *Journal of Applied Psychology, 74,* 187–192.

Barrick, M. R., & Mount, M. K. (1991). The Big Five personality dimensions and job performance: A meta-analysis. *Personnel Psychology, 44,* 1–26.

Beck, A. T. (1987). Cognitive models of depression. *Journal of Cognitive Psychotherapy, 1,* 5–37.

Bell, N. E., & Staw, B. M. (1989). People as sculptors versus sculptor: The roles of personality and personal control in organizations. In M. B. Arthur, D. T. Hall, B. S. Lawrence (Eds.), *The Handbook of Career Theory* (pp. 232–251). New York: Cambridge University Press.

Block, J. (1971), in collaboration with Norma Haan. *Lives through time.* Berkeley, CA: Bancroft.

Block, J. (1977). Advancing the science of personality: Paradigmatic shift or improving the quality of research? In D. Magnusson and N. Endler (Eds.), *Personality at the crossroads: Current issues in interactional psychology* (pp. 37–63). Hillsdale, N.J.: Erlbaum.

Bouchard, T. J., Jr., Lykken, D. T., McGue, M., Segal, N. L., & Tellegen, A. (1990). Sources of human psychological differences: The Minnesota study of twins reared apart. *Science, 250*, 223–250.

Bower, G. H. (1981). Mood and memory. *American Psychologist, 36*, 129–148.

Brief, A. P., Butcher, A., & Roberson, L. (1995). Cookies, disposition, and job attitudes: The effects of positive mood inducing events and negative affectivity on job satisfaction in a field experiment. *Organizational Behavior and Human Decision Processes, 62*, 55–62.

Cacioppo, J. T., & Berntson, G. G. (1999). The affect system: Architecture and operating characteristics. *Current Directions in Psychological Science, 8*, 133–137.

Cacioppo, J. T., Gardner, W. L., & Berntson, G. G. (1999). The affect system has parallel and integrative processing components: Form follows function. *Journal of Personality and Social Psychology, 76*, 839–855.

Cardy, R. L., & Dobbins, G. H. (1986). Affect and appraisal accuracy: Liking as an integral dimension in evaluation performance. *Journal of Applied Psychology, 71*, 672–678.

Chatman, J. A. (1991). Matching people and organizations: Selection and socialization in public accounting firms. *Administrative Science Quarterly, 36*, 459–484.

Clausen, J. A. (1985). *Life course: A sociological perspective.* Upper Saddle River, N.J.: Pearson Education.

Costa, P. T., & McCrae, R. R. (1980). Influence of extraversion and neuroticism on subjective well-being: Happy and unhappy people. *Journal of Personality and Social Psychology, 38*, 668–678.

Costa, P. T., McCrae, R. R., & Zonderman, A. B. (1987). Environmental and dispositional influences on well-being: Longitudinal follow-up of an American national sample. *British Journal of Psychology, 78*, 299–306.

Cropanzano, R., & James, K. (1990). Some methodological considerations for the behavior genetic analysis of work attitudes. *Journal of Applied Psychology, 75*, 433–439.

Davidson, R. J., & Tomarken, A. J. (1989). Laterality and emotion: An electrophysiological approach. In F. Boller & J. Grafman (Eds.), *Handbook of neuropsychology* (pp. 419–441). Amsterdam: Elsevier.

Davis-Blake, A., & Pfeffer, J. (1989). Just a mirage: The search for dispositional effects in organizational research. *Academy of Management Review, 14*, 385–400.

Eisenberg, N., Fabes, R. A., Guthrie, I. K., Reiser, M. (2000). Dispositional emotionality and regulation: Their role in predicting quality of social functioning. *Journal of Personality and Social Psychology, 78*, 136–157.

Epstein, S. (1979). The stability of behavior: I. On predicting most of the people much of the time. *Journal of Personality and Social Psychology, 37*, 1097–1126.

Erez, A., & Judge, T. A. (1994). *Dispositional source of job satisfaction: The role of self-deception* (Working paper 94-14). Ithaca, N.Y.: New York School of Industrial and Labor Relations, Cornell University.

George J. M. (1989). Mood and absence. *Journal of Applied Psychology, 74*, 314–324.

George, J. M., & Brief, A. P. (1992). Feeling good-doing good: A conceptual analysis of the mood at work-organizational spontaneity relationship. *Psychological Bulletin, 112*, 310–329.

Gerhart, B. (1987). How important are dispositional factors as determinants of job satisfaction: Implications for job design and other personnel programs. *Journal of Applied Psychology, 72*, 366–373.

Gilligan, S. G., & Bower, G. H. (1984). Cognitive consequences of emotional arousal. In C. E. Izard, J. Kagan, & R. G. Zajonc (Eds.), *Emotions, cognition, and behavior.* New York: Cambridge University Press.

Goffman, E. (1969). *Strategic interaction.* Philadelphia: University of Pennsylvania Press.

Goiten, B. (1977). Identifying sources of instability in measures of working conditions and work-related attitudes and behaviors. In R. P. Quinn, *Effectiveness in work roles: Employee responses to work environments* (pp. 251–366). University of Michigan, Ann Arbor.

Gray, J. A. (1981). A critique of Eysenck's theory of personality. In H. J. Eysenck (Ed.), *A model for personality* (pp. 246–276). New York: Springer.

Gray, J. A. (1994). Personality dimensions and emotion systems. In P. Ekman & R. J. Davidson (Eds.), *The nature of emotion: Fundamental questions* (pp. 329–331). New York: Oxford University Press.

Green, D. P., Salovey, P., & Truax, K. M. (1999). Static, dynamic, and causative bipolarity of affect. *Journal of Personality and Social Psychology, 76*, 856–867.

Greenwald, A. G. (1980). The totalitarian ego: Fabrication and revision of personal history. *American Psychologist, 35*, 603–618.

Griffen, R. W. (1983). Objective and social sources of information in task redesign: A field experiment. *Administrative Science Quarterly, 28*, 184–200.

Gross, J. J., & John, O. P. (1997). Revealing feelings: Facets of emotional expressivity in self-reports, peer ratings, and behavior. *Journal of Personality and Social Psychology, 72*, 435–448.

Gross, J. J., & John, O. P. (1998). Mapping the domain of emotional expressivity: Multi-method evidence for a hierarchical model. *Journal of Personality and Social Psychology, 74*, 170–191.

Gross, J. J., John, O. P., & Richards, J. M. (2000). The dissociation of emotion expression from emotion experience: A personality perspective. *Personality and Social Psychology Bulletin, 26*, 712–726.

Guilford, J. P. (1965). *Fundamental statistics in psychology and education.* New York: McGraw-Hill.

Hackman, J. R., & Oldham, G. R. (1975). Motivation trough the design of work: Test of a theory. *Organizational Behavior and Human Performance, 16*, 250–279.

Hackman, J. R., Oldham, G., Janson, R., & Purdy, K. (1975). A new strategy for job enlargement. *California Management Review, 17*, 57–71.

Hall, D. T., & Nougaim, K. E. (1968). An examination of Maslow's need hierarchy in an organizational setting. *Organizational Behavior and Human Performance, 3*, 12–35.

Herzberg, F. (1966). *Work and the nature of man.* Cleveland: World.

Hochschild, A. R. (1983). *The managed heart.* Berkeley, CA: University of California Press.

House, R. J., Shane, S. A., & Herold, D. M. (1996). Rumors of the death of dispositional research are vastly exaggerated. *Academy of Management Review, 21*, 203–224.

House, R. J., & Wigdor, L. A. (1967). Herzberg's dual-factor theory of job satisfaction and motivation: A review of the evidence and a criticism. *Personnel Psychology, 20*, 369–389.

Imada, A. S., & Hakel, M. D. (1977). Influence of nonverbal communication and rater proximity on impressions and decisions in simulated employment interviews. *Journal of Applied Psychology, 62*, 295–300.

Isen, A. M., & Baron, R. A. (1991). Positive affect as a factor in organizational behavior. In L. L. Cummings & B. M. Staw (Eds.) *Research in organizational behavior:* Vol. 13 (pp. 1–53), Greenwich, CN: JAI.

Judge, T. A. (1992). The dispositional perspective in human resources research. In G. R. Ferris & K. M. Rowland (Eds.), *Research in personnel and human resources management:* Vol. 10 (pp. 31–72), Greenwich, CN: JAI.

Judge, T. A., & Bono, J. E. (2001). Relationship of core self-evaluations traits—self-esteem, generalized self-efficacy, locus of control, and emotional stability—with job satisfaction and job performance: A meta-analysis. *Journal of Applied Psychology, 86*, 80–92.

Judge, T. A., Bono, J. E., & Locke, E. A. (2000). Personality and job satisfaction: The mediating role of job characteristics. *Journal of Applied Psychology, 85*, 237–249.

Judge, T. A., & Larsen, R. L. (2001). Dispositional source of job satisfaction: A review and theoretical extension. *Organizational Behavior and Human Decision Processes, 86*, 67–98.

Judge, T. A., & Locke, E. A. (1993). Effect of dysfunctional thought processes on subjective well-being and job satisfaction. *Journal of Applied Psychology, 78*, 475–490.

Judge, T. A., Locke, E. A., & Durham, C. C. (1997). The dispositional causes of job satisfaction: A core evaluations approach. *Research in Organizational Behavior, 19*, 151–188.

Judge, T. A., Locke, E. A., Durham, C. C., & Kluger, A. N. (1998). Dispositional effects on job and life satisfaction: The role of core evaluations. *Journal of Applied Psychology, 83*, 17–34.

Kanter, R. M. (1977). *Men and women of the corporation.* New York, NY: Basic Books.

Krzystofiak, F., Cardy, R. C., & Newman, J. (1988). Implicit personality and performance appraisal: The influence of trait inferences on evaluations of behavior. *Journal of Applied Psychology, 73*, 515–521.

Kunda, Z. (1990). The case of motivated reasoning. *Psychological Bulletin, 108*, 480–498.

Larsen, R. J., & Diener, E. (1992). Problems and promises with the circumplex model of emotion. *Review of Personality and Social Psychology, 13*, 25–59.

Larsen, R. J., & Ketelaar, T. (1989). Extraversion, neuroticism, and susceptibility to positive and negative mood induction procedures. *Personality and Individual Differences, 10*, 1221–1228.

Larsen, R. J., & Ketelaar, T. (1991). Personality and susceptibility to positive and negative emotional states. *Journal of Personality and Social Psychology, 61*, 132–140.

Lawler, E. E., & Suttle, J. L. (1972). A causal correlational test of the need hierarchy concept. *Organizational Behavior and Human Performance, 7*, 265–287.

Leventhal, H., & Tomarken, A. J. (1986). Emotion: Today's problems. *Annual Review of Psychology, 37*, 56–610.

Levin, I., & Stokes, J. P. (1989). Dispositional approach to job satisfaction: Role of negative affectivity. *Journal of Applied Psychology, 74*, 752–758.

Locke, E. A. (1976). The nature and causes of job satisfaction. In M. Dunnette (Ed.), *Handbook of industrial and organizational psychology.* Chicago: Rand McNally.

Lyubomirsky, S., & Ross, L. (1997). Hedonic consequences of social comparison: A contrast of happy and unhappy people. *Journal of Personality and Social Psychology, 73*, 1141–1157.

Magnusson, D., & Endler, N. S. (1977). Interactional psychology: Present status and future prospects. In D. Magnusson & N. Endler (Eds.), *Personality at the crossroads: Current issues in interactional psychology.* Hillsdale, NJ: Lawrence Erlbaum Associates, Inc.

Maslow, A. H. (1954). *Motivation and personality.* New York: Harper & Row.

Maslow, A. H. (1970). *Motivation and personality* (2nd ed.). New York: Harper & Row.

Mayer, J. D., & Salovey, P. (1993). The intelligence of emotional intelligence. *Intelligence, 17*, 433–442.

McCrae, R. R., & John, O. P. (1992). An introduction to the five-factor model and its applications. *Journal of Personality, 60*, 175–215.

McGovern, T. V., & Tinsley, H. E. (1978). Interviewer evaluations of interviewee nonverbal behavior. *Journal of Vocational Behavior, 13*, 163–171.

Mischel, W. (1968). *Personality and assessment.* New York: Wiley.

Mischel, W., & Peake, P. K. (1982). Beyond déjà vu in the search for cross-situational consistency. *Psychological Review, 90*, 730–755.

Mitchell, T. R., Thompson, L., Peterson, E., & Cronk, R. (1997). Temporal adjustments in the evaluation of events. *Journal of Experimental and Social Psychology, 33*, 421–448.

Monson, T. C., Hesley, J. W., & Chernick, L. (1982). Specifying when personality traits can and cannot predict behavior: An alternative to abandoning the attempt to predict single act criteria. *Journal of Personality and Social Psychology, 43*, 385–399.

Motowidlo, S. J. (1996). Orientation toward the job and organization. In K. R. Murphy (Ed.), *Individual differences and behavior in organizations* (pp. 175–208). San Francisco: Jossey-Bass.

Oldham, G. R., & Hackman, J. R. (1980). Work design in the organizational context. In B. Staw and L. L. Cummings (Eds.), *Research in Organizational Behavior, 2*, 247–278.

O'Reilly, C. A., & Caldwell, D. F. (1979). Informational influence as a determinant of perceived task characteristics and job satisfaction. *Journal of Applied Psychology, 64,* 157–165.

Paulhus, D. L. (1984). Two-component models of socially desirable responding. *Journal of Personality and Social Psychology, 46,* 598–609.

Paulhus, D. L. (1986). Self-deception and impression management in test responses. In A. Angleitner & J. S. Wiggins (Eds.), *Personality assessment via questionnaire* (pp. 142–165). New York: Springer.

Peterson, C., & Seligman, M. (1984). Causal explanations as a risk factor for depression: Theory and evidence. *Psychological Review, 91,* 347–374.

Plomin, R., & Neiderhiser, J. M. (1992). Genetics and experience. *Current Directions in Psychological Science, 1,* 160–163.

Price, J. L. (1977). *The study of turnover.* Ames: Iowa State University Press.

Quinn, R. P. (1977). *Effectiveness in work roles: Employee responses to work environments.* University of Michigan, Ann Arbor.

Rasmussen, Jr., K. G. (1984). Nonverbal behavior, verbal behavior, resume credentials, and selection interview outcomes. *Journal of Applied Psychology, 69,* 551–556.

Richards, J. M., & Gross, J. J. (2000). Emotion regulation and memory: The cognitive costs of keeping one's cool. *Journal of Personality and Social Psychology, 79,* 410–424.

Russell, J. A., & Barrett, L. F. (1999). Core affect, prototypical emotional episodes, and other things called emotion: Dissecting the elephant. *Journal of Personality and Social Psychology, 76,* 805–816.

Rusting, C. L., & Larsen, R. J. (1997). Extraversion, neuroticism, and susceptibility to positive and negative affect: A test of two theoretical models. *Personality and Individual Differences, 22,* 607–612.

Sackeim, H. A., & Gur, R. C. (1979). Self-deception, other deception and self-reported psychopathology. *Journal of Consulting and Clinical Psychology, 47,* 213–215.

Salancik, G. R., & Pfeffer, J. (1977). An examination of need satisfaction models of job attitudes. *Administrative Science Quarterly, 22,* 427–456.

Salancik, G. R., & Pfeffer, J. (1978). A social information processing approach to job attitudes and task design. *Administrative Science Quarterly, 22,* 427–456.

Schein, E. H. (1983). The role of the founder in creating organizational culture. *Organizational Dynamics,* Summer, 13–28.

Schneider, B. (1983). Interactional psychology and organizational behavior. In L. L. Cummings & B. Staw (Eds.), *Research in Organizational Behavior, 5,* 1–31.

Schneider, B. (1987). The people make the place. *Personnel Psychology, 40,* 437–453.

Schneider, B., & Dachler, P. H. (1978). A note on the stability of the job description index. *Journal of Applied Psychology, 63,* 650–653.

Schneider, J., & Locke, E. A. (1971). A criticque of Herzberg's incident classification system and a suggested revision. *Organizational Behavior and Human Performance, 6,* 441–457.

Selltiz, C., Wrightsman, L. S., & Cook, S. W. (1976). *Research Methods in Social Relations* (3rd ed.). Holt, Rinehart & Winston.

Smither, J. W., Collins, H., & Buda, R. (1989). When ratee satisfaction influences performance evaluations: A case of illusory correlation. *Journal of Applied Psychology, 74,* 599–605.

Staw, B. M. (1985). Repairs on the road to relevance and rigor: Some unexplored issues in publishing organizational research. In P. Frost and L. L. Cummings (Eds.), *Publishing in the Organizational Sciences.* Homewood, IL: Irwin.

Staw, B. M., & Barsade, S. G. (1993). Affect and managerial performance: A test of the sadder-but-wiser vs. happier-and-smarter hypotheses. *Administrative Science Quarterly, 38,* 304–331.

Staw, B. M., Bell, N. E., & Clausen, J. A. (1986). The dispositional approach to job attitudes: A lifetime longitudinal test. *Administrative Science Quarterly, 31,* 56–77.

Staw, B. M., & Ross, J. (1985). Stability in the midst of change: A dispositional approach to job attitudes. *Journal of Applied Psychology, 70,* 469–480.

Staw, B. M., Sutton, R. I., & Pelled, L. H. (1994). Employee positive emotion and favorable outcomes at the workplace. *Organization Science, 5,* 51–71.

Steel, R. P., & Rentsch, J. R. (1997). The dispositional model of job attitudes revisited: Findings of a 10-year study. *Journal of Applied Psychology, 82,* 873–879.

Taylor, S. E., & Brown, J. D. (1988). Illusion and well-being: A social psychological perspective on mental health. *Psychological Bulletin, 103,* 193–210.

Tellegen, A., Lykken, D. T., Bouchard, T. J., Wilcox, K. J., Segal, N. L., & Rich, S. (1988). Personality similarity in twins reared apart and together. *Journal of Personality and Social Psychology, 54,* 1031–1039.

Thoresen, C. J., & Judge, T. A. (1997). *Trait affectivity and work-related attitudes and behaviors: A meta-analysis.* Paper presented at the annual convention of the American Psychological Association, Chicago, IL.

Tomarken, A. J., Davidson, R. J., & Henriques, J. B. (1990). Resting frontal brain asymmetry predicts affective responses to films. *Journal of Personality and Social Psychology, 59,* 791–801.

Tomarken, A. J., & Keener, A. D. (1998). Frontal brain asymmetry and depression: A self-regulatory perspective. *Cognition and Emotion, 12,* 387–420.

Watson, D. (1988). The vicissitudes of mood measurement: Effects of varying descriptors, time frames, and response formats on measures of positive and negative affect. *Journal of Personality and Social Psychology, 55,* 128–141.

Watson, D., & Clark, L. A., (1992). On traits and temperament: General and specific factors of emotional experience and their relation to the five-factor model. *Journal of Personality, 60,* 441–476.

Watson, D., Clark, L. A., & Tellegen, A. (1988). Development and validation of brief measures of positive and negative affect: The PANAS Scales. *Journal of Personality and Social Psychology, 54,* 1063–1070.

Watson, D., & Slack, A. K. (1993). General factors of affective temperament and their relation to job satisfaction over time. *Organizational Behavior and Human Decision Processes, 54,* 181–202.

Watson, D., & Tellegen, A. (1985). Toward a concensual structure of mood. *Psychological Bulletin, 98,* 219–225.

Watson, D., & Tellegen, A. (1999). Issues in dimensional structure of affect: Effects of descriptors, measurement error, and response formats. *Psychological Bulletin, 125,* 601–610.

Weiss, H. M., & Adler, S. (1984). Personality and organizational behavior. In B. Staw & L. L. Cummings (Eds.), *Research in Organizational Behavior, 6,* 1–50.

Weiss, H. M., & Shaw, J. B. (1979). Social influences on judgements about tasks. *Organizational Behavior and Human Performance, 24,* 126–140.

Weissman, A., & Beck, A. T. (1978). *Development and validation of the dysfunctional attitude scale.* Paper presented at the annual convention of the Association for Advancement of Behavior Therapy, Chicago.

White, S. F., & Mitchell, T. R. (1979). Job enrichment versus social cues: A comparison and competitive test. *Journal of Applied Psychology, 64,* 1–9.

Wright, T. A., & Staw, B. M. (1999). Affect and favorable work outcomes: Two longitudinal tests of the happy-productive worker theses, *Journal of Organizational Behavior, 20,* 1–23.

Zelenski, J. M., & Larsen, R. J. (1999). Susceptibility to affect: A comparison of three personality taxonomies. *Journal of Personality, 67,* 761–791.

8

Personality and Work-Related Distress

Jennifer M. George
Rice University

Arthur P. Brief
Tulane University

The study of how personality affects the emotional lives of workers is not new (Weiss & Brief, 2001). For example, Fisher and Hanna (1931), in their classic *The Dissatisfied Worker*, addressed the problem of emotional maladjustment, which they described as a variety of "disturbances of personality which affect individual adjustment in every phase of life" (Viteles, 1932, p. 586). In regard to this maladjustment, Fisher and Hanna observed that it "breeds within him [the worker] dissatisfaction and thwarts him in his search for happiness and success. Inasmuch as his feelings and emotions are inherent aspects of himself, he carries them with him, so to speak, into every situation he enters. Now, since he does not usually know the reason of his dissatisfaction, does not understand the why for and nature of his maladjustment, it is not surprising that he very frequently attaches or attributes it (his dissatisfaction) to his work or his working situation" (pp. vii–viii).

More than 50 years later, organizational researchers unknowingly advanced the same argument, relying on different language (e.g., Brief, Burke, George, Robinson, & Webster, 1988; Payne, 1988). Following the lead of personality psychologists (e.g., Watson & Clark, 1984), these researchers suggested that the personality trait of negative affectivity (or neuroticism) had the potential to influence self-reports of work-related distress. Here, our intent is to move beyond this perspective to a fuller consideration of the role of personality in work-related distress. We believe a broader view is needed because, all too often, the work-related distress literature has been characterized by rather petty disagreements over the specific role a particular personality construct plays. That is, the organizational literature does not adequately reflect the varied ways in which multiple aspects of personality influence the experience of work-related distress.

What is to come is dependent on two points of view, one pertaining to personality, the other to work-related distress. In the tradition of Allport (e.g., 1937), Cattell (e.g., 1965), and Eysenck (e.g., 1982), we generally assume that people possess broad dispositions (or traits) that predispose them to respond in particular ways in terms of their thoughts, feelings, and actions. Thus, our orientation toward personality is aligned more with trait approaches than, for example, with psychodynamic theory (e.g., Freud, 1933) or phenomenological approaches (e.g., Rogers, 1951). Therefore, our treatment of the relationship between personality and stress is limited. The second point of view that flavors this chapter is our concern with the whole person, not just with what has been called job-specific well-being (e.g., Warr, 1999). That is, we are interested in the circumstances of work (e.g., discrete events, chronic conditions) that may adversely affect people's lives in terms of impairing their subjective well-being (SWB; Brief & Atieh, 1987). (For a review of the SWB literature see, for example, Diener, Suh, Lucas, & Smith, 1999. For alternative approaches to the study of stress, see, for example, Baum, 1990; Cohen and Kessler, 1995; Kasl, 1996; and McGrath, 1970.) Thus, this chapter focuses on how personality influences the extent to which the workplace is a significant source of distress in life.

The chapter unfolds as follows. First, given the fact that personality has the potential to directly influence subjective well-being in life, we address theorizing and research on this relationship. Next, we explore several mechanisms through which personality may influence the extent to which experiences emanating from the workplace have the potential to impair psychological well-being. These mechanisms include the role that personality plays in the choice of settings and creation of the conditions of work, the influence of personality on the appraisal of and reactions to settings and conditions of work, and the role that personality plays in coping with distress emanating from the workplace. Lastly, we discuss implication of our analysis and directions for future research. Again, our intent is to help move the work-related distress literature forward by providing a portrayal of personality that more fully depicts its varied influences on how people experience their lives.

Before moving on to what was just outlined, a very brief comment on conceptual clarity in the stress literature may be in order. Although we believe readers will not find it difficult to infer accurately the meanings of the terms we will be using, they also will not encounter concept definitions that can be described as clear, precise, and widely accepted in the scholarly community. So, readers will not find a neatly packaged definition, for example, of *work-related distress*; rather, we will expect they can infer accurately that the term loosely refers to a reaction to work (e.g., anxiety or depression) that constitutes an impairment to one's well-being. This loose state of affairs in the stress literature recently has been addressed by Kasl (1996). He observed that key issues surrounding the concept of stress—for example, "How useful is it as a scientific concept?," "What is the optimal conceptualization?," and "How does it over-lap with other concepts?" (p. 13)—persist after decades of research; and, this persistence is associated with the fact that "[s]tress is obviously a broad, high-level construct which performs different functions for investigators from different disciplines. ... " (p. 14). For those readers who want to dig into this ambiguity, we suggest you start with Seyle (1971) for an historical account; move on to Schuler (1980) for an organizational perspective and, perhaps, a false sense of security; and, end up with Cohen and Kessler (1995) and Kasl for an accurate portrayal of where we now stand.

PERSONALITY AND SUBJECTIVE WELL-BEING

Subjective well-being (SWB), according to Diener et al. (1999), comprises three basic components: positive or pleasant affect (i.e., moods and emotions), negative or unpleasant affect, and life satisfaction (a cognitive evaluation).[1] Although the extent to which a person experiences positive and negative affect may be related to judgments of life satisfaction, life satisfaction assessments are conceptually and empirically distinct from the experience of positive and negative affective states (Andrews & Withey, 1976; Lucas, Diener, & Suh, 1996). Impairment of SWB can be indicated by the absence of positive affect in one's life, an abundance of negative affect in one's life, and/or to feelings of dissatisfaction with the circumstances and conditions of one's life.

In their recent review, Diener et al. (1999, p. 279) stated that "personality is one of the strongest and most consistent predictors of subjective well-being." Evidence in support of the influence of personality on SWB comes from at least three kinds of studies: investigations of the stability of SWB over time and across situations, research on the relation between personality traits and SWB, and studies exploring the effects of life events on SWB.

---

[1]It should be noted that we are sidestepping an important controversy that entails the structure of affect (e.g., Cacioppo, Gardner, & Berntson, 1999; Green, Salovy, & Truax, 1999; Russell & Barrett, 1999; Watson, Wiese, Vaidya, & Tellegen, 1999). Here, we assume it remains appropriate to rely on a two-dimensional (positive and negative) structure of affect (e.g., Watson, 2000; Watson & Tellegen, 1985).

Stability of SWB Over Time and Across Situations

Given the relative stability of personality traits over time (e.g., Costa & McCrae, 1988; McCrae & Costa, 1994; but also see Pervin, 1994), if personality is a causal influence on SWB, then SWB also should be relatively stable (Diener & Lucas, 1999). Operationally, this implies that positive and negative affective states as well as life satisfaction exhibit a degree of stability. Such a degree, in fact, has been demonstrated empirically (Watson, 2000). For example, Diener and Larsen (1984) collected momentary mood ratings from 42 students twice a day over a 6-week period. They then computed separate mean affect scores for the first and second halves of the rating period. The two mean positive affect scores correlated .79; and, the two mean negative affect scores correlated .81. Watson has constructively replicated (Lykken, 1968) these results and, in a similar vein, Headey and Wearing (1989) found that people eventually return to a baseline of positive and negative affect following the occurrence of good and bad events. The life satisfaction component of SWB also has been shown to exhibit a degree of stability. For example, correlations of over .50 between ratings of life satisfaction taken over 4 years apart have been reported, even when the two ratings were obtained from different sources (i.e., self and family/friends) (Magnus & Diener, 1991, as cited in Diener & Lucas. On the stability of SWB over time also see, for example, Spielberger, Gorsuch, Lushene, Vagg, and Jacobs, 1983; Watson and Clark, 1994; Watson, Clark, and Tellegen, 1988; Watson and Walker, 1996).

Although the issue of cross-situational consistency is more complex than that of longitudinal consistency, there is considerable evidence supporting the consistency of the effects of personality traits across a range of situations in which the traits can be expressed (e.g., Block, 1977; Buss & Craik, 1983; Caspi & Bem, 1990; Epstein, 1983). Correspondingly, it appears that indicators of SWB do exhibit a degree of stability across situations. For example, Diener and Larsen (1984), in the previously noted article, also observed that average levels of pleasant affect at work correlated .70 with average pleasant affect in recreation settings; and, average levels of negative affect at work correlated .74 with average negative affect in recreation settings.

In sum, given the relative stability of personality traits and a personality–SWB relationship, one would expect relative stability of SWB. Evoking a variety of evidence, we have shown that indicators of SWB, in fact, do exhibit a degree of stability across time and situations.

Personality Traits and SWB

Extensive evidence suggests that global dimensions of personality, namely neuroticism or negative affectivity (NA) and extraversion or positive affectivity (PA), are consistently related to SWB (DeNeve & Cooper, 1998; Diener & Lucas, 1999; Diener, Sandvik, Pavot, & Fujita, 1992).[2] The traits of NA and PA have been linked repeatedly to the experience of negative and positive affective states, respectively (e.g., Watson & Clark, 1992), two of the three components of SWB. Similarly, life satisfaction has been found to be positively related to PA and negatively related to NA (e.g., Hart, 1999). As Watson (2000, p. 182) concludes, "... individual differences in negative affective experience are strongly correlated with Neuroticism but are essentially unrelated to Extraversion; conversely, individual differences in positive affective experience are strongly correlated with Extraversion but only weakly related to Neuroticism."

In a study of monozygotic and dizygotic twins reared together and apart, Tellegen et al. (1988) found substantial heritabilities for PA and NA, which suggest that approximately 50% of the variance in personality is genetically determined. Results such as these, coupled with studies suggesting that personality is a key determinant of SWB, imply that SWB also has genetic components (Costa, McCrae, & Zonderman, 1987; but also see Veenhoven, 1994). Consistent with this reasoning, Tellegen et al. also found considerable heritabilities for a trait measure of well-being. Supporting the genetic underpinning of SWB is theorizing and research that suggest a biological basis for SWB. For example, Gray (1981, 1987) proposed that the behavioral activation system is that part of the central nervous system that is responsible for positive or pleasant affect; such states are experienced when signals of reward are detected by this system. Similarly, he posited that the behavioral inhibition system is the part of the brain that is responsible for negative or unpleasant affect; such states are experienced when signals of punishment are detected by this system. The sensitivity of these two systems results in individual differences in the tendency to experience the corresponding affective states. Aligned with this thinking, Larsen and Ketelaar (1991) found that people who were high on extraversion were more responsive to a positive mood induction and people who were high on neuroticism were more responsive to a negative mood induction (also see Brief, Butcher, & Roberson, 1995; Derryberry & Reed, 1994; Rusting & Larsen, 1997).

---

[2] Are extraversion and PA one and the same? Similarly, are neuroticism and NA analogous traits? These questions have received much attention in the literature and have been revisited recently by Watson (2000). In multiple data sets, neuroticism has been found to be related significantly to trait negative affect or NA and extraversion has been found to be related significantly to trait positive affect or PA (Meyer & Shack, 1989; Watson). Some researchers in this field have even suggested that the traits of neuroticism and extraversion actually should be relabeled to indicate the fact that they reflect dispositions towards negative and positive affect, respectively (e.g., Tellegen, 1985), and others have suggested that NA forms the core of neuroticism (e.g., Costa & McCrae, 1992) and PA is the essential core of extraversion (e.g., Watson & Clark, 1984, 1992, 1997).

Life Events and SWB

Suggesting that personality influences SWB by no means implies that situational influences or life events are unimportant. However, theorizing and research on the role of life events in SWB suggest that although life events do matter, their observed pattern of influence underscores a prominent role for personality in SWB. For example, Headey and Wearing (1991, 1992), whose research was noted in our discussion of the stability of SWB over time, have proposed a dynamic equilibrium model of SWB. They asserted that people tend to have a stable level of SWB; and, although life events may move a person away from this equilibrium level, the movement likely is temporary because of the influence of personality on the equilibrium level. Moreover, Headey and Wearing argued that personality influences the kinds of events people tend to experience.

Available research findings tend to support Headey and Wearing's (e.g., 1992) model. In terms of the posited influences of personality on life events, research indicates, for instance, that being high on extraversion results in the experience of more objective positive life events and being high on neuroticism results in the experience of more objective negative life events (Magnus, Diener, Fujita, & Pavot, 1993). Examples of objective events, according to Magnus et al. include "promotion/raise" and "parents gave me a major gift (over $1000 value)" (good events) and "fired/laid off" and "divorce/marital separation" (bad events). Evidence also indicates that personality influences self-reports of subjective life events (e.g., "had trouble with boss"; Brett, Brief, Burke, George, & Webster, 1990; Schroeder & Costa, 1984). (For more on the objective–subjective distinction, see, for example Frese & Zapf, 1988, and Kasl, 1996.) In total, ample evidence suggests, consistent with Headey & Wearing's (1992) thinking, that personality influences the occurrence and/or reporting of life events, either of which could affect SWB (e.g., Fergusson & Horwood, 1987; Headey, Glowacki, Holmstrom, & Wearing, 1985; Ormel & Wohlfarth, 1991). Later, we pick up a similar theme in considering the influence of personality on the choice of settings and creation of the conditions of work.

Research also suggests that people tend to revert to their equilibrium SWB levels rather quickly; thus, it seems that only relatively recent life events affect SWB. For example, Suh, Diener, and Fujita (1996) found that life events do not have much influence on SWB beyond a 3-month period. Such a result can be interpreted as indicating how adaptable people are (see Frederick & Loewenstein, 1999), even in response to life-changing events like a spinal cord injury or winning a lottery (e.g., Brickman, Coates, & Janoff-Bulman, 1978; Krause & Steinberg, 1997; Mehnert, Krause, Nadler, & Boyd, 1990).

Clearly, the theorizing and research discussed previously underscore the pervasive role that personality plays in SWB (e.g., Brief, Butcher, George, & Link, 1993; Costa et al., 1987; DeNeve & Cooper, 1998; Diener et al., 1999; Diener & Lucas, 1999). In fact, we have just touched the surface of an extensive and growing body of literature on the determinants of SWB, which attests to the influence of personality. Indeed, we have not attended to the range of theories that have been advanced to explain often-observed personality–SWB relationships (e.g., consequence, cognitive, and goal models). Although some of the ideas associated with these models will be touched on later in the chapter, the interested reader should turn elsewhere for a comprehensive theoretical treatment of personality–SWB relationships (e.g., Diener & Lucas). We also have not attended to the range of personality traits that might influence SWB. For instance, Scheier and Carver (1985) have argued that dispositional optimism influences SWB through expectations about the future. Thus, our treatment of personality–SWB relationships truly has been limited; and, as of yet, we have ignored the setting of interest, the workplace. It is to that context that we now turn.

PERSONALITY, DISTRESS IN LIFE, AND THE WORKPLACE

At this point, you may be wondering if we really needed to write the rest of this chapter and if it makes sense to read it. We have shown, for example, that personality helps to determine equilibrium levels of SWB, with life events boosting or lowering SWB only for relatively short periods of time. Given personality's considerable influence on SWB, one might wonder if the workplace has the potential to significantly impair well-being in life. We clearly believe that it does for at least four related reasons.

First, research evidence suggests that there are conditions of work that can have significant consequences for SWB (e.g., Ganster & Schaubroeck, 1991); key among these, we believe, are those conditions related to the economic instrumentality of work in people's lives (Brief & Atieh, 1987). For example, becoming unemployed has the potential to have devastating effects on workers and their families, and these effects can persist over time (e.g., Kahn, 1981; Kasl & Cobb, 1970; Warr, 1983). Second, factors emanating from the workplace can have repercussions in multiple domains of one's life ranging from the quality of child care and availability of health insurance to the ability to develop and sustain long-term meaningful interpersonal relationships and actualize one's creative potential. Third, exposure to certain chronic conditions of work that are psychologically or physically threatening can impair SWB; the continual or recurring nature of such conditions may even have the potential to alter equilibrium levels of SWB over the long run. Finally, sheer consideration of the amount of time many people spend working both on a weekly basis and over the course of a lifetime (e.g., Leete & Schor, 1994; Rones, Ilg, & Gardner, 1997), in conjunction with the premise that the frequency of the experience of positive and negative affect are important contributors to SWB (Diener, Sandvik, & Pavot, 1991), points to the importance of the world of work as a causal factor in SWB. That is, positive and negative affect clearly can be and are experienced while at work (e.g., George, 1989, 1996; Weiss, Nicholas, & Daus, 1999); and, the more time spent working, the more relative frequencies of positive and negative affect (components of SWB) will be influenced by affect experienced while working.

Given our focus on personality, we will not discuss the diverse range of conditions and situations related to work that might impair well-being in life (e.g., see Warr, 1999). Rather, we will explore how personality can result in distress that impairs well-being through three major mechanisms: the choice of settings and creation of the conditions of work, appraisal of and reactions to settings and the conditions of work, and coping with work-related distress. The mechanisms we chose to explore loosely imply an event/condition–appraisal–coping–outcome type of model—that obviously reflects Lazarus' (e.g., Lazarus, 1966; Lazarus & Folkman, 1984, 1987) orientation toward the stress process; but it should be noted that elsewhere (Brief & George, 1995) we have registered some concerns with that orientation as an exclusive guide to research in the workplace. Our concerns stemmed from Lazarus' phenomenological perspective, which yielded a strong emphasis on individual patterns that seemingly excluded a focus on those conditions of life that adversely affect most people; we believe that the study of work stress must, in part, be about identifying those events/conditions in the workplace that most workers have difficulty coping with effectively. So, although this chapter addresses personality and thus individual patterns, we appreciate that some work events/conditions produce almost uniformly negative effects that vary in form, intensity, and duration across people.

Choice of Settings and Creation of the Conditions of Work

A considerable body of research suggests that people choose settings, including work settings, in part based on their personalities (Ickes, Snyder, & Garcia, 1997). In fact, this premise has a relatively long history (Allport, 1937). In the organizational behavior literature, Holland's (1985) theory of careers, Schneider's attraction-selection-attrition model (e.g., Schneider, Smith, Taylor, & Fleenor, 1998), and theorizing and research on person–organization fit (for a recent review, see Kristof, 1996) all point to the role that personality plays in attraction to, and thus, choice of work settings.

Given that personality appears to play a significant role in the choice of work settings and that these work settings, in turn, have the potential to result in the experience of distress (e.g., Warr, 1999), one mechanism through which personality may adversely affect SWB is through its role in job choice. For example, research suggests that individuals who are high on extraversion or PA engage in more social activity, spend more time in social rather than solitary pursuits, are more likely to work in social occupations, and live in larger households than individuals who are low on extraversion (e.g., Diener et al., 1992; Emmons, Diener, & Larsen, 1986; Watson, Clark, McIntyre, & Hamaker, 1992). To the extent that such individuals gravitate toward jobs that allow for and foster social interaction, their SWB may be enhanced as social activity tends to elevate levels of positive affect (McIntyre, Watson, Clark, & Cross, 1991; Watson, 2000). Conversely, it could be reasoned that individuals who are low on extraversion may gravitate toward jobs that do not require extensive social interaction, which may serve to lower their levels of positive affect and SWB.

As another example, given that individuals who are high on neuroticism or NA are more self-critical, focus more on the negative aspects of themselves, and have lower self-concepts than individuals who are low on this trait (Watson & Clark, 1984), they may seek out less challenging positions, may be less likely to choose jobs commensurate with their abilities, and, all else equal, may gravitate toward jobs that are relatively inferior. While we know of no empirical research that directly investigates this speculation, indirect evidence is consistent with this line of reasoning. For instance, Judge, Higgins, Thoreson, and Barrick (1999) found that a measure of neuroticism obtained in childhood was significantly and negatively related to measures of job satisfaction, annual income, and occupational status.

In addition to personality affecting job choice, personality may also play a role in the creation of work conditions that, in turn, influence distress and SWB. Such an instrumental role for personality is consistent with the tenets of interactional psychology and notions of reciprocal action–transaction (e.g., George, 1992; McCrae & Costa, 1991; Pervin & Lewis, 1978) as well as research that has found that personality predicts the experience of objective life events (e.g., Magnus et al., 1993). McCrae and Costa (1991), for example, found that the five-factor (e.g., Digman, 1990) dimensions of agreeableness and conscientiousness were associated positively with life satisfaction; they reasoned that these relationships may be due to the fact that each of these traits can contribute to the creation of situations that, in turn, influence levels of SWB. That is, individuals who are high on agreeableness may have more positive social experiences, which, in turn, may have a positive influence on SWB; individuals who are high on conscientiousness may have relatively more success in achievement-oriented situations, which has the potential to enhance their SWB.

Moreover, one can imagine how individuals who are high on neuroticism or NA may creative negative work conditions for themselves that, in turn, come back to haunt them in terms of lowering levels of SWB. For instance, individuals who are high on NA may be more critical, harder to get along with, and unpleasant to be around; their supervisors may have a less favorable view of them because of their overall negative outlook, which may result in lower levels of job security when downsizings or cutbacks take place (George, 1992). As a final example, individuals who are high on extraversion may be more likely to develop supportive social networks in an organization, which, in turn, may have the potential to enhance their SWB.

Consistent with an instrumental perspective suggesting that personality traits may contribute to the creation of conditions of work that have the potential to influence well-being are findings that suggest that personality influences the incidence of injuries in the workplace. More specifically, Iverson and Erwin (1997) found that positive affectivity was negatively associated and negative affectivity positively associated with occupational injuries.

In sum, it is easy to think of people exerting influence over where they work and over what they experience (events/conditions) in those settings. Moreover, it is easy to think of personality playing a role in these influence processes. Finally, it also is easy to think of where people work and what they experience in those settings affecting, at least temporarily, how frightened, sad, guilty, or angry as well as how happy, proud, or alert they feel in their lives. It was our intent in this section to demonstrate that these easy thoughts are well grounded scientifically. This is the case even though it appears that work stress researchers have not embraced fully the consequences of personality for the choice of work settings and the creation of work conditions. We optimistically anticipate they will and further enlightenment will result.

Reactions to Settings and Appraisal of the Conditions of Work

The implications of personality for SWB through the choice of work settings and the creation of work conditions are consistent with differential exposure models of understanding the effects of personality on distress (e.g., Bolger & Zuckerman, 1995; Fogarty et al., 1999; Ormel & Wohlforth, 1991). Essentially, these models, in agreement with the material reviewed in the previous section, posit that personality affects exposure to stressors. Supplementing exposure models are differential reactivity models suggest that personality traits influence how individuals appraise and react to conditions, which, in turn, effect distress and well-being. Exposure models and reactivity models should not be viewed as competitors; rather, it is plausible, indeed probable, that both models hold. Consistent with a differential reactivity model, Bolger and Zuckerman found that individuals who were high on neuroticism were more reactive to interpersonal conflicts in terms of experienced distress. Supportive of their results are findings that extraverts (compared to introverts) are more reactive to standard positive mood inductions whereas neurotics (compared to non-neurotics) are more reactive to standard negative mood inductions (Larsen & Ketelaar, 1991) and that high NA individuals are more reactive to work demands than low NA individuals (Parkes, 1990). Larsen and Ketelaar invoked the theorizing of Gray (1971, 1981, 1987) to explain their findings (recall the previously mentioned behavioral activation and inhibition systems and their role in understanding PA and NA; also see Gable, Reis, and Elliot, 2000). Essentially, individual differences in sensitivity to rewards and punishments may be responsible for reactivity differences and the differential experience of positive and negative affective states for those high and low on PA and NA (Zelenski & Larsen, 1999).

Bolger and Shilling's (1991) findings provide additional support for a differential reactivity model. In a daily diary study, these researchers sought to determine if individuals who are high on neuroticism experience more stressful events or react more negatively to the events they do experience. They found exposure and reactivity explained over 40% of the distress difference between people high and low in neuroticism; moreover, Bolger and Shillings observed that reactivity to stressors accounted for twice as much of the distress difference as did exposure to stressors. Other researchers also have found that personality influences reactivity (e.g., Gross, Sutton, & Ketelaar, 1998; Suls, Green, & Hillis, 1998). (For reactivity results pertaining to personality traits other than PA and NA, see, for example, Abramson, Metalsky, and Alloy, 1989; Kobasa, Maddi, and Kahn, 1982; Parkes, 1984; and Suls and Fletcher, 1985.)

Personality also appears to influence the appraisal of daily activities. For example, individuals who are high on extraversion have been found to have more positive opinions of themselves and others in the context of day-to-day interactions whereas individuals who are high on neuroticism may have lower self-esteem in daily social interactions (Barrett & Pietromonaco, 1997). As another example, individuals high on neuroticism appraise daily stressors more negatively (Gunthert, Cohen, & Armeli, 1999) and also are more likely to appraise chronic features of a work environment such as an incentive compensation program more negatively (George, Brief, Webster, & Burke, 1989).

Thus, research suggests that personality likely influences how people react to the stressful events/conditions they encounter in their places of work. This reactivity, for example, may take the form of differences in sensitivity to (i.e., recognition of) an event/condition or in the intensity of the emotional response to a recognized event/condition. Moreover, personality likely influences the cognitive appraisal of a workplace event/condition, for instance, as benign, an opportunity, a threat, or even as harmful. It is important to note that these likelihoods are not presented as alternatives to the exposure consequences of personality; rather, they are additional ways personality may affect the experience of work stress.

PERSONALITY AND COPING

Links between personality and coping have a long-standing history in psychology. For example, psychoanalytical and ego development perspectives tended to posit close connections between the two (e.g., Bryne, 1964; Freud, 1964; Haan, 1977). However, the popular transactional approach, advocated by such researchers as Lazarus and Folkman, downplayed the role of personality per se and focused more on individual patterns of cognitive appraisals of environmental demands and the resources to cope with them (e.g., Folkman & Lazarus, 1980; Lazarus & Folkman, 1984; Suls, David, & Harvey, 1996). Contemporary approaches to understanding the role of personality in coping tend to acknowledge the merits of both perspectives and examine the role of stable dispositions in coping processes while recognizing that coping as a process often unfolds in response to situational stressors (Suls et al., 1996). The more applied orientation of the organizational behavior literature perhaps has led to a heavier focus on transactional-type approaches (e.g., Latack, Kinicki, & Prussia, 1995); yet here too, there is increasing recognition of the multiple roles that personality may play in coping viewed as a process (e.g., George & Brief, 1996). In the sections that follow, we focus on the role that personality plays in choice of coping mechanisms, the extent to which coping may mediate certain personality effects, and coping effectiveness.

Choice of Coping Mechanisms

Because personality refers to the enduring ways in which a person thinks, feels, and behaves, it stands to reason that personality may influence how a person reacts when exposed to work-related stressors. One such reaction is to engage in coping, for example, by attempting to eliminate or reduce the source of stress or by attempting to divert one's attention away from the stressful situation. By choice of coping mechanisms, we mean the strategies a person can be thought of as selecting to deal with a stressful encounter, in the current case, at work. Again, we assert that these choices are influenced by personality.

In fact, research suggests that personality does influence the choice of coping mechanisms. For instance, in two community-based samples, McCrae and Costa (1986) found that high neuroticism was associated with neurotic-type coping behaviors such as hostility, escapism through fantasy, blaming the self, sedation, withdrawal, passive responses, difficulty making decisions, and wishful thinking. They also found that high extraversion resulted in the use of more mature types of coping mechanisms such as positive thinking, direct action, seeking satisfaction elsewhere, and exercising restraint. High openness to experience resulted in more use of humor whereas low openness to experience resulted in more reliance on faith. Although these results were based on self-reports of both personality and coping mechanisms, similar patterns were found when peers or spouses provided ratings of personality and self-reports of coping mechanisms were used.

McCrae and Costa's (1986) findings have been replicated, although the specific patterning of the links between personality and coping mechanism choice has not always been consistent. For example, Bolger (1990) found that neuroticism was positively associated with wishful thinking, self-blame, and distancing in a sample of premedical students coping with a major exam, consistent with McCrae and Costa (1986). However, while Bolger and Zuckerman (1995) found neuroticism to be positively associated with escape/avoidance and confrontation, they also found it to be positively associated with problem solving, self-control, and social support seeking. O'Brien and DeLongis' (1996) results are more consistent with McCrae and Costa's (1986) as these researchers found that being high on neuroticism resulted in less use of problem solving and more use of escape/avoidance and confrontation. High openness to experience led to increased use of positive reappraisal, and high agreeableness led to more seeking of social support and less use of confrontation. Additionally, conscientiousness was positively associated with accepting responsibility and negatively associated with escape/avoidance in this study.

Watson and Hubbard's (1996) results suggest that each of the five factor traits are related to coping choices in ways that would be expected based on descriptions of these traits and their nomological networks. That is, neuroticism was related positively to passive coping mechanisms, disengagement, fantasy, venting, and denial; conscientiousness was related positively to active, problem-oriented, planful, and persistent coping; extraversion was related positively to social support seeking; openness to experience was related negatively to relying on religion/faith and related positively to trying to grow and develop from stressful experiences; and, agreeableness was related positively to trying to interpret things in a positive light. Somewhat consistent with these findings are (a) results that indicate that negative affectivity is related negatively and positive affectivity is related positively to use of rational/cognitive coping mechanisms (Fogarty et al., 1999) and (b) results that indicate that conscientiousness is associated positively with active, utilitarian kinds of coping mechanisms (Shewuck, Elliott, MacNair-Semands, & Harkins, 1999).

Generally, it appears that personality does influence choice of coping mechanisms in ways that would be expected based on descriptions of the relevant traits. (Also see, for example, Costa & McCrae, 1987; Smith, Pope, Rhodewolt, & Poulton, 1989; Terry, 1994). This generalization masks considerable complexity. Methodologically, for instance, it downplays the real difficulties associated with measuring coping in natural settings (e.g., Ptacek, Smith, Espe, & Raffety, 1994; Stone et al., 1998); just imagine developing a self-report measure of denial as a coping response. Conceptually, it downplays the real possibility that coping is entwined with personality in other ways; for example, in the next section we address the likelihood that coping mediates the influence of personality on experienced distress. Moreover, a concern with choice of coping mechanisms, in part, presumes that coping helps; but, evidence is accumulating that self-reports of coping choices are associated with poorer, not better, outcomes (e.g., Aldwin & Revenson, 1987; Carver & Scheier, 1994; also see Watson & Hubbard, 1996). Nevertheless, it appears that for stress researchers interested in the ways people choose to cope with the stressors they encounter in the workplace, to ignore personality would be akin to baking bread with no rising agent—things will fall flat.

Coping as a Mediator

The potential role of coping as a mediator of relationships between neuroticism and distress and performance was examined by Bolger (1990) in the previously mentioned study of premedical students. He found that students who were high on neuroticism were more likely to engage in wishful thinking and blaming the self; and, these coping mechanisms accounted for more than half of the effects that neuroticism had on levels of anxiety. As noted previously, such a result, at least partially, would appear to drive concern with choice of coping mechanism, for this choice is integral to the causal chain of focal interest: personality–coping–strain (e.g., Bolger & Zuckerman, 1995; Fogarty et al., 1999). But recall that research to date, at least research relying on self-report coping scales, has not consistently yielded the sought after coping–reduced strain finding. Watson and Hubbard (1996, p. 767) have noted that this disappointing result may be due to the fact that the coping scales in use "appear to be heavily laden with content that is positively correlated with neuroticism, and so should tend to be associated with increased, rather than decreased, distress." They go on to suggest that the content of coping measures should be expanded to include more positively balanced response mechanisms. All of these findings, for work stress researchers focusing on personality–coping–strain relationships, highlight that they need to exercise extreme care in selecting coping measures. The choice of a coping scale may dictate one's results, which may indicate that coping with workplace stressors does not help.

Coping Effectiveness

Not considered thus far is a model most clearly articulated by Bolger and Zuckerman (1995), what they called a differential coping-effectiveness model. They assert, "... some people may experience adverse outcomes following a stressful event not because they choose normatively maladaptive strategies but because they choose strategies that are ineffective for them alone" (p. 892). Bolger and Zuckerman also noted that this possibility implies that personality moderates the effectiveness of coping and that, prior to their research, the model had not been applied to the study of personality in the stress process. However, McCrae and Costa (1986) did observe in their study that the association between coping and well-being was reduced when personality measures were partialled out.

In a 2-week daily diary study, Bolger and Zuckerman (1995) had students self-report interpersonal conflicts, how they coped with them, and negative emotions. As would be expected, students high in neuroticism reported more interpersonal conflicts and appeared to be more effected by them. As previously mentioned, students high on neuroticism also relied more on escape/avoidance, confrontation, problem solving, self-control, and social support seeking than those low on neuroticism. Interestingly enough, for some of the coping mechanisms and outcome variables (i.e., negative emotions), neuroticism appeared to be a significant moderator such that the effects of coping on negative emotions varied depending on whether one was high or low on neuroticism. Thus, for example, while individuals who were high on neuroticism and used self-control to deal with conflicts became more depressed, those low on neuroticism became less depressed. As another example, although the use of escape/avoidance had no effect on levels of depression for those high on neuroticism, it had a positive effect on depression for those low on neuroticism.

Bolger and Zuckerman's (1995) findings are intriguing and suggest the differential coping-effectiveness model is worthy of the attention of work stress researchers. If the model is pursued, logic would dictate that the following also be considered: Some people may experience relatively favorable outcomes following a stressful event not because they choose normatively adaptive strategies but because they choose strategies that are effective for them alone. That is, a more fully articulated differential coping-effectiveness model would recognize that some personality traits may promote the benefits of a chosen coping mechanism, thereby protecting or enhancing SWB.

In sum, our very brief treatments of how personality may affect choice of coping mechanisms, of the personality–coping-effectiveness causal sequence, and of the differential coping-effectiveness model (i.e., personality as a moderator of coping–distress/SWB relationships) all perhaps are best viewed as mere examples of the ways in which personality is entwined with coping and its outcomes. Once again, we do not see the approaches to the role of personality in coping process we have outlined as competitors. Rather, we anticipate that enlightened work stress researchers will come to see all of the approaches outlined as viable, either simultaneously or variably across contexts. That is, we do not expect future understandings of personality and coping to be simple ones, dominated by a single approach.

SUMMARY AND CONCLUSION

In this chapter, we have strived to provide a glimpse of the multiple roles that personality plays in stress and coping processes. There clearly are multiple paths, as depicted in Fig. 8.1, by which personality may influence the extent to which distress emanating from the workplace has the potential to impair SWB. Rather than summarizing what we have covered thus far, at this point, perhaps it is most useful for us to reflect on what we feel are some promising directions for future theorizing and research in the area.

First, we think that work stress research will advance by viewing workers as whole people. Clearly, personality plays several distinct and important roles in stress and coping processes. A cynical response to this realization might be to ask, "Who cares about work-related distress and coping?" That is, by virtue of their personalities, people may be choosing, creating, and reacting to work settings and coping with them in a somewhat

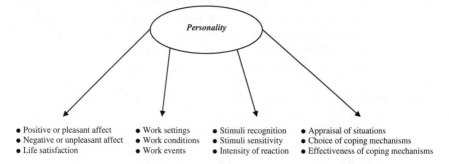

FIG. 8.1 Examples of the ways in which personality influences stress and coping processes.

predetermined manner; in other words, some people may experience more distress than others because of who they are and not necessarily because of what goes on in the workplace. Although such a cynical view is a gross oversimplification, it also neglects the fact that work can affect multiple aspects of people's lives. Thus, to really understand the extent to which work impairs well-being in life and why it can have detrimental effects, we need to look at workers as whole people and the repercussions of both acute (e.g., job loss) and chronic (e.g., excessive working hours) conditions of work on SWB as well as various important domains of life such as family. Fulfilling this research need clearly requires going beyond currently in vogue investigations of work–family conflicts where such conflicts typically are construed in broad and vague terms (e.g., Kopelman, Greenhaus, & Connolly, 1983; but also see Edwards & Rothbart, 1999). Early studies of emotional adjustment and work examined specific aspects of family life (e.g., economic discord and sexual dysfunctions) and their associations with work life (see Weiss & Brief, 2001). Maybe it is time to look to those early studies to guide our future ones. Although personality must be taken into account in such investigations, doing so does not relieve work stress researchers from the obligation to explore conditions of work that may be truly stressful for workers exposed to them such that well-being in life is impaired (Brief & Atieh, 1987). That is, although personality most certainly matters, it is not all of what stress and coping is about. Bad things do happen to people at work (and away from it), and these events/conditions in combination with personality influence SWB. Our job, as work stress researchers, is to identify the bad things that happen to people at work while not neglecting the role of personality in regard to the origins and consequences of those bad things.

Second, issues of timing seem especially crucial in terms of understanding the role of personality and workplace conditions both in the creation and experience of distress. Over the long term, self-reports of stressors, ways of coping, and distress may show trait-like properties. Again, however, real stressors (i.e., objective events/conditions) exist that have real effects. Untangling these complex relationships (e.g., between the subjective and the objective) necessitates a consideration of multiple aspects of time as they relate to personality and distress, including the role of the past and the future in the present and the subjective experience of time, time aggregations, duration of steady states and rates of change, incremental versus discontinuous change, frequency, rhythms, and cycles, and spirals over time (George & Jones, 2000). For example, although we know that people generally return to their equilibrium levels of SWB within 3 months after exposure to a stressful event, is this the case for varying types of stressful events at work? And what about exposure to chronically stressful working conditions? Moreover, how do the effects of exposure to multiple stressful events over time at work accumulate? If personality contributes to the creation of stressful working conditions (e.g., in terms of relationships with subordinates, peers, and/or bosses), how does this problematic process unfold over time (does it take days, months, or years)? And, assuming certain personality traits are associated with hyperreactivity to stressful events at work, how long does such hyperreactivity last and in what pattern does it fade? Obviously, when work stress researchers take into consideration time, they will be faced with the opportunity of constructing a seemingly unlimited number of puzzles of their own to be solved. Solving those puzzles is bound to advance the field in significant ways.

Third, although we have simplistically approached the construct of personality by considering one trait at a time in the examples provided, we fully recognize that people are more complex. Therefore, it is important to explore, first theoretically, then empirically, the role of different personality profiles in understanding how distress emanating from the workplace affects SWB in life. For example, recall from our earlier discussion that SWB is indicated by the experience of positive or pleasant affect, the experience of negative or unpleasant affect, and life satisfaction. Through multiple mechanisms, neuroticism is likely to lead to increased negative affect and lower levels of life satisfaction; analogously, through multiple mechanisms, extraversion is likely to lead to increased positive affect and higher levels of life satisfaction. What are the implications of being high on both neuroticism and extraversion? As another example, conscientiousness appears to result in more effective styles of coping; to what extent might a high level of conscientiousness mitigate some of the effects that a high level of neuroticism may have on experienced distress? These are just a sampling of some of the interesting questions that arise when we consider that each of the five factor traits are relatively independent of each other and, taken together, can be used to describe the whole of one's personality at a global level.

Fourth and most obvious, throughout the chapter we have addressed how personality broadly interacts with situational characteristics, kinds of appraisals, ways of coping, and coping effectiveness associated with distress tied to the workplace. These interactions, conceptualized more precisely and richly than we have done here, provide perhaps the most promising territory for work stress researchers to explore in the years ahead. We say this believing that personality truly captures enduring individual differences and, thereby, provides a means for understanding why people vary in how they emotionally adjust to the settings in which they work. The settings matter, but so do the people in them.

Finally, although the previous four issues raised each have methodological implications, we thought it appropriate to close by addressing methodology per se. Once again, we turn to Kasl (1996) for insight. He, like others before him (e.g., Frese & Zapf, 1988), emphasized the importance of the choice between objective and subjective measures of exposure to stressful conditions/events. Kasl went on to state his preference for the objective approach (also see Ganster & Schaubroeck, 1991) based on several considerations, including the following: the objective approach (a) "provides a clearer picture of etiology, since subjective appraisers can be influenced by many variables, including preexisting stable traits," (b) "is associated with less measurement confounding if our outcomes are based on self-reports and involve similar psychological processes to the subjective appraisals," and (c) "allows for clearer and more appropriate separation of stimuli and responses of independent and dependent variables, since the subjective appraisals may be the first step in a number of tightly linked reactions" (p. 24). Particularly in light of the current focus on personality and its known potential to influence, for example, subjective appraisals and outcomes (e.g., self-reports of SWB), we wholeheartedly endorse Kasl's preference for the objective approach. Indeed, we see inclusion of objective measures of exposure to stressful conditions/events in the study of personality and work-related distress as a necessity in order to disentangle the various roles personality plays in stress and coping processes. This belief does not mean that every study in the area must include objective indicators of exposure; rather, the body of literature should be weighted in the objective direction. That is, we, like Kasl, recognize a place for the subjective approach too. For example, how personality might influence the relationship between objective and subjective indicators of job stressors may be worthy of consideration. If the subjective approach is adopted, we recommend that the previously noted research of Nial Bolger and his colleagues (e.g., Bolger & Schilling, 1991; Bolger & Zuckerman, 1995) be viewed as supplying excellent examples of how to go about studying the multiple roles of personality in stress and coping processes. This research recognizes that stress and coping truly are processes and that static portrayals of personality's influences on them provide an incomplete, or worse, inaccurate picture. For instance, Bolger and Zuckerman, in part to assess the influence of neuroticism on reactivity to interpersonal conflict, conducted a 14-day diary study and employed a statistical model that considered that distress experienced today may be a product of the conflicts and distress experienced yesterday. Results based on the model contributed to their conclusion that neuroticism influences anger and depression indirectly through exposure to interpersonal conflicts as well as moderates relationships between conflicts and anger/depression. Although it is not known if results based on a static model would have lead to these conclusions, it is clear that, merely because of the dynamic nature of the data from which they were derived, Bolger and Zuckerman's findings inspire a higher degree of confidence.

All in all then, we hope we have demonstrated that personality plays many important roles in the extent to which distress emanating from the workplace has the potential to impair SWB. Rather than continuing to focus on ongoing debates in the existing literature (e.g., Burke, Brief, & George, 1993; Chen & Spector, 1991; Spector, Zapf, Chen, & Frese, 2000; Williams, Gavin, & Williams, 1996), we believe the time is ripe to move on. We hope that our chapter will serve as a springboard for such work. As we implied earlier, we trust that the contents of this chapter will not be taken to pit one proposed role of personality against another. Although we appreciate the value of debate in the conduct of science, it is clear to us that work stress researchers have so much to learn (ourselves included) that it is simply wasteful to focus too many resources on any particular debate about the role of personality. Perhaps in a decade or two, we might be in a position to concentrate our energies on debating a specific role of personality. For now, however, theoretical and empirical eclecticism should reign.

REFERENCES

Abramson, L. Y., Metalsky, G. I., & Alloy, L. B. (1989). Hopelessness depression: A theory-based subtype of depression. *Psychological Review, 96*, 358–372.

Aldwin, C. M., & Revenson, T. A. (1987). Does coping help? A reexamination of the relation between coping and mental health. *Journal of Personality and Social Psychology, 53*, 337–348.

Allport, G. W. (1937). *Personality: A psychological interpretation.* New York: Holt, Rinehart & Wilnston.

Andrews, F. M., & Withey, S. B. (1976). *Social indicators of well-being: America's perception of life quality.* New York: Plenum.

Barrett, L. F., & Pietromonaco, P. R. (1997). Accuracy of the Five-Factor Model in predicting perceptions of daily social interactions. *Personality and Social Psychology Bulletin, 23*, 1173–1187.

Baum, A. (1990). Stress, intrusive imagery, and chronic distress. *Health Psychology, 9*, 653–675.

Block, J. (1977). Advancing the psychology of personality: Paradigmatic shift or improving the quality of research? In D. Magnusson & N. Endler (Eds.), *Personality at the crossroads* (pp. 37–64). Hillsdale, NJ: Lawrence Erlbaum Associates, Inc.

Bolger, N. (1990). Coping as a personality process: A prospective study. *Journal of Personality and Social Psychology, 59*, 525–537.

Bolger, N., & Shilling, E. A. (1991). Personality and the problems of everyday life: The role of neuroticism in exposure and reactivity to daily stressors. *Journal of Personality, 59*, 355–386.

Bolger, N., & Zuckerman, A. (1995). A framework for studying personality in the stress process. *Journal of Personality and Social Psychology, 69*, 890–902.

Brett, J. F., Brief, A. P., Burke, M. J., George, J. M., & Webster, J. (1990). Negative affectivity and the reporting of stressful life events. *Health Psychology, 9*, 57–68.

Brickman, P., Coates, D., & Janoff-Bulman, R. (1978). Lottery winners and accident victims: Is happiness relative? *Journal of Personality and Social Psychology, 36*, 917–927.

Brief, A. P., & Atieh, J. M. (1987). Studying job stress: Are we making mountains out of molehills? *Journal of Occupational Behaviour, 8*, 115–126.

Brief, A. P., Burke, M. J., George, J. M., Robinson, B., & Webster, J. (1988). Should negative affectivity remain an unmeasured variable in the study of job stress? *Journal of Applied Psychology, 73*, 193–198.

Brief, A. P., Butcher, A. H., George, J. M., & Link, K. E. (1993). Integrating bottom-up and top-down theories of subjective well-being: The case of health. *Journal of Personality and Social Psychology, 64*, 646–653.

Brief, A. P., Butcher, A. H., & Roberson, L. (1995). Cookies, disposition, and job attitudes: The effects of positive mood-inducing events and negative affectivity on job satisfaction in a field experiment. *Organizational Behavior and Human Decision Processes, 62*, 55–62.

Brief, A. P., & George, J. M. (1995). Psychological stress and the workplace: A brief comment on Lazarus' outlook. In R. Crandall & P. L. Perrewe (Eds.), *Occupational stress: A handbook. Series in health psychology and behavioral medicine*, (pp. 15–19). Philadelphia: Taylor & Francis.

Bryne, D. (1964). Repression-sensitization as a dimension of personality. In B. A. Maher (Ed.), *Progress in experimental personality research* (pp. 169–220). New York: Academic.

Burke, M. J., Brief, A. P., & George, J. M. (1993). The role of negative affectivity in understanding relations between self-reports of stressors and strains: A comment on the applied psychology literature. *Journal of Applied Psychology, 78*, 402–412.

Buss, D. M., & Craik, K. H. (1983). The act frequency approach to personality. *Psychological Review, 90*, 105–126.

Cacioppo, J. T., Gardner, W. L., & Berntson, G. G. (1999). The affect system has parallel and integrative processing components: Form follows function. *Journal of Personality and Social Psychology, 76*, 839–855.

Carver, C. S., & Scheier, M. F. (1994). Situational coping and coping dispositions in a stressful transaction. *Journal of Personality and Social Psychology, 66*, 184–195.

Caspi, A., & Bem, D. J. (1990). Personality continuity and change across the life course. In L. A. Pervin (Ed.), *Handbook of personality: Theory and research*, (pp. 549–575). New York: Guilford.

Cattell, R. B. (1965). *The scientific analysis of personality*. Baltimore: Penguin.

Chen, P. Y., & Spector, P. E. (1991). Negative affectivity as the underlying cause of correlations between stressors and strains. *Journal of Applied Psychology, 76*, 398–407.

Cohen, S., & Kessler, R. C. (1995). Strategies for measuring stress in studies of psychiatric and physical disorders. In S. Cohen, R. C. Kessler, & L. G. Gordon (Eds.), *Measuring stress: A guide for health and social scientists*, (pp. 3–26). New York: Oxford University Press.

Costa, P. T., & McCrae, R. R. (1987). Neuroticism, somatic complaints and disease: Is the bark worse than the bite? *Journal of Personality, 55*, 299–316.

Costa, P. T., & McCrae, R. R. (1988). Personality in adulthood: A six-year longitudinal study of self-reports and spouse ratings on the NEO Personality Inventory. *Journal of Personality and Social Psychology, 54*, 853–863.

Costa, P. T., & McCrae, R. R. (1992). *Revised NEO Personality Inventory (NEO-PI-R) and NEO Five Factor Inventory (NEO-FFI) professional manual*. Odessa, FL: Psychological Assessment Resources.

Costa, P. T., McCrae, R. R., & Zonderman, A. B. (1987). Environmental and dispositional influences on well-being: Longitudinal follow-up of an American national sample. *British Journal of Psychology, 78*, 299–306.

DeNeve, K. M., & Cooper, H. (1998). The happy personality: A meta-analysis of 137 personality traits and subjective well-being. *Psychological Bulletin, 124*, 197–229.

Derryberry, D., & Reed, M. A. (1994). Temperament and attention: Orienting toward and away from positive and negative signals. *Journal of Personality and Social Psychology, 66*, 1128–1139.

Diener, E., & Larsen, R. J. (1984). Temporal stability and cross-situational consistency of affective, behavioral, and cognitive responses. *Journal of Personality and Social Psychology, 47,* 871–883.

Diener, E., & Lucas, R. E. (1999). Personality and subjective well-being. In D. Kahneman, E. Diener, & N. Schwarz (Eds.), *Well-being: The foundations of hedonic psychology* (pp. 213–229). New York: Russell Sage Foundation.

Diener, E., Sandvik, E., & Pavot, W. (1991). Happiness is the frequency, not the intensity, of positive versus negative affect. In F. Strack & N. Schwarz (Eds.), *Subjective well-being* (pp. 119–139). New York: Pergamon.

Diener, E., Sandvik, E., Pavot, W., & Fujita, F. (1992). Extraversion and subjective well-being in a U.S. national probability sample. *Journal of Research in Personality, 26,* 205–215.

Diener, E., Suh, E. M., Lucas, R. E., & Smith, H. L. (1999). Subjective well-being: Three decades of progress. *Psychological Bulletin, 125,* 276–302.

Digman, J. M. (1990). Personality Structure: Emergence of the Five-Factor Model, *Annual Review of Psychology, 41,* 417–440.

Edwards, J. R., & Rothbart, N. P. (1999). Work and family stress and well-being: An examination of person-environment fit in the work and family domains. *Organizational Behavior and Human Decision Processes, 77,* 85–129.

Emmons, R. R., Diener, E., & Larsen, R. J. (1986). Choice and avoidance of everyday situations and affect congruence: Two models of reciprocal interactionism. *Journal of Personality and Social Psychology, 51,* 815–826.

Epstein, S. (1983). A research paradigm for the study of personality and emotions. In M. M. Page (Ed.), *Personality: Current theory and research* (pp. 91–154). Lincoln, Nebraska: University of Nebraska Press.

Eysenck, H. J. (1982). *Personality genetics and behavior.* New York: Praeger.

Fergusson, D. M., & Horwood, L. J. (1987). Vulnerability to life events exposure. *Psychological Medicine, 17,* 739–749.

Fisher, V. E., & Hanna, J. V. (1931). *The dissatisfied worker.* New York: Macmillan.

Fogarty, G. J., Machin, M. A., Albion, M. J., Sutherland, L. F., Lalor, G. I., & Revitt, S. (1999). Predicting occupational strain and job satisfaction: The role of stress, coping, personality, and affectivity variables. *Journal of Vocational Behavior, 54,* 429–452.

Folkman, S., & Lazarus, R. S. (1980). An analysis of coping in a middle-aged community sample. *Journal of Health and Social Behavior, 21,* 219–239.

Frederick, S., & Loewenstein, G. (1999). Hedonic adaptation. In D. Kahneman & E. Diener (Eds.), *Well-being: The foundations of hedonic psychology* (pp. 302–329). New York: Russell Sage Foundation.

Frese, M., & Zapf, D. (1988). Methodological issues in the study of work stress: Objective vs. subjective measurement of work stress and the question of longitudinal studies. In C. L. Cooper & R. Payne (Eds.), *Causes, coping and consequences of occupational stress at work* (pp. 375–410). Chichester, UK: Wiley.

Freud, S. (1933). *New introductory lectures on psychoanalysis.* New York: Norton.

Freud, S. (1964). The neuro-psychoses of defense. In J. Strachey (Ed. & Trans.), *The standard edition of the complete psychological works of Sigmund Freud* (Vol. 3, pp. 45–61). London: Hogarth. (Original work published in 1894)

Gable, S. L., Reis, H. T., & Elliot, A. J. (2000). Behavioral activation and inhibition in everyday life. *Journal of Personality and Social Psychology, 78,* 1135–1149.

Ganster, D. C., & Schaubroeck, J. (1991). Work stress and employee health. *Journal of Management, 17,* 235–271.

George, J. M. (1989). Mood and absence. *Journal of Applied Psychology, 74,* 317–324.

George, J. M. (1992). The role of personality in organizational life: Issues and evidence. *Journal of Management, 18,* 185–213.

George, J. M. (1996). Trait and state affect. In K. R. Murphy (Ed.), *Individual differences and behavior in organizations* (pp. 145–171). San Francisco: Jossey-Bass.

George, J. M., & Brief, A. P. (1996). Negative affectivity and coping with job loss. *Academy of Management Review (Dialogue), 21,* 7–12.

George, J. M., Brief, A. P., Webster, J., & Burke, M. J. (1989). Incentive compensation as an injurious condition of work: A study of labeling. *Journal of Organizational Behavior, 10,* 155–167.

George, J. M., & Jones, G. R. (2000). The role of time in theory and theory building. *Journal of Management, 26,* 657–684.

Gray, J. A. (1971). The psychophysiological basis of introversion-extraversion. *Behavior Research and Therapy, 8,* 249–266.

Gray, J. A. (1981). A critique of Eysenck's theory of personality. In H. J. Eysenck (Ed.), *A model for personality* (pp. 246–276). New York: Springer.

Gray, J. A. (1987). Perspectives on anxiety and impulsivity: A commentary. *Journal of Research in Personality, 21,* 493–509.

Green, D. P., Salovey, P., & Truax, K. M. (1999). Static, dynamic, and causative bipolarity of affect. *Journal of Personality and Social Psychology, 76,* 856–867.

Gross, J. J., Sutton, S. K., & Ketelaar, T. (1998). Relation between affect and personality: Support for the affect-level and affective-reactivity views. *Personality and Social Psychology Bulletin, 24,* 279–288.

Gunthert, K. C., Cohen, L. H., & Armeli, S. (1999). The role of neuroticism in daily stress and coping. *Journal of Personality and Social Psychology, 77,* 1087–1100.

Haan, N. (1977). *Coping and defending: Processes of self-environment organization.* New York: Academic.

Hart, P. M. (1999). Predicting employee life satisfaction: A coherent model of personality, work and nonwork experiences, and domain satisfactions. *Journal of Applied Psychology, 84,* 564–584.

Headey, B., & Wearing, A. (1989). Personality, life events, and subjective well-being: Towards a dynamic equilibrium model. *Journal of Personality and Social Psychology, 57,* 731–739.

Headey, B., & Wearing, A. (1991). Subjective well-being: A stocks and flows framework. In F. Strack, M. Argyle, & N. Schwarz (Eds.), *Subjective well-being: An interdisciplinary perspective* (pp. 49–73). New York: Pergamon.

Headey, B. W., & Wearing, A. J. (1992). *Understanding happiness: A theory of subjective well-being.* Melbourne, Australia: Longman.

Headey, B. W., Glowacki, T., Holmstrom, E. L., & Wearing, A. J. (1985). Modelling change in perceived quality of life. *Social Indicators Research, 17,* 276–298.

Holland, J. L. (1985). *Making vocational choices: A theory of vocational personality and work environments* (2nd ed.). Englewood Cliffs, NJ: Prentice Hall.

Ickes, W., Snyder, M., & Garcia, S. (1997). Personality influences on the choice of situations. In R. Hogan, J. Johnson, & S. Briggs (Eds.), *Handbook of personality psychology* (pp. 165–195). San Diego: Academic.

Iverson, R. D., & Erwin, P. J. (1997). Predicting occupational injury: The role of affectivity. *Journal of Occupational and Organizational Psychology, 70,* 113–128.

Judge, T. A., Higgins, C. A., Thoresen, C. J., & Barrick, M. R. (1999). The Big Five personality traits, general mental ability, and career success across the life span. *Personnel Psychology, 52,* 621–652.

Kahn, R. L. (1981). *Work and health.* Wiley: New York.

Kasl, S. V. (1996). Theory of stress and health. In C. L. Cooper (Ed.), *Handbook of stress, medicine, and health* (pp. 13–26). Boca Raton, FL: CRC Press.

Kasl, S. V., & Cobb, S. (1970). Blood pressure changes in men undergoing job loss: A preliminary report. *Psychosomatic Medicine, 32,* 19–38.

Kobasa, S. C., Maddi, S. R., & Kahn, S. (1982). Hardiness and health: A prospective study. *Journal of Personality and Social Psychology, 42,* 168–177.

Kopelman, R. E., Greenhaus, J. H., & Connolly, T. F. (1983). A model of work, family, and interrole conflict: A construct validation study. *Organizational Behavior and Human Decision Processes, 32,* 198–215.

Krause, J. S., & Steinberg, M. (1997). Aging and adjustment after spinal cord injury: The roles of chronologic age, time since injury, and environmental change. *Rehabilitation Psychology, 42,* 287–302.

Kristof, A. L. (1996). Person-organization fit: An integrative review of its conceptualizations, measurement, and implications. *Personnel Psychology, 49,* 1–49.

Larsen, R. J., & Ketelaar, T. (1991). Personality and susceptibility to positive and negative emotional states. *Journal of Personality and Social Psychology, 61,* 132–140.

Latack, J. C., Kinicki, A. J., & Prussia, G. E. (1995). An integrative process model of coping with job loss. *Academy of Management Review, 20,* 311–342.

Lazarus, R. S. (1966). *Psychological stress and the coping process.* New York: Mcgraw-Hill.

Lazarus, R. S., & Folkman, S. (1984). *Stress, appraisal, and coping.* New York: Springer.

Lazarus, R. S., & Folkman, S. (1987). Transactional theory and research on emotions and coping. *European Journal of Personality, 1,* 141–169.

Leete, L., & Schor, J. B. (1994). Assessing the time-squeeze hypothesis: Hours worked in the United States, 1969–89. *Industrial Relations, 33,* 25–43.

Lucas, R. E., Diener, E., & Suh, E. (1996). Discriminant validity of well-being measures. *Journal of Personality and Social Psychology, 71,* 616–628.

Lykken, D. T. (1968). Statistical significance in psychological research. *Psychological Bulletin, 70,* 151–159.

Magnus, K., & Diener, E. (1991, May). A longitudinal analysis of personality, life events, and subjective well-being. Paper presented at the sixty-third annual meeting of the Midwestern Psychological Association, Chicago. Cited in E. Diener & R. E. Lucas (1999), Personality and subjective well-being. In D. Kahneman, E. Diener, & N. Schwarz (Eds.), *Well-being: The foundations of hedonic psychology* (pp. 213–229). New York: Russell Sage Foundation.

Magnus, K., Diener, E., Fujita, F., & Pavot, W. (1993). Extraversion and neuroticism as predictors of objective life events: A longitudinal analysis. *Journal of Personality and Social Psychology, 65,* 1046–1053.

McCrae, R. R., & Costa, P. T. (1986). Personality, coping, and coping effectiveness in an adult sample. *Journal of Personality, 54,* 385–405.

McCrae, R. R., & Costa, P. T. (1991). Adding *Liebe und Arbeit*: The Full Five-Factor Model and well-being. *Personality and Social Psychology Bulletin, 17,* 227–232.

McCrae, R. R., & Costa, P. T. (1994). The stability of personality: Observation and evaluations. *Current Directions in Psychological Science, 3,* 173–175.

McGrath, J. E. (1970). *Social and psychological factors in stress.* New York: Holt, Rinehart & Winston.

McIntyre, C. W., Watson, D., Clark, L. A., & Cross, S. A. (1991). The effect of induced social interaction on positive and negative affect. *Bulletin of the Pscychonomic Society, 29,* 67–67.

Mehnert, T., Krauss, H. H., Nadler, R., & Boyd, M. (1990). Correlates of life satisfaction in those with disabling conditions. *Rehabilitation Psychology, 35,* 3–17.

Meyer, G. J., & Shack, J. R. (1989). Structural convergence of mood and personality: Evidence for old and new directions. *Journal of Personality and Social Psychology, 57,* 691–706.

O'Brien, T. B., & DeLongis, A. (1996). The interactional context of problem-, emotion-, and relationship-focused coping: The role of the big five personality factors. *Journal of Personality, 64,* 775–813.

Ormel, J., & Wohlfarth, T. (1991). How neuroticism, long-term difficulties, and life situation change influence psychological distress: A longitudinal model. *Journal of Personality and Social Psychology, 60,* 744–755.

Parkes, K. R. (1984). Locus of control, cognitive appraisal, and coping in stressful episodes. *Journal of Personality and Social Psychology, 46,* 655–668.

Parkes, K. R. (1990). Coping, negative affectivity and the work environment: Additive and interactive predictors of mental health. *Journal of Applied Psychology, 75,* 399–409.

Payne, R. (1988). A longitudinal study of the psychological well-being of unemployed men and the mediating effect of neuroticism. *Human Relations, 41,* 119–138.

Pervin, L. A. (1994). Personality stability, personality change, and the question of process. In T. F. Heatherton & J. L. Weinberger, (Eds.), *Can personality change?* (pp. 315–330). Washington, DC: American Psychological Association.

Pervin, L. A., & Lewis, M. (1978). Overview of the internal-external issue. In L. A. Pervin & M. Lewis (Eds.), *Perspectives in interactional psychology* (pp. 1–22). New York: Plenum.

Ptacek, J. T., Smith, R. E., Espe, K., & Raffety, B. (1994). Limited correspondence between daily coping reports and retrospective coping recall. *Psychological Assessment, 6,* 41–49.

Rogers, C. R. (1951). *Client-centered therapy.* Boston: Houghton Mifflin.

Rones, P. L., Ilg, R. E., & Gardner, J. M. (1997). Trends in the hours of work since the mid-1970s. *Monthly Labor Review, 120*(4), 3–14.

Russell, J. A., & Barrett, L. F. (1999). Core affect, prototypical emotional episodes, and other things called emotion: Dissecting the elephant. *Journal of Personality and Social Psychology, 76,* 805–819.

Rusting, C. L., & Larsen, R. J. (1997). Extraversion, neuroticism, and susceptibility to positive and negative affect: A test of two theoretical models. *Personality and Individual Differences, 22,* 607–612.

Scheier, M. F., & Carver, C. S. (1985). Optimism, coping, and health: Assessment and implications of generalized outcome expectancies. *Health Psychology, 4,* 219–247.

Schneider, B., Smith, D. B., Taylor, S., & Fleenor, J. (1998). Personality and organizations: A test of the homogeneity of personality hypothesis. *Journal of Applied Psychology, 83,* 462–470.

Schroeder, D. H., & Costa, P. T. (1984), Influence of life event stress on physical illness: Substantive effects or methodological flaws? *Journal of Personality and Social Psychology, 46,* 853–863.

Schuler, R. S. (1980). Definition and conceptualization of stress in organizations. *Organizational Behavior and Human Performance, 24,* 115–130.

Seyle, H. (1971). The evolution of the stress concept—stress and cardiovascular disease. In L. Levi (Ed.), *Society, stress, and disease: The psychological environment and psychosomatic diseases, Vol. 1.* London: Oxford.

Shewuck, R. M., Elliott, T. R., MacNair-Semands, R. R., & Harkins, S. (1999). Trait influences on stress appraisal and coping: An evaluation of alternative frameworks. *Journal of Applied Social Psychology, 29,* 685–704.

Smith, T. W., Pope, M. K., Rhodewalt, F., & Poulton, J. L. (1989). Optimism, neuroticism, coping, and symptom reports: An alternative interpretation of the Life Orientation Test. *Journal of Personality and Social Psychology, 56,* 640–648.

Spector, P. E., Zapf, D., Chen, P. Y., & Frese, M. (2000). Why negative affectivity should not be controlled in job stress research: Don't throw out the baby with the bath water. *Journal of Organizational Behavior, 21,* 79–95.

Spielberger, C. D., Gorsuch, R. L., Lushene, R., Vagg, P. R., & Jacobs, G. A. (1983). *Manual for the State-Trait Anxiety Inventory (Form Y).* Palo Alto, CA: Consulting Psychologists Press.

Stone, A. A., Schwartz, J. E., Neale, J. M., Shiffman, S., Marco, C. A., Hickcox, M., Paty, J., Porter, L. S., & Cruise, L. J. (1998). A comparison of coping assessed by ecological momentary assessment and retrospective recall. *Journal of Personality and Social Psychology, 74,* 1670–1680.

Suh, E., Diener, E., & Fujita, F. (1996). Events and subjective well-being: Only recent events matter. *Journal of Personality and Social Psychology, 70,* 1091–1102.

Suls, J., David, J. P., & Harvey, J. H. (1996). Personality and coping: Three generations of research. *Journal of Personality, 64*, 711–735.

Suls, J., & Fletcher, B. (1985). The relative efficacy of avoidant and nonavoidant coping strategies: A meta-analysis. *Health Psychology, 4*, 249–288.

Suls, J., Green, P., & Hillis, S. (1998). Emotional reactivity to everyday problems, affective inertia, and neuroticism. *Personality and Social Psychology Bulletin, 24*, 127–136.

Tellegen, A. (1985). Structure of mood and personality and their relevance to assessing anxiety with an emphasis on self-report. In A. H. Tuma & J. D. Maser (Eds.), *Anxiety and the anxiety disorders* (pp. 681–706). Hillsdale, NJ: Erlbaum.

Tellegen, A., Lykken, D. T., Bouchard, T. J., Wilcox, K. J., Segal, N. L., & Rich, S. (1988). Personality similarity in twins reared apart and together. *Journal of Personality and Social Psychology, 54*, 1031–1039.

Terry, D. J. (1994). Determinants of coping: The role of stable and situational factors. *Journal of Personality and Social Psychology, 66*, 895–910.

Veenhoven, R. (1994). Is happiness a trait? Tests of the theory that a better society does not make people any happier. *Social Indicators Research, 32*, 101–160.

Viteles, M. S. (1932). *Industrial psychology*. New York: Norton.

Warr, P. B. (1983). Work, jobs, and unemployment. *Bulletin of the British Psychological Association, 36*, 305–311.

Warr, P. (1999). Well-being and the workplace. In D. Kahneman, E. Diener, & N. Schwarz (Eds.), *Well-being: The foundations of hedonic psychology* (pp. 392–412). New York: Russell Sage Foundation.

Watson, D. (2000). *Mood and temperament*. New York: Guilford.

Watson, D., & Clark, L. A. (1984). Negative affectivity: The disposition to experience aversive emotional states. *Psychological Bulletin, 96*, 465–490.

Watson, D., & Clark, L. A. (1992). On traits and temperament: General and specific factors of emotional experience and their relation to the Five-Factor Model. *Journal of Personality, 60*, 441–476.

Watson, D., & Clark, L. A. (1994). *The PANAS-X: Manual for the Positive and Negative Affect Schedule—Expanded Form*. Unpublished manuscript, University of Iowa, Iowa City.

Watson, D., & Clark, L. A. (1997). Extraversion and its positive emotional core. In R. Hogan, J. Johnson, & S. Briggs (Eds.), *Handbook of personality psychology* (pp. 767–793). San Diego: Academic.

Watson, D., Clark, L. A., McIntyre, C. W., & Hamaker, S. (1992). Affect, personality and social activity. *Journal of Personality and Social Psychology, 63*, 1011–1025.

Watson, D., Clark, L. A., & Tellegen, A. (1988). Development and validation of brief measures of positive and negative affect: The PANAS scales. *Journal of Personality and Social Psychology, 54*, 1063–1070.

Watson, D., & Hubbard, B. (1996). Adaptational style and dispositional structure: Coping in the context of the Five-Factor Model. *Journal of Personality, 64*, 737–774.

Watson, D., & Tellegen, A. (1985). Toward a consensual structure of mood. *Psychological Bulletin, 98*, 219–235.

Watson, D., & Walker, L. M. (1996). The long-term stability and predictive validity of trait measures of affect. *Journal of Personality and Social Psychology, 70*, 567–577.

Watson, D., Wiese, D., Vaidya, J., & Tellegen, A. (1999). The two general activation systems of affect: Structural findings, evolutionary considerations, and psychobiological evidence. *Journal of Personality and Social Psychology, 76*, 820–838.

Weiss, H. M., & Brief, A. P. (2001). Affect at work: An historical perspective. In R. L. Payne & C. L. Cooper (Eds.), *Emotions at work: Theory, research and applications in management* (pp. 133–172). Chichester: Wiley.

Weiss, H. M., Nicholas, J. P., & Daus, C. S. (1999). An examination of the joint effects of affective experiences and job beliefs on job satisfaction and variations in affective experiences over time. *Organizational Behavior and Human Decision Processes, 78*, 1–24.

Williams, L. J., Gavin, M. B., & Williams, M. L. (1996). Measurement and nonmeasurement processes with negative affectivity and employee attitudes. *Journal of Applied Psychology, 81*, 88–101.

Zelenski, J. M., & Larsen, R. J. (1999). Susceptibility to affect: A comparison of three personality taxonomies. *Journal of Personality, 67*, 761–791.

IV

The Role of Personality in Understanding Micro Organizational Processes

The three chapters in this section explore three traditional topics in organizational psychology: motivation, leadership, and citizenship behavior. The three topics go from within-person issues (motivation) to dyadic leader-follower relationships (leadership) to a kind of performance in organizations, citizenship behavior, which has been receiving increasingly significant attention.

In chapter 9, James and Rentsch present an overview of a new approach to thinking about personality in the workplace, implicit justification. Their reasoning is that the way people explain, or justify, behavior is a key to their personality. James and Rentsch argue that personality and motivation are inextricably entwined, and furthermore, that understanding their linkage is possible via a new measurement procedure called conditional reasoning. This procedure, which requires people to explain or justify vignettes presented to them, seems to offer insights into the prediction and understanding of behavior in ways that yield improved validity over more traditional self-descriptive reports.

In chapter 10, Spangler, House, and Palrecha explore the relationship between personality and leadership. Their focus on the intersection of motives and personality provides a second look (after James and Rentsch in chap. 9) at this personality–motive nexus and shows how this combined perspective offers insights into understanding leadership effectiveness. Furthermore, Spangler and his colleagues show how a focus on motives sheds light on the consistently modest relationships that exist in the literature on the personality prediction of leadership.

Chapter 11, by Organ and Paine, reviews the expanding literature attempting to provide insight into citizenship behavior at work via individual differences correlates. Thus, the early work on citizenship behavior (also known as contextual performance) focused on job satisfaction and situational correlates of job satisfaction (like fairness or justice). In this chapter, Organ and Paine explore various conceptualizations of the relationship between personality and citizenship behavior in an attempt to explain the modest relationships between them shown to date. They then offer an alternative research paradigm for exploring these relationships, one that focuses less on hunting for new individual traits that might correlate with citizenship behavior and more on capitalizing on what we know by using a more configural approach.

9

J-U-S-T-I-F-Y to Explain the Reasons Why: A Conditional Reasoning Approach to Understanding Motivated Behavior

Lawrence R. James and Joan R. Rentsch
The University of Tennessee

Personality consists of those components of cognitive structure and cognitive process that determine individuals' emotional and behavioral adjustments to environments (see Allport, 1937; James & Mazerolle, 2002). Many of these components are primarily motivational in content, the prime example being the motives (needs) that lie at the core of the cognitive structure (Murray, 1938) and that strongly influence the direction, intensity, and persistence of the characteristic behavioral adjustments that we commonly refer to as traits. To illustrate, differences in the strength of the need to achieve influence the difficulty levels of the tasks that different individuals choose to perform and the varying levels of intensity and persistence that these individuals are willing to devote to tasks to attempt to satisfy their need to achieve. Intervening between the motives and the behaviors they stimulate are various affective (e.g., sense of challenge, anticipation, and excitement) and cognitive (e.g., goals, expectancies, valences) mechanisms that shape and sustain the direction, intensity, and perseverance of the motivated behaviors. In a real sense, the study of personality is a study of motivation because the core explanatory mechanisms of personality—motives—shape the individual differences in behaviors that define traits. We shall refer to this functional link or connection between motives and the behaviors intended to serve these motives as the *personality–motivation nexus*.

In organizational research, almost all the studies of this personality–motivation nexus are based at least in part on self-reports (Schwarz, 1999). This fact implies that investigations of the motivational shaping of behavioral and emotional adjustments to environments are predicated almost exclusively on individuals' conscious cognitions. *Conscious cognitions* consist of those components of cognitive structure and cognitive process that are accessible to introspection by the individual. Measures of personality based on conscious cognitions are often referred to as being *self-ascribed* (as in self-ascribed motive; see Greenwald & Banaji, 1995).

Mounting evidence suggests that implicit or unconscious cognitions provide an additional, important, and often unique (in relation to conscious cognitions) source of information about the personality–motivation nexus (see Greenwald & Banaji, 1995; Winter, John, Stewart, Klohnen, & Duncan, 1998). *Implicit cognitions* are (a) components of cognitive structure and cognitive process that determine individuals' perceptual, emotional, and behavioral adjustments to environments (see Allport, 1937; James & Mazarolle, 2002) that (b) are not accessible to introspection by the individual (cf. Greenwald & Banaji; Kilstrom, 1999; Nisbett & Wilson, 1977; Winter et al.). Implicitness is believed to be a function of one or more factors such as the following:

Basic biological drives that have not reached consciousness (e.g., implicit motives).

Developmental or learning experiences that have been lost to memory (e.g., conditioned associations between stimuli and emotions).

Cognitive processing that was at one time consciously controlled but has become automatic and lost to introspection (e.g., an unrecognized propensity to prefer internal over external attributions to explain success/failure).

Cognitive processes that unconsciously serve to enhance or to protect self-esteem and subjective well-being (e.g., rationalization or denial; see Fiske & Taylor, 1984, 1991; Greenwald & Banaji; Kilstrom; Nisbett & Wilson; Winter et al.).

Substantial breakthroughs in the understanding of how implicit cognitive structures and processes are employed by humans to give meaning to, and to determine their functioning in, social contexts have been provided primarily by research in social cognition. In general terms, research in *social cognition* involves examinations of the inferences, judgments, explanations, and theories that people have about the causes and effects of their own behavior and the behavior of others in social environments. The specific domains of research in social cognition that involve implicit cognitions include framing, attribution errors, illusionary correlations or halo, confirmatory biases in hypothesis testing, categorization/protoyping (e.g., stereotyping), downward comparison, implicit personality theories, rationalization and self-justification, discounting, positive and negative leniency in evaluation and judgment, self-handicapping, escalating commitment, felt contentment, and defense mechanisms underlying ego protection and ego enhancement (cf. Fiske & Taylor, 1984, 1991; Greenwald & Banaji, 1995; Kilstrom, 1999; Nisbett & Wilson, 1977; Winter et al., 1998).

It is our belief that the evolving field of implicit cognition has great potential for advancing our understanding of the personality–motivation nexus in work settings. An indication of the potential of this field is given by a comparison of validities furnished by self-report measures of conscious cognitions compared to validities furnished by a new procedure for measuring implicit cognitions. With respect to self-report or self-attributed measures, it is well documented that a major problem for personality measured via conscious cognition is a ceiling on validity coefficients. Mischel (1968) observed that correlations between self-report measures of personality and consequential behaviors infrequently exceeded .30 and therefore accounted for 10% or less of the variance in salient behavioral criteria. Researchers have made amazingly little progress to improve the measurement of personality in the past 30 years. For example, recent meta-analyses have indicated that the average, uncorrected validities for single predictors against behavioral criteria rarely exceed .30 and have a mean of approximately .12 even when the review is limited to studies of theoretically predicted relationships—see Barrick & Mount, 1993; Ghiselli, 1966. (*Uncorrected* refers to lack of adjustment for unreliability in the criterion, unreliability in the predictor, or range restriction.). It appears reasonable to conclude, therefore, that personality measures tend to have significant but modest—make that low and generally unimpressive—criterion-related validities. Explaining slightly more than 01% of the variance in behavior on the average suggests that conscious cognitions may not have captured all there is to know about how personality affects motivated behavior.

Recently, instruments have been developed to measure implicit aspects of the personality–motivation nexus. These instruments have produced much more impressive validities against independently assessed behavioral criteria. For example, James and Mazerolle (2002) reported results for conditional reasoning tests developed to assess implicit motive strength (an assessment of whether the implicit motive to achieve is stronger or weaker than the implicit motive to avoid failing) and implicit cognitive readiness to aggress (a measure of implicit preparedness to engage in aggression). A crucial test of the construct validity of these conditional reasoning tests was whether empirical validation analyses confirmed that the tests predicted behavioral indicators of achievement and aggression. The predicted links for aggression were tested in eight studies, which included one experimental study and seven field studies. The inferential links for

TABLE 9.1
Uncorrected Validities for Conditional Reasoning Tests (CRTs) for
Aggression and Achievement Motivation

A. Aggression

	Criterion	Sample	Instrument	Research Design	Uncorrected Validity*
1.	Supervisory rating—overall performance	140 Patrol officers	CRT	Predictive	−.49
2.	Absences—lack of class attendance	188 Undergraduates	CRT	Predictive	.37
3.	Lack of truthfulness about extra credit	60 Undergraduates	VCRT	Experiment	.49
4.	Absences—work attendance	97 Nuclear facility operators	CRT	Postdictive	.42
5.	Student conduct violations	225 Undergraduates	VCRT	Postdictive	.55
6.	Attrition	135 Restaurant employees	CRT	Predictive	.32
7.	Absences—lack of work attendance	105 Package handlers	CRT	Predictive	.34
8.	Work unreliability	111 Temporary employees	CRT	Predictive	.43

B. Achievement Motivation

	Criterion	Sample	Instrument	Research Design	Uncorrected Validity*
9.	Average test score over a semester	336 Undergraduates	CRT	Predictive	.52
10.	Overall grade point average	110 Undergraduates	CRT	Postdictive	.32
11.	Sign petition advocating curriculum change	67 MBA students	CRT	Natural Experiment	.62
12.	In-basket performance in assessment center	263 Middle-level managers	CRT	Predictive	.39
13.	Final grade in course	359 Undergraduates	CRT	Predictive	.35
14.	Final grade in course	101 Undergraduates	CRT	Predictive	.30

*All correlations are statistically significant ($p < .05$). *Uncorrected* means not corrected for either range restriction or attenuation because of unreliability in either the predictor or the criterion. VCRT refers to a verbal–visual version of the test.

achievement motivation were tested in five studies of which one was a natural experiment and four were field studies.

The absolute values of the uncorrected validities were all statistically significant and ranged from .30 to .62. These validities, all of which are predictive or cross validities, are reported in Table 9.1. The mean validity in this table is approximately .43. If one compares the variance accounted for by this average validity (i.e., $.43^2 = .1849$) to the variance accounted for by the average self-report measure ($.12^2 = .0144$), then indications are that implicit measures of personality offer the opportunity to enhance prediction of behavior by approximately 1200% (i.e., [.1849 − .0144]/.0144) in comparison to explicit measures. This result serves to indicate that measures of implicit cognitions are likely to add substantially to our understanding of the personality–motivation nexus. It also suggests that personality is as important as cognitive problem solving skills in regard to predicting salient behaviors in the workplace.

What is the secret to developing highly valid personality tests? Of initial note is that by virtue of being hidden from introspection, implicit social cognitions cannot be assessed by self-report (cf., Greenwald & Banaji, 1995; Nisbett & Wilson, 1977). Rather, indirect procedures must be used to capture what for respondents are unconscious cognitive processes. The conditional reasoning measurement system taps into the unconscious, habitual reasoning biases that humans use to justify motive-based behaviors (James, 1998). Individuals with different implicit motives behave differently and develop different implicit biases to enhance the rational appeal of their respective behaviors. It follows that whether an individual engages in the use of a specific bias is dependent or conditional on whether he or she is motivated to engage in the behaviors that are served (e.g., protected) by this bias. Having respondents solve what on the surface appear to be inductive reasoning problems is the method used to assess the conditional use of implicit biases. Unknown to respondents, different answers are based on different reasoning biases. The intent of measurement is that only those individuals who are prone to implicitly use a particular justification will see the answer based on this bias as logical or rational. How one answers the problems is thus indicative of one's underlying justification propensities and implicit motive structure.

The social cognitive studies of implicit cognition noted previously made it possible to develop the conditional reasoning measurement system. The purpose of this chapter is to overview the essentials of these studies, the objective being to introduce the reader to implicit cognition and its role in motivation. Specific topics of discussion include implicit motives, unconscious framing proclivities, implicit assumptions, and the implicit role of justification mechanisms in what individuals believe to be rational reasoning. We shall also discuss the relationship between implicit and explicit cognitions. We have found that it is helpful to introduce implicit cognition using exemplars. The exemplars employed here, achievement motivation and fear of failure, were chosen because of their centrality to the study of motivation in work settings. We begin by examining the personality–motivation nexus in greater depth, beginning with the two building blocks of personality, motives and traits.

THE PERSONALITY–MOTIVATION NEXUS

The personality–motivation nexus exists because motives engender the individual differences in behaviors that define traits. For example, to say that a person is *achievement motivated* or high in the trait of achievement motivation means that he or she consistently, over time and evocative situations, directs intense and persistent effort toward accomplishing demanding tasks. Note that we are describing this person's behavior. Now suppose we ask: Why does this person approach (select) demanding tasks and then devote intense and persistent effort toward accomplishing them? In other words, why does he or she behave in ways that we describe as achievement motivated? An answer to this question appears to be that people who aim intense and persistent effort at achieving demanding objectives have a strong need (motive, desire) to do things better (McClelland, 1985).

A similar question could be posed regarding people who experience considerable anxiety or fear over failing and engage in avoidance or other forms of inhibitory behaviors. Why do they react this way to evocative situations? Consider that one of the reasons that an achievement-oriented objective is considered an achievement is because it is difficult. People fail out of college or are not accepted into graduate schools. It is not uncommon to be passed over for promotion at least once in one's life. A majority of new business ventures fail. One may practice unrelentingly for an athletic event and yet still fail to win or even place among the top finishers. Basically, striving to achieve carries with it a degree of uncertainty, a risk that the venture may be unsuccessful. These types of situations may stimulate the need in some individuals to protect themselves from undertaking actions that put them at risk of experiencing psychological discomfort. These individuals have a strong need (or motive) to avoid failure. These two examples illustrate the inextricable link between personality and motivation, or the personality–motivation nexus. We continue this discussion in the following sections, where we look at motives and traits more fully and add the intervening implicit cognitions.

IMPLICIT COGNITIONS IN THE
PERSONALITY–MOTIVATION NEXUS

As noted earlier, personality refers to dynamic mental structures and coordinated mental processes (i.e., cognitive structures and processes) that determine individuals' emotional and behavioral adjustments to their environments (see Allport, 1937). The term *dynamic* suggests that personality continues to evolve throughout one's lifetime. Evolution for a given individual is predictable, however, because there is also considerable coherence in personality over time. For example, *mental structures* include motives, memories, and self-images. These attributes may adjust and modify to correspond to changes in activity level, development, education, occupation, marital status, health, socioeconomic status, and so on. But we also witness consistency over time. To illustrate, over time and across situations, the achievement-oriented person will continue to seek success, whereas the person high in fear of failure will continue to avoid demanding tasks. The same is true for *mental processes* such as perception and reasoning. Over time, one's attributions for why one acts in particular ways may sharpen and reflect increased understanding. However, unrecognized rationalizations in these attributions may remain with one throughout the life span. We shall focus on these unrecognized rationalizations, or justifications, because they play key roles in the implicit processing that underlies motivated behavior. The treatment of justifications begins by reviewing the attributes that they serve, namely traits and motives.

TRAITS

The term *trait* refers to a disposition to behave in a relatively consistent manner over time and across situations. The three salient aspects of a trait are as follows: A number of related behaviors can be grouped into one general category, this category can be operationally defined in terms of these behaviors, and the behaviors representing the trait are consistently manifested over time and situations (James & Mazerolle, 2002).

Traits become evident when individuals are faced with difficult decisions (see Stagner, 1977). These are decisions that are evocative—that is, they are important to the individual—and imply that the individual is free to make a choice about behavior. In the workplace, these decisions often involve whether to approach or to avoid a demanding task or objective. Whether to approach or to avoid often becomes a form of approach–avoidance conflict (Atkinson, 1978). How these conflicts tend to be resolved provides the foundation for two primary traits, namely achievement motivation and fear of failure.

The Trait of Achievement Motivation

Over their life spans, some people exhibit a recurring pattern in which they resolve approach–avoidance conflicts in favor of approaching achievement-oriented objectives. An achievement-oriented goal is one that

(a) relative to one's skill and ability, is personally challenging or demanding, (b) requires intense and persistent effort to attain, and (c) is perceived by the individual as an important and worthwhile accomplishment. A recurring pattern of seeking successively more challenging goals and tasks is also likely to include a willingness to devote intense effort to the selected objective. Intensity is reflected by competitiveness, devoting long hours to honing the skills required for success, and a level of involvement in goal accomplishment that may result in neglecting other aspects of one's life. Accompanying intensity is tenacity, exemplified by a willingness to persevere for long periods of time to accomplish the demanding objectives. Individuals who consistently resolve approach–avoidance conflicts in favor of approaching high-press-for-achievement tasks and who are willing to devote intense and persistent effort to accomplishing these tasks are displaying consistent behavioral tendencies that define the trait of achievement motivation (see McClelland, 1985; Wright & Mischel, 1987).

The Trait of Fear of Failure

Fear of failure refers to the anticipatory feeling of uneasiness, apprehension, dread, and anxiety about attempting a difficult task, failing, and appearing incompetent (Atkinson, 1978). Fear of failing, or more precisely the desire to reduce anxiety over failing, serves to dampen the enthusiasm for achievement and stimulates affected individuals to avoid achievement-oriented tasks completely, or to withdraw from such tasks if success is not immediately forthcoming. It is also the case that the fear and foreboding over possible failure may become a self-fulfilling prophecy if demanding tasks are not avoided. Heightened apprehension over substandard performance can increase anxiety to such a level that it interferes with performance on difficult tasks.

The trait of fear of failure refers to a behavioral tendency to resolve approach–avoidance conflicts in favor of avoiding achievement-oriented tasks and objectives. To be precise, the trait of fear of failure is indicated by *inhibitory behaviors* (cf., Atkinson, 1978), which are actions that serve to minimize anxiety over failing by dampening—inhibiting—the undertaking of achievement-oriented activities. As noted earlier, avoidance of, or withdrawal from, achievement-oriented tasks is the most direct behavioral indicator of fear of failure. However, avoidance may not be socially desirable or even possible, in which case inhibitory behaviors may take on subtle forms. Included are compensatory behaviors, defensive withholding of effort, and self-handicapping (see James & Mazerolle, 2002). These types of manifestations of the trait of fear of failure can be devastating to businesses.

MOTIVES (NEEDS)

Traits enable us to describe what people do, but not why they are doing it. Many researchers consider *motives*—innate strong needs and desires—as likely causes of the consistent behavior patterns represented by traits (see James & Mazerolle, 2002). For example, some people are attracted to high-press-for-achievement objectives and are willing to devote intense and persistent effort to accomplishing these objectives, because they have a motive (need, desire) to show that they are capable of mastering challenging tasks (see Atkinson, 1978; McClelland, 1985). The motive to achieve derives its potency or forcefulness from the natural incentives of positive emotions or feelings, wherein the pursuit of demanding tasks is associated with enthusiasm, excitement, and involvement. Pride in having demonstrated mastery is also to be considered, as are winning approval and recognition for having competed successfully, given that many achievement-oriented tasks involve competition with others.

By way of contrast, people who exhibit the trait of fear of failure are motivated by different need(s). As mentioned earlier, an achievement-oriented objective is considered an achievement because it is difficult. An individual striving to achieve risks experiencing failure and faces uncertainty. The sense of uncertainty is strongest when the probability of success is approximately 5 in 10, for it here that one is least able to predict the outcome and thus is most likely to experience apprehension about the result (Atkinson, 1978).

Uncertainty and risk suggest that when an achievement-oriented opportunity triggers the need to achieve and anticipations of the thrill of the chase, it also stimulates an opposing or antagonistic motive that performs a self-protective function. This motive is a form of a safety mechanism designed to protect individuals from engaging in activities that will cause them psychological damage. The protective mechanism consists of a natural proclivity to consider the downside of achievement striving, which is failure and the resulting humiliation, embarrassment, and sense of incompetence that follow failing. The motive is therefore referred to as the *motive (or need) to avoid failure.*

Everyone who cognizes normally has some concern with avoidance of failure. Nevertheless, people vary in the strength of the need to avoid failure. Those who have an intense aversion to uncertainty, and are strongly concerned with protecting themselves from failure, are predisposed to experience considerable fear of failure (e.g., apprehension, anxiety, dread, worry) when faced with high-press-for-achievement goals or tasks (see Atkinson, 1978; Nicholls, 1984).

Basically, these people have an overriding need to avoid experiencing humiliation, shame, and embarrassment. When presented with an achievement-oriented opportunity, the motive to avoid failing acts to counterbalance the motive to achieve by stimulating concerns about the ramifications of attempting to succeed and falling short. The opposing forces of the motive to achieve and the motive to avoid failing create what we referred to earlier as approach–avoidance conflicts.

Attempts to resolve approach–avoidance conflicts when faced with achievement-oriented goals or tasks involve what Atkinson (1978, p. 16) designated the "resultant achievement-oriented tendency," or simply the "resultant tendency." For a given task or objective, the resultant tendency varies on a continuum from a high probability of approach to a high probability of avoidance. These probabilities are determined in part by which of the two motives is stronger and by the degree of this dominance.

For some people, the resultant tendency is represented by an approach or excitatory tendency because the motive to achieve is stronger than the motive to avoid failure. When the need to achieve is strong, and the need to avoid failure is only modest or weak, then the excitatory tendency or probability of approach is quite high. Indeed, when a strong need to achieve dominates a modest or weak need to avoid failure, people tend not only to resolve approach–avoidance conflicts by engaging in achievement activities, but also to devote intense and persistent effort to succeeding at these activities. As a pattern of approach and effort expenditure recurs over time and situations, individuals who exhibit the pattern are identified as achievement motivated or are said to possess the trait of achievement motivation.

For other people, the motive to avoid failure is stronger than the motive to achieve. These people are prone to avoid or at least to dampen their enthusiasm for achievement-oriented activities in an attempt to relieve anxiety and apprehension (i.e., fear of failure). These individuals are thus said to possess an "avoidant" or "inhibitory" resultant tendency (Atkinson, 1978, p. 16). When a strong need to avoid failure dominates a modest or weak need to achieve, the inhibitory tendency is quite high. People with this motive pattern consistently tend to resolve approach–avoidance conflicts by avoiding achievement-related activities or engaging in inhibitory behaviors. Over time and situations, people who consistently experience fear of failure and exhibit inhibitory tendencies are described as possessing the trait of fear of failure.

In sum, the personality–motivation nexus refers to the fact that motives shape and direct behavior. Dominant motives are more influential than weak motives, although even a weak motive is likely to exert some effect (e.g., people with strong approach tendencies are not immune to humiliation). We now elaborate the discussion by turning to social cognition to explain how motives influence behavior. We are particularly interested in the implicit cognitions that are expected to mediate the effects of motives on traits.

IMPLICIT COGNITIONS: MEDIATORS
OF MOTIVE–TRAIT RELATIONSHIPS

Motives explain why some individuals approach demanding tasks while others avoid these tasks. To explain how motives trigger behavior, we must dig deeper into personality, which is to say into cognitive structure and processes. By seeking to understand how motives engender the behaviors that define traits, we enter the social cognitive domain of personality. *Social cognition* is formally defined as the "... cognitive processes and structures (e.g., self-conceptions, standards, goals) through which individuals assign personal meaning to events, plan courses of action, and regulate their motivation, emotion, and interpersonal behavior" (Cervone, 1991, p. 372). James and Mazerolle (2002) presented models in which social cognition mediates the effects of motives on traits (i.e., motives → social cognition → traits). By nature of being a mediator, social cognition seeks to explain the processes by which motives act on or produce behavior.

It is our belief that a complete account of personality requires discussion of both the trait and social cognitive perspectives, with emphasis placed on how the approaches unite and synthesize to explain behavior (Cervone, 1991). We shall not attempt to be complete or exhaustive in this accounting, in part because it is an evolving endeavor. Fortunately, much has already been written on how explicit (social) cognitions are believed to shape and guide behavior. Indeed, treatments of motivation in organizational contexts have long had a strong cognitive orientation, albeit one devoted to introspective and self-attributed constructs. These treatments typically include discussions of explicit constructs such as expectancies, valences, instrumentalities, goals, strategies, plans, and self-concepts (e.g., self-esteem, test anxiety), not to mention self-attributed motives such as achievement motivation, conscientiousness, occupational interests, and values. We shall not review this literature inasmuch as it can be found in introductory texts. Rather, we shall focus on what is new and promising, namely implicit cognitions and their roles as mediators of motive–trait relationships.

To illustrate the role of implicit cognitions, consider that when presented with an evocative decision, it is necessary to process information cognitively to make sense of it. For example, when faced with a personally evocative and demanding goal or task, one might consider the answers to such questions as: To what extent is success determined by how intensely I work and by my willingness to persist over time? In order to answer such questions, the individual must interpret what a demanding task, success, intensity, and persistence mean to him or her. This process is called *framing*, and it is indicated by the adjectives that an individual uses to interpret (perceive, assign meaning to) events. For example, some people frame working hard on a demanding task as being overloaded and stressed. Others frame working hard on a demanding task as being intrinsically motivated and job-involved.

To frame an event is to place the event in a cognitive schema. *Cognitive schemas* are internal prisms through which external stimuli pass and are translated into interpretative adjectives that indicate personal meaning. Each individual tends to use the same cognitive schemas repeatedly to interpret events, which results in framing proclivities. *Framing proclivities* are unrecognized (unconscious, implicit, latent) dispositions to use only certain adjectives to interpret the same or similar events (e.g., most achievement-oriented people are framed as "obsessive"). It is these unrecognized framing proclivities that implicitly shape how one consciously interprets evocative events and that determine input into the mental analyses undertaken to decide whether to approach or avoid evocative situations (James, 1998).

The mental analyses are often grounded in *implicit assumptions,* which are unconscious hypotheses and theories that shape and guide reasoning, the product of which is experienced consciously as rational thinking and decision making (see Wegner & Vallacher, 1977). For example, some individuals possess an implicit or unconscious proclivity to assume that internal causes are more important than external causes when making attributions about the causes of performance on demanding tasks. Analyses to determine the causes of success or failure on actual tasks are unknowingly shaped and guided by this implicit assumption. That is, these individuals are unconsciously biased toward finding that internal factors (e.g., intensity, commitment) are the primary causes of performance. The result is that these individuals arrive at conscious judgments that success or failure was largely a function of internal factors such as how hard an individual was willing to work. If asked, these individuals would affirm that their reasoning was purely rational. They are unaware of their implicit disposition to favor internal attributions when they reason about the causes of performance on hard tasks.

Other people's reasoning may evidence an unconscious proclivity to assume that external forces are the primary causes of success or failure on demanding tasks. This unconscious proclivity will unknowingly orient conscious reasoning toward judging factors such as resources or leadership to be the principal causes of performance on demanding tasks. These individuals will also believe that their reasoning was purely rational. The unconscious or implicit tendency to favor external explanations is neither recognized nor available to introspection.

Cognitive schemas, framing proclivities, and implicit assumptions are permanent fixtures of cognitive structure, which means that they are used repeatedly to guide analyses and thinking. The fact that people are not aware of their influences on reasoning is indicated by referring to them as implicit (social) cognitions (Greenwald & Banaji, 1995). In general terms, *implicit cognition* refers to the operation of framing proclivities and implicit assumptions that are beyond the awareness of, or are not accessible to introspection by, the individual (Greenwald & Banaji; Kilstrom, 1999; Nisbett & Wilson, 1977).

Motives affect implicit cognitions. Consider that assignment of meaning based on framing proclivities, followed by analysis based on both framing proclivities and implicit assumptions, are reasoning processes. Four especially interesting features of these reasoning processes are:

1. People with different dominant motives often interpret evocative events differently (James, 1998, referred to individual differences in framing as differential framing).
2. The reasoning of people with different dominant motives is often grounded in different implicit assumptions, in part because of differential framing.
3. Irrespective of which motive(s) is dominant, the unconscious shaping of framing and analysis by the dominant motive(s) is designed to enhance the rational appeal of behavior that serves the motive(s).
4. Irrespective of individual differences in inferences and conclusions, almost every individual believes that his or her reasoning is rational and sensible.

We shall again use the exemplars of achievement motivation and fear of failure to illustrate these points. Below, we demonstrate how people with a strong motive to achieve reason differently than people with a strong motive to avoid failing. These differences in reasoning are said to be conditional on the personalities of the reasoners (James, 1998; James & McIntyre, 2000). Specifically, *conditional reasoning* is defined as reasoning that is dependent on personality, which occasions when framing and analyses are dependent on the particular motives, framing proclivities, and implicit assumptions of the reasoner (James & Mazerolle, 2002). Thus, whether framing and analyses identify approach or avoidance as being the more reasonable behavioral adjustment to a demanding task is conditional (i.e., dependent) on whether the person doing the reasoning is motivated more by the motive to achieve or the motive to avoid failure.

CONDITIONAL REASONING AS A PRODUCT
OF JUSTIFICATION MECHANISMS

We shall first adopt a form of shorthand to facilitate discussion. The term *AM* (for achievement motivated) will be used to refer to people for whom the motive to achieve dominates the motive to avoid failure. By contrast, people for whom the motive to avoid failure dominates the motive to achieve will be referred to as *FFs* (for fear of failure).

As discussed earlier, reasoning is conditional because AMs and FFs have different ideas about what constitutes a reasonable adjustment to an environment. Differing judgments about what is a reasonable adjustment are in turn a product of differential framing and the use of different implicit assumptions by AMs and FFs. James (1998; James & Mazerolle, 2002) proposed that these differences in framing proclivities and implicit assumptions be viewed as forms of implicit reasoning biases that AMs and FFs rely on to justify engaging in their respective desired behaviors. He introduced the term *justification mechanism* to refer to the biases. Justification mechanisms are defined as implicit biases whose purpose is to define, shape, and otherwise influence reasoning so as to enhance the rational appeal of behaving in a manner consistent with a disposition or motive.

Justification mechanisms are unknowingly mapped into conscious thought via the (a) cognitive schemas (interpretative categories) used to frame events and the (b) implicit assumptions that are used to determine whether it is more sensible to approach or to avoid a demanding task. For example, given a high-press-for-achievement decision, justification mechanisms for AMs consist of implicit biases whose purpose is to define, shape, and otherwise influence reasoning so as to enhance the rational appeal of approach behaviors. Justification mechanisms for FFs consist of implicit biases whose purpose is to define, shape, and otherwise influence reasoning so as to enhance the rational appeal of avoidance (or inhibitory) behaviors.

Some of the more salient justification mechanisms, or *JMs,* are described in the paragraphs that follow for AMs and then for FFs. This presentation is drawn from a recent article by James (1998) and a book on personality by James and Mazerolle (2002). It is important to reiterate that the individuals who rely on these JMs are unaware of the conditional nature of their reasoning and the biases in their thinking. To them, their analyses involve natural framing and sensible assumptions that offer logical guides for inferences about the effects of behaviors (e.g., approach to or avoidance of demanding tasks) on such things as success/failure at work, health, interrelationships with others, and a general sense of emotional well-being (see Wegner & Vallacher, 1977).

Justification Mechanisms of AMs

As noted briefly, AMs have an unrecognized tendency to attribute behavior to personal responsibility (see McClelland & Boyatzis, 1982; Weiner, 1979). They are predisposed to reason from the perspective that people should, if the opportunity arises, take initiatives and be responsible for decisions and strategies. They are also predisposed to reason from the perspective that people should be held personally accountable for the success or failure of these endeavors. The implicit assumption that people should be held personally accountable for success or failure on demanding tasks engenders a tendency to favor internal attributions (initiative, perseverance, conscientiousness) as explanations for performance in achievement situations. Predilections to invoke internal attributions (explanations) indicates a lack of inclination to use external attributions (e.g., helpful coworkers contributed to success when performance is good, inadequate resources restricted performance when one fails) for explanatory purposes.

Note that an exclusively rational analysis might uncover reasonable support for both internal (e.g., effort, skills) and external (e.g., leadership, resources) explanations for performance. Highly motivated individuals, however, are unknowingly predisposed to reason from the perspective (i.e., have an implicit assumption) that success or failure on demanding tasks is largely a function of personal initiative, intensity, and persistence (i.e., internal attributions). Thus, in their attempts to justify approach to demanding goals and objectives and the pursuit of achievement, AMs are inclined to give greater emphasis to internal factors than is deserved (see Weiner, 1979). This is what is meant by an *implicit* or *unconscious bias.*

Bias does not denote error, because internal factors constitute one plausible explanation for performance. But, a purely rational model calls for a dialectic, where both personal and external factors are viable as causes of performance. The connotation of bias is thus a predilection to favor one side of a dialectic when a rational analysis can identify two (or more) alternative, often conflicting, plausible explanations for which there is no logical basis for favoring one explanation over any other.

AMs may well subscribe consciously to the idea of a dialectic, and may even express strong beliefs in the validity of explanatory models that espouse both internal and external causes. However, when asked to analyze specific events and to rationally determine causes of success or failure, AMs have a propensity to favor internal causes as rational explanations. We return to this point later when we discuss the relationship between explicit and implicit cognitions.

AMs tend to favor explanations based on personal responsibility because (a) they want to believe consciously that success on demanding tasks is not only possible but also controllable via their efforts, and (b) attributing success to personally controllable factors such as initiative and perseverance indirectly suggests that they are competent, self-reliant, and talented. It is also noteworthy that a predilection to attribute success on demanding tasks to internal, personal agents fosters an optimistic view of the likelihood of one's success, which is to say the likelihood that demanding goals and tasks will succumb to one's intense and persistent efforts.

TABLE 9.2
Justification Mechanisms for Achievement Motivation

Personal responsibility inclination	Tendency to favor personal factors such as initiative, intensity, and persistence as the most important causes of performance on demanding tasks.
Opportunity inclination	Tendency to frame demanding tasks on which success is uncertain as challenges that offer opportunities to demonstrate present skills, to learn new skills, and to make a contribution.
Positive connotation of achievement striving	Tendency to associate effort (intensity, persistence) on demanding tasks to dedication, concentration, commitment, and involvement.
Malleability of skills	Tendency to assume that the skills necessary to master demanding tasks can, if necessary, be learned or developed via training, practice, and experience.
Efficacy of persistence	Tendency to assume that continued effort and commitment will overcome obstacles or any initial failures that might occur on a demanding task.
Identification with achievers	Tendency to empathize with the sense of enthusiasm, intensity, and striving that characterize those who succeed in demanding situations. Selectively focus on positive incentives that accrue from succeeding.

This is then a form of unconscious bias, although not necessarily error (see Funder, 1987), whose purpose is to enhance the logical appeal of approach behaviors. It illustrates the presence of a JM—namely a personal responsibility bias—in framing and analyses. Reasoning that has been unconsciously shaped, defined, and guided by the personal responsibility bias is said to be conditional because framing and analyses are dependent on the reasoner having a strong motive to achieve.

An implicit affinity to personal responsibility is just one illustration of how JMs shape, define, and otherwise influence the framing and analyses of AMs. Other JMs for AMs are presented in Table 9.2. Included in this set is the positive connotation of achievement striving bias. This JM often affects AMs' framing of working long hours, with minimal rest and attention to other facets of their lives. A sustained and single-minded concentration on the attainment of a demanding goal is framed or interpreted as a demonstration of dedication, intensity, commitment, involvement, or tenacity. Tacit in this framing is an unrecognized predilection on the part of AMs to ignore or to discount the many forms of stress (e.g., overload, conflict between work and nonwork roles) that they are likely to encounter in their quests to achieve (McClelland, 1985; Spence & Helmreich, 1983).

One of the reasons that AMs do not frame working on demanding tasks as stressful is that they tend to regard these tasks as challenges or opportunities (Spence & Helmreich, 1983). This framing is reflective of an implicit bias to assume that demanding activities are opportunities to take on important objectives, to demonstrate noteworthy skills, and to make contributions in areas that count. This is the opportunity bias JM.

Note how this framing contrasts with that of FFs. The essence of being an FF is to associate threat and anxiety with the same demanding tasks that AMs perceive as challenges and opportunities. AMs are able to take this perspective because they expect to succeed. Indeed, unlike FFs, who fixate on the downside of achievement striving, AMs attend selectively to the upside. This orientation is manifested by a selective focus on the positive incentives that accrue to successful achievers, both material (e.g., promotion) and emotional (e.g., involvement, excitement, a sense of efficacy).

Another important JM for AMs is the efficacy of persistence bias. A hallmark of being an AM is to reason from the perspective that continued effort and perseverance will ultimately result in successful accomplishment of achievement-oriented objectives (McClelland, 1985; Weiner, 1979). The JM entitled efficacy of persistence bias is especially likely to influence reasoning when AMs must overcome obstacles and transitory failures. Examples include the following: (a) a scientist who attributes a failed experiment to learning experiences, and moves on to continue experimentation; (b) an entrepreneur who begins anew after a business failure, with even greater determination to build a successful enterprise; (c) an athlete who persists and intensifies practice sessions after having failed to meet his or her standards in competition, and (d) aspiring authors such as Alex Haley, who continue to submit manuscripts even though they are rejected repeatedly.

An alternative explanation could have been invoked in each of these illustrations. A number of these alternative explanations could have resulted in abandoning the objectives (e.g., attributions to uncontrollable outside forces). However, an unrecognized willingness to invoke reasoning that justifies persisting on the tasks demonstrates the efficacy of persistence bias and the dominant motivational force—that is, the motive to achieve—that this JM serves. It is also noteworthy that the tendency of AMs to slant their reasoning to favor efficacy of persistence is often accompanied by a corollary and supporting tendency to think that the skills necessary to accomplish a demanding task can, if necessary, be learned or developed via training, practice, and experience (see Dweck & Leggett, 1988). This reasoning is often at least partially influenced by the JM entitled the malleability of skills bias.

In sum, JMs serve the motive to achieve by implicitly shaping, defining, and guiding the reasoning that AMs use to enhance the rational appeal of approaching demanding tasks. It is thus JMs that make it possible for AMs to approach and to persevere on personally challenging tasks without experiencing debilitating anxiety about the uncertainty of success or being intimidated by the risk to security that often accompanies failure on important tasks. Indeed, the conscious reasoning engendered by JMs encourages AMs to engage in steadfast pursuit of difficult objectives because this reasoning frames the objectives as opportunities worth commitment and sacrifice, where willingness to expend intense and persistent effort will eventually produce success.

Justification Mechanisms of FFs

Achievement commands respect in our culture, and demanding tasks, which herald achievement, are imbued with considerable valence. As we have seen, this valence triggers approach tendencies on the part of AMs. Approach is corroborated and sanctioned as being rational by a set of JMs that lionize demanding goals and render success as primarily a function of dedication and commitment. FFs are also aware of the importance of achievement and the rewards that accrue to those who succeed on difficult tasks. However, this knowledge does not engender the attraction to the tasks experienced by AMs. Rather, for FFs the recognized significance of doing well on difficult tasks stimulates fear and anxiety about the consequences of not doing well, the primary concern being whether one will be perceived as incompetent. Basically, the types of goals and tasks that serve as challenges and opportunities for AMs create psychological hazards (e.g., apprehension, debilitating anxiety, threat) for FFs.

FFs seek relief from their fear of failing by avoiding the achievement-oriented activities on which they see themselves as likely to fail. As discussed, avoidance and other, nondestructive types of inhibitory behaviors are often viewed as self-protective processes, or coping mechanisms, for FFs (see Atkinson, 1978; Nicholls, 1984; Sorrentino & Short, 1986). Especially important ingredients of this coping process are means to justify avoiding the tasks, goals, problems, and environments in which failure is perceived as probable. FFs want to believe that the avoidance/inhibitory behaviors they engage in to relieve their anxiety about failing are both reasonable and will produce the desired results.

The framing and inferences employed by FFs to justify avoidance behaviors are often based on some aspect of the justification mechanisms (JMs) summarized in Table 9.3. Several of these JMs are described in greater detail below.

TABLE 9.3
Justification Mechanisms for Fear of Failure

External attribution inclination	Tendency to favor external factors such as lack of resources, situational constraints, intractable material, or biased evaluations as the most important causes of performance on demanding tasks.
Liability inclination	Tendency to frame demanding tasks as personal liabilities or threats because one may fail and be seen as incompetent. Perceptions of threat are euphemistically expressed in terms such as risky, costly, or venturesome.
Negative connotation of achievement striving	Tendency to frame effort (intensity, persistence) on demanding tasks as overloading or stressful. Perseverence on demanding tasks after encountering setbacks or obstacles is associated with compulsiveness and lack of self-discipline.
Fixed skills	Tendency to assume that problem-solving skills are fixed and cannot be enhanced by experience, training, or dedication to learning. Thus, if one is deficient in a skill, then one should not attempt demanding tasks or should withdraw if one encounters initial failures.
Leveling	Tendency to discount a culturally valent but, for the reasoner, a psychologically hazardous event (e.g., approaching demanding situations) by associating that event with a dysfunctional and aversive outcome (e.g., cardiovascular disease).
Identification with failures	Tendency to empathize with the fear and anxiety of those who fail in demanding situations, selectively focus on negative outcomes that accrue from failing.
Indirect compensation	An attempt to increase the logical appeal of replacing a threatening situation with a compensatory (i.e., less-threatening) situation by imbuing the less-threatening situation with positive, socially desirable qualities.
Self-handicapping	An attempt to deflect explanations for failure away from incompetence in favor of self-induced impairments such as not really trying or not being prepared (e.g., defensive lack of effort).

FFs often reason that engaging in achievement striving is stressful (see Atkinson, 1978; McClelland, 1985; Nicholls, 1984). Such reasoning is often implicitly shaped by the JM entitled negative connotation of achievement striving bias. Basically, FFs are unconsciously disposed to frame achievement striving in negative terms, which is their framing proclivity. Illustrative occasions in which this JM is revealed include FFs' framing of achievement-oriented activities such as intensity and persistence as overloading and sources of potential burnout. These are the same activities that AMs regard as indicators of perseverance and commitment. Dedication for AMs becomes mental or physical overload for FFs, from which springs feelings of anxiousness, strain, and tension.

A corollary to framing demanding tasks as stressful is a predilection by FFs to see the intense and persistent efforts of AMs to achieve as signs of compulsiveness and obsessiveness. The flipside of this corollary is that FFs tend to reason that people who take a more relaxed approach to work are less likely to demonstrate symptoms of stress such as exhaustion, illness, burnout, and chronic anxiety about how one's career is progressing (Crocker & Major, 1989). Such reasoning is also a product of an implicit tendency to justify avoidance of demanding tasks by invoking the negative connotation of achievement bias.

Other JMs are reflected in FFs' reasoning. For example, FFs possess a strong predilection to conclude that the failure on which they have focused their attention is due to external agents that are beyond their control (e.g., lack of resources, societal inequities, poor leadership). Such reasoning often reveals an underlying JM entitled the external attribution bias (see the first JM in Table 9.3 and Crocker & Major, 1989).

As a specific illustration of reasoning based on this JM, consider FF students who conclude that low to moderate scores on an important, difficult exam were products of uncontrollable external agents such as lack of resources (e.g., inadequate study time), situational constraints (e.g., loud roommates), impregnable material, or biased professors. Thus, whereas AMs tend to reason from the perspective that less than stellar performance can be improved by control of internal factors (e.g., increase study time), FFs tend to focus reasoning on external factors over which they have no control and that will likely nullify whatever effort they expend to master material. It is also the case that FFs are less than enthusiastic about AMs' tendency to hold people personally accountable for performance on demanding tasks. To FFs, it hardly seems reasonable to be held personally responsible for failures that were caused by factors over which one had little or no control.

AMs' tendency to champion the efficacy of intense and persistent effort comes under logical attack by FFs from yet another perspective. Research has shown that people who concentrate their attention on failure and its aversive consequences also tend to conclude that basic cognitive problem-solving abilities and critical intellectual skills are fixed and cannot be enhanced by experience, training, or dedication to learning. This reasoning is frequently shaped by a JM designated as the fixed skills bias (see Crocker & Major, 1989; Dweck & Leggett, 1988; Nicholls, 1984; Weiner, 1979). Reasoning engendered by a fixed skills bias contrasts sharply with the reasoning of AMs, who, as noted, tend to analyze behavior from the perspective that the skills necessary to accomplish a demanding task can, if not present at the onset of a difficult assignment, be developed via training, experience, and learning (i.e., effort) as the assignment progresses. FFs, by contrast, are skeptical of pursuing assignments for which they perceive themselves as having deficient critical skills (i.e., they experience an inhibitory or restraining tendency).

The preceding discussion paints a picture in which FFs logically associate achievement-oriented activities with such things as stress, uncontrollable agents, risk, intractable difficulties, and a sense of helplessness. These logical connections furnish FFs with an excuse for avoiding demanding tasks. In place of high-press-for-achievement situations, FFs seek secure and safe environments, where the futures of their jobs and careers are predictable and certain. Such jobs and careers are often less glamorous or prestigious, which stimulates the implicit operation of a JM entitled the indirect compensation bias. Indirect compensation consists of an attempt to justify replacing threatening goals and tasks (i.e., high-press-for-achievement objectives) with less threatening (i.e., compensatory) goals and tasks by imbuing the latter objectives with positive qualities (e.g., reasoning that emphasizes the valence of job security).

To conclude, the JMs possessed by FFs encourage them to reason from the standpoint that venting inhibitory tendencies is feasible and sensible as opposed to unrealistic, defensive, or foolish. Framing and inferences based on these JMs help make it possible for FFs to avoid demanding tasks without seeing themselves as unmotivated, indecisive, untalented, risk avoidant, or lacking in initiative. In particular, JMs and the reasoning they shape, define, and sustain assist FFs in arriving at conclusions that they are cautious and patient individuals who, in the interest of maintaining a realistic, stable, and predictable lifestyle, are making decisions and engaging in behaviors that promote balance, security, lack of stress, and tranquillity.

HOW JMS IMPLICITLY SHAPE REASONING STRATEGIES

Justification mechanisms are basic elements of personality as personality is represented in framing and thinking about what is a justifiable behavioral adjustment in an environment. Justification mechanisms have content; they involve identifiable biases that produce reasoning that attempts to enhance the logical appeal of specific behaviors. Justification mechanisms may also influence the strategies that individuals use to reason. For example, a bias toward personal responsibility is likely to stimulate a directed search process wherein the reasoner seeks occasions on which initiative, intensity, and persistence did in fact lead to success. Such a directed search represents a reasoning strategy that is known as a confirmatory bias. The term *confirmatory* denotes that the reasoner selectively seeks out only that information (evidence, data, historical events) that supports his or her underlying JM. Reasoning strategies are temporary mental actions that serve JMs, but are not themselves associated with indigenous content. A particular process such as a directed search for confirming evidence may serve any number of JMs. Thus, we do not think of reasoning strategies as JMs, but rather as implicit biases in reasoning that are shaped and directed by JMs. These points are developed more fully in the following paragraphs.

People judge whether behavior is rational or sensible by attempting to (a) discriminate among degrees of truth and falsity of assumptions about what is the best course of action; (b) identify unstated premises in advocacies for different behavioral adjustments; (c) distinguish among degrees of relevance and irrelevance of information (evidence, data, historical events, testimony) in regard to decision making and judgment; and (d) make valid inferences or generalizations based on what is often incomplete data (e.g., what is the likely or expected outcome of a behavioral choice). Justification mechanisms may be mapped directly into these reasoning processes. To illustrate, FFs may map an external attributional bias (e.g., professors are biased against me) into a query about the controllability of a specific event (e.g., grade on a particular test). In this case, reasoning (inference about grade) is given content by a JM. That is, the JM implicitly shapes the inference that a low grade should be expected because the professor is biased. Alternatively, JMs may be mapped onto reasoning via their influences on the strategies by which one reasons. Confirmatory and disconfirmatory biases, primary versus peripheral relevance of evidence, and selective attention are categories of reasoning strategies that serve JMs.

As noted, a confirmatory bias involves a directed search designed to seek out information (evidence, data, historical events) that corroborates what are considered justified behavioral adjustments. A *disconfirmatory bias* involves a directed search designed to seek out information that discredits or discounts displeasing (e.g., opposing, conflicting, contrasting, critical) arguments about what constitutes a justifiable behavioral adjustment. For example, FFs may seek out cases in which lack of resources or other uncontrollable factors engendered failure on demanding tasks. This evidence is then used to discount AMs' reasoning that success on demanding tasks is largely a function of personal effort. FFs would generally be unaware that an external attribution bias stimulated the directed search for evidence that failure is often beyond personal control.

Primary versus peripheral relevance of evidence is an unrecognized predilection to judge evidence as (a) primary or relevant if it supports personally favored biases, but (b) peripheral or irrelevant if it is critical of what is considered reasonable or offers alternatives to one's conclusions. *Selective attention* is a tendency in perception to attend principally to evidence that corroborates one's JMs. *Selective inattentiveness* implies an analogous tendency in which evidence that is inconsistent with one's JMs fails to reach the threshold of consciousness. An example of selective attention is AMs' proclivity to attend primarily to positive incentives resulting from a promotion, such as greater decision-making power and greater rewards. Accompanying this focused mindfulness is inattentiveness to potential negative outcomes, such as the enhanced stress that accompanies more consequential decision making. It might be noted that selective attention is a passive process in which receptiveness to information in perception is the issue. Confirmatory and disconfirmatory biases are proactive processes in which people seek out information that confirms or disconfirms reasoning.

TO EXPLAIN WHY, ONE MUST JUSTIFY

We have attempted to identify prominent domains of social cognition that explain how and why different individuals make divergent behavioral adjustments in the same environment. Simply stated, people who behave differently think differently. Salient components of these differences in thinking are (a) differential framing of the same situational context, and (b) analyses that on the surface appear sensible to the reasoner (at least) but in reality are implicitly influenced by biasing mechanisms (i.e., JMs) whose purpose is to enhance the logical plausibility, and thereby justifiability, of that reasoner's motives or behavioral dispositions.

Interestingly, in constructing rationales for their behaviors, individuals often try to overcome their self-perceptions of their biases through employing what they believe to be principles of reasoning (cf., Feldman & Lindell, 1989). The conviction that they have been successful in their pursuit of objectivity may be at least partially true. What individuals fail to realize, however, is that the arguments that they have carefully constructed via reasoned judgments are subject to biasing processes of which they are unaware and over which they have no control. Their reasoning may thus be characterized by what we have referred to as conditional. The term *conditional* connotes that the probability that a person will judge a behavior to be reasonable is dependent on the strength of that person's motive to engage in the behavior. A related connotation of *conditional* is that what one considers a reasonable behavioral adjustment to a given context is dependent on one's underlying personality.

The unrecognized, indeed unconscious, nature of justification processes may seem a vexing problem to those who wish to believe that their behavioral adjustments are based on truly objective reasoning. To these individuals we note that a large and accumulating body of research indicates that justification processes are not likely to be recognized by even highly skilled reasoners who search for logical fallacies in their own reasoning (see Atkinson, 1978; Nisbett & Wilson, 1977; McClelland, 1985). The simple fact is that the reasoning people use to justify their behavior is key to understanding why they behave as they do and to predict how they will behave in the future. Unless biases in reasoning are being used to rationalize illegal and/or pathological behavior, it is perhaps best to think of them as a natural part of adaptive human functioning. People want to believe that their choices of behavior are justified, which is to say rational as opposed to irrational. It is often, although not always, functional and healthy psychologically to engage in nonconscious processes that assist in realizing this belief.

THE RELATIONSHIP OF IMPLICIT AND EXPLICIT COGNITIONS

Implicit cognitions have a history of low and frequently nonsignificant correlations with explicit cognitions. This is the case irrespective of whether the measures of implicit cognitions are based on conditional reasoning scales (James, 1998; James & McIntyre, 2000) or projective techniques (Greenwald & Banaji, 1995; Kilstrom, 1999; Winter et al., 1998). Low correlations are consistent with the theoretical perspective that different constructs are represented by implicit and explicit cognitions. The idea of different constructs is a complex subject that we shall broach via a brief scenario.

Suppose that we have a knowledgeable and seasoned researcher who has published repeatedly in prestigious journals on the interaction between traits and situations. The commitment, intensity, and perseverance indicated by an extensive publication record indicate that this researcher is an AM. Moreover, the subject matter of many of these articles indicates a strong, conscious belief in interactional psychology (i.e., perceptions, emotions, and behaviors are products of the interactive influences of dispositions and organizational contexts). Indeed, this individual is well known for passionately sponsoring interactional concepts such as person–environment fit.

Suppose that we ask this investigator, whom we shall refer to as Professor X, to analyze specific, evocative events and then to furnish rational inferences as to why these events occurred. Note that we are not asking for a general theory or a set of abstract beliefs regarding why people, in general, behave. Rather, we are asking for analyses of specific, real-time events involving real people, culminating in rational conclusions as to why each specific event occurred. These problems are to explain (a) why an assistant professor in Professor X's department was denied tenure, (b) why a student known to Professor X passed doctoral exams, (c) why a recent manuscript prepared by a colleague of Professor X's was rejected, and (d) why a peer of Professor X's recently received an award for contributions to research.

Professor X analyzes each problem independently. He attempts to frame premises, evidence, and outcomes in terms of their meaning and significance to the problem of finding behavioral causes for an event. He then tries to determine which facts are relevant to solving the problem and which facts are not. Included here are endeavors to ascertain which testimony is trustworthy, which evidence is untainted, and which samples of behavior are representative. After arriving at initial rational explanations for each of the four events, Professor X attempts to identify premises that would weaken each inference or that might furnish a viable alternative explanation. Finally, the explanation for each event that is most clearly supported by confirming evidence is decided on.

Just described is what Professor X considers to be a rational and reasonably objective process. Yet, to the trained observer, biases unrecognized by Professor X are evident in Professor X's analyses. In particular, Professor X has a tendency to attribute success to initiative, intensity, commitment, and perseverance. Failure is attributed to missed opportunities to take initiatives, to lack of commitment to a research career, or to an unwillingness to make sacrifices in other parts of one's life that promote scientific productivity. Basically, Professor X possesses an implicit proclivity to favor personal motivation over situational factors when making attributions about the most reasonable causes of success or failure in scientific endeavors by students, colleagues, peers.

A proclivity to attribute the success or failure of others to (the lack of) motivation and commitment to science is indicative of an implicit cognitive system devoted to justifying the expression of a strong motive to achieve. What is thought by Professor X to be logical and sensible analyses are in fact guided and shaped by implicit biases, which developed to enhance the rational appeal of Professor X's own achievement-oriented activities. When it is pointed out to Professor X that his analyses of these four specific events are partially inconsistent with his explicit belief in interactional models, he simply surmises that these four events are anomalies that fail to disconfirm his general theory. In other words, Professor X has no capacity to introspect and identify his own implicit biases and remains convinced that his analyses are sensible even though inconsistent with his conscious belief system.

We hasten to note that implicit cognitive systems may or may not be congruent with explicit, self-attributed motives, values, and beliefs. Professor X may, for example, think of himself as achievement motivated even though he is not aware that his reasoning is affected by JMs for achievement motivation. As noted previously, converging lines of evidence suggest that explicit cognitive systems are not highly, or even moderately, related to explicit cognitive systems. Thus, AMs such as Professor X may subscribe consciously to the idea of a dialectic and may even express strong beliefs in the validity of explanatory models that espouse both internal and external causes (e.g., interactional models). However, when asked to analyze specific events and to rationally determine causes of success or failure, AMs will consistently favor internal causes as rational explanations. FFs, of course, will tend to favor external attributions.

SUMMARY AND CONCLUSION

Our purpose here has been to argue the case that implicit cognition is a fundamental component of the personality–motivation nexus. We have attempted to introduce and to overview implicit cognition via some of the key components of a new theory of measurement. The new theory of measurement is conditional reasoning, and the foundation for conditional reasoning is implicit cognitions in the form of JMs. The next logical step would be to describe the conditional reasoning measurement system. Unfortunately, space limitations require that we direct the interested reader to other sources for this information (James, 1998; James & Mazerolle, 2002; James & McIntyre, 2000). We note here that the conditional reasoning measurement system maps implicit cognitions that reflect JMs into logical reasoning problems. The strategy is that people will solve reasoning problems using the same biases that they use to justify their own behavior. In other words, what is seen as logical reasoning in regard to behavior will also be seen as logical reasoning when solving reasoning problems. As mentioned previously, the measurement system designed to measure implicit cognitions produced an average validity of .43, which is undeniably superior to the average validity of .12 obtained from self-report measures. These measures of implicit cognition have produced an increase in explained variance of approximately 1200%. Moreover, they provide a partial resolution to the long search for an effective, indirect measurement system for implicit cognitions (see Greenwald & Banaji, 1995).

REFERENCES

Allport, G. W. (1937). *Personality: A psychological interpretation.* New York: Holt.

Atkinson, J. W. (1978). The mainsprings of achievement-oriented activity. In J. W. Atkinson & J. O. Raynor (Eds.), *Personality, motivation, and achievement* (pp. 11–39). Washington, DC: Hemisphere.

Barrick, M. R., & Mount, M. K. (1993). Autonomy as a moderator of the relationship between the big five personality dimensions and job performance. *Journal of Applied Psychology, 78,* 111–118.

Cervone, D. (1991). The two disciplines of personality psychology. *Psychological Science, 2,* 371–372.

Crocker, J., & Major, B. (1989). Social stigma and self-esteem: The self-protective properties of stigma. *Psychological Review, 96,* 608–630.

Dweck, C. S., & Leggett, E. L. (1988). A social-cognitive approach to motivation and personality. *Psychological Review, 95,* 256–273.

Feldman, J. M., & Lindell, M. K. (1989). On rationality. In I. Horowitz (Ed.), *Organization and decision theory* (pp. 83–164). Boston: Kluwer Academic.

Fiske, S. T., & Taylor, S. E. (1984). *Social cognition.* Reading, MA: Addison-Wesley.

Fiske, S. T., & Taylor, S. E. (1991). *Social cognition* (2nd ed.). New York: McGraw-Hill.

Funder, D. C. (1987). Errors and mistakes: Evaluating the accuracy of social judgment. *Psychological Bulletin, 101,* 75–90.

Ghiselli, E. E. (1966). *The validity of occupational aptitude tests.* New York: Wiley.

Greenwald, A. G., & Banaji, M. R. (1995). Implicit social cognition: Attitudes, self-esteem, and stereotypes. *Psychological Review, 102,* 4–27.

James, L. R. (1998). Measurement of personality via conditional reasoning. *Organizational Research Methods, 1,* 131–163.

James, L. R., & Mazerolle, M. (2002). *Personality at work.* Beverly Hills: Sage.

James, L. R., & McIntyre, M. D. (2000). *Conditional Reasoning Test of Aggression Test Manual.* Knoxville, TN: Innovative Assessment Technology.

Kilstrom, J. F. (1999). The psychological unconscious. In L. A. Pervin & O. P. John (Eds.), *Handbook of personality: Theory and research* (2nd ed.) (pp. 424–442). New York: Guilford.

McClelland, D. C. (1985). *Human motivation.* Glenview, IL: Scott, Foresman.

McClelland, D. C., & Boyatzis, R. E. (1982). Leadership motive pattern and long-term success in management. *Journal of Applied Psychology, 67,* 737–743.

Mischel, W. (1968). *Personality and assessment.* New York: Wiley.

Murray, H. A. (1938). *Explorations in personality.* New York: Oxford University Press.

Nicholls, J. C. (1984). Achievement motivation: Conceptions of ability, subjective experience, task choice, and performance. *Psychological Review, 91,* 328–346.

Nisbett, R. E., & Wilson, T. D. (1977). Telling more than we can know: Verbal reports on mental processes. *Psychological Review, 84,* 231–259.

Schwarz, N. (1999). Self-reports: How the questions shape the answers. *American Psychologist, 54,* 93–105.

Sorrentino, R. M., & Short, J-A. C. (1986). Uncertainty orientation, motivation, and cognition. In R. M. Sorrentino & E. T. Higgins (Eds.), *Handbook of motivation and cognition: Foundations of social behavior* (pp. 379–403). New York: Guilford.

Spence, J. T., & Helmreich, R. L. (1983). Achievement-related motives and behavior. In J. T. Spence (Ed.), *Achievement and motives* (pp. 7–74). San Francisco: Freeman.

Stagner, R. (1977). On the reality and relevance of traits. *The Journal of General Psychology, 96,* 185–207.

Wegner, D. M., & Vallacher, R. R. (1977). *Implicit psychology: An introduction to social cognition.* New York: Oxford University Press.

Weiner, B. (1979). A theory of motivation of some classroom experiences. *Journal of Educational Psychology, 71,* 3–25.

Winter, D. G., John, O. P., Stewart, A. J., Klohnen, E. C., & Duncan, L. E. (1998). Traits and motives: Toward an integration of two traditions in personality research. *Psychological Review, 105,* 230–250.

Wright, J. C., & Mischel, W. (1987). A conditional approach to dispositional constructs: The local predictability of social behavior. *Journal of Personality and Social Psychology, 53,* 1159–1177.

10

Personality and Leadership

William D. Spangler
School of Management and Center for Leadership Studies
State University of New York at Binghamton

Robert J. House
The Wharton School of Management
University of Pennsylvania

Rita Palrecha
School of Management and Center for Leadership Studies
State University of New York at Binghamton

For millennia, historians, social critics and philosophers have inquired into the personality and motivation of great and not-so-great leaders. The systematic social–scientific study of leadership and personality goes back at least seventy-five years. Stogdill (1974) estimated 3000 empirical studies had been conducted. Since then, thousands more have undoubtedly appeared.

Despite this intense interest in leadership in general and personality and leadership specifically, numerous critics have expressed skepticism about the value of such research. Some have attacked the notion that personality characteristics explain leader behavior. On the basis of social learning theory, Mischel (1973) argued that situations explain individual behavior. Systematic differences in individual behavior are due to learned differences that may be modified or extinguished as situational characteristics change. On the basis of attribution theory, Davis-Blake and Pfeffer (1989) and Meindl, Ehrlich, and Dukerich (1985) argued that leadership is an attribution observers make to leaders on the basis of the observers' theories and their observations.

Other writers have expressed dismay at the state of leadership research in general:

... Probably more has been written and less known about leadership
than any other topic in the behavioral sciences" (Bennis, 1959, p. 259).
"After 40 years of accumulation, our mountain of evidence about leadership seems to offer few clear-cut facts" (McCall, 1976).
"It is difficult to know what, if anything, has been convincingly demonstrated by replicated research. The endless accumulation of empirical
data has not produced an integrated understanding of leadership"
(Stogdill, 1974, p. vii).

Three purposes motivated us to write this chapter: to summarize the
research in the field, to evaluate the scientific merit of this research, and
to integrate the available research according to a single framework. First,
we summarize the various mainstreams of personality and leadership research. We then evaluate each area. Our conclusion from this review is
that research in each area suffers from major weaknesses or limitations.
Furthermore, each research area seems to be unrelated to the others. This
evaluation gives credence to the pessimistic appraisals cited previously.
However, our position is that studying leadership in the context of personality has been and continues to be a fruitful endeavor. We reach this
unexpected conclusion by looking at the various areas of research through
a new lens. That is, if we organize previous research according to a general theory of personality and behavior, we see that we have accomplished
much more than is apparent. We will use the work of McClelland et al.
(McClelland, 1975, 1976, 1980, 1985a; Smith, 1992) to facilitate this reorga-
nization.

First we need to define the concept of personality as we use it in this
chapter. In a review of personality psychology, McAdams (1997) distinguishes three major themes: the whole person, the problem of motivation,
and differences among people. The whole person approach investigates
how people integrate their lives and make sense of the world. Topics include (a) cognitive processes of self-perception and (b) development of the
self over time toward greater integration and autonomy. The problem of
motivation is concerned with the internal springs of human action. These
springs include biological and learned drives and cognitive processes.
Individual differences focus on those dimensions or nomothetic factors
that may serve to distinguish individuals from one another. McAdams
singles out the five-factor model of Costa and McCrae (McAdams, 1997;
McCrae & Costa, 1999) as an attempt to explain behavior and compare people in terms of a universal set of characteristics. Winter and Barenbaum
(1999) subdivide these individual differences into traits such as the Big
Five and motives. Motives energize and focus behavior. Traits are stable
consistencies in expressive or stylistic behavior that affect the expression of
motives.

We suggest that personality is a small part of personality theory. A key task of personality theory is to explain how individuals negotiate their way in the social world. A fundamental axiom of personality theory is that individuals do not exhibit the same behavior in different situations merely because they have stable personality characteristics (Eysenck & Eysenck, 1980; McAdams, 1994, 1996, 1997). Winter and Barenbaum (1999) argue that the importance of social context is one of the major lessons of history that personality psychologists have learned. With respect to personality and leadership specifically, Stogdill (1948) concluded, from a review of more than 100 studies, "It becomes clear that an adequate analysis of leadership involves not only a study of leaders, but also of situations (p. 65)."

In this chapter we will limit our analysis to two aspects of personality psychology: individual differences (or nomothetic characteristics) and motivation. We limit our analyses to well-defined and fundamental characteristics with special consideration of social context. For example, research has identified drive as a prerequisite for leadership (Kirkpatrick & Locke, 1991). Drive is the result of a variety of individual characteristics and environmental characteristics interacting (McClelland, 1985a); we need to identify the components of drive and the processes whereby these components result in drive.

As a further limitation, we focus on personality and leadership from the viewpoint of the leader; we do not investigate how personality affects the reactions of followers or subordinates. This is a limitation imposed by the complexity of the topic.

SUMMARY OF PERSONALITY AND LEADERSHIP RESEARCH

Complexity characterizes the field of personality and leadership research. In this section we summarize seven rather distinct bodies of research: early trait research, the work of McClelland on leader motivation, leadership and the Big Five personality characteristics, anecdotal and formal research on the Myers-Briggs Type Indicator (MBTI), flexibility and self-monitoring, proactive behavior, and development of leadership skills.

Early Trait Research

The social–scientific study of leadership started in the early 1930s with an initial focus on the search for individual characteristics that universally differentiate leaders from nonleaders. Five reviews of the literature concerning leadership traits, published in the 1940s and 1950s, summarized findings of leadership trait research (Bird, 1940; Gibb, 1947; Jenkins, 1947;

Mann, 1959; Stogdill, 1948). These reviews indicated that leadership traits often correlated with measures of effectiveness of managers, assumed to be leaders, in the range of .25 to .35 and frequently much higher. House and Baetz (1979) found that when studies of adolescents and children were eliminated from Stogdill's review, intelligence, prosocial assertiveness (e.g., dominance as measured by the California Personality Inventory), self-confidence, energy–activity, and task-relevant knowledge consistently showed high correlations with leadership. For example, self-confidence and intelligence often had correlations with leadership in the range of .40 to .50. Lord, DeVader, and Alliger (1986) conducted a meta-analysis of 35 of the studies reviewed by Stogdill and found that intelligence, dominance, and masculinity were significantly related to follower perceptions of leadership. In a summary of the trait literature, Kirkpatrick and Locke (1991) reached similar conclusions: They highlighted drive, leadership motivation, honesty and integrity, self-confidence, cognitive ability, and knowledge of the business.

House and Aditya (1997) noted several problems associated with the early trait research. These deficiencies include failure to distinguish between leadership and management, a primary emphasis on empirically rather than theory-driven research, inadequate sampling, inadequate measures, inconsistency of operationalizations of the same constructs across different studies, and a primary focus on main effects of personality on outcomes to the neglect of interactions of personality and environmental or situational variables. In addition, the early trait studies were primarily based on single personality variable models and paid little attention to combinations of personality traits or culture and gender effects.

McClelland and Motives

McClelland and associates have studied the motivational bases of behavior over several decades. Much of their work has focused on the effects of achievement, power, and affiliation motives as measured by a specific testing procedure, the Thematic Apperception Test (TAT) (Smith, 1992). Subjects in these studies write short stories to a set of pictures. Researchers have found that it is also possible to use text from speeches or other sources. Trained coders subsequently score the textual material for the three motives. Three major findings from this research tradition are that (1) the achievement motive is positively related to entrepreneurial behavior and success (McClelland, 1976), (2) the power motive predicts success of managers in traditional organizations and politics, and (3) specific profiles or combinations of motives are related to performance and success of leaders such as American presidents (House, Spangler, & Woycke, 1991). McClelland et al. have also emphasized that motive scores alone do not predict behavior well. Motives operating in the presence of environmental incentives predict behavior. For example, someone high on need for achievement is motivated by situations that provide a challenge or an opportunity to excel in individual performance (McClelland, 1985a). We will return to this body of research later in the chapter.

Leadership and the Big Five

A substantial amount of previous research on personality has converged in the five-factor taxonomy of personality traits, known as the Big Five. The Big Five factors are neuroticism, extraversion, openness, agreeableness, and conscientiousness (McCrae & Costa, 1990, 1999). Research has related these traits to numerous outcomes including subjective well-being and happiness, job satisfaction, job performance, and leadership.

Neuroticism (N) is defined as emotional instability or liability. Individuals characterized as highly neurotic tend to worry about unpleasant situations that might arise, tend to react emotionally to unexpected and negative events, and take a long time to return to a normal emotional state. Individuals who score low on a neuroticism scale tend to worry less about unpleasant eventualities, to react less violently to such events, and to return to a normal state sooner than do high-N individuals. John and Srivastava (1999) view negative emotionality as the core of the construct. Costa and McCrae (1992) have summarized various aspects of neuroticism into six facets: anxiety, angry hostility, depression, self-consciousness, impulsiveness, and vulnerability.

Extraversion (E) as an object of scientific study stretches back at least a century, and during that time a number of conceptualizations have emerged (John & Srivastava, 1999; Watson & Clark, 1997). Recently, something of a consensus has emerged about the basic meaning of the concept. John and Srivastava consider extraversion to be an "energetic approach to the social and material world..." Similarly, Watson and Clark view positive emotionality to be the core of the concept. Within this general construct, researchers have identified a number of facets. For instance, Costa and McCrae (1992) define and measure six facets of extraversion: gregariousness, assertiveness, activity, excitement-seeking, positive emotions, and warmth.

Openness (O) is receptiveness to new ideas, approaches, and experiences. It may be also described as interest in experience for its own sake. Low openness is reflected in a preference for what is practical, familiar, and concrete. Openness is not related to self-disclosure or willingness to talk about one's inner feelings (McCrae & Costa, 1990), and it is distinct conceptually from measured intelligence, intellect, and conscientiousness (McCrae & Costa, 1997)

Agreeableness (A) is an individual difference in personality ranging from antagonism, tough-mindedness, and hardheadedness to selfless concern for others and trusting feelings. Those high on agreeableness tend to be compassionate, good-natured, eager to cooperate, and desirous of avoiding conflict. Those low on this trait tend to be ruthless, suspicious, stingy, antagonistic, critical, and irritable.

Conscientiousness (C) refers to individual differences in organization and achievement. Conscientious individuals are dutiful, self-disciplined, ambitious, hardworking, and persistent. Those low in conscientiousness tend to be more easy-going and less exacting with themselves and others, negligent, lazy, disorganized, late, and aimless.

Judge, Bono, Ilies, and Werner (2001) developed hypotheses relating the Big Five traits to leadership emergence, leadership effectiveness, and charismatic/transformational leadership. Judge and his coauthors expected neuroticism and leadership to be negatively related because neuroticism interferes with productive leader–other relationships, and is negatively related to self-confidence. They hypothesized that extraversion would be positively related to energy and social interaction, which are aspects of leadership. They hypothesized openness to have a positive relationship to charismatic–transformational leadership. Finally, they expected conscientiousness to be positively related to transformational/charismatic leadership that often requires persistence in the face of defeat. A meta-analysis based on 275 correlations from 94 studies supported these hypotheses. The multiple correlation of the Big Five traits with transformational leadership was a respectable .47.

Kirkpatrick and Locke (1991) described the role of persistence (conscientiousness), emotional stability (neuroticism reversed scored), and cognitive ability (possibly related to openness). Hogan, Curphy, and Hogan (1994) mapped much of the early trait research onto the five-factor model. These results suggest that the five-factor model may substantially advance our understanding of personality and leadership.

However, there are several unresolved difficulties. First, there is considerable controversy about the theoretical standing of the five factors. Block (1995, 2001) asserted that the five-factor model is not a theory but a collection of ad hoc characteristics. McAdams (1992, 1994) has argued that the model fails to provide compelling causal explanations for human behavior and experience. Others (Costa & McCrae, 1995; Goldberg & Saucier, 1995; McCrae, 2001) disagree.

A related issue concerns the comprehensiveness of the five-factor model. From the perspective of our definition of personality psychology given at the beginning of this chapter, the five-factor model primarily measures one domain of personality, namely nomothetic traits. McAdams (1994, 1997) has stressed that personality psychology includes an attempt to understand the person as a whole and an attempt to understand the motivational bases of behavior. Within this limited domain of nomothetic traits, the five-factor model may not be complete. Winter and Barenbaum (1999) stated that nomothetic personality characteristics might be subdivided into traits and motives. Motives energize and direct behavior into global behavioral patterns, that is, general achievement, power, and affiliation behavioral patterns. Traits channel the manner of expression of these general behavioral patterns. For example, achievement motivation may be expressed in an extraverted or introverted manner.

In an attempt to show the overlap or universality of the five-factor model, Costa and McCrae (1988) related five-factor scores with measures of motives as defined by Murray and McClelland. They used the Jackson (1989) Personality Research Form (PRF) questionnaire measures of motives. They concluded that motives as measured by the PRF might be interpreted within the framework of the five-factor model. However, they did not relate five-factor scores to motives as measured by the TAT. The TAT method is based on the content analysis of stories or other texts written by subjects. According to McClelland (1980), TAT-based measures of motives and survey-based measures of motives with the same name are fundamentally different.

We may illustrate this limitation of the five-factor model as follows. If we know that extraverts are more successful than introverts in managerial positions, we still do not know why such people are motivated to pursue management work as opposed to some other outlet for their extraversion (Winter, John, Stewart, Klohnen, & Duncan, 1998). In other words, the model does not deal extensively with motivation.

Perhaps the major limitation of the model, with respect to leadership research, is that it does not specify the conditions under which specific traits operate (McAdams, 1992). For example, under what conditions of organizational level, type of work, organizational type, and environmental conditions such as turbulence and uncertainty, would these traits play a significant role? Similarly, the model does not specify how profiles of traits may operate under specific conditions. Finally, the model does not explain the basic mechanisms by means of which personality traits and environmental characteristics work together to produce observed leader behavior and outcomes.

These difficulties with the five-factor model are not intrinsic or inevitable. Later in this chapter, we show that motives as defined and studied by McClelland et al., together with traits as defined and studied by Costa, McCrae, et al., provide a basis for exploring leadership that is more powerful than either approach used alone. Further, the inability of the model to describe conditions under which factors relate to leader behavior is not a fatal flaw of the model itself. Leadership researchers have not yet developed and tested propositions relating the five factors to organizational and social environments. The potential of this research is great, particularly for the factors of extraversion and neuroticism. We have accumulated a huge reservoir of research on the nature, bases, correlates, and outcomes of extraversion and neuroticism (John & Srivastava, 1999; Eysenck, 1967; Watson & Clark, 1997), which may be used to develop propositions relating traits, environmental characteristics, and motives.

From this discussion, we conclude that the five-factor model as elaborated by Costa and McCrae provides an important building block for understating leadership. However, it does not provide a stand-alone explanation of behavior.

The MBTI and Leadership

Practitioners have used the MBTI for personnel selection and management development for decades. The MBTI, derived from the work of Jung, measures four factors, namely extraversion–introversion, sensing–intuition, thinking–feeling, and judgment–perception (Myers & McCaulley, 1985). The basic notion is that there are distinct personalities types, so individuals' scores on each factor are dichotomized—for example, extraversion versus introversion on the extraversion–introversion scale. Sixteen personality types result. According to the theory behind of the MBTI, each personality type is optimal for some kinds of work. For instance, someone characterized by extraversion, intuition, thinking, and judgment supposedly thrives in situations requiring public speaking. Because practitioners use the MBTI in real-world situations, large sets of data are available and, potentially, this material avoids the problem of external validity or generalizability that afflicts instruments tested in laboratory situations and with students.

Despite the potential of the MBTI, formal research, as opposed to anecdotal evidence, has been limited (Gardner & Martinko, 1996). From an empirical study relating the MBTI to the NEO measures of the five factors, McCrae and Costa (1989) concluded that the MBTI does not measure dichotomous or distinct types, but rather four continuous dimensions that may be interpreted in term of the five-factor model. Furnham (1996) correlated NEO scores and MBTI scores in a sample of 160 working adults; he found a complex set of correlations among the MBTI and NEO scales. In our opinion, because MBTI scores are highly correlated with five-factor scores derived from the NEO, any relationships between MBTI scores and management behavior or effectiveness may be due to five-factor effects and not the unique effects of MBTI types.

Flexibility and Self-Monitoring

Zaccaro, Foti, and Kenny (1991) conducted a laboratory study of leader emergence. The objective of the study was to enhance understanding of the personality characteristic called self-monitoring. Self-monitoring includes three characteristics: a concern for social appropriateness, sensitivity to social cues, and an ability to control one's behavior in response to those cues (Snyder, 1974, 1979). There were four group tasks and participants were rotated through four group situations, each involving a different task and different people. Zaccaro et al. found that self-monitoring was significantly correlated with above-average supervision rankings and with task-relevant behaviors on two of the four tasks. Mumford, Zaccaro, Harding, Jacobs, and Fleishman (2000) found further support for a relationship between self-monitoring and emergent leadership. These two sets of results provide partial support for the proposition that emergent leaders recognize different group member requirements (social perceptiveness) and respond accordingly (behavioral flexibility).

Proactive Behavior

It is often one of the major functions of leadership to challenge the status quo (Bennis & Nanus, 1985; Kouzes & Posner, 1995). It is almost always a major function of leaders to continuously improve organizational performance. Proactivity, a tendency to take initiative to influence and improve one's environment is a personality trait that is especially relevant to these two functions.

Extraversion and openness to experience have been shown to be positively related to proactive socialization behavior in a longitudinal study of individuals seeking employment in various job sites (Wanberg & Kammeyer-Mueller, 2000) and to charismatic/transformational leadership among a sample 156 managers, as rated by their immediate superiors (Bateman & Crant, 1993). Archival measures of proactivity have also been found to be positively associated with U.S. presidential performance as rated by presidential historians (Deluga, 1998). Thus, proactivity is a personality trait that appears to be characteristic of effective leaders, especially with respect to innovation and the introduction of change.

It is likely that self-monitoring behavior, as defined by Zaccaro et al. (1991) and Mumford et al. (2000) is relevant to relationships with others, whereas proactive behavior is relevant to the elimination of constraints on the leader's behavior. Research needs to be conducted to test this speculation.

Leader Personality and the Development of Leadership Skills

Mumford et al. (2000) have advanced a theory of leadership effectiveness based on specific leadership-related skills. The model proposes that leader performance is based on three key types of skills: (1) skills relevant to ill-defined, complex, novel, social problems in organizations, (2) solution construction skills, and (3) social judgment skills. Skills develop as a function of the interaction between traits and experience. Accordingly, individuals with selected traits seek out developmental experiences, which result in skill development. Individuals high on these traits develop the relevant skills more readily than individuals who are not high on these traits.

The leadership skills model of Mumford et al. (2000) does not specify traits, but the authors used the following example to support the previous argument. Snow and Lohman (1984) showed that the rate with which people acquire abstract, principle-based knowledge structures is influenced by intelligence. Intelligence also appears to influence the acquisition of complex problem-solving skills (Baughman, 1997). Thus intelligence as a trait can influence the individual's capability for skill acquisition. Given the role of traits in understanding leadership skills, it is important to examine the relationships of various personality characteristics, leader skills, and leader behavior. The Mumford et al. model provides a framework that can be extended to explain the role of personality traits in developing the leadership skills.

SPECIFICATION OF ENVIRONMENTAL AND SITUATIONAL CONTINGENCIES

Throughout this chapter we have emphasized that personality characteristics do not necessarily predict leader behavior and outcomes; we need to consider the specific situation in which leaders function. In the previous section we briefly mentioned the importance of incentives. These incentives are contextual variables on which the enactment of the motives is contingent. In addition, we discuss here six classes of contextual moderators of relationships between leader personality characteristics and leader behavior and effectiveness.

Strong Versus Weak Situations

Mischel (1973) argued that the psychological strength of situations influences the degree to which individual dispositions such as motives or personality traits are expressed behaviorally. Strong situations are situations in which there are strong behavioral norms, strong incentives for specific types of behaviors, and clear expectations concerning what behaviors are rewarded. Accordingly, in strong situations, motivational or personality tendencies are constrained and there will be little behavioral expression of individual dispositions. Lee, Ashford, and Bobko (1990) and Monson, Hesley, and Chernick (1982) demonstrated empirical support for this argument. Thus, in organizations that are highly formalized and governed by well-established role expectations, norms, rules, policies, and procedures, there is less opportunity for organizational members to behaviorally express their dispositional tendencies.

In contrast, in less formalized and more flexible organizations individuals have more opportunity to express their dispositional tendencies behaviorally. Thus, in strong psychological situations, we expect leader traits to be less strongly correlated with leader behavior than in weak psychological situations. Furthermore, in strong psychological situations, we expect leader behavior to have less influence on others. Strength of situations presented to both leaders and followers or subordinates influences the degree to which leaders can behaviorally express their dispositions and the degree to which followers or subordinates have latitude in responding to their managers or leaders.

Environmental Stress

Stress experienced by followers presents opportunities for individuals so inclined to be leaderlike and more effective in leadership roles (Weber, 1947). According to Sales (1972), under highly stressful conditions followers look to their leaders for guidance and reduction of the stressful aspects of the situation. Stress can result from external threat, frustration, internal organizational conflict, or a high degree of uncertainty experienced by followers.

Sales (1972) conducted a series of laboratory experiments as well as studies based on analyses of archival data. He demonstrated convincingly that under adverse social or economic conditions leaders are given more decision making discretion and are even, at times, expected to be authoritarian in the actions they take and in their decision making. Mulder and Stemerding (1963) and Mulder, van Eck, and de Jong (1971) reported similar findings in field settings in which stress in the environment occurred naturally due to economic competition.

Waldman, Ramirez, House, and Puranam (2001) found that when followers of CEOs perceive the organizational environment as highly uncertain, at the time the CEO leadership was assessed, socialized charismatic CEOs had a positive effect on their organizations' financial performance over a four-year period. In contrast, when the environment was perceived as less uncertain at the time the CEO leadership was assessed, charismatic leadership had a modest but significant negative effect on firm profitability throughout the subsequent four years. After four years, the initial effect of the charismatic CEOs' behavior began to wane. One of the significant implications of the study is that it helps specify the duration of effects of leader behaviors on organizations' financial performance.

Presence of Trait-Relevant Arousal Variables

Critics of trait theories argue that traits must be stable and predict behavior over substantial periods of time and across widely varying situations (Davis-Blake & Pfeffer, 1989). Schneider (1983) observed, however, that traits are predictive of an individual's characteristic behavior in select situations only rather than across all situations. For example, when authority, leadership, and influence are made salient, their salience arouses tendencies to engage in prosocial assertiveness. Megargee, Bogart, and Anderson (1966) found that in experimental emergent leadership situations, when situational cues make leadership, influence, power, and hierarchical relationships salient, fourteen of sixteen subjects, who scored high on the dominance scale of the California Personality Inventory, engaged in more leader behaviors than individuals who scored low on this scale. Only two low-dominance subjects engaged in such behaviors. The California Personality Inventory scale measures prosocial assertiveness and not authoritarian, domineering, or aggressive tendencies. When the task was emphasized and leadership was de-emphasized, there was no relationship between dominance and the assumption of leadership roles. This study illustrates how traits are likely to predict behavior under conditions of trait-relevant arousal. In neutral or nonarousing situations, traits are not likely to predict behavior.

Fit Between Leader Motives and Organizational Orientation

It is also necessary for leader motives to be congruent with the primary orientation of their organizations. Kirkpatrick and Baum (2000) found that the achievement and power motives expressed in vision statements of entrepreneurs predicted subsequent organizational growth over a two-year time span. The expression of the power motive was primarily concerned with projecting a favorable or prestigious image, influencing customers to buy, or developing and maintaining positive relationships with customers. In a second study, Kirkpatrick, Wofford, and Baum (2000) found that the affiliation motive, as expressed in vision statements, predicted group effectiveness of a government engineering services agency. As noted earlier, and in line with the above study, House et al. (1991) found the power motive to predict U.S. presidential socialized charismatic behavior, and Spangler and

House (1991) found the power motive to be predictive of objective measures of presidential economic and social domestic performance, frequency of great decisions such as the Louisiana Purchase by Thomas Jefferson and the Emancipation Proclamation by Abraham Lincoln, as well as ratings of presidential greatness by political historians. Also, House, Delbecq, Taris, & Sully de Luque (2001) found the achievement motive to be highly related to indicators of effective CEO leadership.

These findings suggest that the relevance of a particular motive depends on the orientation of the organization being lead. For entrepreneurial organizations, which are achievement-oriented collectives, the achievement motive is the most relevant leader motive. For politically or combat-oriented organizations, the power motive is the most relevant. For small, intimate, socially oriented or service-oriented organizations, the affiliative motive is the most relevant. The proposition that motives are differentially relevant to leader effectiveness, contingent on the orientation of the organizations being lead, has been largely overlooked in the leadership literature. While having a fair degree of support, this proposition deserves further empirical investigation.

Organizational Role Demands

Miner (1993) has developed a set of four role motivation theories that relate organizational productivity to the congruence between organizational role requirements and member motivation. The four types of organizations, specified by Miner, are hierarchical, professional, task or entrepreneurial, and group. Each type of organization brings with it a distinct set of leader role requirements and associated motivations.

Miner (1978) hypothesized that managers with a motivational profile congruent with the demands of their organizational roles in hierarchical organizations would be more successful, as indicated by the organizational level they had obtained. Using a projective test, which required managers to finish a series of incomplete sentences (the Miner Sentence Completion Scale, Miner, 1964), Miner found that in hierarchical organizations the motivations most strongly linked to promotion were desire to exercise power, desire to compete with peers, and a positive attitude towards superiors. These aspects of managerial motivation are consistent with a high need for implicit power.

In contrast, Miner (1993) argued that professional organizations require members who desire to learn and acquire knowledge, desire to exhibit independence, desire to acquire status, desire to help others, and wish to exhibit professional commitment. These motivations, as measured by the professional form of the Miner Sentence Completion Scale, predict success in professional organizations (Miner, 1993). These findings may be related to the implicit achievement and socialized power motives as defined and studied by McClelland (1985b). Later in his chapter we will discuss the concepts of personalized versus socialized power. Briefly, socialized power motivation leads to power-related behavior that benefits others rather than the leaders personally.

Miner (1993) identified five motivations that were associated with success in task/entrepreneurial organizations: preference to achieve through one's own effort, desire to avoid risk, desire for performance feedback, desire to introduce innovative solutions, and desire to plan and establish goals. Miner (1993) cited the work of McClelland et al. (McClelland, 1985b) on achievement and entrepreneurship as a major source for these motivations. Several studies, summarized by Miner (1993), demonstrate that these motivations are related to organizational success, primarily for chief executives of high-growth, small entrepreneurial firms.

Miner (1993) defined group organizations as organizations based on small, cohesive groups. These groups are units where decisions are made by consensus or majority, face-to-face communication is the norm, and concerted group pressure enforces desired behavior. Larger organizations based on such groups may use a pervasive common intraorganizational culture and overlapping group membership to achieve coordination and unity of purpose. Miner (1993) argued that five motivations correspond to five role requirements in group-based organizations. Members in these organizations desire to interact socially and affiliate, wish to maintain their affiliative relationships in groups, have favorable attitudes towards peers, desire to have collaborative/cooperative relationships, and prefer democratic processes. To date, there appears to be no form of the Miner Sentence Completion Scale to measure these types of motivation, and we have found no research testing Miner's proposition that these motivations are related to effectiveness of group-based organizations. We speculate that the implicit affiliation motive may provide one source for these motivations.

Situation-Specific, Trait-Relevant Contextual Variables

It is likely that in almost all situations there are unique trait-relevant contextual variables that facilitate the enactment of individual characteristics. For example, physical prowess was found to be correlated with emergent leadership under conditions requiring physical abilities such as in boys' gangs and adolescent boys' groups (Stogdill, 1974). Korman (1968) found that intelligence differentiates effective from ineffective first-line supervisors, but that at high levels in the hierarchy there were no significant differences in intelligence between effective and ineffective managers, most likely because of restriction in the range of intelligence scores at high levels.

Summary

In this section we have reviewed six sets of environmental or situational variables that affect the expression of personality. In addition, we have alluded to the role of incentives in the expression of motives for achievement, affiliation, and power. Although all of this work is valuable, the sheer complexity and apparent unrelatedness of these studies limit their utility. In the next sections we will try to integrate and simplify these findings.

McCLELLAND'S THEORY OF MOTIVATION

From this review of the personality and leadership literature, we draw two conclusions. First, within each area, there are a number of weaknesses or limitations. The second and more important observation is that there appears to be little if any connection among these sets of findings. These two results appear to justify the pessimism of the scholars we cited at the beginning of this chapter. We offer the somewhat counterintuitive suggestion that these results represent a substantial increase of our understanding of personality and leadership. The value of the research becomes evident if we organize the various research streams according to a single theoretical framework. We have chosen the perspective of McClelland et al. (McClelland, 1980; McClelland, 1985a; Smith, 1992; Winter et al., 1998).

We choose McClelland et al. for several reasons. First, their perspective covers in detail the two domains of personality psychology that we are pursuing in this chapter, namely nomothetic characteristics and motivation. This perspective also makes a distinction between motives and traits. McClelland and his associates have done much of the work in the personality and leadership domain. Other researchers, particularly those investigating traits such as dominance, have also used this approach. Other findings, for example, those relating intelligence to leadership, may be understood within his framework. Finally, the McClelland perspective allows us to make some sense of social context, which we have specified as a key element in any understanding of personality and leadership.

From McClelland's perspective, motives are aspects of a person or animal that drive, direct, and select behavior:

Hunger in a rat (or any other animal) makes it more active (*drives*), focuses its attention on some stimuli more than others (*directs*), and facilitates learning a maze to get food. That is, if there is a food reward, its satisfaction of the hunger drive *selects* out responses that lead to the food reward (McClelland, 1980, p. 56).

Motives may be consciously held or nonconscious (McClelland, Koestner, & Weinberger, 1989; Koestner, Weinberger, & McClelland, 1991); both types of motives drive, direct, and select behavior. Winter et al. (1998) reviewed a number of definitions of motives extending from Empedocles (5th century BCE) to Freud and included McClelland's view. The common thread or theme of these definitions appears to be the notion of motives as goals or ends that impel behavior until a state of satiation is achieved. Atkinson and Birch (1970) claimed that this state of satiation is dynamic and temporary: Once a need is satisfied, the individual pursues some other goals or ends until the first need again requires satiation.

Winter et al. (1998) further clarified the meaning of the concept of motive by describing what motives are not. They are not traits such as extraversion and other of the Big Five factors of personality. The distinction between motive and trait for Winter et al. is that motives involve goals or end states; traits are individual differences that influence the ways in which these end states are achieved. That is, traits channel (Winter's term) or direct the ways in which motives are expressed. Traits are stylistic consistencies across individuals in goal-directed behavior. For example, a person who is high on the achievement motive may pursue satisfaction of that motive in an extroverted or introverted manner. Extraversion, in this case, channels the manner by which the motive is pursued.

McClelland and associates have distinguished two classes of motives, implicit and self-attributed or explicit motives. A major difference between implicit and explicit motives is the method of measurement. A number of researchers developed survey or questionnaire measures of need for social influence, commonly referred to as need for power (e.g., Edwards, 1959; Gough, 1957). Some of these instruments were based explicitly on the work of McClelland and his associates or Murray (1938). Others used an atheoretical approach. These measuring devices differ from the TAT used by McClelland (1985a). The TAT requires subjects to write stories in response to pictures that are subsequently content analyzed by trained coders. In contrast, survey instruments require respondents to check off responses to questions, which are then added up to provide measures of need for power as well as other motives such as need for achievement and need for affiliation.

McClelland argued that the dispositions measured by the TAT are implicit motives. Implicit motives are dispositions that have traditionally been labeled needs, e.g., need for achievement (nAchievement), need for power (nPower), and need for affiliation (nAffiliation). McClelland considered these TAT-measured dispositions to be motives because they "drive behavior (i.e., energize it), direct behavior (i.e., focus attention on relevant activity), and select behavior (i.e., produce better learning or performance)" (McClelland et al., 1989, p. 696). These motives are labeled *implicit* motives because the individual writing stories in response to a set of pictures is not explicitly describing himself or herself. Rather, the stories reflect nonconscious motives of the author.

There is evidence that implicit motives drive, direct, and select behavior through physiologically based reinforcement processes. McClelland et al. (1989) discussed a study in which the presentation of a romantic film was associated with the increased release of dopamine, a pleasurable experience for those high in nAffiliation. Also, a study by Steele (1977) revealed that upon viewing President J. F. Kennedy's inspirational inaugural address, which was intended to be an empowering experience for the audience, subjects' power motivation was aroused and increased significantly. The increase in power motivation was strongly and significantly correlated with increases in epinephrine ($r = .71$, $p < .05$).

Explicit motives differ from implicit motives in at least four fundamental ways: They are relatively conscious perceptions of what is valued by the individual whereas implicit motives are relatively nonconscious; they are uncorrelated with measures of implicit motives; they predict short-term behavior. For example, implicit need for achievement predicts entrepreneurial success, and a combination of low need for implicit affiliation and high need for implicit power predicts long-term success in management (see McClelland, 1985b, for a review of relevant studies), whereas self-attributed or explicit motives predict responses to immediate and specific situations and choice behavior. Fourth, explicit and implicit motives have different developmental histories. Implicit motives develop early in life as a result of experiences with various incentives and are rooted in early, preverbal experiences. Explicit motives develop somewhat later in life, require the presence of language, and come from the individual's understanding of social incentives and demands made verbally by others in the environment.

As a result of these distinct developmental histories, implicit motives are related to physiological processes such as release of norepinephrine and dopamine and activation of the sympathetic nervous system; self-attributed motives evidently are not related to such physiological processes. Recent evidence suggests that both kinds of motives are also likely to be, to a large extent, genetically transmitted through inheritance (Bouchard, Lykken, McGue, Segal, & Tellegen, 1990).

In the following pages we discuss the relevance of motives to leadership and management.

The Implicit Achievement Motive

This motive is a nonconscious concern for excellence in performance—a continuing concern for doing better all the time. This motive concerns achieving excellence through one's individual efforts (McClelland, Atkinson, Clark, & Lowell, 1958). Achievement motivated individuals set challenging goals for themselves, assume personal responsibility for goal accomplishment, persist in the pursuit of goals, take calculated risks to achieve goals, and actively collect and use information for feedback purposes. Theoretically, high achievement motivated managers are predicted to be effective under conditions of autonomy and strong achievement incentives. Achievement incentives are intrinsic attributes of tasks that have achievement motivation potential. We discuss these incentives in more detail further on in this chapter.

Achievement motivation is positively related to the effectiveness of leaders of small task-oriented groups (Litwin & Stringer, 1968) and leaders of relatively small entrepreneurial firms (McClelland, 1985b). However, achievement motivation does not always have a positive influence on outcomes. House et al. (1991) found that achievement motivation of U.S. presidents was inversely related to archival measures of presidential effectiveness. House et al. (2001) found that the achievement motives of chief operating executives of divisions of large organizations were not related to indicators of performance of their organizations. Theoretically, individuals high in achievement motivation identify with tasks too personally to delegate effectively, and they tend to meddle in the work of their subordinates. Consequently, they are more successful in small organizations, where the leader's input is proportionately much higher, and there are fewer constraints on the leader, than in large complex organizations. It remains to be empirically determined whether or not the achievement motive is dysfunctional at higher organizational levels, as our interpretation of the theory of achievement motivation (McClelland, 1985b) suggests.

The Implicit Affiliative Motive

This motive is defined as a nonconscious concern for establishing, maintaining, and restoring close personal relationships with others. Individuals with high affiliative motivation are concerned about establishing, maintaining, and re-establishing close personal relationships with others (McClelland, 1985b).

Theoretically, highly affiliative motivated managers are reluctant to monitor the behavior of subordinates, to convey negative feedback to subordinates even when required, to discipline subordinates for ethical transgressions or violations of organizational policies. Woodward (1974) found that U.S. presidents with high affiliative motivation had more scandals and legal transgressions in their administrations than presidents with low affiliation motivation. Presumably, this finding reflects the reluctance of high affiliative motivated presidents to monitor the work of their subordinates and take disciplinary action when required.

Highly affiliative motivated managers manage primarily on the basis of personal relationships with subordinates and therefore show favoritism toward some. House et al. (1991) found that affiliative motivated U.S. presidents were less effective than other presidents with respect to economic and social–domestic performance. Further, House et al. (2001) found that the affiliative motivation of CEOs was significantly negatively correlated with indicators of effectiveness of the organizations they lead.

The Implicit Power Motive

This motive is defined as a nonconscious concern for acquiring status and having an impact on others. Individuals with high power motivation enjoy asserting social influence, being persuasive, drawing attention to themselves, and having an impact on their immediate environment including the people with whom they interact. Theoretically, if enacted in a socially constructive manner, high power motivation should result in effective managerial performance in high-level positions (McClelland, 1975; 1985b). However, unless constrained by a disposition to exercise power in a moral and constructive manner, high power motivated managers will exercise power in an impetuously aggressive manner for self-aggrandizing purposes to the detriment of their subordinates and organizations.

High power motivation induces highly competitive behavior. Therefore, when unconstrained by moral inhibition, power motivation is theoretically predictive of leader effectiveness when the role demands of leaders require strong individual competitiveness, the use of threats and punishment, aggressiveness, manipulative exploitative behavior, or the exercise of substantial political influence. The power motive was found by House et al. (1991) significantly to predict U.S. presidential charismatic behavior and archival measures of presidential effectiveness. Theoretically, the power motive, when constrained by a strong concern for the moral use of power, is most likely to lead to effective leader behavior at upper management levels in hierarchical organizations and in political endeavors.

The Responsibility Disposition

Winter and Barenbaum (1985) developed and validated a projective measure of concern for moral responsibility, which they label the *responsibility disposition*. The authors do not label this trait as a motive because they have not demonstrated that it has all of the properties of a motive, that is, that it drives, directs, and selects behavior. Indicators of high concern for responsibility are expressions of concern about meeting moral standards and obligations to others, concern for others, concern about consequences of one's own action, behavior according to a personal code of ethics, and critical self-judgment. The responsibility measure is based on quantitative content analysis of narrative text material such as speeches or written documents. Theoretically, the responsibility disposition should be predictive of socialized (altruistically oriented nonexploitive, non-self-aggrandizing, nonimpulsive) charismatic leader behavior, supportive leader behavior, fairness, integrity, follower trust and respect for the leader, and commitment to the leader's vision, and consequently organizational effectiveness. House et al. (2001) found support for this expectation among a sample of CEOs and chief operating officers of divisions of large corporations.

In the following section we discuss the leader motive profile (LMP) theory (McClelland, 1975). This theory involves the power and affiliative motives and the disposition to use power in a morally responsible manner. House et al. (2001) found that when the responsibility disposition was used as an indicator of concern for the moral exercise of power, as part of the leader motive profile, the LMP scores predicted socialized charismatic leader behavior. Similarly, Winter (1991) found that when the responsibility disposition was used as part of the LMP scores of AT&T managers, the LMP scores of entry-level managers predicted managerial success over a 16-year period.

The Need for Appropriate Incentives

According to McClelland's theory, motives predict behavior more strongly in the presence of appropriate incentives because enactment of the motive in the presence of selected incentives will lead to reinforcing outcomes for the individual.

McClelland et al. (1989) have made a distinction between social incentives and activity incentives. Social incentives are rewards, prompts, expectations, demands, and norms that come from others. These incentives may be provided by a boss, experimenter, coworkers, or by a group. Social achievement incentives include challenging goals set by an experimenter or boss and achievement work norms. Social power incentives include power goals set by the experimenter or some other person and power work-group norms. Social affiliative incentives include norms and expectations that reward individuals contingent on their collaborative and courteous behavior.

In contrast to social incentives, activity incentives are characteristics of the task itself. Performing the task directly reinforces the individual high on some implicit motive. Activity achievement incentives include opportunities to act independently, to set challenging goals, and to take moderate risks. Activity power incentives include opportunities for strong, vigorous action that affects other people, actions that have a strong emotional impact on others, and a position, job, or task that provides the incumbent or subject with fame, reputation, or status. Affiliative activity incentives are opportunities to voluntarily make and maintain close personal relationships. Thus tasks that offer opportunity for close and harmonious personal interaction with others, opportunity for cooperation, and opportunity to serve others personally are examples of tasks with high affiliative incentives.

The relevance of this distinction between social and activity incentives is the proposition that specific classes of incentives interact with specific types of motives (McClelland et al., 1989). Specifically, social incentives interact with explicit motives but not implicit motives, and activity incentives interact with implicit motives but not explicit motives. A number of studies have shown that social incentives but not activity incentives interact with self-attributed motives to predict behavior (deCharms, Morrison, Reitman, & McClelland, 1955; McClelland et al., 1989; Patten & White, 1977). Activity incentives but not social incentives interact with implicit motives to produce behavior.

Based on a meta-analysis of 190 correlations reported in 102 empirical articles, Spangler (1992) found that achievement motivation in combination with intrinsic achievement incentives had a multiple regression coefficient of .66 with a combined measure of such outcomes as subject's income, job level, professional rank, publications (of researchers), and voluntary participation in leadership activities. In a meta-analysis of research on power motivation, Spangler (2001) found that the implicit power motive interacted with power activity incentives to predict outcomes, and the explicit power motive interacted, as expected, with power social incentives. To date there have been no studies, to our knowledge, that have tested the combined effects of the affiliative motive and relevant incentives.

It is worthwhile to compare these concepts of social and activity incentives with the work of Deci et al. (Deci, 1971; Deci, Koestner, & Ryan, 1999a; Deci, Koestner, & Ryan, 1999b; Ryan & Deci, 2000). The McClelland approach and the Deci et al. approach share two characteristics. First, both provide similar definitions of intrinsic versus extrinsic motivation. Second, both suggest that extrinsic motivation undermines intrinsic motivation.

In the McClelland framework, activity incentives are intrinsic to activities performed. The activity is its own reward. Motivation, behavior, and satisfaction result from the interaction of these intrinsic rewards with a high need for such rewards, that is, high need for implicit achievement. This motivation might be labeled *intrinsic motivation*. Likewise, social incentives are external to the activity itself; they are incentives residing in environments— for example, goals set by a superior, expectations of coworkers, or prevalent organizational norms. According to McClelland et al. (1989), these incentives interact with self-attributed motives, that is, the need for these external rewards. Therefore, motivation resulting from the interaction of social incentives and self-attributed needs might be labeled *extrinsic motivation*. Similarly, Deci et al. (e.g., Ryan & Deci, 2000) define extrinsic motivation as that dependent on external rewards such as money.

A major, replicated finding in the intrinsic versus extrinsic research literature is that extrinsic motivation reduces intrinsic motivation (Deci, Koestner, & Ryan, 1999b). For example, in the Magic Marker experiment (Lepper, Greene, & Nisbett, 1973), preschool children played with colored paper and Magic Markers with great enthusiasm. Then some of the children were told that they would be rewarded for exceptional performance. All children in this group received the exceptional performance award. At a subsequent date, the children who had been promised and had received the extrinsic reward were less interested in playing with the materials than other children in the experiment who had not been extrinsically rewarded. Similarly, Spangler (1992), in a meta-analysis of 102 achievement-motivation articles, found that social incentives reduced the correlation between implicit need for achievement and outcomes.

Operant Versus Respondent Behavior

McClelland and his associates also distinguish operant from respondent behavior. *Operant behavior* is behavior that the subject generates spontaneously and is freely emitted. It is not possible to specify or control the stimuli that elicit operant behavior. In contrast, *respondent behavior* is behavior that is controlled by characteristics of the subject's environment. It is behavior elicited by known stimuli in the environment. Of course, behavior is not either entirely operant or entirely respondent. It is possible to arrange behavior along a continuum from behavior and outcomes enacted or attained under extreme environmental control to behavior and outcomes that are relatively free from explicit environmental control. Relatively operant outcomes include attained income, job level attained in an organization, professional rank, publications, and social behavior occurring under natural conditions. Respondent outcomes include school grades, intelligence and achievement test scores, and results of personality inventories and opinion surveys. Behavior or performance typically measured in laboratory experiments falls somewhere between these extremes and may be labeled *semi-operant*.

Sets of Motives: The Leader Motive Profile (LMP)

As stated earlier, one of the deficiencies of early trait theory research was that it focused on individual traits that would be associated with effective leadership. To date, only one multiple trait theory of leadership has been advanced: McClelland's leader motive profile (LMP) theory, which is promising and enjoys more than modest empirical support. According to LMP theory, the following combination of nonconscious motives is generic to, and predictive of, leader effectiveness: high power motivation, high concern for the moral exercise of power (the responsibility dispositions), and power motivation greater than affiliative motivation. Following is a brief description of the underlying rationale of LMP theory.

According to LMP theory, the power motive is necessary for leaders to be effective because it induces them to engage in social influence behavior and such behavior is required for effective leadership. Furthermore, highly power motivated individuals obtain more satisfaction from the exercise of influence, and this satisfaction sustains their interest in the exercise of leadership.

When the self-aggrandizing tendency usually associated with high power motivation is inhibited by a high concern for morally responsible exercise of power (or social influence), individuals are predicted to engage in the exercise of power in an effective and socially constructive manner. The combination of high power motivation and a strong disposition toward the moral exercise of power should thus result in leadership that induces follower trust, respect for the leader, and commitment to the leader's vision.

Also, the power motive, according to LMP theory, needs to be higher than the affiliative motive. Theoretically, when the power motive is higher than the affiliative motive, individuals do not engage in the dysfunctional behaviors usually associated with high affiliation motivation described previously. House et al. (2001) confirmed these theoretical expectations in their study of CEOs and chief operating officers of divisions of large organizations.

Theoretically, the leader motive profile predicts managerial effectiveness under conditions where leaders need to exercise social influence in the processes of making decisions and motivating others to accept and implement decisions. In formal organizations, these conditions are found at middle and higher organizational levels and in nontechnical functions. By contrast, in smaller technology-based organizations, where group leaders can rely on technological knowledge and direct contact with subordinates rather than delegation through multiple organizational levels to make decisions, the achievement motive is theoretically predictive of leaders' effectiveness. Thus LMP theory is theoretically limited to the boundary conditions of moderate to large nontechnologically oriented organizations and to managers who are separated from the work of the organization by more than one organizational level.

Several studies have demonstrated support for the LMP theory (House et al., 2001; McClelland, 1975; McClelland & Boyatzis, 1982; McClelland & Burnham, 1976; Spangler & House, 1991; Winter, 1978, 1991). The study by House et al. (2001) revealed that LMP theory was most predictive of constructive and positive charismatic leader behavior in small entrepreneurial organizations. This finding is inconsistent with the boundary conditions specified for LMP theory—large complex nontechnical organizations. However, this finding is consistent with Mischel's argument that dispositions are most likely enacted under weak psychological conditions. In entrepreneurial organizations, chief executives are less constrained by formal organizational rules and policies than are managers of large organizations.

A major deficiency in this literature concerns the specific behaviors associated with LMP. Only the study by House et al. (2001) addresses this issue. These authors found that LMP is rather strongly associated with follower reports of their superiors as being charismatic, displaying integrity, and being supportive. The major research issues confronting LMP theory concern the need to specify the boundary conditions under which the theory holds and the need for a better understanding of the behavioral manifestations of the LMP motive syndrome.

UNEXPECTED YIELD FROM PAST PERSONALITY AND LEADERSHIP RESEARCH: A THEORY OF PERSONALITY AND LEADERSHIP

Complexity and confusion appear to characterize the personality and leadership research that we have summarized in this chapter. Under the heading of personality and leadership research, we summarized six rather distinct research streams such as early trait research and work linking the Big Five traits to leadership. In the subsequent section, we reviewed a further six sets of studies that attempted to introduce environmental characteristics into the study of personality and leadership. Despite the apparent confusion and the apparent lack of substantial relationships among these twelve sets of research findings, we believe that an integration and simplification, on the basis of the work or McClelland et al., is possible.

The Early Trait Research: Explicit Motives and Leadership

As a consequence of limitations such as reliance on atheoretical and single-variable studies, and because of the fact that the early leadership trait studies were seldom replicated, disenchantment with the study of leadership traits grew. However, this disenchantment did not adequately reflect the true status of leadership trait research. Stogdill's (1948) article is credited as the coup de grace of leadership trait research. Contrary to the popular interpretations of the time, which seem to have persisted to this day, Stogdill concluded that there is a cluster of personality traits that differentiate leaders from followers, effective from ineffective leaders, and higher- from lower-level leaders. These traits are intelligence, self-confidence, energy–activity level, and dominance. Stogdill also concluded that traits should be studied in interaction with situational variables.

Despite these problems with early trait research, and the misinterpretation of Stogdill's conclusion, there was a substantial yield from the early trait research, which has gone largely unrecognized. Early trait research yielded three payoffs.

First, it identified a number of personality characteristics that are reliably associated with various measures of leadership: intelligence, energy–activity, masculinity, adjustment, dominance, and self-confidence and self-assurance in interacting with others (see House & Beatz, 1979; Lord et al., 1986). Second, studies by Ghiselli (1971) and Goodstein and Schrader (1963) demonstrated the practical application of trait research by showing that valid scales could be constructed that differentiate individuals in positions of leadership from others and that also differentiate individuals in positions of leadership according to the hierarchical organizational levels that they had acquired.

Early research into personality measures had a third and related payoff for understanding leadership, namely an understanding of need for power and a set of measures of the construct. Ostrand (1980) discussed a number of instruments that measure such constructs as dominance, ascendance, and ascendancy. Measures are available for concepts labeled *abasement, authoritarianism,* and *aggression.* In some cases, a single instrument measures constructs that are seemingly related. The Jackson Personality Research Form (PRF; Jackson, 1989) purportedly measures both dominance and abasement. The Adjective Check List (ACL; Megargee, 1972) measures both dominance and aggression. Is abasement just need for power reverse-scored? Possibly, need for power is the same as dominance and aggression. This issue is important for an understanding of the concept of need for power: Is it a prosocial motive or a selfish and aggressive tendency?

Ostrand (1980) argued that the measures labeled *dominance, ascendance,* and *ascendancy* focus on a common underlying construct, self-confidence and the ability to interact well with others. Furthermore, these measures intercorrelate as expected. Jackson (1989) reported a correlation of .78 between PRF Dominance and the CPI Dominance. Megargee (1972) reported positive and significant correlations of the CPI Dominance scale with the corresponding scales of the Edwards Personal Preference Schedule (EPPS), the Cattell 16 PF, and the Guilford-Zimmerman Temperament Survey.

These measures also possess discriminant validity. Ostrand (1980) noted that these measures are not related to a set of superficially similar measures, namely authoritarianism and aggression in terms of underlying construct or observed correlations. The common thread of this latter set of measures appears to be a lack of self-confidence and an inability to interact well with others.

Although it was not clear at the time, subsequent research conducted by McClelland and his associates (e.g., McClelland, Koestner, & Weinberger, 1989) established that these paper-and-pencil instruments measure one specific type of need for social influence, namely explicit or self-attributed need for power, as opposed to implicit or nonconscious need for power.

The Role of Intelligence

One of the consistent findings in the personality and leadership literature is the role of intelligence or intellect (Stogdill, 1948; Kirkpatrick and Locke, 1991). This research raises several important questions. One is the definition of *intelligence*. A second concerns the conditions under which intelligence promotes leader effectiveness. A third is the relationship of intelligence to other personality factors such as traits and motives.

In our review of the literature, we have cited intelligence (Stogdill, 1948; Kirkpatrick & Locke, 1991), complex problem-solving skills (Mumford et al., 2000), proactivity, and openness to experience and conscientiousness (Hogan et al., 1994). All appear to be related to leadership in one way or another. McCrae and Costa (1997) discuss similarities and differences among measured intelligence, openness to experience, conscientiousness, and intellect. They find all are related but different. In particular, they assert that openness to experience is distinct from the other concepts. Openness to experience includes a need for experience, curiosity, and creativity. Future research may examine the differential relationships of each to leadership. In part because of this confusion of concepts, we have made little headway in understanding the specific situations under which each is related to leadership.

We do have some interesting evidence concerning the third question, the relationship of intelligence to other personality characteristics. McCrae and Costa (1997) argue that openness to experience contains a motivating component; people high on this dimension are intrinsically motivated to seek out new experiences. Whether or not intelligence contains a motivating component is not clear to us. However, there is evidence that intelligence may interact with motives to affect behavior and performance. That is, intelligence may be a capacity to learn and perform well; motives provide the motivation to do so. Ray and Singh (1980) found that nonverbal intelligence and achievement motivation interacted to predict improvement in agricultural productivity of 200 Punjab farmers over a 5-year period.

Search for a Parsimonious Set of Situational Variables

It is often said that effective leaders are the right individuals in the right place at the right time. Being the right person means having the personality traits and motives specified in this chapter. Being in the right place at the right time means being in at least one of the six situation circumstances that we have identified plus being in situations that provide appropriate incentives for the implicit and explicit motives specified earlier. In addition, Bass (1998), Jacobsen and House (2001), and Shamir, House, and Arthur (1993), have theoretically specified a substantial number of additional situational variables that they hypothesize to moderate relationships between transformational–charismatic leader behaviors and their effects. Clearly such a long list of situational contingency variables lacks theoretical parsimony. What is now necessary is to discover the relative strengths of these variables and determine which are necessary and which are sufficient conditions for the two major classes of leadership—transformational–charismatic and transactional–exchange leadership—to be effective. It is also necessary to determine whether these variables are additive in their moderating effects or whether only a small set of such variables is necessary and/or sufficient to facilitate and enhance the emergence and effectiveness of leaders.

We see three mechanisms that may help to reduce the complexity of these findings concerning situations and leadership. First, in the McClelland theory, motives are not fixed. Their strength increases and decreases in response to recent behavior and external stimuli (Atkinson & Birch, 1970). Only the average strength level of motives distinguishes one person from another. Therefore, situational variables that arouse specific motives will lead to more forceful and persistent leader behavior. Second, motives do not create behavior in the absence of incentives. In organizations, embedded incentives will interact with motives. It is likely that organizational orientation discussed previously creates incentives for the expression of specific leader motives. Also, Miner's work on organizational role demands suggests that motive-related role demands provide relevant incentives. Third, Mischel's (1973) concept of strong versus weak situations explains variation from one situation to another. The stronger or more coercive an organizational situation, the weaker the relation will be between leader motives and leader behavior and between leader behavior and effectiveness.

Multiple Motives: The Extended Leadership Motive Profile (LMP)

There is substantial evidence relating implicit motives to manager and leader behavior specified in McClelland's LMP theory. However, the theory was intended to explain behavior in hierarchical nontechnical organizations and has been tested primarily with samples of male managers. The traditional command-and-control organizational form is giving way to new management styles. It is noteworthy that House et al. (2001) found that the responsibility disposition was positively related to effectiveness indicators for both CEOs of entrepreneurial firms and chief operating officers of autonomous divisions of large organizations.

Organizational environments are becoming more complex and uncertain as competition intensifies. A large proportion of current organizations are becoming increasingly technical because of the internationalization of markets and the competitive advantages of using the Internet. Purchasing, coordination, and transfer of information within organizations, communication with other organizations, information storage, and the like depend more and more on high technology. Provision of services and products likewise has become increasingly specialized and complicated, so a relatively high proportion of managers need to master increasingly complicated bodies of technical knowledge. At the same time, small high-technology start-up companies are becoming increasingly important as sources of new products and services.

Both of these trends, the increase in technical requirements for managerial work and the prominence of small start-up companies, suggest that need for achievement is a more important component of managerial success and leader motivation than in the past. Further, a long stream of research (e.g., McClelland, 1962, 1976) has demonstrated a strong link between entrepreneurial behavior and need for achievement.

Because of these trends, more collegial organizations are replacing traditional command and control organizations (Pfeffer, 1994). Contemporary organizations have fewer levels than traditional organizations and fewer managers as a percentage of total employees. At the same time, because of available information processing technology, there has been considerable decentralization of decision making and jobs of nonmanagers are becoming more complex. Hence the span of control of the typical manager has increased and more responsibility and authority has been delegated to subordinates. Given the need for adjustment to constant change in a turbulent world, organizational members need continuously to learn new technologies. Thus, a major focus of many managers is likely to be the development of subordinates through coaching and empowerment, as well as participation in professional development activities offered by outside agencies such as consultants and universities.

Furthermore, because organizations are facing more complex environments and must rely on a larger number of stakeholders, their leaders need to be effective negotiators and sometimes engage in hard-nosed negotiations, alliance building, and frequently manipulative behavior with respect to external stakeholders and competition. Many traditional hierarchical organizations have given way to an organizational form where personal relationships are likely to be extremely crucial for association with external organizations as well as the management of a highly educated workforce.

Despite the trend toward less hierarchy, all organizations with over approximately 150 employees of necessity must become somewhat hierarchical. Organizational levels, job titles, work specialization, and role definitions become imperative to avoid chaos. Role demands in such organizations will most likely require a mix of personality characteristics and skills to deal with the changes described above as well as many of the elements of the traditional model of managerial behavior, as indicated by Miner's work and research concerning the leader motive profile. These suggestions lead us to conclude that need for socialized power will remain an important personality factor in modern organizations

It is possible that a new leader motive profile will include a different set of motives than those specified in the original LMP theory. In the traditional theory, power was positively related to effectiveness, and achievement and affiliation were negatively related to effectiveness for hierarchical organizations and political leaders. In the emerging typical organizations of the 21st century, both power and achievement may be positively related to leader effectiveness. Indeed, a variety of different motive profiles may be required for a variety of types of organizations. At the present time we have no theory to suggest a comprehensive range of profiles corresponding to organizational types. Miner's (1993) work on organizational role demands may provide guidance in elucidating relationships between motive profiles and organizational types. Clearly this is a topic for future theoretical development and empirical research.

The Channeling Hypothesis: The Interaction of Motives and Traits

Major advances in recent research have included elaboration of McClelland's motivation theory, simplification and testing of traits, and a realization that sets of personality characteristics and individual differences need to be studied simultaneously (e.g., the LMP). However, no empirical studies have tested the profile approach by combining McClelland's motives with the Big Five traits as defined by McCrae and Costa (1990).

According to Winter et al. (1998), personality theorists and researchers have tended to follow one of two paths for the past 75 years or so. Researchers in one camp have investigated individual differences that may be referred to as traits. This tradition has culminated in some degree of agreement that there are five major traits, colloquially referred to as the Big Five. In developing measures of these traits, researchers have relied on correlational techniques to produce survey or questionnaire instruments.

Other researchers have pursued the study of motives experimentally as well as longitudinally in field settings and generally have measured motives by means of the TAT or similar devices. McClelland et al. (see McClelland, 1985b) developed these TAT measures in the form of stories that were neutral with respect to motive content. The stories written about these pictures by subjects were then content analyzed for motive imagery, and the motive imagery scores were then used to predict behavior under varying experimental conditions.

To some extent, these two approaches exemplify the two scientific disciplines discussed by Cronbach (1957). Both Cronbach and Winter et al. (1998) argued that the split of research into these two camps has had unfortunate consequences. Winter et al. concluded that the split has produced an incomplete understanding of the phenomena. Winter et al. suggested that motives from the McClelland tradition explain the energizing of general categories of behavior, but not the specific ways such behavior may be manifested. They also suggested that, in contrast to motives, traits do not explain the energizing of behavior or motivation of behavior. Conscientiousness, for example, describes a particular behavioral style but does explain the type of behavior someone persists in or why any behavior should be pursued. Therefore, Winter et al. have proposed that motives and traits are part of complementary systems. Specifically, they have suggested that traits and motives interact to influence behavior. Motives energize and create general classes of behavior, for example, achievement behavior; traits guide or channel behavior in specific directions. To test this channeling hypothesis, Winter et al. investigated interactions of needs for affiliation and power with extraversion. Both interactions were supported in two longitudinal studies.

Research summarized earlier has demonstrated relationships between Big Five traits and leadership (Judge et al., 2001). Research in the McClelland motive tradition has demonstrated substantial relationships between implicit motives and leader behavior and success, most notably, the LMP. We may combine the two streams of research according to the channeling hypothesis and seek to explain leader and managerial behavior in terms of interactions of specific motives and specific traits. We suggest the following equation as a subject for future research:

Leader effectiveness

$$= f(\text{implicit power, achievement, affiliation motivation})$$

$$+ f(\text{neuroticism, extraversion, openness, agreeableness,}$$

$$\text{conscientiousness})$$

$$+ f(\text{interactions of implicit motives and traits}).$$

A hypothesis may be created for each of the fifteen interactions (3 implicit motives × 5 traits) found in the equation. For example, we would expect need for power and extraversion to have a positive interactive effect on leader behavior. Extraversion is related to sociability, risk-taking, dominance, and happiness (or subjective well-being). Sociability enhances the effect of need for power by facilitating relationships with others; risk-taking leads to less conservative strategies and also to taking risks in making contacts with others; dominance enhances need for power, which is need for social influence; and subjective well-being will make the leader more attractive to others and hence more susceptible to his or her influence attempts.

In addition to linking leader behavior to specific trait × motive interactions, we may suspect that some combinations of motives and traits are not likely. Perseverance is a characteristic of implicit need for achievement, so it unlikely that implicit need for achievement would be channeled by low conscientiousness or low perseverance. It is not likely that someone with a high need for implicit affiliation would act in a disagreeable way.

We suggest an alternative. Winter et al. (1998) argue that motives and traits are independent but interacting systems. The issue is whether or not traits and motives are correlated. Little research has been done on this issue, but if traits and motives are uncorrelated, we would expect cases where a high need for implicit achievement might be combined with low perseverance, or a high need for affiliation might coexist with a low level of agreeableness. Such combinations might produce dissatisfaction, frustration, and unexpected behavior.

This model appears to apply to both transactional and transformational leader effectiveness. That is, motive research has shown the relationship of motives to traditional management or transactional leader behavior as well as to charismatic–transformational behavior. Furthermore, Judge et al. (2001) demonstrated that traits explain both traditional and transformational behavior. However, we can formulate hypotheses that differentiate transactional from transformational leadership. As an example, Bass (1985) identified intellectual stimulation as a basic facet of transformational leadership. According to House and Aditya (1997), one of the basic functions of the charismatic leader is to create new ideas and a new vision and mission. Openness to experience in combination with a high need for power will create an intellectually curious leader. Such leaders will tend to associate with and to attract similar people. Therefore the interaction of need for socialized power and openness will be positive. The interaction of socialized power and openness will also likely lead to the emergence of transformational rather than transactional leaders. Creative thinking is less important in traditional bureaucratic organizations, so we expect that the interaction of power and openness will be negatively related to transactional leadership or will have a positive but small effect. We also expect that leaders high on the need for power and openness in bureaucratic positions will tend to move to other positions.

Research cited elsewhere in this chapter allows us to specify the conditions under which we expect leaders' behavior to be predicted by the previous equation. Motives are mission relevant. In the examples of interactions given earlier, we had in mind managerial and political situations where the LMP has been shown to predict behavior. In other cases, achievement or affiliation will be the relevant positive motive and power may be negatively related to success. Related to this criterion of mission relatedness are incentives. We suggest the first equation function predicts leader behavior when activity incentives corresponding to the mission-related motives are available. Finally, the equation functions should be more predictive under weak psychological conditions.

Future research may also investigate the independent and interactive effects of explicit motives and traits. In this case leader behavior is a function of explicit motives such as explicit need for power, achievement, and affiliation, and traits. Once again effective behavior will be a function of mission-relevant motives. Incentives in this case will be the social incentives that have been shown to interact with explicit motives but not implicit motives. The type of behavior predicted by the equation would be different from that predicted by implicit motives and traits. McClelland (1980) argued that implicit motives are related to long-term operant behavior such as long-term leader success; explicit behavior is related to short-term respondent behavior, namely intentions, plans, and choices. Perhaps explicit motives and traits predict emergent behavior and perceptions of behavior (Judge et al., 2001) whereas implicit motives and traits predict long-term managerial effectiveness and transformational leadership effectiveness. We believe the speculation is worth testing as it goes to the heart of the two major extant categories of leadership theory.

Management Versus Leadership

There has been a substantial discussion in the leadership literature concerning differences between leaders and managers (Bennis & Nanus, 1985; Yukl, 1994; Zaleznik, 1977, 1989). Yukl (1994) clarified the issue by noting that leadership and management involve separate processes, but need not involve separate people. Yukl (p. 4) notes that "... the essence of the argument seems to be that managers are oriented toward stability and leaders are oriented toward innovation; managers get people to do things more efficiently, whereas leaders get people to agree about what things should be done." Bass (1985) has made a similar distinction between transactional leadership and transformational leadership.

The distinction between leadership and management suggests that research concerning leadership should include measurement of the degree to which the individuals studied are perceived by knowledgeable informants to be leaders, managers, or both. It is likely that some of the personality characteristics that differentiate effective from ineffective leaders are different from those that differentiate effective from ineffective managers. To date, we have not identified these differences.

McClelland's work suggests an avenue of investigation. McClelland (McClelland, 1980) distinguished respondent from operant behavior. Respondent behavior reacts to external stimuli; operant behavior is not conditioned by environmental influences. McClelland argued that respondent behavior results in part from the interaction of explicit motives and social incentives. Operant behavior arises from implicit motives interacting with activity incentives embedded within tasks themselves. Transactional leadership or traditional management shares some similarities with respondent behavior, and transformational leadership shares some characteristics of operant behavior. A testable hypothesis is that traditional managers may be motivated more by explicit motives and social incentives whereas transformational leaders are motivated by implicit motives and activity incentives.

Sex, Gender, Personality, and Leadership

There is substantial research relating sex and gender to personality characteristics, as well as research relating sex and gender to manager and leader behavior. However, previous research has not simultaneously studied relationships among sex, gender, personality, and leader or manager behavior. In this section we outline one possible direction for future research.

First we need to make a distinction between sex and gender. *Sex* refers to male and female biological differences. *Gender* is a psychological and sociological phenomenon. The term refers to the cultural meanings that are attributed to biological differences (Kimmel, 1996).

Sex effects are evident if men and women differ intrinsically independently of situation or culture. If we find that men on average score higher than women on some measure of need for power, for example, and this relationship is invariant across situation and culture, and particularly, if we can link the difference to some biological characteristic, for example testosterone that varies on average between men and women, then we have a sex effect.

Also, if the expression of some characteristics depends invariantly on sex, this is also a sex effect. For example, if men typically and regardless of situation or circumstance differ from women in the expression of the need for power, we have evidence of a sex effect.

Gender effects may manifest themselves in at least two ways. If levels of motives or some other personality characteristics are linked to sex but these relationships change across situations, we have a gender effect. Also, if other processes such as gender-based socialization account for the differences, we have gender effects. Furthermore, through socialization men and women acquire distinct sets of beliefs and behavior. If men and women manifest a high need for power differently, as a reflection of differential socialization, the differential expression is a gender effect, even if there is an underlying physical sex-linked difference in need for power.

A topic of some importance is the relationship of sex and gender to traits, motives, and their behavioral enactment in managerial behavior. Limited research suggests there is no direct effect of sex on motive level. That is, women, on average, are not higher or lower than men on implicit motives. Winter (1988) argued that women show no sex differences in the ways in which the power motive is aroused, in average levels of nPower, or in relationships between nPower and power-related outcomes. In a study of 211 male and 180 female managers over a 12-year period, Jacobs and McClelland (1994) found that the implicit need for power predicted the level of success of both the men and women. In our literature review for this chapter, we found no research that indicates any direct sex effect on implicit motives.

However, there is evidence that indicates that men and women do not express motives in the same way (Winter, 1988). The difference is that women are much more likely than men to have a highly developed responsibility disposition. Winter attributed this difference to the differential socialization experiences of men and women. Jacobs and McClelland (1994) found that two distinct power-related themes distinguished successful men from successful women. Men were more likely to use reactive power themes whereas women were likely to use proactive and more resourceful power themes.

Moore (1997) hypothesized that serotonin affects affiliation, aggression, and dominance behavior. She gave an antidepressant that affects serotonin, or a placebo, to 28 men and 21 women involved in an intimate relationship. Men and women responded differently to the drug; women tended to become less needful, more emotionally resilient, and more self-assured in their relationship.

Gender role theory and research lend credence to these findings. Societal gender roles (Eagly, 1987) are those shared expectations that apply to individuals solely on the basis of their socially identified sex. Gender stereotype research (Best & Williams, 1997) has consistently supported the proposition that there are different expectations for men's and women's attributes and social behavior. Gender stereotypes (Best & Williams) lead to gender-specific early child rearing and socialization processes. It has been argued that women are typically socialized into communal values reflecting a concern for others, selflessness, and a desire to be at one with others. Men are typically socialized into agentic values involving self-expansion, self-assertion, competence, and mastery (Eagly, 1987; Eagly, Karau, & Makhijani, 1995; Eagly, Makhijani, & Klonsky, 1992).

SUMMARY AND CONCLUSION

In this review of personality and leadership research, we began with early research. These studies explored relationships between single personality variables and leadership. Although this body of research has been criticized for several deficiencies and has been relatively ignored for several decades, it provided the basis for subsequent research by identifying importance dimensions of personality and by providing measures of personality characteristics. Subsequent research has expanded on this base. We have reviewed major advances such as the elaboration of the work of McClelland and the consolidation of traits into the Big Five. We have also summarized much of the research that has examined the role of environments. Finally, we develop a theory of personality and leadership based on the theoretical work of McClelland et al. Pessimism about the past or future of research into the personality and leadership seems to be misplaced.

REFERENCES

Atkinson, J. W., & Birch, D. (1970). *The dynamics of action.* New York: Wiley.

Bass, B. M. (1985). *Leadership and performance beyond expectations.* New York: Free Press.

Bass, B. M. (1998). *Transformational leadership: Industrial, military, and educational impact.* Mahwah, NJ: Lawrence Erlbaum Associates, Inc.

Bateman, T. S., & Crant, J. M. (1993). The proactive component of organizational behavior. *Journal of Organizational Behavior, 14,* 103–118.

Baughman, W. A. (1997). *The role of relational preferences in the development of knowledge and skills.* Unpublished doctoral dissertation, George Mason University.

Bennis, W. (1959). Leadership theory and administrative behavior: The problem of authority. *Administrative Science Quarterly, 4,* 259–301.

Bennis, W., & Nanus, B. (1985). *Leaders: The strategies for taking charge.* New York: Harper & Row.

Best, D., & Williams, J. (1997). Sex, gender, and culture. In J. W. Berry, M. H. Segall, & C. Kagitcibasi (Eds.), *Handbook of cross-cultural psychology* (Vol. 3: Social behavior and applications, 2nd ed., pp. 163–213). Needham Heights, MA: Allyn & Bacon.

Bird, C. (1940). *Social psychology.* New York: Appelton-Century-Crofts.

Block, J. (1995). Going beyond the five factors given: Rejoinder to Costa and McCrae (1995) and Goldberg and Saucier (1995). *Psychological Bulletin, 117*(2), 226–229.

Block, J. (2001). Millennial contrarianism: The five-factor approach to personality description 5 years later. *Journal of Research in Personality, 35*(1), 98–107.

Bouchard, T. J., Jr., Lykken, D. T., McGue, M., Segal, N. L., & Tellegen, A. (1990). Sources of human psychological differences: The Minnesota study of twins reared apart. *Science, 250,* 223–228.

Costa, P. T., & McCrae, R. R. (1988). From catalog to classification: Murray's needs and the five-factor model. *Journal of Personality and Social Psychology, 55*(2), 258–265.

Costa, P. T., & McCrae, R. R (1992). *NEO PI-R Professional Manual.* Odessa, FL: Psychology Assessment Resources.

Costa, P. T., & McCrae, R. R. (1995). Solid ground in the wetlands of personality: A reply to Block. *Psychological Bulletin, 117*(2), 216–220.

Cronbach, L. (1957). The two disciplines of scientific psychology. *American Psychologist, 12*, 671–684.

Davis-Blake, A., & Pfeffer, J. (1989). Just a mirage: The search for dispositional effects in organizations. *Academy Of Management Review, 14*, 385–401.

deCharms, R., Morrison, H. W., Reitman, W., & McClelland, D. C. (1955). Behavioral correlates of directly and indirectly measured achievement motivation. In D. C. McClelland (Ed.), *Studies in motivation*. Englewood Cliffs, NJ: Prentice Hall.

Deci, E. (1971). Effects of externally mediated rewards on intrinsic motivation. *Journal of Personality and Social Psychology, 18*(1), 105–115.

Deci, E., Koestner, R., & Ryan, R. (1999a). A meta-analytic review of experiments examining the effects of extrinsic rewards on intrinsic motivation. *Psychological Bulletin, 125*(6), 627–668.

Deci, E., Koestner, R., & Ryan, R. (1999b). The undermining effect is a reality after all—Extrinsic rewards, task interest, and self-discrimination: Reply to Eisenberger, Pierce, and Cameron (1999), and Lepper, Henderlong, and Gingras (1999). *Psychological Bulletin, 125*(6), 692–700.

Deluga, R. (1998). American presidential proactivity, charismatic leadership, and rated performance. *Leadership Quarterly, 9*, 265–292.

Eagly, A. H. (1987). *Sex differences in social behavior: A social-role interpretation*. Hillsdale, NJ: Lawrence Erlbaum Associates, Inc.

Eagly, A. H., Karau, S. J., & Makhijani, M. G. (1995). Gender and the effectiveness of Leaders: A meta-analysis. *Psychological Bulletin, 117*, 125–145.

Eagly, A. H., Makhijani, M. G., and Klonsky, B. G. (1992). Gender and the evaluation of leaders: A meta-analysis. *Psychological Bulletin, 111*, 3–22.

Edwards, A. L. (1959). *Edwards Personal Preference Schedule*. New York: The Psychological Corporation.

Eysenck, H. J. (1967). *Biological basis of personality*. Springfield, IL: Thomas.

Eysenck, M. W., & Eysenck, H. J. (1980). Mischel and the concept of personality. *British Journal of Psychology, 71*(2), 191–204.

Furnham, A. (1996). The big five versus the big four: The relationship between the Myers-Briggs Type Indicator (MBTI) and NEO-PI five factor model of personality. *Personality and Individual Differences, 21*(2), 303–307.

Gardner, W. L., & Martinko, M. J. (1996). Using the Myers-Briggs Type Indicator to study managers: A literature review and research agenda. *Journal of Management, 22*(1), 45–83.

Ghiselli, E. E. (1971). *Exploration in managerial talent*. Pacific Palisades, CA: Goodyear.

Gibb, C. A. (1947). The principles and traits of leadership. *Journal of Abnormal and Social Psychology, 42*, 267–284.

Goldberg, L. R., & Saucier, G. (1995). So what do you propose we use instead? A reply to Block. *Psychological Bulletin, 117*(2), 221–225.

Goodstein, L. D., & Schrader, W. J. (1963). An empirically derived key for the California Psychology Inventory. *Journal of Applied Psychology, 47*, 42–45.

Gough, H. G. (1957). *Manual for the California Psychological Inventory*. Palo Alto, CA: Consulting Psychologists Press.

Hogan, R., Curphy, G. J., & Hogan, J. (1994). What we know about leadership: Effectiveness and personality. *American Psychologist, 49*(6), 493–504.

House, R. J., & Aditya, R. N. (1997). The social scientific study of leadership: Quo vadis? *Journal of Management, 23*, 409–474.

House, R. J., & Baetz, M. L. (1979). Leadership: Some empirical generalizations and new research directions. In B. Staw (Ed.), *Research in organizational behavior* (Vol. 1, pp. 341–423). Greenwich, CT: JAI.

House, R. J., Delbecq, A., Taris, T., & Sully de Luque, M. (2001). *Charismatic leadership theory: An empirical test based on CEO Leader behavior and effects.* Working paper, Department of Management, The Wharton School, University of Pennsylvania.

House, R. J., Spangler, W. D., & Woycke, J. (1991). Personality and charisma in the U.S. Presidency: A psychological theory of leadership effectiveness. *Administrative Science Quarterly, 36,* 364–396.

Jackson, D. N. (1989). *Personality Research Form manual.* Port Huron, MI: Sigma Assessment Systems.

Jacobs, R. L., & McClelland, D. C. (1994). Moving up the corporate ladder: A longitudinal study of the leadership motive profile and managerial success in women and men. *Consulting Psychology Journal: Practice and Research, 46*(1), 32–41.

Jacobsen, C., & House, R. J. (2001). The dynamics of charismatic leadership. *Leadership Quarterly, 12*(1), 75–112.

Jenkins, W. O. (1947). A review of leadership studies with particular references to military problems. *Psychological Bulletin, 44,* 54–79.

John, O. P., & Srivastava, S. (1999). The big-five taxonomy: History, measurement, and theoretical perspectives. In L. A. Pervin and O. P. John (Eds.), *Handbook of personality: Theory and research* (pp. 102–138). New York: Guilford.

Judge, T. A., Bono, J. E., Ilies, R., & Werner, M. (2001). Personality and leadership: A review. Under review.

Kimmel, M. S. (1996). Series Editor's Introduction. In C. Cheng (Ed.), *Masculinities in organizations.* Thousand Oaks, CA: Sage.

Kirkpatrick, S. A., & Baum, J. R. (2000, August). *What makes the vision work? How entrepreneurs' motives and organizational goals impact long-term venture growth.* An interactive paper presented at the Academy of Management Meeting, Toronto.

Kirkpatrick, S., & Locke, E. A. (1991). Do traits matter? *The Executive, 5*(2), 48–61.

Kirkpatrick, S. A., Wofford, J. C., & Baum, J. R. (2000, April). *Leader motives and performance in service and manufacturing organizations.* Paper presented at the annual conference of the Society for Industrial and Organizational Psychology, New Orleans, LA.

Koestner, R., Weinberger, J., & McClelland, D. C. (1991). Task-intrinsic and social-extrinsic sources of arousal for motives assessed in fantasy and self-report. *Journal of Personality, 59,* 57–82.

Korman, A. K. (1968). The prediction of managerial performance: A review. *Personnel Psychology, 21,* 295–322.

Kouzes, J. M., & Posner, B. Z. (1995). *The leadership challenge: How to keep getting extraordinary things done in organizations* (2nd ed.). San Francisco, CA: Jossey-Bass.

Lee, C., Ashford, S. J., & Bobko, P. (1990). Interactive effects of "type A" behavior and perceived control on worker performance, job satisfaction, and somatic complaints. *Academy of Management Journal, 33,* 870–881.

Lepper, M., Greene, P., & Nisbett, R. (1973). Undermining children's intrinsic interest with extrinsic reward: A test of the "overjustification" hypothesis. *Journal of Personality and Social Psychology, 28*(1), 129–137.

Litwin, G. H., & Stringer, R. A., Jr. (1968). *Motivation and organizational climate.* Boston: Harvard Business School Press.

Lord, R. G., DeVader, C. L., & Alliger, G. M. (1986). A meta-analysis of the relation between personality traits and leadership perceptions: An application of validity generalization procedures. *Journal of Applied Psychology, 71,* 402–411.

Mann, R. D. (1959). A review of the relationship between personality and performance in small groups. *Psychological Bulletin, 56,* 241–270.

McAdams, D. P. (1992). The five-factor model in personality: A critical appraisal. *Journal of Personality, 60*(2), 329–361.

McAdams, D. P. (1994). A psychology of the stranger. *Psychological Inquiry, 5*(2), 145–148.

McAdams, D. P. (1996). Alternative futures for the study of human individuality. *Journal of Research in Personality, 30*(3), 374–388.

McAdams, D. P. (1997). A conceptual history of personality psychology. In R. Hogan, J. Johnson, & S. Briggs (Eds.), *Handbook of personality psychology* (pp. 3–39). San Diego, CA: Academic.

McCall, M. W. (1976). Leadership research: Choosing gods and devils on the run. *Journal of Occupational Psychology, 49*(3), 139–153.

McClelland, D. C. (1962). Business drive and national achievement. *Harvard Business Review, 40*(4), 99–112.

McClelland, D. C. (1975). *Power: The inner experience.* New York: Irvington.

McClelland, D. C. (1976). *The achieving society.* New York: Irvington.

McClelland, D. C. (1980). Motive dispositions: The merits of operant and respondent measures. In L. Wheeler (Ed.), *Review of personality and social psychology* (Vol. 1, pp. 53–81). Beverly Hills, CA: Sage.

McClelland, D. C. (1985a). How motives, skills, and values determine what people do. *American Psychologist, 40*, 812–825.

McClelland, D. C. (1985b). *Human motivation.* Glenview, IL: Scott, Foresman.

McClelland, D. C., Atkinson, J. W., Clark, R. A., & Lowell, E. L. (1958). A scoring manual or the achievement motive. In J. W. Atkinson (Ed.), *Motives in fantasy, action, and society.* New York: Van Nostrand.

McClelland, D. C., & Boyatzis, R. E. (1982). Leadership motive pattern and long-term success in management. *Journal of Applied Psychology, 67*, 737–743.

McClelland, D. C., & Burnham, D. H. (1976). Power is the great motivator. *Harvard Business Review, 54*(2), 100–110.

McClelland, D. C., Koestner, R., & Weinberger, J. (1989). How do self-attributed and implicit motives differ? *Psychological Review, 96*, 690–702.

McCrae, R. R. (2001). 5 years of progress: A reply to Block. *Journal of Research in Personality, 35*(1), 108–113.

McCrae, R. R., & Costa, P. T., Jr. (1989). Reinterpreting the Myers-Briggs Type Indicator from the perspective of the five-factor model of personality. *Journal of Personality, 57*(1), 17–37.

McCrae, R. R., & Costa, P. T., Jr. (1997). Conceptions and correlates of openness to experience. In R. Hogan, J. Johnson, & S. Briggs (Eds.), *Handbook of personality psychology* (pp. 825–847). San Diego, CA: Academic.

McCrae R. R., & Costa, P. T., Jr. (1990). *Personality in adulthood.* New York: Guilford.

McCrae, R. R., & Costa, P. T., Jr. (1999). A five-factor theory of personality. In L. A. Pervin & O. P. John (Eds.), *Handbook of personality: Theory and research* (pp. 139–153). New York: Guilford.

Megargee, E. I. (1972). *The California Psychological Inventory handbook.* San Francisco, CA: Jossey-Bass.

Megargee, E. I., Bogart, P., & Anderson, B. J. (1966). Prediction of leadership in a simulated industrial task. *Journal of Applied Psychology, 50*, 292–295.

Meindl, J. R., Ehrlich, S. B., & Dukerich, J. M. (1985). The romance of leadership. *Administrative Science Quarterly, 30*(1), 78–102.

Miner, J. B. (1964). *Scoring guide for the Miner Sentence Completion Scale.* Atlanta, GA: Organizational Measurement System Press.

Miner, J. B. (1978). Twenty years of research on role-motivation theory of managerial effectiveness. *Personnel Psychology, 31*, 739–760.

Miner, J. B. (1993). *Role motivation theories.* London: Routledge.

Mischel, W. (1973). Toward a cognitive social learning reconceptualization of personality. *Psychological Review, 80*, 252–283.

Monson, T. C., Hesley, J. W., & Chernick, L. (1982). Specifying when personality traits can and cannot predict behavior: An alternative to abandoning the attempt to predict single act criteria. *Journal of Personality and Social Psychology, 3*, 385–499.

Moore, A. A. (1997). Effects of serotonin-specific reuptake inhibitors on intimacy. *Dissertation Abstracts International, 58*(5-B), 2744.

Mulder, M., & Stemerding, A. (1963). Threat, attraction to group, and need for strong leadership. *Human Relations, 16*, 317–334.

Mulder, M., van Eck, J. R. R., & de Jong, R. D. (1971). An organization in crisis and non-crisis Situations. *Human Relations, 24*, 19–51.

Mumford, M. D., Zaccaro, S. J., Harding, F. D., Jacobs, T. O., & Fleishman, E. A. (2000). Leadership skills for a changing world: Solving complex social problems. *Leadership Quarterly, 11*, 11–35.

Murray, H. A. (1938). *Explorations in personality.* New York: Oxford University Press.

Myers, I. B., & McCaulley, M. H. (1985). *A guide to the development and use of the Myers-Briggs Type Indicator.* Palo Alto, CA: Consulting Psychologists Press.

Ostrand, J. L. (1980). Dominance. In R. H. Woody (Ed.), *Encyclopedia of clinical assessment* (Vol. 1, pp. 481–489). San Francisco, CA: Jossey-Bass.

Patten, R. L., & White, L. A. (1977). Independent effects of achievement motivation and overt attribution on achievement behavior. *Motivation and Emotion, 1*, 39–59.

Pfeffer, J. (1994). *Competitive advantage through people: Unleashing the power of the work force.* Boston: Harvard Business School Press.

Ray, J. J., & Singh, S. (1980). Effects of individual differences on productivity among farmers in India. *Journal of Social Psychology, 112*(1), 11–17.

Ryan, R., & Deci, E. (2000). Intrinsic and extrinsic motivation: Classic definitions and new directions. *Contemporary Educational Psychology, 25*(1), 54–67.

Sales, S. (1972). Authoritarianism: But as for me, give me liberty, or give me maybe, a great big, strong, powerful leader I can honor, admire, respect and obey. *Psychology Today, 94–98*, 140–143.

Schneider, B. (1983). Interactional psychology & organizational behavior. In L. L. Cummings & B. M. Staw (Eds.). *Research in organizational behavior* (Vol. 5, pp. 1–31). Greenwich, CT: JAI.

Shamir, B., House, R. J., & Arthur, M. B. (1993). The motivational effects of charismatic leadership: A self-concept based theory. *Organization Science, 4*(4), 577–595.

Smith, C. P. (1992). *Motivation and personality: Handbook of thematic content analysis.* New York: Cambridge University Press.

Snow, R. E., & Lohman, D. R. (1984). Toward a theory of cognitive aptitude for learning from instruction. *Journal of Educational Psychology, 76*, 347–375.

Snyder, M. (1974). Self-monitoring of expressive behavior. *Journal of Personality and Social Psychology, 30*, 526–537.

Snyder, M. (1979). Self-monitoring processes. In L. Berkowitz (Ed.), *Advances in experimental social psychology* (Vol. 12, pp. 86–128). San Diego, CA: Academic.

Spangler, W. D. (1992). The validity of questionnaire and TAT measures of need for achievement: Two meta analyses. *Psychological Bulletin, 112*, 140–154.

Spangler, W. D. (2001). *A meta-analysis of TAT and questionnaire measures of need for power.* Unpublished manuscript.

Spangler, W. D., & House, R. J. (1991). Presidential effectiveness and the leadership motive profile. *Journal of Personality and Social Psychology, 60*, 439–455.

Steele, R. S. (1977). Power motivation, activation, and inspirational speeches. *Journal of Personality, 45*, 53–64.

Stogdill, R. M. (1948). Personal factors associated with leadership: A survey of the literature. *Journal of Psychology, 25*, 35–71.

Stogdill, R. M. (1974). *Handbook of leadership: A survey of theory and research*. New York: Free Press.

Waldman, D., Ramirez, G., House, R. J., & Puranam, P. (2001). Does leadership matter? CEO leadership attributes and profitability under conditions of perceived environmental uncertainty. *Academy of Management Journal, 44*, 134–144.

Wanberg, C. R., & Kammeyer-Mueller, J. D. (2000). Predictors and outcomes of proactivity in the socialization process. *Journal of Applied Psychology, 85*, 373–385.

Watson, D., & Clark, L. A. (1997). Extraversion and its positive emotional core. In R. Hogan, J. Johnson, and S. Briggs (Eds.), *Handbook of personality psychology* (pp. 767–793). San Diego, CA: Academic.

Weber, M. (1947). *The theory of social and economic organization*. New York: Oxford University Press.

Winter, D. G. (1978). *Navy leadership and management competencies: Convergence among tests, interviews, and performance ratings*. Boston: McBer.

Winter, D. G. (1988). The power motive in women—and men. *Journal of Personality and Social Psychology, 54*(3), 510–519.

Winter, D. G. (1991). A motivational model of leadership: Predicting long-term management success from TAT measures of power motivation and responsibility. *Leadership Quarterly, 2*(2), 67–80.

Winter, D. G., & Barenbaum, N. B. (1985). Responsibility and the power motive in women and men. *Journal of Personality, 53*, 335–355.

Winter, D. G., & Barenbaum, N. B. (1999). History of modern personality theory and research. In L. A. Pervin & O. P. John (Eds.), *Handbook of personality*. New York: Guilford.

Winter, D. G., John, O. P., Stewart, A. J., Klohnen, E. C., & Duncan, L. E. (1998). Traits and motives: Toward an integration of two traditions in personality research. *Psychological Review, 105*, 230–250.

Woodward, C. V. (1974). *Responses of the presidents to charges of misconduct*. New York: Dell.

Yukl, G. (1994). *Leadership in organizations* (3rd ed.). Englewood Cliffs, NJ: Prentice Hall.

Zaccaro, S. J., Foti, R. J., & Kenny, D. A. (1991). Self-monitoring and trait-based variance in leadership: An investigation of leader flexibility across multiple group situations. *Journal of Applied Psychology, 76*, 308–315.

Zaleznik, A. (1977, May/June). Managers and leaders: Are they different? *Harvard Business Review, 55*(3), 67–77.

Zaleznik, A. (1989, January/February). Executives and organizations: Real work. *Harvard Business Review, 89*(1), 57–64.

11

Personality and Citizenship Behavior in Organizations

Dennis W. Organ
Kelley School of Business
Indiana University

Julie Beth McFall
Carlson School of Management
University of Minnesota

Essentially the same theoretical reasons for believing job satisfaction to influence organizational citizenship behavior (OCB) would argue for an effect of personality on OCB. Yet, to date, the evidence in support of an effect of job attitudes is more consistent and robust than comparable evidence relating personality and OCB. We assume, first, that the data can be taken at face value and ask how that would lead us to revise our framework for thinking about personality and OCB. We then examine the prevailing paradigm for research on OCB and personality and offer explanations as to why that paradigm might militate against detecting relationships between OCB and certain traits. We offer suggestions for future research that could provide a basis for stronger inferences about the role of disposition in OCB.

PERSONALITY, SATISFACTION, AND ORGANIZATIONAL CITIZENSHIP BEHAVIOR

Whenever people first began to develop intuitive, informal models about the causes of individual performance in organizations, among the earliest truths they took as self-evident were that morale and character had much to do with a person's work contributions. A century or more later, folk conceptions of job performance probably still hold to that view, having never seen much reason to question it. Experience and casual observation, it would seem, continually support the reasoning that (a) job satisfaction plays a substantial role in determining a person's job performance and that (b) personality traits predispose some individuals to work harder and better than do other individuals.

Yet, until recently, industrial and organizational psychology took a dim view of such thinking. The proposition that job satisfaction appreciably influenced performance simply did not stand up to the hard glare of systematic empirical research. Influential reviews by Brayfield and Crockett (1955) and Vroom (1964) laid waste to the simplistic view that individual satisfaction had much if any bearing on individual productivity. Job satisfaction might still be important, mainly for humanistic reasons; it might have a marginal effect on absences and turnover, and I/O psychologists continued to measure and study job satisfaction (more than any other single variable), all the while reminding us not to be seduced by Pollyannaish thinking that we could use job satisfaction to leverage productivity.

Meanwhile, I/O psychology, while borrowing and devising many measures of individual differences, had little success in finding personality traits that reliably predicted a person's productivity. A scholarly review of the extant evidence concluded that no basis existed for thinking "that personality measures can be recommended as good or practical tools for employee selection" (Guion & Gottier, 1965, p. 159). The one measurable individual difference variable that did reliably suggest itself as a substantial predictor of job performance was intelligence, in particular the g factor (discussed later) that appears to underlie any measure of mental ability. Thus, while some people indeed work more productively than others, they do so because they're smarter—not because of the differences in temperament, mood, sociability, and values that we normally associate with the idea of personality.

The I/O psychology model of individual performance thus came down to cognitive ability as the major (if not sole) individual characteristic that accounted for much variance in individual performance. The rest could be chalked up to training, experience, work design, work incentives, competent supervision, and technology.

But in the last decade or so, I/O psychology seems to have taken a turn toward meeting folk wisdom halfway. Scholars and researchers have hit on a framework that seems to bring both job satisfaction and personality back into the picture as worthwhile constructs in models of performance.

RETHINKING PERFORMANCE

The revisionist stance in I/O psychology regarding job satisfaction and personality comes about largely because of an altered conception of what we mean by an individual's performance. For much of the 20th century, scientific research on the causes of individual performance pursued a paradigm in which performance was operationally defined in terms of measurable output—dollar value of sales, number of cases processed, tons of lumber harvested, boxes of shoes packaged, and the like. Studies that coupled the output measure with one pertaining to quality also generally took the form of discrete counting, as in number or percentage of rejects or errors. When hard measures of performance were not at hand, I/O psychologists fashioned rating systems for use by supervisors, but care was taken to tailor these rating forms as objectively as possible to the specific, formally defined activities of the job description. If such ratings actually were found to correlate significantly with a measure of satisfaction or personality, researchers and reviewers were inclined to qualify the finding by noting the imperfect validity of subjective ratings.

One can well understand the appeal of such a paradigm for serious researchers in I/O psychology. The paradigm boasted the virtues that we associate with objective, reliable, valid measures and replicable procedures. The paradigm screened out the noise and error to which casual observation and anecdotal evidence—the kind of evidence leading people to believe that satisfaction and personality shape performance—are prone.

But the implicit model of organization in such a paradigm is that organizational effectiveness is the sum of the individual performances in terms of the latter's measurable output and execution of specifically assigned task requirements. If such were not the case, then the organization structure or plan was faulty—the plan had failed to specify the important activities and locate them appropriately and formally within the responsibilities of designated positions.

A much different model of organizational effectiveness had been sketched by Barnard (1938). Barnard saw the essence of organizations as cooperative systems that cannot be reduced to the sum of individual productivity measures. He recognized willingness to cooperate as a dynamic that transcends measurable task performance. Furthermore, and significantly for the present discussion, he recognized that willingness to cooperate is not invariant—it varies across individuals (i.e., according to some more or less stable traits or characteristics), as well as within individuals according to the "net satisfactions or dissatisfactions experienced or anticipated" (Barnard, p. 84–85).

Katz and Kahn (1966) echoed the strains of Barnard with their emphasis on innovative and spontaneous contributions by individuals to organizational functioning. They noted that organizations require more than reliable performance of job duties and task productivity to be successful. Unforeseen contingencies continually arise, necessitating spontaneous actions by individuals beyond the purview of their job descriptions. Cooperation, good will, initiative, forbearance, consideration of others, and information sharing all matter in a general and pervasive sense that cannot be reduced to job descriptions. They are contributions that frequently are taken for granted, seldom documented, and hard to measure, but they are the stuff of which organized action is made.

Recently, I/O psychology has begun to enrich its conception of performance by going beyond objective measures of output and job-specified activities to embrace Barnard's willingness to cooperate and Katz and Kahn's (1966) innovative and spontaneous contributions. Much of the impetus to redefine performance has developed from the work done by I/O psychologists involved in the Army's Project Alpha on the selection, classification, and deployment of personnel (Campbell and Zook, 1990; Rumsey, Walker, and Harris, 1994). Linked to that work is the research and theory development associated with contextual performance (e.g., Borman and Motowidlo, 1993), individual contributions that sustain the organizational and interpersonal context for task performance and that have generalized value and significance across different jobs and organizations.

Independently of Project Alpha, our own work and that of close colleagues (Organ, 1988, 1990; Organ and Painc, 1999; Podsakoff, Ahearne, and MacKenzie, 1997; Podsakoff and MacKenzie, 1994; Smith, Organ, and Near, 1983) has sought to account for variance in OCB, or the individual contributions—such as helping others, consideration of others'needs, protection of and care for organizational resources, constructive suggestions— that go beyond the strict job definition and seldom qualify for guaranteed remuneration by the reward system. Various other research programs have addressed similar expansion of our rendering of performance, looking at broad conceptions of extra-role behavior (e.g., Van Dyne, Cummings, and Parks, 1995).

At the risk of slighting the valued contributions of numerous contributors to the literature concerning this broadened conception of performance, we wish to simplify the discussion that follows by limiting it largely to the programs of research and theory development associated with contextual performance and OCB.

REVISIONIST VIEWS OF PERSONALITY AND JOB SATISFACTION RELATED TO CITIZENSHIP BEHAVIOR

Contextual Performance Approach

Following the work of the Army Alpha project, and proceeding largely in the vein of the traditional industrial psychology interest in selection and placement, researchers in contextual performance focused on stable, measurable attributes of individuals. For several decades prior to Alpha,

I/O psychology had concentrated its interest in individual attributes to differences in g, the general intelligence factor that most or all mental ability tests have in common. The work of Hunter, Schmidt, and others (e.g. Hunter and Hunter, 1984; Schmidt, Ones, & Hunter, 1992) had firmly established the role of g as a valid and generalizable predictor of task performance, whereas measures of noncognitive aspects of personality had been found wanting in that regard.

Now, however, with a notion of performance that went beyond the task or job description, researchers in contextual performance could see greater scope in which noncognitive aspects of personality might well explain important variance. While g seemed to provide the best individual difference predictor of task performance, it seemed eminently plausible that aspects of temperament, values, sociability, and character would account for differences in levels of contextual performance. Contextual performance need not be constrained by technical skills, nor by the constraints of work flow and technology; it typically manifests itself in weak situations in which neither obvious cues nor overpowering incentives dictate specific responses. These should be precisely the situations in which personality influences behavior.

Moreover, about this same time the community of scholars in the measurement and description of personality began to settle on the framework of the Big Five model of personality, which provided an accepted model within which to specify, define, and measure the characteristics of people that would predict contextual performance.

OCB Approach

On the other hand, the work on OCB began with a focus on job satisfaction (and, perforce, related attitudes and perceptions). Indeed, it is not much of an overstatement to say that OCB research had its origins in a determined effort to find something that is predicted by job satisfaction. The approach taken essentially was to define some aspects of performance other than task productivity with which job satisfaction would correlate. Defining and measuring OCB such that it included contributions by way of informal cooperation and accommodation, going beyond the minimally enforced or rewarded levels of attendance and punctuality, and constructive involvement in workplace governance, researchers reasoned that here we would find scope for the expression of attitudes such as job satisfaction. Unlike narrowly defined task productivity, OCB would not be constrained by technology, work design, or technical skills.

Thus, the work on contextual performance and on OCB both pointed toward the kind of performance that lies more at the discretion of the individual. Each approach described a kind of performance that is defined by many repetitions, over long intervals, of seemingly modest, mundane behaviors that nonetheless aggregate so as to render organizations more viable, more efficient in their operations, and more effective in meeting the inevitable unforeseen contingencies that arise. Research by Podsakoff and MacKenzie (1994), Podsakoff et. al. (1997), and Walz and Niehoff (1996) strongly supports the association of contextual performance or OCB with organizational effectiveness.

Differences in the Approaches

The difference between the two programs of research—on contextual performance and OCB—is that I/O psychologists have sought to explain contextual performance by using personality predictors, whereas those interested in what they call OCB have tended to think in terms of job attitudes and the antecedents of those attitudes. It is as if the researchers in contextual performance hoped to have their work culminate in more valid systems for selection and placement, whereas OCB researchers had their eyes on what managers could do in order to shape attitudes favorable to organizational functioning.

Yet both camps appear to have found good theoretical footing for their aims. Personality and attitudes have in common the record that they seldom fare well in predicting specific behaviors at specific times in specific places. They predispose persons in certain directions, but those predispositions can be overridden by salient cues and powerful incentives to act or to refrain from acting in certain ways. Even absent such cues and incentives, people are subject to transient states—fatigue, mood, preoccupation—that inhibit actions to which they would otherwise be predisposed. The result is that personality and attitudes better predict what people do of their own inclination over an extended time interval, aggregated across many situations, in varying forms, and in the absence of strictly enforced requirements or strong incentives. Those conditions go far to characterize much of what we mean by contextual performance or OCB.

A meta-analysis (Organ & Ryan, 1995) of more than a decade of research on OCB provided strong, cumulative evidence for a link between job attitudes and OCB. The estimated population correlation coefficient (corrected for attenuation caused by unreliability of measures) between job satisfaction and the interpersonal helping dimension of OCB was .28; excluding studies with self-ratings of OCB, and thus common method variance with the satisfaction measure, the correlation was .26. The correlations with the impersonal conscientiousness dimension of OCB were .28 and .24. Other measures (fairness in the workplace, affective commitment, supervisor supportiveness) that demonstrably have much in common with job satisfaction, in terms of reflecting affectively toned descriptions of the job environment, registered comparable correlations with various dimensions of OCB.

By contrast, the meta-analysis of various measures of personality showed little support for a robust link to OCB. Measures that could plausibly be interpreted as markers of the Big Five dimensions of agreeableness, emotional stability, and extraversion failed to connect with any dimension of OCB beyond .15 in absolute value. Measures that, on their face, could be taken as reflective of the Big Five dimension of conscientiousness fared slightly better, .22 (but only .04 when excluding studies with self-ratings) with interpersonal helping, and .30 (.23 when considering only other-ratings) with the OCB dimension pertaining to excellence in attendance, punctuality, use of time, and compliance with workplace rules and procedures.

Individual studies (e.g., Konovsky & Organ, 1996; Organ & Lingl, 1995) that have sought to compare the predictive power of job attitudes and specific traits, as well as test causal models of OCB, have found rather much the same result. When OCB measures are first regressed on job satisfaction and/or perceived fairness as predictors, the addition of personality measures adds little or nothing to explained variance. Conspicuously, and most surprisingly, measures of agreeableness contribute essentially nil. Conscientiousness adds a modest amount of explained variance in impersonal forms of OCB (e.g., generalized compliance).

Moreover, although researchers following up on the work of Project Alpha have provided consistent evidence for the ability of conscientiousness (and specific traits that fall within the larger domain of this aspect of the Big Five) to predict contextual performance, the findings, even though significant in a strictly statistical sense, are comparable to the results of Organ & Ryan's (1995) meta-analysis. Thus, Van Scotter & Motowidlo (1996) report correlations of .16 between conscientiousness and job dedication, .11 between conscientiousness and interpersonal facilitation. None of the correlations involving agreeableness, extraversion, or positive affectivity exceeded .16.

Three notable exceptions to the foregoing trend can be found in research reported by Kamp and Hough (1988), Campbell (1990), and Motowidlo and Van Scotter (1994). Kamp and Hough's findings came from a meta-analysis of correlations between measures of eight personality variables and criteria that included measures of job proficiency, school success, training performance, and delinquency. The delinquency criterion was operationalized by incidents of absence without leave and unfavorable discharges in military samples and, in civilian samples, by documented cases of company rule violations and employee theft. Personality measures regarded as theoretically relevant to these delinquency measures were those interpreted as adjustment and dependability, which correlated (when corrected for reliability and attenuation caused by range restriction) −.43 and −.42, respectively, with the delinquency criterion.

Campbell's (1990) research (which was part of Project Alpha) reported a correlation of .30 between dependability and personal discipline—the latter being, of course, a criterion quite suggestive of OCB and contextual performance. Motowidlo and Van Scotter's (1994) study found correlations of .36, .31, and .22 between contextual performance and, respectively, work orientation, dependability, and cooperativeness.

The levels of correlations shown in the Kamp and Hough (1988), Campbell (1990), and Motowidlo and Van Scotter (1994) reports clearly command attention. However, two questions necessarily arise in the interpretation of these results in regard to the relationship between personality and OCB:

1. The delinquency measures studied by Kamp and Hough would seem to pose as referents for something rather different from either OCB or contextual performance. They have to do with extreme incidents of unconstructive, injurious, or otherwise objectionable behaviors. Moreover, one has little reason to regard them as simply mirror opposites of OCB. Granted, one would generally anticipate that people who render frequent and substantial OCB would also be the persons least likely to commit such objectionable behaviors. But one would not necessarily suspect that those who contribute relatively less OCB are, on that account alone, prone to engage actively in deliberate wrongdoing. Many citizens are at best passively involved in voluntary contributions to the community, but that does not mark them as likely felons. Still, the findings from Kamp and Hough do argue for a useful role of certain predictors of behavior that is highly relevant to the larger picture of performance in organizations.

2. The Campbell and the Motowidlo and Van Scotter studies involve measures of dependability and work orientation. The question that one might raise here is whether these measures fit the generally understood notion of personality. To the extent that these measures capture a stable dimension of behavior, then we would understandably think of them as personality. However, the measure of dependability sounds very much like Hogan and Hogan's (1989) reliability, which they derived by selecting and weighting (according to empirical validity evidence) items that came from facets of different personality domains. In other words, measures of dependability (and, one might suspect, work orientation and cooperativeness), while of demonstrated utility in predicting criteria relevant to OCB, appear to represent particular mixes of traits that optimize the prediction of certain forms of OCB. The suggestion here is that, if there are connections between personality and OCB, the connections cannot be reduced to simple or univariate dimensions within the Big Five.

We might also regard dependability, work orientation, and cooperativeness not so much as the basic tendencies of personality but as the characteristic adaptations (McCrae & Costa, 1996) that people develop at work. That is, people learn, with varying degrees of effectiveness and from varied intentions, how to cope with life at work—in their relationships with others, how to solve problems, and how to serve their own interests in either the short or long run. Of course, we might also strongly suspect that basic tendencies have much to do with the forms of characteristic adaptations, a point argued eloquently by Motowidlo, Borman, and Schmitt (1997) and a matter to which we shall return in the discussion that concludes this chapter.

Overall then, we are left with an empirical record that is not quite so convincing as we would have hoped in regard to the ability of theoretically accepted personality dimensions to predict OCB. As we have seen, some stable behavior patterns derived from underlying domains of personality clearly have relevance to OCB, and they seem to show particular advantage for predicting the more extreme forms of organizational delinquency. But bivariate correlations between OCB and dimensions of personality have not been impressive.

One has to wonder why measures of the theoretically important personality factors have not shown as much power as job attitude measures in predicting OCB and contextual performance. Intuitively they would both seem to have much to do with OCB and, in fact, much more to do with OCB than with the objective performance measures that are more influenced by skill, training, work methods, and formal reward systems. Both personality and attitudes would seem to contain the tendencies and predispositions that would better predict what people do over extended periods of time and in situations in which neither strong cues and incentives nor requisite skills constrain those tendencies and dispositions. Yet the evidence, although supporting this reasoning with respect to various theoretically specified attitudes (job satisfaction, affective commitment, perceived fairness, supervisor supportiveness), remains marginal for personality measures. The one instance in which a personality variable lives up to what we would intuitively expect is conscientiousness—when the criterion is something like job dedication or generalized compliance. Especially disappointing is the general lack of predictive power for the Big Five dimension of agreeableness. Considering how much of OCB (particularly in the dimensions of interpersonal helping, sportsmanship, courtesy) or contextual performance (interpersonal facilitation) seems like a sketch of the agreeable person—one who is easy to get along with, trusting and trustworthy, patient, slow to anger or resentment—one can only scratch one's head at the consistent failure to find correlations above .10 to .15.

Let's assume we have enough empirical data now to decide how we want to proceed in terms of how we think about personality and OCB. First, we can discuss whether we should take the extant data at face value and rethink the basis for the link between personality and OCB. What considerations, given the evidence we now have, might give us compelling reasons for relegating personality to a subordinate role in determining OCB (however much our a priori or intuitive thinking might have suggested otherwise)? Second, we can question whether, in fact, the extant data should be taken at face value. Can we marshal other findings to suggest why we should strenuously qualify that data? Is there something about the research paradigm of OCB that systematically works against the chances for personality to predict OCB?

SUPPOSE WE TAKE THE DATA AT FACE VALUE

Indirect Rather Than Direct Effects of Personality

One means of interpreting the cumulative findings is to think in terms of a causal model in which job attitudes exert direct effects on OCB, whereas personality, for the most part, has its influences indirectly via job attitudes (exceptions being a direct effect of conscientiousness on job dedication or generalized compliance or other aspects of OCB that are harder to separate from in-role performance). Certainly we now have substantial reason to think that something in the individual (other than demographic status or intelligence) predisposes the person to report more or less job satisfaction (Arvey, Bouchard, Segal, & Abraham, 1989; Judge, Bono, & Locke, 2000; Staw, Bell, & Clausen, 1986; Staw & Ross, 1985; Steel & Rentsch, 1997). People who report greater satisfaction at one time in one organization tend to report greater satisfaction at a later time (even decades later) in a different organization.

Yet, as we might suspect, the tendency of some trait(s) to lead individuals to greater or lesser satisfaction can be overridden by factors in the job environment (e.g., Steel & Rentsch, 1997). Thus, if job attitudes pose direct links to OCB, the measurable correlations between personality and OCB would be smaller, because some variance in attitudes arises from nondispositional sources.

Such a model would place personality in a subordinate role for determining OCB, but only in a statistical sense. From another perspective, the model would make personality more like a primal source of the dynamics determining OCB. That is, selection of people would already have gone far toward determining who will be more satisfied (or perceive more fairness, or feel greater affective commitment to the group or organization), and thus who will contribute more to the organization in the form of OCB. If a firm's management is limited in how far it can go toward structuring the workplace so as to increase satisfaction, or prevent dissatisfaction, it will be important to management to have a predominance of individuals who, of their own inclinations, will experience and report more positive attitudes.

Making our causal model more complex, we might also think that dispositional variables (e.g., such as those we would associate with agreeableness) incline individuals to certain ongoing, informal behavior patterns that have the result of making those persons more or less likely to experience rewarding consequences to their behavior. For example, a person high in agreeableness plausibly interacts with peers so as to be well-liked by others, to have considerable informal status in the group, to benefit from the give-and-take of small favors, to enjoy the camaraderie and support of those around him or her. The consequences of these characteristic behavior patterns would, therefore, naturally cause people with those underlying dispositions to derive greater satisfaction in the workplace. Of course, these effects are far from invariant; some work situations might offer scant opportunity for pleasurable interactions with coworkers and superiors, and impersonal factors determining work arrangements, polices, and formal rewards might more than offset the otherwise natural tendencies of agreeable people to get along handsomely with others. Therefore, this more elongated, indirect link between personality and OCB would still further attenuate measurable correlations between the two sets of variables.

Personality Determines Manner or Motive Rather Than Substance of OCB

One could also make a case for the assertion that personality more likely determines the manner, style, or method of rendering OCB, rather than the frequency or substantive value of the OCB. In making this case, we might well find it instructive to go beyond the gross level of generality represented by the familiar Big Five and think in terms of more specific facet traits that lie within those five dimensions. Individuals characterized as, for example, high in nurturance or empathic concern for others, as a facet trait within the dimension agreeableness, would manifest those traits when proffering aid to others—that is, the evident focus of the aid would be on the target of the aid and that target's discomfort. Conversely, those individuals lower in nurturance and empathy might provide as much or more substantive help, but with focus on the task and perhaps with a more impersonal, detached manner, suggestive of an achievement orientation within the conscientiousness dimension.

A case might also be made that personality has more to do with the motives that prompt OCB than with the substance, frequency, or value of the OCB itself. As Penner, Midili, & Kegelmeyer (1997) have noted, OCB can serve vastly different needs or motives for different individuals. Consider, for example, the individual who has a strong need for competitive achievement, not only as a person but also for the group or organization with whom he or she is associated, and a different individual with an equally strong need for affiliation. Conceivably both could be moved to contribute mightily in the form of OCB. But the person with strong need for achievement is motivated by a desire to see the work unit or the firm succeed as an efficient, profitable enterprise, and just happens to think of OCB as a means of making that unit or firm a winner. On the other hand, the colleague with an overriding affiliation motive thinks mainly in terms of the good relationships effected and the positive affect that those around them will experience as they solve their problems and perform efficaciously. Also, it has been noted that some OCBs, particularly those salient to a manager or supervisor, might be narrowly self-serving, intended to have much the same effect as any other form of ingratiation (Bolino, 1999). Although this motive would not command our admiration, the motive need not vitiate the value of the OCB itself.

Does the Workplace Suppress the Effects of Personality?

Finally, in light of the evidence to date, we have to consider the possibility that, as a rule, personality simply accounts for little variance in OCB in any sense. While this approach might seem counterintuitive, perhaps our intuition takes the form of an uncritical extrapolation of what we see in nonwork domains. At home, in the community, while engaged in casual social interaction, much behavior is spontaneous—not directed by conscious means–end calculations or cognitive assessments of the context of the behavior. One could argue that when people engage themselves in a formal work organization, they do so with a heightened consciousness of context and tend to suppress the natural impulses of their temperament. Whether performing within the limits of the specific job requirements and dictates of the formal reward system or contributing in a manner that goes beyond the job description and contractual incentives, participants make deliberate cognitive assessments, such as the fairness of the system around them and the supportiveness of the management and supervision. Such assessments would filter the more natural expressions of traits that would appear more evident in other contexts. Some evidence (Organ & Konovsky, 1989) does support the inference that OCB derives more immediately from cognitive evaluations of the work environment than from affective states.

Following this reasoning further, we might theorize that a specific dimension of individual differences—one not heretofore examined in research on OCB—determines whether the more intuitively suggestive traits, such as agreeableness or extraversion, would find their expression in OCB contributions. Research (e.g., Snyder and Cantor, 1980) indicates that people differ in the extent to which they monitor cues in their environment and accordingly allow those cues to take priority over personal attitudes or temperament in determining behavior. High self monitors search more intensively for such cues, even subtle ones, whereas low self-monitors are less vigilant in this search and more often act according to the logic of their sentiments. To the extent that high self-monitors would suppress the expression of behaviors otherwise consistent with their temperament, some attenuation would result in the association between certain global traits and their manifestation in OCB.

Consider, for example, an individual who would generally score below the median in a trait such as agreeableness. Assuming the validity of this score, such a person would probably be inclined to grouse about petty slights and inconveniences and not be interested in the give-and-take of courtesies, favors, and mutual supportiveness among coworkers. That is, we would predict that this person would not practice sportsmanship, courtesy, and helping to much extent. But if this person fits the description of a high self-monitor, and also senses that constant complaining and a reputation for not being a team player would damage his or her long-run interests, such a person would make some exertions not to behave as their temperaments would otherwise lead them to behave. Thus, we find that self-monitoring moderates the relationship between extraversion and performance in an interview (Osborn, Hubert, & Veres, 1998). We might well expect also that it moderates the relationship between agreeableness or empathic concern and some forms of OCB.

An Information Processing Model

OCB, for the most part, represents actions that we generally regard as good, desirable, and virtuous. Intuitively, we imagine good behaviors as the expression of good qualities in good people; pretty is as pretty does. But this approach might not offer the most instructive mode of thinking about the wellsprings of all or even most constructive behaviors in organized work settings. Consider instead a model in which organizational participants actively think about most of what they would do. They would process information (much of which is subtle or imprecise) as to what specific behaviors would be substantively and materially constructive in situations in which they find themselves. They think about whether they possess the competence with which to enact those behaviors, and just how they might enact them, so as contribute something useful. They would probably think as well not only about the personal costs, but other trade-offs with respect to the net contribution to organizational effectiveness. The point is that not all occurrences of OCB are equally beneficial to organizational functioning. For example, the importance of attendance and punctuality surely varies appreciably from one day or situation to another; one could probably say as much about interpersonal facilitation. At the same time, while OCB has from the start been cast more in terms of mundane and easy-to-perform contributions, in contrast to the skill and aptitude requirements of technical task performance, most likely some instances of OCB do require certain skills—whether they be in the form of knowledge, intelligence, or interpersonal savvy. The point is that some people who might, by dint of their temperament, be quite disposed to practice exemplary conduct, lend aid, and involve themselves in workplace governance, nonetheless might see little real contribution resulting from such actions in numerous instances, and/or think they lack the ability to engage in them in constructive fashion.

BUT CAN THE DATA BE TAKEN AT FACE VALUE?

We now consider reasons why the effects of personality on OCB cannot be assessed conclusively on the basis of the evidence to date. These reasons have to do with the predominant paradigm, methods, and procedures with which the question has been addressed.

Most of the published research on correlates and predictors of individual OCB conforms to the following pattern:

1. The research is conducted within one organization, occasionally two organizations (which are similar in terms of industry, e.g., health care, or geographic location).
2. The measure of OCB, if not a self-rating, takes the form of a supervisor rating of people within that supervisor's group of reports.
3. Measures of job satisfaction or other job attitudes and measures of personality take the form of self-reports, usually administered at the workplace.

Consider now the implications of these features of the research paradigm and how they complicate any inferences we might draw about the true or general relationship between personality and individual OCB.

Attenuation Caused by Confounded Levels of Analysis

When we do our research within the constraints of a single organization, we have de facto excluded sources of variance having to do with the organization itself. That is, we can look at only variance around the mean of personality within the organization and variance around the mean of OCB within that organization. Left out of the picture is the plausible hypothesis that organizations differ substantially in important aspects of personality. In fact, Schneider, Smith, Taylor, & Fleenor (1998) provide evidence that organization is a main effect in measurable aspects of personality, notably in the Myers-Briggs dimension of Thinking/Feeling—a dimension that theoretically would pose much relevance to the incidence of interpersonal helping and interpersonal facilitation in the workplace. Indeed, Schneider et al. also found a main effect caused by industry. These findings indicate that, consistent with Schneider's (1987) attraction–selection–attrition hypothesis, both individuals and organizations engage themselves in a sorting out of persons with traits that provide some degree of fit between people and organizational ambience. We might well suppose that such a process operates even more actively at the level of the department or office within the organization. A study by Cable and Judge (1997) confirms that (a) interviewers can assess with reasonable accuracy how well the values of a prospective hire fit the values of the organization and that (b) interviewers also make hiring decisions or recommendations that take this fit into account.

Thus, we might reason that a valid test of the effect of personality on OCB must do so by taking into account multiple levels of analysis—not just individuals within a group, but across groups, organizations, probably industry. Only recently (e.g., Putka & Vancouver, 2000) have researchers begun to look at OCB at such multiple levels. In principle, a reanalysis of a set of previously reported studies could provide preliminary indications of how much attenuation has occurred in correlations between individual dispositional variables and OCB as a result of restricted ranges of both personality and OCB.

One might counter this argument with the question: If single-organization studies have attenuated the relationships between personality and OCB, why have they not similarly attenuated the correlations with job satisfaction and other job attitudes? The answer is, perhaps they have, but not quite so much as occurred with personality. While no doubt job satisfaction also varies across organizations and organizational units, an individual's cognitive appraisals that determine level of satisfaction inevitably involve some degree of local comparisons. Given finite resources within any organizational unit, not all people can count on receiving the rewards, pleasures, and treatment they think they deserve or have come to expect. Thus, we suspect that whether an individual works in the organization with an overall high or low level of satisfaction, at least a modest level of within-organizational variance in job attitudes would manifest itself.

For the most part, research on individual correlates of OCB has concerned itself with the individual unit of analysis (significant exceptions include George, 1990, and George and Bettenhausen, 1990, both of which used analyses to sort out individual and group level relationships). The analysis of unit or group level relationships is more characteristic of research examining the consequences of OCB (e.g., Podsakoff et. al., 1997). But there is good reason to think of individual OCB and its personal correlates (i.e., dispositional and attitudinal variables) in terms of a cross-level model heterogeneity model (Klein, Dansereau, & Hall, 1994). In other words, individual dispositional variability is attenuated by attraction–selection–attrition dynamics, whereas individual attitudes are shaped in part by environmental influences (e.g., leadership style) common to the group or unit. One would expect that the overall OCB in the group is also affected by experiences common to the group. If group and individual level effects are not properly sorted out in the analysis, what we are likely to be left with is within-group variability in both disposition and OCB—and much of this variability is random error variance (in other words, random noise is then accounting for too great a proportion of the total variance being analyzed). Conceivably, increased attention to the viability of the cross-level heterogeneity model, accompanied by appropriate variance-partitioning tools, would reveal a stronger relationship between personality and OCB.

Supervisor's Rating as a Monomethod Problem

Most of the published research on OCB and personality has used the supervisor's rating as the measure of OCB. Although this procedure is certainly preferable to self-ratings of OCB (which present various kinds of problems of interpretation, because of common method variance in the OCB and personality measures), supervisor ratings have their own problems, particularly in regard to registering the effects of certain traits on certain dimensions of OCB.

One problem has to do with the use of OCB by some subordinates to ingratiate themselves with the supervisor. We have good reason (e.g., MacKenzie, Podsakoff, and Fetter, 1991) to suspect that managers' perceptions of subordinates' OCB influence their impressions of subordinates' overall performance (of course, the reverse direction of causation might also operate, i.e., perceptions of overall performance might bias ratings of OCB). Some subordinates probably suspect as much, and if so inclined, might well practice their OCB in a selective manner so as to be sure the supervisor is aware of it, while giving little thought to forms of OCB that would probably not come to the attention of the boss. In other words, OCB becomes an instrument of ingratiation, and the motive base of such OCB is quite different from OCB that more regularly flows from the influence of personality traits such as agreeableness or empathic values.

Also, recall that the one personality trait that seems to pose some robust association with OCB measures is conscientiousness. Conscientiousness has a strong task connotation and is likely to manifest itself in forms—attendance, punctuality, use of time at work, strict adherence to rules—that are much more amenable to supervisor notice. If supervisors rate subordinates on various dimensions of OCB, they probably tend to use what they know about attendance, punctuality, and use of work time as a proxy for inferences about other forms of going beyond strict job requirements as contributions. Thus, we note that research using multiple dimensions of OCB invariably finds high intercorrelations—from .35 to .60 and up—between the dimensions. The levels of these correlations most likely are overstated because of common method variance (supervisor's ratings) in how the dimensions of OCB are measured. This effect would work against the detection of personality determinants of those forms and instances of OCB not easily available to the supervisor's observation. For example, OCB that consists of informal helping, courtesies to and cooperation with colleagues, and cheerleading for peer contributions—and that plausibly follows more from traits suggestive of agreeableness and empathic concern—represents a portion of OCB that many supervisors would not know about. In sum, the kind of OCB that actually is influenced by traits other than conscientiousness would not often be accurately gauged by supervisor ratings.

There arises, as well, the question of whether such supervisory ratings do not reflect the volume or frequency of OCB so much as the importance or perceived value (at least in managerial thinking) of the OCB that subordinates render. Even the most vigilant manager cannot capture in memory all of the day-to-day gestures that we would incorporate within OCB. Managers' memories, and thus impressions, of subordinate behavior patterns become disproportionately shaped by critical incidents, that is, an instance of helping a coworker that at the time proved decisive in averting a major foul-up in the workflow. Attendance and punctuality during crunch times would register more durably in managers' recall than they would during smooth or routine business periods. While personality might have more to do with OCB in a day-in, day-out sense over the long sweep of time, the OCB that managers recall when they rate people is probably based on the relatively small percentage of situations in which the value-added contribution of the OCB was greatest, or otherwise because the time and situation made those specific contributions salient to the manager. Personality might have little to do with an individual's heroic response to such situations. Intelligence, judgment, skill, possibly even combined with the less admirable assessment of "here's how I can score big," would loom larger.

Self-Descriptions of Personality and Job Satisfaction

Research has established that, in general, self-descriptions of personality— when meeting the usual standards for reliability, format, and content validity—have reasonable predictive validity. However, we might well wonder if this validity is not compromised when researchers administer these measures in the work setting. There can be no mistaking that many of the items purportedly measuring, for example, agreeableness, neuroticism, or extraversion, have value-laden connotations, especially in their apparent (i.e., apparent to the responder) implications for what makes a good employee in certain organizations or jobs. Whatever promises of anonymity might be offered by researchers and administrators, one can understand why respondents might tilt their self-descriptions in a fashion that would not be the case if they answered the same questions in a more neutral, less potentially threatening environment.

Measures of job satisfaction, however, at least on their face, appear not to focus on the person's traits, but rather on the evaluation of the environment itself. It is not nearly so much a reflection on one's self to say that one is not pleased with, for example, the salary structure or the hours of work, as it is to say that one is not a very agreeable person. Yet we have abundant evidence, as noted earlier, that indeed the person accounts for substantial variance in job satisfaction measures. Some people characteristically report higher job satisfaction at any particular time and in any particular job or organization.

We thus have to consider the possibility that, when measures of job satisfaction and measures of personality are administered at the same time and in the work setting, responses to job satisfaction actually function as unobtrusive measures of personality—and, because of the unobtrusiveness and nontransparency, perhaps even have more validity as a measure of certain traits than the personality measures themselves. Therefore, the somewhat stronger relation of job satisfaction measures to OCB could be due as much to personality as it is to job satisfaction, at least that portion of job satisfaction that actually arises from treatment and experience in the workplace.

Finally, we should note that, just as there are good reasons to make more use of other sources (such as coworkers) of OCB ratings in addition to, or in lieu of, supervisory ratings, some considerations argue for other sources of personality descriptions. For example, Mount, Barrick, and Strauss (1994) examined the validity of observer ratings of the Big Five personality dimensions. Coworker ratings of subject extraversion correlated .34 with supervisor performance ratings, and supervisor ratings of extraversion correlated .24 with coworker ratings of performance. Customer ratings of subject extraversion correlated .27 and .21 with, respectively, performance ratings by supervisors and coworkers. Customer accounts of subject agreeableness correlated .30 and .34 with coworker and supervisor performance ratings, respectively. By comparison, self-ratings of extraversion correlated only .06 and .12 with performance ratings by supervisor and coworker, and self-descriptions of agreeableness correlated only .05 and .04 with supervisor and coworker performance ratings. Because the measure of overall performance included items regarding interpersonal skills, commitment to the job, initiative, and customer communications, one can assume that OCB weighed strongly in the performance ratings. The results, incidentally, cannot be chalked up to any differences in attenuation or compression in self versus other ratings of personality. Of course, interpretation of these findings involves some regard for just what we mean by personality. Is personality properly viewed as the internal states that can only be accessed and described by the individual, or should we think of personality as patterns of behavior comprising a social reputation that is described with some consensus by external observers (Hogan, 1991)?

SUMMARY AND CONCLUSION

Where do we go from here? First, we would argue that what we do not need is some search in the form of a fishing expedition for yet another trait measure that would finally register the effect of personality on OCB—not, at least, if research using that measure follows the same paradigm involving supervisor ratings in one organization and self-reports of personality descriptions. Already, we think, we have a serviceable framework for thinking about personality within the Big Five and some variations on that (e.g., as fashioned by Hogan, Hogan, & Busch, 1984). Also, existing theory already points quite strongly toward what we should expect the relevant traits to be. The problem isn't whether we've found the right traits or not; the issue is, first, has the prevalent paradigm given these traits a good chance to emerge as robust correlates of OCB; and second, if altering the paradigm to give them a better chance makes little difference in the results, then we have to rethink our intuitive or implicit model about personality and OCB.

As noted earlier in the research by Kamp and Hough (1988), Campbell (1990), and Motowidlo and Van Scotter (1994), the attributes of dependability (or reliability) and work orientation show promise for predicting OCB. Most likely these attributes do relate to the Big Five, but probably not in a direct or simple fashion. Conceivably they represent something like profiles or combinations of some of the more specific facet traits that reside within the Big Five structure. While straightforward measures of extraversion or agreeablness might not pose strong statistical associations with OCB, some aspects of those dimensions of personality, or some mixture of them with certain aspects of conscientiousness, might well define the stable behavior patterns that we associate with discretionary contributions to organizational context. For example, a person who is very agreeable would no doubt earn the affection of peers, but only if that agreeableness is tinged with a streak of achievement orientation would it manifest itself in value-added contributions to organizational functioning. Thus, while we do not need to invent measures of still more basic dimensions of personality, we would do well to think more in terms of some combinatorial profiles of those dimensions. This approach was urged by Dunnette (1993), who speculated that we could mine more gold from the ore of personality theory by conceiving of work-relevant traits not as atoms of elements, but molecules of compounds of those elements. Hogan (1991) also has endorsed such an approach, as well as used it by constructing measures with items chosen on the basis of predictive validity rather than factorial purity.

Another promising approach comes from Motowidlo et al.'s (1997) distinction between basic tendencies and characteristic adaptations. Basic tendencies refer to deep-seated aspects of temperament, such as those captured by the Big Five and similarly well-established, parsimonious frameworks. These aspects of people date from formative stages of life, if not from birth. Characteristic adaptations, on the other hand, develop later in life, taking the form of habits, values, attitudes, orientations; they are learned from interacting with many and varied environmental contexts. Some of these adaptations would come to resemble, in everyday perception and parlance, what we think of as personality, particularly if we observe these adaptations within a delimited context (e.g., work) or at maturity. So far as work organizations are concerned, not all of these characteristic adaptations are equally beneficial, nor are they learned by all people equally well. Again, one could plausibly maintain that these adaptations have some linkage to basic tendencies as defined by, for example, the Big Five, but again, not in a simple fashion. Perhaps agreeableness provides an advantage in developing a characteristic adaptation in the form of work-related helping behavior. But since we regard characteristic adaptations as learned, some cognitive abilities probably come into play as well.

The framework of Motowidlo et. al. (1994) positions these characteristic adaptations as more causally proximal to OCB and contextual performance. Defining, measuring, and validating such adaptations could potentially provide a much more compelling view of how personality dimensions figure into OCB.

But there is much work to do on the paradigm even before we reject out of hand a more direct connection between basic dimensions of personality and OCB. More attention to levels of analysis—whether this involves new studies or a sorting out of old data—could enable us to gauge how much we have confounded the effects of personality and organization. Increased use of customer and coworker ratings, instead of or in addition to ratings by supervisors, will probably give us a more holistic account of individuals' contributions in the form of OCB (some might argue for the usefulness of self-ratings of OCB, but that has been tried and the results do not argue for more of this: Organ & Ryan, 1995). Measures of personality taken away from the work setting, perhaps even provided by nonwork associates of the individual, and somewhat less obviously value-laden items in those measures, could prove instructive.

Whatever the findings and outcomes of varying the research paradigm for studying personality and OCB, one could suppose that they will be rife with implications for how we think about personality, OCB, and organization.

How much of what we call *organization* pertains to strong or weak situations? A situation might well qualify as strong even if formal incentives and authority symbols do not intrude themselves. Indeed, some theoretical work is needed on this useful, yet still rather hazy, concept of strength of the situation. Much of that strength might pertain more to issues of self-definition of the context rather than specific external features.

Should we construe OCB in terms of value-added contribution or frequency? If we reason that these are distinguishable attributes of behavioral contributions, then some attention probably needs to be given to the measures we prepare for external raters, be they peers, customers, or superiors.

Do organizations and/or organizational units already tend to select persons according to how important OCB is to their effectiveness? It would be surprising if, at least informally, such were not the case. One suspects that interviewers, for example, make some effort to gauge a person's potential for OCB when recruiting candidates for positions in which OCB is important.

Do motives for OCB make no difference in the value of that OCB, or do motives determine how reliable, enduring, and generalized OCB will be? A narrowly instrumental motive—emphasizing present and future emoluments for oneself—probably means that OCB will be carefully targeted so as to be observable by those in a position to further one's ends. A more obvious task-oriented motive might result in the OCB having more real leverage on unit or departmental effectiveness. An affiliation-oriented motive, however, might sustain a more consistent level or frequency of OCB across varied groups, including peers and customers.

Is OCB as much or more a function of skills, intelligence, and judgment, rather than just sentiment or disposition? Some skills, especially interpersonal ones, almost certainly enter into the effectiveness of some forms of OCB. Are cognitive skills at issue as well? For example, the capacity to see the larger picture or to think in terms of longer-run effects of how present problems are addressed and resolved, have obvious links to mental ability, and they no doubt figure into the judicious choice of how to allocate finite energies toward particular instances of OCB.

Whose assessments of OCB—managers, coworkers, customers—provide the most theoretically meaningful measure? We would like to see all of these forms of OCB ratings, but are they equally important in all situations, or does one form or another make more sense as a function of the work context?

Whose assessments of disposition—people themselves, work associates, nonwork associates—offer the most useful predictors of workplace behavior? If we use assessments by work associates, are we tapping into personality or into characteristic adaptations?

Answers, even partial and tentative answers, to such questions can only enrich our frameworks for understanding collective action.

REFERENCES

Arvey, R. D., Bouchard, T. J., Jr., Segal, N. L., and Abraham, L. M. (1989). Job satisfaction: Environmental and genetic components. *Journal of Applied Psychology, 74*, 187–192.

Barnard, C. I. (1938). *The Functions of the executive.* Cambridge, MA: Harvard University Press.

Bolino, M. C. (1999). Citizenship and impression management: Good soldiers or good actors? *Academy of Management Review, 24*, 82–98.

Borman, W. C., & Motowidlo, S. J. (1993). Expanding the criterion domain to include elements of contextual performance. In N. Schmitt & W. C. Borman (Eds.), *Personality selection* (pp. 71–98). San Francisco: Jossey-Bass.

Brayfield, A. H., & Crockett, W. H. (1955). Employee attitudes and employee performance. *Psychological Bulletin, 52*, 396–424.

Cable, D. M., & Judge, T. A. (1997). Interviewers' perceptions of person-organization fit and organizational selection decisions. *Journal of Applied Psychology, 82*, 546–561.

Campbell, J. P. (1990). An overview of the army selection and classification project (Project A). *Personnel Psychology, 43*, 231–239.

Campbell, J. P., & Zook, L. M. (Eds.). (1990). *Improving the selection, classification, and utilization of Army enlisted personnel: Final report on Project A.* Alexandria, VA: U.S. Army Research Institute.

Dunnette, M. (1993, April). Moderator comments presented at symposium, *Personality at Work,* annual conference of Society for Industrial and Organizational Psychology, San Francisco.

George, J. M. (1990). Personality, affect, and behavior in groups. *Journal of Applied Psychology, 75*, 107–116.

George, J. M., & Bettenhausen, K. (1990). Understanding prosocial behavior, sales performance, and turnover: A group-level analysis in a service context. *Journal of Applied Psychology, 75,* 698–709.

Guion, R. M., & Gottier, R. F. (1965). Validity of personality measures in personnel selection. *Personnel Psychology, 18,* 135–164.

Hogan, R. (1991). Personality and personality measurement. In M. D. Dunnette & L. M. Hough (Eds.), *Handbook of industrial and organizational psychology* Vol. 2 (pp. 873–919). Palo Alto, CA: Consulting Psychologists Press.

Hogan, J., & Hogan, R. (1989). How to measure reliability. *Journal of Applied Psychology, 69,* 273–279.

Hogan, J., Hogan, R., & Busch, C. M. (1984). How to measure service orientation. *Journal of Applied Psychology, 69,* 3–11.

Hunter, J. E., & Hunter, R. F. (1984). Validity and utility of alternate predictors of job performance. *Psychological Bulletin, 96,* 72–98.

Judge, T. A., Bono, J. E., & Locke, E. A. (2000). Personality and job satisfaction: The mediating role of job characteristics. *Journal of Applied Psychology, 85,* 237–249.

Kamp, J. O., & Hough, L. M. (1988). Utility of temperament for predicting job performance. In L. M. Hough (Ed.), *Literature review: Utility of temperament, biodata, and interest assessment for predicting job performance* (ARI Research Note 88-02). Alexandria, VA: U.S. Army Research Institute for the Behavioral and Social Sciences.

Katz, D., & Kahn, R. L. (1966). *The Social psychology of organizations.* New York: Wiley.

Klein, K. J., Dansereau, F., & Hall, R. J. (1994). Levels issues in theory development, data collection, and analysis. *Academy of Management Review, 19,* 195–229.

Konovsky, M. A., & Organ. D. W. (1996). Dispositional and contextual determinants of organizational citizenship behavior. *Journal of Organizational Behavior, 17,* 253–266.

MacKenzie, S. B., Podsakoff, P. S, & Fetter, R. (1991). Organizational citizenship behavior and objective productivity as determinants of managerial evaluations of salespersons' performance. *Organizational Behavior and Human Decision Processes, 50,* 123–150.

McCrae, R. R., & Costa, P. T., Jr. (1996). Toward a new generation of personality theories: Theoretical contexts for the five-factor model. In J. S. Wiggins (Ed.), *The five-factor model of personality: Theoretical perspectives.* New York: Guilford.

Motowidlo, S. J., Borman, W. C., & Schmit, M. J. (1997). A theory of individual differences in task and contextual performance. *Human Performance, 10,* 71–83.

Motowidlo, S. J., & Van Scotter, J. R. (1994). Evidence that task performance should be distinguished from contextual performance. *Journal of Applied Psychology, 79,* 475–480.

Mount, M. K., Barrick, M. R., & Strauss, J. P. (1994). Validity of observer ratings of the Big Five personality factors. *Journal of Applied Psychology, 79,* 272–280.

Organ, D. W. (1988). *Organizational citizenship behavior: The Good Soldier syndrome.* Lexington, MA: Lexington.

Organ, D. W. (1990). The motivational basis of organizational citizenship behavior. In B. M. Staw & L. L. Cummings (Eds.), *Research in Organizational Behavior, 12,* 43–72. Greenwich, CT: JAI.

Organ, D. W., & Konovsky, M. A. (1989). Cognitive versus affective determinants of organizational citizenship behavior. *Journal of Applied Psychology, 74,* 157–164.

Organ, D. W., & Lingl, A. (1995). Personality, satisfaction, and organizational citizenship behavior. *Journal of Social Psychology, 135,* 339–350.

Organ, D. W., & Paine, J. B. (1999). A New kind of performance for industrial and organizational psychology: Recent contributions to the study of organizational citizenship behavior. In C. L. Cooper & I. T. Robertson (Eds.), *International Review of Industrial and Organizational Psychology* Vol. 14, 337–368.

Organ, D. W., & Ryan, K. (1995). *Personnel Psychology, 48,* 775–802.

Osborn, S. M., Hubert, S. F., & Veres, J. G. (1998). Introversion-extraversion, self-monitoring, and applicant performance in a situational panel interview: A field study. *Journal of Business and Psychology, 13,* 143–156.

Penner, L. A., Midili, A. R., & Kegelmeyer, J. (1997). Beyond job attitudes: A personality and social psychology perspective on the causes of organizational citizenship behavior. *Human Performance, 10,* 111–131.

Podsakoff, P. M., Ahearne, M., & MacKenzie, S. B. (1997). Organizational citizenship and the quantity and quality of work group performance. *Journal of Applied Psychology, 82,* 262–270.

Podsakoff, P. M., & MacKenzie, S. B. (1994). Organizational citizenship behavior and sales unit effectiveness. *Journal of Marketing Research, 31,* 351–363.

Putka, D. J., & Vancouver, J. B. (2000, August). Decomposing the variance in employees' engagement in OCB: A multi-level investigation. Paper presented at Academy of Management meetings, Toronto.

Rumsey, M. G., Walker, C. B., & Harris, J. H. (1994). *Personnel selection and classification.* Hillsdale, NJ: Lawrence Erlbaum Associates, Inc.

Schmidt, F. L., Ones, D. O., & Hunter, J. E. (1992). Personnel selection. *Annual Review of Psychology, 43,* 627–670.

Schneider, B. (1987). The people make the place. *Personnel Psychology, 40,* 437–454.

Schneider, B., Smith, D. B., Taylor, S., & Fleenor, J. (1998). Personality and organizations: A test of the homogeneity of personality hypothesis. *Journal of Applied Psychology, 83,* 464–470.

Smith, C. A., Organ, D. W., & Near, J. P. (1983). Organizational citizenship behavior: Its nature and antecedents. *Journal of Applied Psychology, 68,* 653–663.

Snyder, M., & Cantor, N. (1980). Thinking about ourselves and others: Self-monitoring and social knowledge. *Journal of Personality and Social Psychology, 39,* 222–234.

Staw, B. M., Bell, N. E., & Clausen, J. A. (1986). The dispositional approach to job attitudes. *Administrative Science Quarterly, 31,* 56–77.

Staw, B. M., & Ross, J. (1985). Stability in the midst of change: A dispositional approach to job attitudes. *Journal of Applied Psychology, 70,* 469–480.

Steel, R. P., & Rentsch, J. R. (1997). The dispositional model of job attitudes revisited: Findings of a ten-year study. *Journal of Applied Psychology, 82,* 873–879.

Van Dyne, L., Cummings, L. L., & Parks, J. M. (1995). Extra-role behaviors: In pursuit of construct and definitional clarity (a bridge over muddied waters). In L. L. Cummings & B. M. Staw (Eds.), *Research in Organizational Behavior, 17,* 215–285. Greenwich, CT: JAI.

Van Scotter, J. R., & Motowidlo, S. J. (1996). Interpersonal facilitation and job dedication as separate facets of contextual performance. *Journal of Applied Psychology, 81,* 525–531.

Vroom, V. H. (1964). *Work and motivation.* New York: Wiley.

Walz, S. M., & Niehoff, B. P. (1996). Organizational citizenship behaviors and their effect on organizational effectiveness in limited menu restaurants. In J. B. Keys & L. N. Dosier (Eds.), *Academy of Management Best Papers Proceedings,* 307–311.

V

The Role of Personality in Understanding Meso Organizational Processes

In these three chapters we jump the level of analysis away from a focus on individual differences to group and organizational processes. These chapters come closest in tone and level of analysis to Argyris's (1957) and McGregor's (1960) notions that the personality of people, in the aggregate, is important as a basis for understanding and prediction.

Moynihan and Peterson in chapter 12 open the discussion with a focus on groups and group composition, with individual personality as the group composition variable of interest. Just this is a departure because the group composition literature has been dominated by a focus on demographic variables. In any case, they show that there have been three fairly distinct approaches to understanding group composition via a focus on personality but that no one of these approaches alone is satisfactory. Thus, after they review the research literature in the three approaches, they conclude that no one approach is best and that the three together make the most sense as the research paradigm of choice.

Schneider and Smith in chapter 13 argue in a rather straightforward fashion that the personality of the leader of an organization, and the personality of the members of an organization in the aggregate, are an important source of information if one wishes to understand the locus of the cause of organizational climate and culture (and even structure). In the former case, personality of the leader, they propose that leaders enact their personality by the way they design the organization to function; in the latter case they argue that members of organizations accrue together through a natural process of what has come to be called the attraction–selection–attrition (ASA) model of organizational functioning (Schneider, 1987). They find a surprising amount of research scattered about that suggests this model has some useful validity.

Argyris presents an informative perspective on the times in which he wrote *Personality and Organization* (1957). Argyris makes clear in this chapter that the goal of his research and writings was to provide frameworks for action that might improve organizational functioning. He hoped this would happen by providing managers with insights into the psychology of workers, thus offering them new lenses or frames with which to view or anticipate employees' reactions. By making predictions about likely employee reactions to management decisions and behaviors, he hoped to convince them that these insights into the psychology of workers had external validity. As becomes clear in the chapter, Argyris is still at it, attempting to show management how insight into the psychology of workers and their own psychology can have important action implications.

REFERENCES

Argyris, C. (1957). *Personality and organization*. New York: Harper & Row.
McGregor, D. M. (1960). *The human side of enterprise*. New York: McGraw-Hill.
Schneider, B. (1987). The people make the place. *Personnel Psychology, 40*, 437–453.

12

The Role of Personality in Group Processes

Lisa M. Moynihan and Randall S. Peterson
London Business School

This chapter discusses the role of personality in group processes. We specifically focus attention on the importance of member personality as a group composition variable by providing a review of the relevant theory and research. We argue here for three basic theoretical perspectives explaining the nature of personality effects in group process and team performance: (1) universal—certain traits always predict teamwork success, (2) contingent—certain traits predict team performance depending on the task or organizational culture, and (3) configurational—the mix of traits within a group, or the fit of individual members with each other, predicts team performance. Each of these three approaches to personality in groups finds significant empirical support in the literature and has some shortcomings. We conclude that a full understanding of the role of personality in group processes must integrate all three of these approaches.

Composition effects have long been of interest to researchers interested in group processes and team performance. There are scores of studies and reviews (e.g., Williams & O'Reilly, 1998), even edited volumes focusing on composition effects in group performance (e.g., Neale, Mannix, & Gruenfeld, 1998). This research has, however, largely focused on demographic and knowledge diversity. Team member personality has not played a central role in this theoretical development. This chapter aims to focus attention on the importance of member personality as a group composition variable by providing a review of the relevant theory and research findings. We specifically discuss (a) how personality affects group process,

(b) the specific types of effects member personality has on performance, and (c) directions for future research in the area.

Traditional small group research has been described by McGrath (1984) and Hackman (1987) in terms of systems theory with inputs, processes, and outputs. To date, groups researchers have focused on a range of input variables, primarily skills and abilities and demographic characteristics such as age, sex, race, and functional background. Researchers interested in composition have been drawn to the use of demographic variables because of the relative ease of data collection and have often assumed these variables are proxies for an individual's values, perspectives, or cognitive orientation (e.g., Pfeffer, 1983; Williams & O'Reilly, 1998). However, these assumptions are tenuous at best and risk reliance on stereotypical views of individual differences. Although age, sex, race, and functional background may shape values and orientations, they are not the primary roots of individual differences. Greater differentiation between people and definition of individual differences come to light in personality.

Personality scholars have defined *personality* as the essence of a person, the part of a person that is most representative of him or her, not only because it differentiates between people, but because it embodies what a person is (Allport, 1937; Hall & Lindzey, 1957). Personality is the pattern of relatively enduring ways in which a person thinks, feels, and behaves (Pervin, 1980). Personality is thus an important factor in accounting for how employees behave in groups and in organizations. Personality has been shown to influence career choice (Holland, 1966), job satisfaction (Staw & Ross, 1985), and leadership (Bass, 1990). Because personality influences career choice, it is an earlier antecedent to cognitive and affective orientation than functional background. Similarly, teamwork skills stem from personality that affects individual behavior and then intragroup relations. Personal attributes are often recognized as important individual characteristics in productive work teams (Kinlaw, 1991; Yeatts & Hyten, 1998). In short, personality is more closely linked to the cognitive and affective orientations of a team than demographic variables and is thus likely to be a more powerful predictor of group processes and performance than demographic characteristics.

The other major reason personality is a more predictive composition variable than demographic characteristics is because of the rise of team-based work in firms (Ilgen, 1999). In the last two decades, attention has shifted from research on small groups of strangers in laboratory settings to existing teams grounded in organizations. Historically, the group composition literature developed around demographic variables because visible and underrepresented attributes were the most immediately salient and thus powerful drivers of composition effects on group processes. Personality, being a less visible aspect of group interaction, received far less attention as a composition variable. More recent social cognition research has discovered, however, that demographic characteristics of other group members become less salient over time as members of a group or team get to know each other better. Underlying personal characteristics, such as personality traits, become more salient over time (Harrison, Price, & Bell, 1998; Levine & Moreland, 1998). Thus, personality variables have become more important predictors of team processes and performance as intact teams are increasingly the subject of study. What is more, the role of personality is particularly important in self-managed teams. Unlike teams with prescribed group role structures that may suppress the role of personality (Berkowitz, 1956; Heslin, 1964), in self-managed team environments individual group roles are allowed to evolve autonomously over time, enhancing the power of personality effects (Barry & Stewart, 1997).

Although personality has not received as much attention as demographic composition variables have in the systems model of group processes, a body of literature has accumulated examining personality as an input. We review that literature here and use the systems model of inputs, process, and outputs as a framework for the research in the personality and group processes. We argue that this literature has taken three basic approaches—universal, contingent, and configuration[1]—each with differing views of the nature of what the inputs, processes, and outputs are in the systems model. These perspectives describe three interrelated mechanisms by which personality has an impact on group processes.

THEORETICAL PERSPECTIVES ON PERSONALITY'S EFFECT IN GROUPS—DIFFERING VIEWS OF INPUTS, PROCESSES, AND OUTPUTS

Research taking the universal perspective views personality as the primary input in the systems model. Member personality is assumed to have a universal direct effect on individual behavior and interpersonal processes in groups, which then affects group outcomes. Personality inputs affect individual-level cognition, motivation, and affective states. These states in turn shape group-level task and interpersonal process behavior in teams (Bales, 1958; Jackson, May, & Whitney, 1995) and ultimately shape team-level information processing and cohesion (Hackman, 1987). Cognitive traits, those that refer to individual differences in perceptual and information processing, are hypothesized to operate via individuals' perceptions of the group task or challenge. For example, field independence is the

---

[1]This categorization scheme is borrowed from the strategic human resource management literature, specifically Delery and Doty (1996).

autonomous predisposition to analytically structure ambiguous situations (e.g., DeBasio, 1986). Field-independent individuals rely less on others for social information when encountering ambiguous situations (Witkin & Goodenough, 1977; Witkin, Moore, Goodenough, & Cox, 1977). A group composed of field-dependent members is likely to have greater difficulty structuring an ambiguous task. Conversely, a group composed entirely of field-independent members may not consult extensively with each other while working on an ambiguous task because each member may tend to rely on his or her own cognitive structuring of the problem. This lack of consultation then leads to reduced information sharing and lower-quality group performance. Motivational traits, on the other hand, are those individual differences that influence how an individual's energy is directed. These traits are hypothesized to affect interpersonal relations in groups. Extraversion, emotional stability, and agreeableness, for example, are all linked to how people interact with others in groups (e.g., Barrick, Stewart, Neubert, & Mount, 1998). For example, high levels of emotional stability among members have long been associated with cohesive group process. Member personality, in sum, shapes group process and performance through individual behavior.

The contingent perspective has a more complex view of the inputs in the systems model of group functioning. This perspective views inputs as being both personality traits as well as task characteristics or organizational culture. The process by which personality has an impact on group outcomes is assumed to be through the interaction between personality and situation. This perspective has become increasingly popular as social psychologists have generally accepted an interactionist perspective toward personality (Magnusson & Endler, 1977). This perspective recognizes that the same situation can affect different people in different but predictable ways, depending on personality. For example, in situations of high task complexity, employees who are high on need for achievement have a desire to perform challenging tasks well. Thus they will perform better on those challenging tasks than those who are low on this trait (but not on tasks that are not challenging). It is the interaction of personality and situational factors that determine how people think, feel, and behave. Thus, the group task or social context will interact with the individual group members' personality to affect group process and performance.

The configuration perspective takes an even more complex view of the inputs in the systems model, viewing inputs as the configuration of traits within the group. This view differs from the universal perspective, which considers the mean group level of only one or two particular traits rather than how a variety of traits interact with each other. Configurationists recognize that people do not display their personalities one trait at a time and that something may be missing when research focuses solely on the relationship between aggregate team levels on a personality dimension and team performance. An individual's behavior is the result of the simultaneous influence of multiple traits and the situation (Brandt & Devine, 2000). High performance is theorized to be caused by the harmonious interaction of members with complementary personalities.

MEASURING PERSONALITY AT THE GROUP LEVEL

The three theoretical perspectives just mentioned vary in their conceptualization of the inputs in the group process model. Individual scores are aggregated to represent the group in many different ways (Barrick et al., 1998; LePine, Hollenbeck, Ilgen, & Hedlund, 1997; Mohammed, Angell, & Ringseis, 2000). For example, team composition of personality can be operationalized by the use of the mean, measures of dispersion or variability, the maximum individual score, or the minimum individual score (Chan, 1998). Aggregating based on the mean is most appropriate for tasks that are additive in nature, meaning that the group outcome is a result of the summative combination of the contributions of all group members.[2] Use of the minimum individual score in a group is most appropriate if the task is conjunctive, meaning the groups tasks are highly interdependent and their performance is dependent on the level of the lowest member (or weakest link). Use of the maximum score is most appropriate when the task is disjunctive, meaning that the group outcome is determined by the performance of the best member in the group. Use of variance is most appropriate when the task is compensatory, meaning the group score is created by averaging team members' inputs. The use of a measure of variability is also particularly useful to test hypotheses about diversity (or consensus) on team outcomes (Chan; O'Connor, 1998).

In the universal and contingent approaches specifically, the assumption is usually for homogeneity in a group or organization (Klein, Dansereau, & Hall, 1994). A mean score is thus often used as the group-level measurement with these two perspectives. Indeed, groups researchers have focused almost exclusively on mean level of individual characteristics to represent the group level on a particular variable of interest. Use of the mean suggests an assumption that it accurately reflects the group as a whole and that there are low levels of variability about the mean (O'Connor). This assumption is often false and can result in both Type I error where one finds effects that do not exist and Type II errors where one does not detect differences where they do exist because the wrong aggregation method has been used (see Barrick et al., 1998; Steiner, 1972).

---

[2]Here we invoke Steiner's (1972) typology of group task types.

In the configuration approach, however, the diversity of traits is of specific interest. Personality is often measured as agreement of traits (variance rather than mean). The focus here is on heterogeneity or differences within groups. Thus the choice of an aggregation method is particularly critical for research from this perspective. Use of a theoretically inappropriate operationalization of group personality could lead to (a) lack of finding an effect of interest or (b) finding a relationship that is only an artifact of the data combination method and really does not mean what the researcher intended it to mean (Nunally & Bernstein, 1994; Rousseau, 1985).

THEORETICAL APPROACHES TO PERSONALITY COMPOSITION

As noted earlier, the underlying assumptions about the impact of personality in teams can be grouped into three broad theoretical perspectives: universal, contingent, and configurational. Historically, the literature on composition has focused on identifying simple universal effects. Research taking this perspective began in the 1940s and views the impact of personality traits to have direct effects on group performance, no matter what the task or context. Literature beginning in the 1970s became more differentiated with interest in the fit of personality to task type, organizational culture, or other members of the team. The contingent perspective suggests that personality affects group performance contingent on how personality interacts with task characteristics or organizational culture. The configurational perspective suggests that personality affects group performance through the internal fit of the members with each other, or the configuration of traits within the group. Each of these perspectives has distinct implications for the optimal composition of groups for achieving superior performance.

THE UNIVERSAL APPROACH

The universal approach assumes that some traits are universally better (or worse) for group work, and thus some individuals are better suited for teamwork than others. This assumption is implicit in research that discusses staffing in terms of *teamwork KSAs* or the knowledge, skills, and abilities that are necessary for work in groups that may not be required for individual work (e.g., Klimoski & Jones, 1995; Stevens & Campion, 1994). This perspective takes the position that successful team performance depends not only on the KSA inputs for individual task performance but also on those characteristics of individual team members that facilitate team functioning. The facilitation of team functioning occurs through both task and interpersonal mechanisms (Bales, 1958).

Most studies within the universal framework assume that the impact of personality on group process and performance is additive. That is, it is the sum or total level of a given trait within a group that matters. The underlying assumption of the additive view of personality composition in groups is that certain traits have either a positive or negative effect on groups, and so the higher (or lower) the average level of these traits in the group, the better off it will be (Moreland & Levine, 1992). The operationalization of group personality utilizing the universal perspective is usually the mean level of a particular trait. The variance of traits within a group is not generally considered.

The majority of early studies conducted in the 1950s and 1960s were concerned almost exclusively with identifying the traits that should be universally important inputs into the performance of any group task (Levine & Moreland, 1998). Specifically, this early personality literature focused on the direct effects of personality on the quality of interpersonal relations and group processes. Shaw (1981) summarized this literature into five categories or types of traits. These categories included interpersonal orientation, social sensitivity, ascendant tendencies, dependability, and emotional stability. He futher identified some patterns across studies relating personality traits to types of behaviors in group processes. For example, Shaw's review indicated that individuals with a positive orientation toward others encourage cohesive group process. Specifically, those who are conscientious and emotionally stable facilitate cohesive group functioning, whereas highly anxious individuals inhibit smooth group functioning.

Though this early work provided some generalizable insights, it was limited by uncertainty about which traits were most important to group work and how the large number of traits studied were related to each other (Levine & Moreland, 1998). The field also suffered from lack of integration during this time because of a lack of consensus about what constituted important group outcomes (Barrick et al., 1998). The literature reported on a variety of process and outcome measures, focusing most often on cohesive process. This problem began to improve following Hackman's (1987) categorization of group productivity outcomes into current performance, the ability of a group to work together over time, and the ability of a group to fulfill the individual needs of its members. Researchers then began to focus on both current performance and team viability as simultaneous team outcomes (Ilgen, 1999).

The emergence of the five-factor model of personality has also helped to integrate results because it provides a framework for how traits are organized as well as identifying traits likely to affect work performance (Barrick et al., 1998; Driskell, Hogan, & Salas, 1987; Levine & Moreland,

1998). The five factors include extraversion, conscientiousness, neuroticism, agreeableness, and openness to experience (Barrick & Mount, 1991; Costa & McCrae, 1992). Broadly defined, *extraversion* is characterized by the tendency to be assertive, active, and sociable. *Conscientiousness* is characterized by the tendency to be purposeful, responsible, and determined. *Neuroticism* is characterized by the tendency to experience negative emotions of fear, embarrassment, and guilt. *Agreeableness* is characterized by a desire to get along with and have sympathy for the problems of others. *Openness* is characterized by intellectual curiosity, active imagination, and preference for variety (Costa & McCrae, 1992). Many earlier scales are now recognized as being subsumed under this Big Five taxonomy. For example, the scale of adjustment is now recognized as a part of neuroticism in the five-factor model of personality. Early work also used scales of dominance and authoritarianism, which are now recognized as consistent with the extraversion subscale of assertiveness in the five-factor model (e.g., Haythorn, 1953; Heslin, 1964; Mann, 1959). Thus Shaw's (1981) review can now be better understood with the recognition that these many traits can be collapsed into the broad traits of neuroticism, extraversion, and agreeableness factors in the five-factor model of personality.

Research in the past two decades continues to be concerned with identifying the traits that should be universally important to the performance of any team. These more recent studies are more easily summarized than the early literature, because they consistently utilize the five-factor model of personality and more specific performance criteria that allow a clearer understanding of the effects of personality on performance (Barrick & Mount, 1991; Costa & McCrae, 1992). Four of the five factors have been theoretically and empirically linked to task and interpersonal relations mechanisms in teams (i.e., conscientiousness, extraversion, agreeableness, and neuroticism, but not openness). We now review the research linking four of the five factors to team processes and performance.

Conscientiousness

Conscientiousness has been examined in team performance because it is a reliable predictor of individual performance. Conscientiousness has consistently been found to be positively related to task focus. Neuman and Wright (1999) for example, found that conscientiousness predicted ratings of performance at both the individual and group level in a sample of human resources teams. The group level of conscientiousness was measured as the level of the lowest scoring member of the team, using the rationale that group tasks required interdependence because teams met regularly to discuss human resource policies and procedures and respond to employee benefits claims. The level of the lowest team member on conscientiousness predicted peer ratings of individual performance in the teams beyond the measures of general cognitive ability and specific skills identified through job analysis. The minimum conscientiousness score also predicted supervisor ratings of team performance as well as objective measures of amount and accuracy of work completed. Both mean level and minimum level of conscientiousness have also been found to predict supervisor ratings of manufacturing team performance (Barrick et al., 1998).

Leader conscientiousness has also been found to affect team processes. For example, CEO conscientiousness was found to be positively related to both flexible top management team decision making and firm performance (Peterson, Owens, & Martorana, 2000). The conscientiousness of a team's leader was also found to moderate the effect of team conscientiousness in a laboratory study of hierarchical decision-making teams with distributed expertise (Lepine et al., 1997). The level of team conscientiousness was again operationalized as the level of the lowest member in the group because of the team's high level of interdependence. Team members were trained on specific areas of a military simulation and were required to perform a decision task that required unique information input from each member. In this task, the leader considered staff input and then made a final decision. Conscientiousness positively affected team performance, but only when both the team level conscientiousness (measured by the lowest team member) and the leader conscientiousness were high. In sum, conscientiousness has been found to be a broad predictor of team and individual performance in field and laboratory settings.

We did, however, find several laboratory studies that revealed no effects for conscientiousness (e.g., Barry & Stewart, 1997; Waung & Brice, 1998). These studies are linked together in that they all utilize creativity tasks. For example, a brainstorming study found that when group members were allowed to discuss strategies, groups composed of highly conscientious people produced better-quality performance (in terms of feasibility), whereas groups composed of low-conscientiousness members produced a greater quantity of potential solutions (Waung & Brice). Such studies suggest tasks that require creativity may moderate the relationship between group conscientiousness and task performance. Conscientious individuals prefer consistency and systematic order, and thus are not as likely to generate novel solutions to problems. Therefore, conscientiousness may be broadly applicable across many types of tasks, but may not predict specific types of tasks that require a large degree of creativity.[3]

---

[3]Creativity involves two distinct functions—to generate novel approaches to problems and to identify which novel approaches are useable. Individuals high in conscientiousness are likely to struggle with the first part, and thus may not be considered as creative.

Extraversion

The trait of extraversion has been shown to have positive effects on individual job performance for jobs requiring a high degree of social interaction, such as sales (Barrick & Mount, 1991; Mount, Barrick, & Stewart, 1998). Following the reasoning that most teams also require a good deal of social interaction, researchers have investigated the effect of extraversion in team settings. In a study of 51 work teams in a manufacturing setting, for example, Barrick et al. (1998) investigated the impact of extraversion on team processes, current team performance, and team viability. They found that teams higher in mean levels of extraversion received higher supervisor ratings of team performance than teams low on extraversion. Further, teams higher in extraversion received higher supervisor ratings for team viability. Results showed that the impact of extraversion on team viability was mediated through the group process variable of social cohesion. In other words, teams with more extraverted members tend to be more socially cohesive and ultimately more highly evaluated by their supervisors (see Ancona, 1990, on external boundary spanning). Supporting evidence indicating extraversion is positively related to interpersonal relations within groups was also specifically found in a lab study where results revealed that the amount of talking a member did in a group was perceived by other group members as an indication of degree of expertise (Littlepage, Schmidt, Whisler, & Frost, 1995).

More recently, however, Barry and Stewart (1997) found that groups with high proportions of extraverted members (measured by variance rather than the mean) can have problems of reduced cohesion and performance. The argument is that such groups can have too many people jockeying for dominance in the group. These researchers suggest a curvilinear relationship between extraversion and performance. The results of their study further suggest that the degree of variance of extraversion also has a curvilinear relationship to task focus and performance, suggesting that too many or too few extraverts in a group can be detrimental to the configuration of a group. In general, extraversion appears to facilitate cohesive group process, but only at moderate levels.

Agreeableness

Mixed results have also been found for the effects of mean level of agreeableness on team performance. Hogan, Raza, & Driskell (1988) for example, found that agreeableness had positive effects for performance on mechanical tasks but not on social tasks. Another study found that teams with high mean levels of agreeableness have higher team viability (Barrick et al., 1998). Because agreeableness is characterized by concern for a group over one's individual desires and interests, it is also sometimes called *collectivism* (e.g., Wagner 1995; Wagner & Moch, 1986). Wagner found that for groups of management students working on a case study analysis and presentation task, individuals high on agreeableness were more likely to be rated as cooperative group members by their peers. Researchers have also found that low levels of agreeableness (high individualism) are associated with reduced individual effort or social loafing in groups (Comer, 1995; Earley, 1989, 1993). One additional study found that the effects of group agreeableness were enhanced by the degree of collectivism in the organizational culture (Chatman & Barsade, 1995).

However, some studies have found negative effects of agreeableness on team performance (Berkowitz, 1956; McGrath, 1962; Weick & Penner, 1969). For example, McGrath (1962) found that teams low on agreeableness showed improvement on a marksmanship task, whereas teams composed of highly agreeable individuals showed no improvement. Individuals low on agreeableness tended to be unresponsive to teammates and tended to focus on their own task performance. For individuals in these groups, their individual marksmanship was correlated with their social adjustment in the group, and there was no correlation between social adjustment and esteem for teammates. Conversely, for individuals in highly agreeable groups, their social adjustment was correlated with esteem for teammates and had no relationship with their individual marksmanship performance. Adjustment to the team was a function of the individual's own task performance in low-agreeableness groups but not high-agreeableness groups. Adjustment for individuals in high-agreeableness groups seems to be a function of social success. These results suggest that group members high on agreeableness may be more concerned with interpersonal success than with task success, which can be detrimental to group performance. The fact that results from this study differ from others is likely due to the nature of the group task, however. Marksmanship, in this study, was an individually performed or additive task. Thus the group performance level was solely based on the sum of individual performance—no social interaction of group coordination was required. It could be argued that this task was in fact not a true group task.

Neuroticism

Neuroticism has been identified as a universally detrimental variable for work-team performance. Haythorn (1953) conducted an early study illustrating the influence of this trait on group performance. This study utilized a sample of ROTC sophomores. Participants worked in five unique groups on three types of tasks in order to isolate the impact of individual personality traits in groups. Measured as the mean of the individuals, Haythorn

(1953) found emotional stability—the low end of the neuroticism scale is also often referred to as *emotional stability*—to be positively related to observers' measures of group productivity and job completion of tasks involving syllogistic reasoning, mechanical assembly, and creative story composition. Results of other early studies also found that emotional stability is positively related to team performance (see reviews by Heslin, 1964; Mann, 1959). For example, Heslin's review cites military research findings that ratings of squad effectiveness were positively related to squad member adjustment whereas the neurotic traits of paranoia and nervousness were negatively related to these performance ratings (Greer, 1955). Two more recent field studies employing preexisting teams further supported the importance of this trait. First, in a study of manufacturing teams, emotional stability was positively related to team viability, or the ability to work together in the future (Barrick et al., 1998). This study also examined the minimum level in the group, based on the reasoning that manufacturing teams employ both additive and conjunctive tasks. However, the level of the lowest member on emotional stability (high neuroticism) was not related to team performance the way mean level was. Second, in a study of top management teams, CEO emotional stability was found to be positively related to top management team flexibility, cohesion, and performance (Peterson et al., 2000).

Another closely related study looked at the group level of positive affectivity on group process behaviors in groups of salespeople. The positive affective tone of a group was related to prosocial behavior of its members (George, 1990). Teams with negative affective tone (negative affectivity or neuroticism) experienced higher rates of absenteeism (George). Taken together, the studies reviewed indicate that emotional stability is positively associated with cohesive group process and effective decision making.

Limitations of the Universal Approach

A great deal of progress has been made by looking at direct effects of member personality on team interaction and performance. Our review of the literature revealed empirical support for a positive universal effect of (1) conscientiousness on individual and group performance, except for creative tasks; (2) agreeableness, except on additive tasks; (3) emotional stability on both group cohesion and task performance; and (4) moderately high extraversion on group process and performance. However, because variance of traits is generally ignored in the universal perspective, the implication of using a mean to represent the group score assumes an additive task and that the composition of traits within a group is compensatory.

One weakness in the literature is the lack of attention given to explicating and measuring the mediating processes through which personality affects group processes and outcomes. Few studies develop a theoretical discussion of exactly how group process mediates the relationship between conscientiousness, agreeableness, extraversion, or emotional stability and outcomes. Do groups high in conscientiousness succeed because the individuals are very task focused (assuming an obvious translation from the individual to the group level)? Or do they succeed because they are not distracted by relationship conflict stemming from personal differences in desire for hierarchy and order (assuming a more complex path)? Insufficient theoretical attention to the mediating processes means that many of these studies fail to account for the effects they report.

Another closely related limitation of the universal approach is a lack of attention to type of task or organizational culture being performed (although some of the results reviewed here certainly suggest this lack). There is wide variation in the tasks employed across studies, and little attention is given to how the nature of the task may affect how personality influences group processes and outcomes (Driskell et al., 1987; Neuman & Wright, 1999). Previous research has found that task differences moderate the relationships between group inputs and outcomes (Goodman, 1986; McGrath, 1984; Stewart & Barrick, 2000). Thus careful consideration needs to be given to the effects of personality and measurement in specific task contexts (Barrick et al., 1998; Lepine et al., 1997; Neuman & Wright, 1999). In fact, a number of recent studies identify themselves as being concerned with interdependent tasks and acknowledge that their results may depend on the task or degree of interdependency (Barrick et al.; Lepine et al.; Mohammed et al., 2000). These studies are also exemplary because they sought to employ aggregation statistics (mean or minimum) that matched their research question and the nature of the task, using minimum score for conjunctive tasks and group mean for additive tasks. We now examine the literature that has developed on the nature of personality effects in groups as being contingent on the task or organizational culture.

THE CONTINGENT APPROACH

The contingent approach to personality in groups assumes that group performance is contingent on the nature of the group task or organizational culture. In this theoretical perspective, the inputs in the group process model include both personality traits as well as task or context. These studies conceptualize the mean group level of a trait as being the important factor in the match of group composition to context. In these interaction designs, groups were constructed to be homogenous on level of trait, and no attention was given to variance of traits in a group (e.g., Aronoff, Meese, & Wilson, 1983). Groups that are high or low on a certain trait are examined in situations that are high or low on a certain contextual factor. The implication of this perspective is that the optimal personality composition of a team depends on the nature of the work it performs and/or the organizational culture in which it operates. Here we review representative studies from this approach that have examined the moderating effects of situational variables on the relationship between personality and group process or performance.

Organizational Culture as Moderator

A number of studies have investigated organizational culture as a moderator of the relationship between personality and group performance. These studies conceptualize fit of personality needs to culture as the process mechanisms through which performance effects occur. Aronoff et al. (1983), for example, predicted higher group productivity when individual needs fit the social structure context. They hypothesized that individual needs lead group members to seek specific types of rewards from group processes and outcomes. Using a laboratory study design and a model building task, Aronoff et al. examined individuals with safety needs and esteem needs in egalitarian versus hierarchical contexts. Culture was manipulated by giving instructions to groups in the hierarchical condition to select and utilize a group leader; the egalitarian groups were instructed not to have status distinctions and to be completely democratic. Results revealed that individuals with high needs for esteem were more productive in egalitarian than in hierarchical structures. Individuals with high needs for esteem seek respect from others and demonstrate competence or ability. Such individuals are motivated to demonstrate their competence through active participation and to be respectful of others in order to gain reciprocal respect. Because egalitarian contexts offer more opportunity for individual inputs, they facilitate individual performance of members with high esteem needs (Aronoff et al.).

Chatman and Barsade (1995) studied the influence of individualistic versus cooperatively dispositioned people in collective versus individualistic cultures. In this laboratory study using MBA students and the looking glass simulation task, individualistic and collective culture was again manipulated through task instructions. Results revealed that organizational culture moderated the cooperative behavior of those predisposed to cooperate—they cooperated in a cooperative culture and competed in an individualistic culture. The culture had no effect, however, on those with individualistic dispositions—they were always competitive. Thus individualists are less affected by cultural contexts than those with more collective orientations. Individualists place a high priority on maximizing their own welfare, and so the workplace culture does not alter this priority or their behavior (Argyle, 1991). Collectivists, on the other hand, seek social approval and are more congenial (i.e., high in agreeableness), so they are more likely to be affected by cultural norms guiding behavior in any given context (Chatman & Barsade, 1995).

Task Characteristics as Moderator

Several studies have looked at the effects of fit between characteristics of the group task and personality of group members on group performance. For example, Schneider & Delaney (1972) examined groups varying on need for achievement looking at task complexity in a laboratory study. Need for achievement is characterized by a desire to perform challenging tasks well and to meet one's own high standards (McClelland, 1985). The low-complexity task involved identifying a commonly held symbol, and the high-complexity task was performing arithmetic computations. Results revealed that need for achievement moderated performance on high-complexity tasks, but had no effect on low-complexity tasks. Groups that were high on need for achievement solved complex problems faster than those low on this trait, but had the same solution speed rates as groups low on need for achievement when problems were simple.

DeBasio (1986) examined the fit between field independence and the degree of structure of the group task. *Field independence* is characterized as a cognitive trait of autonomously providing analysis and structure to situations rather than relying on social comparison (Witkin et al., 1977). A laboratory study employing a low- versus high-structure task was used. The low-structure task instructed the group to list five traits for career success. The high-structure task involved asking the group to develop a method of blowing out two candles from an eight-foot distance. Results revealed that both groups took longer to complete the highly structured task, but that speed of task completion of field-dependent groups was more impaired by type of task than field independents. Thus for work that requires fast response on unstructured projects, teams composed of field independents should perform better.

Hogan, Raza, and Driskell (1988) drew on McGrath's (1984) group task typology and investigated the relationship of prudence (conscientiousness), ambition and sociability (two dimensions of extraversion), and likability (agreeableness) on group performance of mechanical versus social tasks. They hypothesized that different types of tasks require different types of behavior, and so the importance of traits depends on the task at hand. Specifically, they used the mechanical task of a Navy simulation requiring the movement of freight from one ship to another. This task requires a great deal of team coordination. The social task involves dealing with or helping others, including training Navy recruiters on persuasion techniques. Results suggest that high levels of conscientiousness, extraversion (ambition only), and agreeableness are related to performance on mechanical tasks. These traits were important because the mechanical task required cohesion, integration, and care to maintain proper procedures. Performance on social tasks, however, found that only conscientiousness had a positive relationship with group performance. Performance on these social tasks was dependent on the quality of oral communication, the degree of adapting the presentation content to the needs of the audience, and informing and advising rather than selling or persuading the audience. Groups with high levels of extraversion (both ambition and sociability) or agreeableness did not perform as well as groups low on these traits. Teams with high mean scores for ambition, sociability, and agreeableness performed poorly primarily because they attempted to persuade the audience to accept their point of view too forcefully (Hogan et al.).

In sum, studies from the contingent perspective have found support for performance benefits stemming from fit of team personality with contextual factors. For example, individuals with high needs for esteem are more productive in egalitarian than in hierarchical cultures. Results also suggest that individuals with dispositions to cooperate are more likely to adapt their behavior to the degree of collectivism in the cultural context than individualistic people. Performance benefits stemming from the fit of personality with characteristics of the task have also been found. Field independents perform complex tasks more efficiently than field dependents. Research also suggests that agreeableness and ambition may facilitate group performance on mechanical tasks but inhibit performance on social tasks (Hogan et al., 1988).

Limitations of the Contingent Approach

The contingent approach also makes a valuable contribution to the literature through its recognition of the interaction of personality with the situation. This approach finds research support for both organizational culture and task type as moderator variables. These findings notwithstanding, there are two important limitations in the current stream of research. The first limitation of the contingent approach is that the few studies available specifically designed to this approach rely exclusively on laboratory designs in order to control for task type or organizational culture. This laboratory approach creates an interpretation problem in that it fails to consider the strength of the situation as a variable in the research design. Situations created in the laboratory are often made to be strong in order to maximize variance of the treatment and minimize individual differences (Weiss & Adler, 1984). Because these studies are interested in the fit between personality and culture or task characteristics, they employ laboratory situations that are intentionally strong situations. As a result, they fail to represent the full range of situational strength that exists in the real world and may not be externally valid.

The second limitation with this line of research, which it shares with the universal approach, is that no attention is given to the composition of the group. In the interaction designs of these lab studies, groups were constructed to be homogenous on level of trait, being either homogeneously high or low. Real groups in organizations are, of course, composed of members with varying levels on a particular trait. The success of a group is dependent on more than a specific trait and the task. Success is also determined by the constellation of people in the group and their individual personality profiles. In other words, every group has a number of individuals in it, and each individual possesses a variety of personality traits that simultaneously influence the individual's interpersonal and task behavior in groups. We now turn our attention to this theoretical approach where variance and configurations of traits within a group are considered.

CONFIGURATION APPROACH

The configuration approach conceptualizes the role of personality in group composition to be more complex than either the universal or contingent approaches. The personality inputs in the group systems model include not only mean or minimum measures of personality, but the variance of a particular trait or the mix of different traits in a group as well. This line of research assumes that it is either (a) the trait similarity or dissimilarity or (b) the mix of complementary traits within a group that leads to performance effects. The fit of members to each other affects interpersonal and task process in the group. Two streams of research have examined the mix of traits within a group, focusing on either homogeneity versus heterogeneity or complementary compatibility. The homogeneity versus heterogeneity approach is generally concerned only with group variance on one trait, whereas the compatibility line of research is concerned with the mix of multiple traits that work well together in a group. Team members are thought to be compatible when they share multiple (congruent) traits or when they possess different but mutually supporting (complementary) traits (Moreland & Levine, 1992). Thus operationalization of group personality is either variance on a single trait or variance/agreement of complementary traits (e.g., need for power and need for affiliation have high agreement if there are a balance of members high and low on those traits in a group).

Homogeneity and Heterogeneity

The homogeneity versus heterogeneity debate in personality runs parallel to the larger body of literature in team composition concerned with heterogeneity or demographic diversity (e.g., Williams & O'Reilly, 1998). This line of research assumes that it is the trait similarity or dissimilarity that leads to performance effects rather than the average level of a trait within the group. The argument in favor of homogeneity in groups is that similarity enhances the cohesion, communication, and motivation to work together on collective tasks. The argument in favor of heterogeneity is that it will encourage seeing the same information in different ways and division of labor amongst group members based on preferences and skills (Haythorn, 1968). In other words, heterogeneity is most likely to facilitate group productivity through task-focusing behaviors and homogeneity should facilitate group productivity through cohesive interpersonal processes (see Steiner, 1972).

Several studies have found support for homogeneity. For example, three studies have found that the variance of conscientiousness as well as the group mean level is important for predicting group performance (Barrick et al., 1998; Bond & Shiu, 1997). Barrick et al. found a negative relationship between variance in conscientiousness and team performance such that high mean levels of conscientiousness are desirable. A mix of high- and low-conscientiousness members may lead to lower performance. Post hoc analyses suggest that teams with a low-conscientiousness member did not perform as well in hierarchically distributed decision-making teams (LePine et al., 1997), suggesting that the distribution of conscientiousness matters for group process issues. Although these and other researchers originally conceptualized conscientiousness as operating through task rather than interpersonal processes, it is possible that the impact of one or a few members low in conscientiousness is detrimental to the interpersonal processes in a team. In other words, the high-conscientiousness members of the group may want to focus closely on the details of the task whereas those low on conscientiousness place a lower priority on these issues, resulting in conflict. For example, an exploratory longitudinal lab study conducted by Bond and Shiu produced some supportive results when examining the effects of conscientiousness on the interpersonal process variable of shared exchange or willingness to share information in a group. The tasks in this study were undirected group projects in an introductory social psychology class. The researchers found that the variance of self-discipline (a subscale of conscientiousness) negatively affected shared exchange. They found that variability in self-discipline in a group reduced the level of free and expressive interaction between members. These results suggest that the variance of conscientiousness among members may alter group performance through interpersonal processes. In other words, highly conscientious members may be irritated or frustrated when working with less conscientious members.

Evidence in support of homogeneity was also found by Toquam, Macaulay, Westra, Fujita, and Murphy (1997). Toquam et al. found that crews of nuclear power plant operators who were homogeneous on social skills (MMPI scale) performed more effectively on control room simulations than heterogeneous crews. Communication is very important for these type of crews (Toquam et al.), and so they theorized that social skill parity leads to enhanced performance though its effect on crew communication patterns. In support of this idea, the same study found that crews that were less consistent in the types of communications provided across various scenarios were rated as less effective. Though the link was not directly tested in this study, the combination of these results suggest that crews that are homogeneous on social skills have more consistent communication patterns, which lead to higher levels of effectiveness. Thus recent literature is recognizing that the homogeneity of conscientiousness and social skills also matters for team performance, and the mediating mechanism for this personality composition effect operates through interpersonal and communication process loss when variance is high.

Heterogeneity of multiple traits, or as the mix of traits within a group rather than the diversity of one trait within a group, has also found support in the literature. The intent of these studies was to construct groups of members similar on global personality orientation rather than on a particular trait or dimension of personality. This line of research found support for multiple-trait heterogeneity positively influencing group performance. A key early study by Hoffman and Maier (1961) suggested that heterogeneity of traits in groups leads to better group outcomes. In this study, groups were formed to be homogeneous or heterogeneous based on the profile similarity of their scores on the Guilford-Zimmerman Temperament Survey (Guilford & Zimmerman, 1949). Participant pairwise similarity was assessed based on the correlations of the ten dimensions of the profile (using Kendall's tau). Groups were composed of members with the most similar or different profiles. The intention was to construct groups of members similar on global personality orientation rather than on one particular trait. Four types of problems were used to test the relative abilities of homogeneous versus heterogeneous groups on the quality of their solutions. All tasks involved problem solving and a range of potential personal value conflicts. Results revealed that heterogeneous groups provided higher-quality solutions than did homogenous groups. Hoffman and Maier concluded that the greater the differences in perceptions among group members, the higher the quality of their problem solving because the presence of opposing viewpoints caused more complete solutions to emerge or new ones to be developed by the group in order to deal with the conflicts or problems raised (see Nemeth, 1986, on minority influence). Other studies also provide consistent results that general personality heterogeneity leads to better group outcomes than homogeneity (Aamodt & Kimbrough, 1982; Ghiselli & Lodahl, 1958). For example, Aamodt and Kimbrough used

global personality types and found support for heterogeneity of generalized behavioral styles enhancing the quality of solutions to group tasks.

In sum, current evidence suggests that homogeneity promotes group
cohesion, especially when looking at a single personality dimension. Heterogeneity, on the other hand, improves group information sharing and
problem solving, especially when looking at very broad indices of variance on multiple traits. It is important to note that these results are not
necessarily in conflict. Some recent studies suggest that whether homogeneity or heterogeneity is preferable depends on the specific personality
trait in question. For example, homogeneity on conscientiousness and social skills, and heterogeneity on extraversion, have been found to have positive influence on group process and performance. The collective results of
these studies further suggest that the group personality input in a systems
model of group processing may be more complex than a simple mean level
on a trait. The most significant implication for groups researchers is that
knowing how group personality is measured is critical—both mean and
variance on a trait can be important. Theory should dictate which is the
proper operationalization of group level personality (Klein et al., 1994).

Congruence and Compatibility

Some team-configuration studies also take multiple traits into consideration as well as taking the nature of a particular trait into account in order to
determine optimal personality composition. Rather than being concerned
only with group variance on one trait or type, this line of inquiry is concerned with the mix of people with different traits that work well together
in a group. These studies are concerned with the ways in which group
members must be compatible in order to work together most effectively.
This view recognizes that people do not display their personalities one
trait at a time, but rather that an individual's behavior is the result of the
simultaneous influence of multiple traits (Brandt & Devine, 2000). Group
performance is assumed to stem from the harmonious interpersonal interaction of members with complementary personalities.

Most of the research on compatibility has used Schutz's (1958) fundamental interpersonal relations orientation (FIRO) theory. Schutz's theory
posits that all interpersonal behavior reflects the degree to which three basic human needs are expressed and wanted from others. These needs are
inclusion, affection, and control. Need for *inclusion* is the need for membership in a cohesive group. Need for *affection* is the need for close and
warm relationships with others. *Control* needs are the need to dominate
others. Members of a group are thought to be compatible when they share
multiple similar traits, or when they possess dissimilar but mutually supporting (complementary) traits (Moreland & Levine, 1992). Both congruent

and complementary groups have a balance of initiators and receivers of control, inclusion, or affection. An incompatible group would include some members who want more affection, inclusion, or control than other members are able to provide.

Schutz (1958) predicted that compatible groups would generally be more efficient and productive than incompatible groups. The evidence for compatibility using the FIRO-B is mixed, however. A supportive laboratory study by Reddy and Byrnes (1972) using manager subjects on a Lego assembly task found that congruence (in terms of similar levels) on control and affection was positively related to speed of assembly. Other studies found support for incompatible groups (Hill, 1975; Shaw & Webb, 1982). In a field study utilizing naturally intact groups of system analysts, Hill found that both congruence and complementarity on needs for inclusion, affection, and control were negatively related to group members' perceptions of performance (measured by one group member per team). In sum, there is support for the idea that individual fit within a group is dependent on how they well members fit within the configuration of traits of the other group members. However, some of these effects are also contingent on the task at hand (a three-way interaction).

Several more recent studies have also examined the effect of personality compatibility in groups. Brandt and Devine (2000) is the only study to examine explicitly how compatibility affects group process. These researchers examined compatibility on dominance (extraversion) and affiliation (agreeableness) on task-related communication and interpersonal conflict. Groups were defined as compatible if they had moderate mean levels of extraversion and high mean agreeableness. In this study, teams of undergraduates performed a managerial decision-making task simulation that required them to decide which of seven applicants to hire as a new manager. Results found that personality compatibility had a significant negative relationship with interpersonal conflict, and that interpersonal conflict was negatively related to the time required to complete the task. Personality compatibility had no effect on the amount of task-related communication.

Another study by Buchanan and Foti (2000) examined the patterns of three personality traits as predictor of group performance on a creative brainstorming task. This study utilized a sample of undergraduate students and looked at the group-level patterns of extraversion, conscientiousness, and openness. This study constructed individuals in groups by clustering them based on their similarity across multiple personality variables in order to better control for the context in which these traits operate. The researchers hypothesized that groups with high levels of conscientiousness and openness but moderate levels of extraversion would be the optimal configuration and would perform best. They reasoned that because openness and conscientiousness had been previously related to group performance (see Barry & Stewart, 1997). Three contrast configurations were used as comparisons. Contrast A groups were high on all three traits, contrast B groups were high on conscientiousness, moderate on extraversion, but low on openness, and contrast C groups were high on openness, moderate on extraversion, but low on conscientiousness. Results revealed that the predicted optimal configuration for a group did indeed predict quantity of ideas generated as well as greater numbers of high-quality ideas than the rest of the contrast configurations. Furthermore, there were no significant differences between the contrast groups. The lack of significant differences in performance among the three contrast configuration patterns indicates that the cause of group performance was due to the pattern of personality traits in the optimal configuration rather than one specific personality trait (Buchanan & Foti, 2000).

Limitations of the Configuration Approach

Our review of the literature revealed general support for the configuration approach—the notion that the array of individuals on the team also predicts process and outcomes. On balance, the findings reviewed earlier suggest that group configurations of high homogeneous levels of conscientiousness, agreeableness, and openness and heterogeneity on extraversion lead to positive group processes and outcomes. As with the other two approaches there are, of course, limitations to the configuration approach. There are at least three problems with the current state of the research. First, these studies generally employ measures of broad personality types (e.g., Aamodt & Kimbrough, 1982; Hoffman, 1959; Hoffman & Maier, 1961). These researchers attempted to group people by broad categories and treated them as mutually exclusive types, but the details of how the particular traits interact with each other are lost. The findings from past studies need to be replicated and a broader range of traits need to be examined in the future.

The second limitation of this approach is its lack of measurement of and attention to affective or cognitive mediators likely to affect relations-oriented or task-oriented behaviors that lead to performance. Such mediating mechanisms are nicely outlined in Jackson et al.'s (1995) general causal model for understanding the dynamics of diversity in teams. In Jackson's model, diversity, which in this case we can think of in terms of personality composition, affects the cognitions, affect, status, and power of group members, which leads to short-term behaviors directed at either tasks or interpersonal relations within the group. These short-term behaviors lead to long-term consequences of norms and patterns relating to task and interpersonal relations. Configuration research needs to focus more attention on such process pieces of the group systems model.

A third limitation of configuration research is its lack of attention to situation or contextual factors. The mixed results of the studies on compatibility may be due to the fact that they employed tasks with different levels of task interdependence. Hill (1975) even suggests that a possible reason for his results in favor of incompatibility stem from the fact that he used a field sample of systems analysts who have a great deal of autonomy in their jobs. Compare this research to Reddy and Byrnes' (1972) assembly task that required a great deal of task interdependence without the chance to remove oneself from the group and work independently on a part of the task. Such interdependence can lead to more destructive aggression and poor interpersonal relations in the group when personalities are not compatible. In short, the effects of personality can be moderated by both the task and the configuration of people in the group (i.e., the three-way interaction).

Finally, it is worth noting that the configuration approach is commonly used in organizational consulting, despite the fact that there has been relatively little empirical research. Several team measures exist in the practitioner domain that are concerned with trait configuration (referred to as *roles*) in a team, such as Belbin's team roles model (Belbin, 1981, 1993) and the team management system (Margerison & McCann, 1984). These models propose that there are various team roles and a balance of these roles leads to optimal team functioning. This theory suggests two things: (1) practitioners may be espousing team personality configurations that have little grounding in research, and (2) there is practitioner interest in further scholarly work in this tradition.

SUMMARY AND CONCLUSION

We found support for all three approaches reviewed in this chapter. There are universal effects of personality on group performance—positive relationships between agreeableness or emotional stability and cohesive group process, and between conscientiousness and task focus (e.g., Barrick et al., 1998; Bond & Shiu, 1997; Lepine et al., 1997). We also found supportive evidence for the contingent approach—organizational culture and task type both moderate the relationship between group-member personality and performance (e.g., Aronoff et al., 1983; Hogan et al., 1988). Finally, we found support for the configuration approach—heterogeneity is helpful for task-related outcomes and homogeneity is helpful for relationship-related outcomes (e.g., Hoffman & Maier, 1961). More important, it is important to recognize that the universal, contingent, and configuration approaches are not necessarily mutually exclusive and may indeed be complementary. Another way to think about these approaches is in terms of degree of specificity. The universal perspective can be thought of as the broadest perspective documenting the effects of personality across all contexts. The contingent perspective helps us look more deeply into organizational phenomena to derive more specific theories about the circumstances under which particular types of personality traits will be most effective for group performance. Finally, the configuration approach helps us to look even more deeply into organizational context by allowing researchers to look into the internal dynamics within the teams and examine how the individual members interact with each other. Thus all three perspectives on the role of personality composition in teams may be operational.

This review has revealed at least four ways in which the literature on the role of personality in groups could be improved. The first is the need to articulate the mediating mechanisms between group personality and performance more often and more clearly. Such tests of mediating links were more likely to be employed in recent research, but it is still not commonplace. We need answers to questions about why and how particular traits have which specific effects. Do groups succeed on highly complex tasks because they work together well (interpersonal relations) or because they stay focused on task? Which personality trait(s) or configuration of traits works best to achieve smooth interpersonal relations and/or task focus? Answers to such questions about which traits lead to interpersonal versus task processes in groups will (a) help scholars understand why certain aspects of organizational culture moderate the relationship between member personality and group outcomes and (b) indicate what other aspects of culture or task might be worth testing as potential moderators.

The literature would also benefit from clarity on the variety of methods for operationalizing team composition uncovered in this review—some prior work has used the mean level of traits in a group with others using the minimum level. More recent studies interested in diversity of a trait in a group have also used variance of a trait. Theoretically, the appropriateness of the operationalization should depend on the nature of the work being done by the group and the degree of task interdependence (Steiner, 1972). Several key works in the groups literature have outlined task typologies that influence the compositional effects and measurement of groups on performance (McGrath, 1984; Steiner). When groups are highly interdependent their performance depends on their weakest link, and thus the level of the lowest member on a particular trait should be the most appropriate measure for the group. Conversely, for groups whose work consists of pooling individual efforts, a mean level of a trait may be the more appropriate measure for the group (Steiner). Future research should clarify when and why each method of operationalizing the composition of group personality is most appropriate. When these theoretical issues are explicitly considered they will serve to advance an integrated understanding of the relationships between personality inputs, group processes, and performance outcomes.

A third way in which the literature on personality and group process should develop is by drawing more specifically on the group process literature. One way this could happen is by utilizing the classic typologies of tasks developed by groups researchers that should theoretically moderate compositional effects of personality in groups (e.g., McGrath, 1984; Steiner, 1972). For example, Steiner's distinction between an additive and conjunctive task suggests that the interdependence associated with a conjunctive task would make heterogeneity or incompatibility of personality problematic. The groups literature can also suggest additional process mechanisms that can lead to enhanced performance that may have their roots in personality traits. One possible example here comes from the notion that personality is also likely to be an important predictor of external boundary spanning and information-gathering activities (drawing on Ancona, 1990). Antecedents of obtaining external resources for the team and engaging in coordination activities across functional units have previously been related to demographic characteristics of functional background and organizational tenure (Ancona & Caldwell, 1992). It is highly probable that personality traits are also a powerful antecedent of these ambassador and task coordinator activities. These are but two examples of where the personality literature could benefit from closer integration with the group process literature.

Most important, the literature on personality and group processes needs to recognize and integrate all three of the approaches discussed here. Each approach makes a distinct contribution to our understanding of the role of personality in groups. For example, future work looking at the optimal tension between heterogeneity and homogeneity of any given trait could benefit from using this strategy. Past research has generally assumed that the effects of homogeneity and heterogeneity are either good or bad (e.g., groups with all extraverts are always good). A more integrated approach suggests that heterogeneity is neither universally good nor bad. Rather, it is likely that optimal levels exist depending on a variety of circumstances. Barry and Stewart (1997) are an excellent example of looking at just such a possibility. They found a curvilinear result for the effect of extraversion on group performance, with a mix of people high and low on extraversion being optimal. Thus, we now recognize that moderate mean-level extraversion almost always encourages greater group cohesion and performance than low mean-level extraversion (universal effect), certain tasks and organizational cultures such as sales strongly favor extraversion (contingent effect), and that too many extraverts in a group create a dysfunctional competition for dominance (configuration effect). Thus the personality effects we would expect when taking a universal perspective may not hold, depending on the task or configuration. If teams engaged in sales activities have a high proportion of extraverts, there may not be negative intrateam competitive effects because these energies are collectively focused on making sales. However, for teams engaged in other types of activities, too many extraverts can be detrimental to interpersonal processes because dominating behaviors are internally focused. Optimal configurations of all traits are likely to depend on both the trait and the context in which the group operates (see Williams & O'Reilly (1998) on demographic diversity).

REFERENCES

Aamodt, M. G., & Kimbrough, W. W. (1982). Effect of group heterogeneity on quality of task solutions. *Psychological Reports, 50*, 171–174.

Allport, G. W. (1937). *Personality: A psychological interpretation*. New York: Holt.

Ancona, D. G. (1990). Outward bound: Strategies for team survival in an organization. *Academy of Management Journal, 33*, 334–365.

Ancona, D. G., & Caldwell, D. F. (1992). Demography and design: Predictors of new product team performance. *Organization Science, 3*, 321–341.

Argyle, M. (1991). *Cooperation: The basis of sociability*. London: Routledge.

Aronoff, J., Meese, L. A., & Wilson, J. P. (1983). Personality factors in small group functioning. In H. H. Blumberg, P. Hare, V. Kent, and M. Davies (Eds.), *Small groups and social interaction* (pp. 79–88). Chichester, England: Wiley.

Bales, R. F. (1958). Task roles and social roles in problem solving groups. In E. E. Maccoby, T. M. Newcomb, and E. L. Hartley (Eds.), *Readings in social psychology*. New York: Holt, Rinehart and Winston.

Barrick, M. R., & Mount, M. K. (1991). The Big Five personality dimensions and job performance: A meta-analysis. *Personnel Psychology, 44*, 1–26.

Barrick, M. R., Stewart, G. L., Neubert, M. J., & Mount, M. K. (1998). Relating member ability and personality to work-team processes and team effectiveness. *Journal of Applied Psychology, 83*, 377–391.

Barry, B., & Stewart, G. L. (1997). Composition, process, and performance in self-managed groups: The role of personality. *Journal of Applied Psychology, 82*, 62–78.

Bass, B. M. (1990). *Bass & Stogdill's handbook of leadership* (3rd ed.). New York: Free Press.

Belbin, R. M. (1981). *Management teams: Why they succeed or fail*. London: Heinemann.

Belbin, R. M. (1993). *Team roles at work: A strategy for human resource management*. Oxford: Butterworth, Heinemann.

Berkowitz, L. (1956). Personality and group position. *Sociometry, 19*, 210–221.

Bond, M. H., & Shiu, W. Y. (1997). The relationship between a group's personality resources and the two dimensions of its group process. *Small Group Research, 28*, 194–217.

Brandt, K. M., & Devine, D. J. (2000, April). Effects of personality compatibility in decision making teams. Paper presented at the 15th annual conference of the Society for Industrial-Organizational Psychology, New Orleans, LA.

Buchanan, L., & Foti, R. J. (2000, April). Personality patterns and creative task performance in teams. Paper presented at the 15th annual conference of the Society for Industrial-Organizational Psychology, New Orleans, LA.

Chan, D. (1998). Functional relations among constructs in the same content domain at different levels of analysis: A typology of composition models. *Journal of Applied Psychology, 83*, 234–246.

Chatman, J. A., & Barsade, S. G. (1995). Personality, organizational culture, and cooperation: Evidence from a business simulation. *Administrative Science Quarterly, 40*, 423–443.

Comer, D. R. (1995). A model of social loafing in real work groups. *Human Relations, 48*, 647–667.

Costa, P. T., Jr., & McCrae, R. R. (1992). *NEO PI-R Professional Manual*. Odessa, FL: Psychological Assessment Resources.

DeBasio, A. R. (1986). Problem solving in triads composed of varying numbers of field-dependent and field independent subjects. *Journal of Personality and Social Psychology, 51*, 749–754.

Delery, J. E., & Doty, D. H. (1996). Modes of theorizing in strategic human resource management: Tests of universalistic, contingency, and configurational performance predictions. *Academy of Management Journal, 39*, 802–835.

Driskell, J. E., Hogan, R., & Salas, E. (1987). Personality and group performance. *Review of Personality and Social Psychology, 9*, 91–112.

Early, P. C. (1989). Social loafing and collectivism: A comparison of the United States and the People's Republic of China. *Administrative Science Quarterly, 34*, 55–581.

Early, P. C. (1993). East meets west meets mideast: Further explorations of collectivistic and individualistic work groups. *Academy of Management Journal, 36*, 319–348.

George, J. M. (1990). Personality, affect, and behavior in groups. *Journal of Applied Psychology, 75*, 107–116.

Ghiselli, E. E., & Lodahl, T. M. (1958). Patterns of managerial traits and group effectiveness. *Journal of Abnormal and Social Psychology, 57*, 61–66.

Goodman, P. S. (1986). Impact of task and technology on group performance. In P. S. Goodman and Associates, *Designing effective work groups* (pp. 120–167). San Francisco: Jossey-Bass.

Greer, F. L. (1955). *Small group effectiveness* (Institute Report No. 6). Philadelphia: Institute for Research on Human Relations.

Guilford, J. P., & Zimmerman, W. S. (1949). *The Guilford-Zimmerman Temperament Survey*. Beverly Hills: Sheridan Supply.

Hackman, R. J. (1987). The design of work teams. In J. W. Lorsch (Ed.), *Handbook of organizational behavior* (pp. 315–342). Englewood Cliffs, NJ: Prentice Hall.

Hall, C. S., & Lindzey, G. (1957). *Theories of personality*. New York: Wiley.

Harrison, D. A., Price, K. H., & Bell, M. P. (1998). Beyond relational demography: Time and the effects of surface- and deep-level diversity on work group cohesion. *Academy of Management Journal, 41*, 96–107.

Haythorn, W. (1953). The influence of individual members on the characteristics of small groups. *The Journal of Abnormal and Social Psychology, 48*, 276–284.

Haythorn, W. W. (1968). The composition of groups: A review of the literature. *Acta Psychologica, 28*, 97–128.

Heslin, R. (1964). Predicting group task effectiveness from member characteristics. *Psychological Bulletin, 62*, 248–256.

Hill, R. E. (1975). Interpersonal compatibility and work group performance. *Journal of Applied Behavioral Science, 11*, 210–219.

Hoffman, L. R. (1959). Homogeneity of member personality and its effect on group problem solving. *Journal of Abnormal and Social Psychology, 58*, 27–32.

Hoffman, L. R., & Maier, R. F. (1961). Quality and acceptance of problem solving by members of homogenous and heterogeneous groups. *Journal of Abnormal and Social Psychology, 62*, 401–407.

Hogan, R., Raza, S., & Driskell, J. E. (1988). Personality, team performance, and organizational context. In P. Whitney and R. B. Ochsman (Eds.), *Psychology and productivity*. New York: Plenum.

Holland, J. L. (1966). *The psychology of vocational choice*. Waltham, MA: Blaisdell.

Ilgen, D. R. (1999). Teams embedded in organizations: Some implications. *American Psychologist, 54*, 129–139.

Jackson, S., May, K. E., & Whitney, K. (1995). Understanding the dynamics of diversity in decision-making teams. In R. A. Guzzo and E. Salas (Eds.), *Team effectiveness and decision making in organizations* (pp. 204–261). San Francisco: Jossey-Bass.

Kinlaw, D. C. (1991). *Developing superior work teams: Building quality and the competitve edge*. San Diego, CA: Lexington Books.

Klein, K. J., Dansereau, F., & Hall, R. J. (1994). Levels issues in theory development, data collection, and analysis. *Academy of Management Review, 19*, 195–229.

Klimoski, R., & Jones, R. G. (1995). Staffing for effective group decision making: Key issues in matching people and teams. In R. A. Guzzo & E. Salas (Eds.), *Team Effectiveness and decision making in organizations* (pp. 291–333). San Francisco: Jossey-Bass.

LePine, J. A., Hollenbeck, J. R., Ilgen, D. R., & Hedlund, J. (1997). Effects of individual differences on the performance of hierarchical decision-making teams: Much more than g. *Journal of Applied Psychology, 82*, 803–811.

Levine, J. M., & Moreland, R. L. (1998). Small groups. In D. T. Gilbert, S. T. Fiske, & G. Lindzey (Eds.), *The handbook of social psychology* (4th ed., pp. 415–469). New York: McGraw-Hill.

Littlepage, G. E., Schmidt, G. W., Whisler, E. W., & Frost, A. G. (1995). An input-process-output analysis of influence and performance in problem-solving groups. *Journal of Personality and Social Psychology, 69*, 877–889.

Magnusson, D., & Endler, S. (1977). Interactional psychology: Present status and future prospects. In D. Magnusson and S. Endler (Eds.), *Personality at the crossroads: Current issues in interactional psychology*. Hillsdale, NJ: Lawrence Erlbaum Associates, Inc.

Mann, R. D. (1959). A review of the relationships between personality and performance in small groups. *Psychological Bulletin, 56*, 241–270.

Margerison, C. J., & McCann, D. J. (1984). *How to lead a winning team*. Manchester: MCB University Press.

McClelland, D. C. (1985). *Human Motivation*. Glenview, IL: Scott, Foresman.

McGrath, J. E. (1962). The influence of positive interpersonal relations on adjustment and interpersonal relations in rifle teams. *Journal of Abnormal and Social Psychology, 65*, 365–375.

McGrath, J. E. (1984). *Groups: Interaction and performance*. Englewood Cliffs, NJ: Prentice-Hall.

Mohammed, S., Angell, L., & Ringseis, E. (2000, April). The effect of team composition on team performance: the role of personality, team orientation, and task type. Paper presented at the 60th annual conference of the Academy of Management Meetings, Toronto, Canada.

Moreland, R. L., & Levine, J. M. (1992). The composition of small groups. In E. J. Lawler, B. Markovsky, C. Ridgeway, & H. A. Walker (Eds.), *Advances in group processes* (Vol. 9, pp. 237–280). Greenwich, CT: JAI.

Mount, M. K., Barrick, M. R., & Stewart, G. L. (1998). Five-Factor Model of personality and performance in jobs involving interpersonal interactions. *Human Performance, 11*, 145–165.

Neale, M. A., Mannix, E. A., & Gruenfeld, D. H (1998). *Research on Managing Groups and Teams: Composition*. Stamford, CT: JAI.

Nemeth, C. J. (1986). Differential contributions of minority and majority influence. *Psychological Review, 93*, 1–10.

Neuman, G. A., & Wright, J. (1999). Team effectiveness: Beyond skills and cognitive ability. *Journal of Applied Psychology, 84*, 376–389.

Nunally, J. C., & Bernstein, I. H. (1994). *Psychometric theory*. New York: McGraw-Hill.

O'Connor, K. M. (1998). Experiential diversity in groups: Conceptualizing and measuring variation among teammates. In M. A. Neale, E. A. Mannix, and D. H. Gruenfeld (Eds.), *Research on Managing Groups and Teams: Composition* (pp. 167–182). Stamford, CT: JAI.

Pervin, L. A. (1980). *Personality theory and assessment*. New York: Wiley.

Peterson, R. S., Owens, P. D., & Martorana, P. V. (2000). How *does* leadership affect organizational performance? Top management team dynamics mediate the relationship between CEO personality and organizational performance. Unpublished manuscript: Cornell University.

Pfeffer, J. (1983). Organizational demography. In L. L. Cummings & B. M. Staw (Eds.), *Research in organizational behavior* (Vol. 5, pp. 299–357). Greenwich, CT: JAI.

Reddy, W. B., & Byrnes, A. (1972). Effects of interpersonal group composition on the problem solving behavior of middle managers. *Journal of Applied Psychology, 56*, 516–517.

Rousseau, D. M. (1985). Issues of level in organizational research: Multi-level and cross-level perspectives. *Research in Organizational Behavior, 7*, 1–37.

Schneider, F. W., & Delaney, J. G. (1972). Effect of individual achievement motivation on group problem solving efficiency. *Journal of Social Psychology, 86*, 291–298.

Schutz, W. C. (1958). *FIRO: A three dimensional interplay of interpersonal behavior*. New York: Holt Rinehart & Winston.

Shaw, M. E. (1981). *Group dynamics: The psychology of small group behavior* (3rd ed.). New York: McGraw-Hill.

Shaw, M. E., & Webb, J. N. (1982). When compatibility interferes with group effectiveness. *Small Group Behavior, 13*, 555–564.

Staw, B. M., & Ross, J. (1985). Stability in the midst of change: A dispositional approach to job attitudes. *Journal of Applied Psychology, 70*, 469–480.

Steiner, I. D. (1972). *Group process and productivity*. New York: Academic.

Stevens, M. J., & Campion, M. A. (1994). The knowledge, skill, and ability requirements for teamwork: Implications for human resource management. *Journal of Management, 20*, 503–530.

Stewart, G. L., & Barrick, M. R. (2000). Team structure and performance: Assessing the mediating role of intrateam process and the moderating role of task type. *Academy of Management Journal, 43*, 135–148.

Toquam, J. L, Macaulay, J. L, Westra, C. D., Fujita, Y., & Murphy, S. E. (1997). Assessment of nuclear power plant crew performance variability. In M. T. Brannick, E. Salas, and C. Prince (Eds.), *Team Performance Assessment and Measurement* (pp. 253–287). Mahwah, NJ: Lawrence Erlbaum Associates, Inc.

Wagner, J. A., III (1995). Studies of individualism-collectivism: Effects on cooperation in groups. *Academy of Management Journal, 38*, 152–172.

Wagner, J. A., III, & Moch, M. K. (1986). Individualism-collectivism: Concept and measure. *Psychologica, 28*, 173–181.

Waung, M., & Brice, T. S. (1998). The effects of conscientiousness and opportunity to caucus on group performance. *Small Group Research, 29*, 624–634.

Weick, K. E., & Penner, D. D. (1969). Discrepant membership as an occasion for effective cooperation. *Sociometry, 32*, 413–424.

Weiss, H. M., & Adler, S. (1984). Personality and organizational behavior. *Research in Organizational Behavior, 6*, 1–50.

Williams, K. Y., & O'Reilly, C. A., III (1998). Demography and diversity in organizations: A review of 40 years of research. *Research in Organizational Behavior, 20*, 77–140.

Witkin, H. A., & Goodenough, D. R. (1977). Field dependence and interpersonal behavior. *Psychological Bulletin, 84*, 661–689.

Witkin, H. A., Moore, C. A., Goodenough, D. R., & Cox, P. W. (1977). Field dependent and field independent cognitive styles and their educational implications. *Review of Educational Research, 47*, 1–64.

Yeatts, D. E., & Hyten, C. (1998). *High-performing self-managed work teams: A comparison of theory to practice*. Thousand Oaks, CA: Sage.

13

Personality and Organizational Culture

Benjamin Schneider
University of Maryland and Personnel Research Associates, Inc.

D. Brent Smith
Rice University

Personality has been central to the study of psychology. The construct—and such related constructs as values and interests—in some sense defines psychology for it is the framing of the internal world of people that differentiates psychology from all other sciences. Personality conjures up thoughts about needs that people attempt to gratify (e.g., Maslow, 1954), the preferences people have for behaving in ambiguous or relatively unstructured situations (e.g., McCaulley, 1990), and the internal enduring interests and values of people that serve as guides or standards for their behavior (e.g., Holland, 1997; Schwarz, 1997). In what follows, we will use the generic term *personality* to refer to all of these classes of individual attributes that give form, structure, and consistency to people's behavior over time and situations.

Culture has been central to the study of anthropology. Anthropology concerns the enduring behavior patterns that characterize entitative groups. *Entitative* groups of people have a sense of their own identity as a group and are viewed by others as belonging to a particular group (Trice & Beyer, 1993). With regard to the culture construct, in discussions of behavior it is the group, not individuals in the group, that is the focus of attention. When the attributes of people are mentioned in thinking about culture, the word *shared* is invariably part of such discussion. This word refers typically to the sharing of ideologies surrounding sets of beliefs about how things work, values that indicate what things are worthwhile and what are not, and norms that tell people—in the collective—how to behave (Schein, 1992; Trice & Beyer). In what follows we will use the term *culture* to refer to beliefs, values, and norms with the understanding that it is the sharedness of these attributes that yield the entitative group that is the focus of interest. In addition, an allied concept, *climate*, which refers to patterns of behavior that are rewarded, supported, and expected in an environment (Schneider, 1990) (the focus is on environmental attributes) will also be included with the word *culture*. Readers will please forgive us if we slip over into other attributes of the organization that might also be conceptualized as a reflection of personality. This extension happens primarily because there is a paucity of work on the cross-level relationship between personality and organizational culture or climate. So, when we found a study, for example on the relationship between CEO personality and organizational structure (Miller & Droge, 1986) we included it.

The formal study of personality has, for the most part, been at the individual level of analysis. We ask questions, for example, about how person A differs in her personality from person B and then ask if and how those internal (needs, values, preferences) individual differences get reflected in observable individual behavior. The formal study of culture has been at the group level of analysis. Here we ask questions, for example, about how group A differs in its culture (values, beliefs, norms, environmental attributes) from group B, and we document the behavioral differences associated with those ideological and environmental differences.

Attempts to make connections between personality and organizational culture have been sparse. This lack is not surprising. The enterprise of science, like all enterprise, is to perfect what differentiates in the marketplace, so in the marketplace of ideas it is not particularly surprising to find psychology and anthropology going their separate ways. This is not to say that there is no such work. Indeed, a major impetus for writing this chapter was to bring to consciousness the cross-level theory and research that has been accomplished and which links work across these two such seemingly different disciplines.

We note here that the attempt to integrate across these different perspectives on organizational behavior is not new even though the literature is still sparse. Williams (1968), for example, reviewed the then-extant literature more than 30 years ago with relatively few citations; our reference list will not be that long either, with the exception of work that has been accomplished within Schneider's (1987) ASA model. Indeed, Williams' (p. 155) early commentary on the issue of integration across levels reads as if it were written today: "Some of the most comprehensive literature on personality and organizational behavior is probably to be found in the cross-cultural anthropology and personality literature, which seldom is utilized or integrated with attempts to look at personality functioning in the organization. Yet it is probably the literature that most closely meets one of the requisites of such a field: the simultaneous consideration of personality and the structure and functioning of the system."

We agree with Williams (1968). Much of what we discuss here is directly analogous at the organizational level to what the anthropologists were attempting to do at the societal level, that is, to understand the dynamic interplay between personality and culture.

In what follows, we first explore the types of multilevel research paradigms that have been used for linking individual attributes to group-level phenomena and outcomes. These views are presented somewhat in the abstract because discussion of these paradigms provides a foundation for a more detailed explication of the actual research that has been accomplished. In the section after consideration of research paradigms in the abstract, we consider research that has been accomplished with regard to how aggregate personality within an organization might be reflected in organizational culture; here the focus is on Schneider's (1987) proposal that over time organizations become relatively homogeneous with regard to the personality of the people in them—and this melding determines their observed and experienced culture. This discussion is followed by a consideration of how the personality of one individual, a CEO for example, might determine the culture of the organization. Here work by Miller and his colleagues (e.g., Miller & Droge, 1986) is the target of attention. Their research suggests that the personality (need for achievement, locus of control) of CEOs is reflected in the structure and strategy organizations adopt. Then a review of some of the applied implications of this crossing of levels of analysis for understanding the role of personality in organizational culture is presented. Finally we present concluding thoughts on cross-level phenomena in general and the role of personality in organizational culture.

ON MULTILEVEL AND RECIPROCAL RESEARCH PARADIGMS

Figure 13.1 is based on Schneider, Smith, and Sipe (2000). The figure shows some of the diverse ways that one can conceptualize cross-level linkages of the sort with which we are concerned in this chapter. In research on personality, of course, the dominant American paradigm has been from an understanding of the facets of personality to the relationship of the facets of individual personality to individual behavior, link 1 in the figure. For culture research the paradigm has been from an understanding of the facets of culture to the relationship of culture to group behavior, link 2 in the figure. In this chapter we essentially ignore links 1 and 2 because (a) research on these linkages is plentiful and has been reviewed elsewhere in great detail (see other chapters in this book on link 1and Ashkanasy, Wilderom,

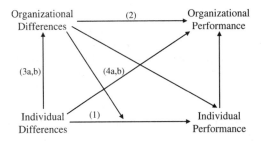

FIG. 13.1 Multilevel framework for understanding links among and between individual and organizational attributes and performance. From "Personnel Selection Psychology: Multilevel considerations," by B. Schneider, D. B. Smiths, and W. P. Sipe, 2000, in K. J. Klein and S. W. J. Kozlowski (Eds.), Multilevel Theory, Research, and Methods in Organizations: Foundations, Extensions, and New Directions, San Francisco: Jossey-Bass.

& Peterson, 2000, for link 2), and (b) our focus is on the cross-level or meso (House, Rousseau, & Thomas-Hunt, 1995) relationships existing between the individual-level variable personality and the organizational-level variable culture.

Link 3a is one variation of the cross-level linkage issue of concern to us here. It shows a relationship between individual personality and organizational culture. Another link, link 3b, is also of concern to us here. It specifies the idea that aggregated individual personality might be reflected in organizational culture. The other linkages shown in the figure will not be as central to our focus but will become relevant later as we explore additional cross-level issues worthy of attention from a personality and culture perspective. For example, we will argue later that links 4a (individual personality to organizational performance) and 4b (aggregated individual personality to organizational performance) are unlikely to be empirically demonstrated unless intermediate mediating linkages are considered. Thus, perhaps the relationships shown as 4a and 4b are really best thought of as being explored by first studying links 3a and 3b and then link 2; conceptually then, personality links to organizational performance through the culture created by personality (either individual or aggregate).

We must stop here for a moment to make the following observation: Personality, an internal personal quality, may relate to external criteria (for instance, culture) only through behavior (of individuals or collectives). From this point forward, we will speak of the relationship between personality and culture always inferring—and sometimes explicitly remembering— that it is behavior, not personality, that yields the culture of an organization. Indeed, in a later section of the chapter we will note the need to conduct further research on this crucial link.

Until this point, the description of Fig.13.1 has focused on unidirectional causal arrows. However, it is also obviously reasonable to conceptualize organizational culture as the cause of personality and, indeed, organizational performance as a cause of organizational culture—or, for that matter, individual performance as a cause of personality. There is some work on these reciprocal relationships, but the literature is sparse to say the least. Our own opinion is that one reason for this relative lack of such research concerns the apparent durability of personality over time and situations (Costa et al., 1986). If personality is relatively invariant over time and situations, then it might be assumed that personality is not reciprocally related to the situations in which people behave. As we will show later, we do not accept this conclusion. Finally, feedback loops also need to be considered a part of Fig.13.1. Here an hypothesized feedback loop might run from individual behavior (say the personality of the founder) to organizational culture (Schein, 1992) and from organizational culture back to aggregated individual personality (the kind of people the culture created by the founder attracts (Schneider, Goldstein, & Smith, 1995). For another example, consider that Argyris (1957) proposed that manager behavior toward employees can create an environment in which the norms that characterize a workplace infantilize workers. That is, by the establishment of rules, procedures, and demands on workers that treat them as children, workers then conceptualize themselves as children and then behave as children, reinforcing manager behavior that treats them like children—and the cycle continues. In a sense we have just begun the discussion of some relationships between personality and culture, so let us proceed with a few more conceptual and research examples of how people have thought about the links between organizational culture and personality.

HOW AGGREGATE PERSONALITY EMERGES IN ORGANIZATIONS

Research proceeding under this paradigm has focused on Schneider's (1987) hypothesis that people are attracted to, selected by, and stay with organizations that fit their personality. He noted that a result of this cycle of attraction–selection–attrition (ASA) is that organizations are characterized by a modal personality and this modal personality is at the root of the culture of an organization. The idea that aggregate personalities in a setting define the culture of that setting was not new with Schneider (1987). He borrowed the notion from Holland (1966; 1973; 1997).

As early as 1961 Holland (Astin & Holland, 1961) developed a measure of college climate called the environmental assessment technique (EAT). The main focus of the measure was the vocational interests of the students in different majors on campuses. Aggregate campus measures of the student interests were used as early as 1965 (Astin, 1965) to characterize 1,000 campuses across the U.S. Holland (1997, p. 41) says this about his view of environments: "An environmental model may be defined as the situation or atmosphere created by the people who dominate a given environment. For instance, a Social environment [one of Holland's six environmental types] would be an environment dominated by Social types." Holland's basic hypothesis was that when person and environment are congruent— when social types enter Social environments—a host of desirable outcomes for the individual are likely. These desirable outcomes include job satisfaction, achievement, and vocational stability.

There are two brilliant insights in this seemingly simple model. First, environments are defined by the attributes of the people who dominate them—not physical structures, decision-making style, managerial authority, and so forth, which are an outcome of the people in a situation. Second, in the absence of an environmental type against which to frame the individual's vocational type, the prediction problems are enormous. If fit is what counts and the person and the environment are characterized in conceptually analogous terms, then the prediction problems are relatively simplified, avoiding an almost infinite number of possible person–environment interactions. Incidentally, Holland credits Linton (1945), one of the early psychological anthropologists studying personality–culture linkages, with the idea that environments can be usefully characterized by the attributes of the people in them.

As Holland's work is very well known and readily available, we shall not go into great detail on the full congruence conceptualization nor the extensive research on the model (see Furnham, 2001, for an excellent overview). This research frequently (though certainly not always) finds some support for the hexagonal framework and its subsequent prediction both in vocational counseling (see Schwartz, 1992) and industrial and organizational settings (see Muchinsky, 1999). Perhaps two examples of environmental types, the artistic and conventional environments, suffice for present purposes:

> The artistic environment is characterized by the dominance of environmental demands and opportunities that entail ambiguous, free, unsystematized activities and competencies to create art forms or products, and by dominance of Artistic types (Holland, 1997, p. 45).
>
> The conventional environment is characterized by the dominance of environmental demands and opportunities that entail the explicit, ordered, systematic manipulation of data such as keeping records, filing materials, reproducing materials, organizing written and numerical data according to a prescribed plan, operating businesses and data processing equipment, and by a population dominated by Conventional types (Holland, 1997, p. 47).

It is very important to note that it is aggregated individual types that, through their behavior there, produce organizational environments (what we here call *cultures*) and that it is fit of an individual to that culture that produces individual outcomes for that individual.

Schneider's (1987; Schneider, Goldstein, & Smith, 1995) model is less sophisticated and complete than the Holland perspective he used as a conceptual analog. Schneider merely suggested a cycle, the ASA cycle, and the idea that an outcome of the cycle was the modal personality and that this mode served as the foundation for the culture of an organization. Thus, whereas Holland noted that environments are defined by the people in them, and that fit of an individual to that environment is important for individual outcomes, he had not identified quite how the people who define them actually got to be in them. This latter issue was a key part of the Schneider framework.

It is obvious that Schneider's ASA cycle is not new in its components because many have suggested that people are differentially attracted to organizations, or that people are differentially selected by organizations, or that people differentially leave organizations; the major contribution of the Schneider proposal is that all of these happen for an organization and that the outcome of all of these happening is relative homogeneity of personality in organizations. The earliest paper we have found that addresses components of the later ASA model is one by Betz and Judkins (1975). Betz and Judkins were sociologists who became interested in the issues of the relative contribution of selective attraction and socialization to long-term organizational member attitudes. They studied 384 high school teachers and which of two unions they joined after becoming teachers. They showed that teachers who joined any union were different from those who did not join a union, and that teachers who joined one of the unions were significantly different from those who joined the other union. Betz and Judkins (p. 238) concluded that "These organizations appear to attract individuals with attitudes largely developed before membership; individuals appear to be attracted toward organizations whose membership will be supportive of their attitudes."

Etzioni (1975), another sociologist, also identified components of the ASA model as a base for understanding organizational behavior. Etzioni (pp. 433–434) discussed the idea that organizations differ in the compliance patterns required for organizational effectiveness: "In addition to positions requiring different types of compliance, there are actors who differ in the type of compliance they can effectively achieve and sustain, and these individuals tend to be recruited into positions requiring the compliance pattern for which they are suited. The distribution, of actors and positions, is related in such a way that effectiveness is supported, though never maximized, because the mechanisms which distribute persons to positions—self-selection and organizational selection—are imperfect." We clearly see in this quotation attraction and selection and, by inference, attrition. In addition, we infer that particular organizations, requiring specific forms of compliance, will have in their management specific kinds of people.

It is perhaps not surprising that early thinking on topics that reflect an ASA conceptualization were done by sociologists. These scholars are used to thinking about people in the aggregate. Unlike psychologists, they have not been overly burdened by the conceptual and methodological issues that have had an inhibitory effect on us moving to levels of analysis above the individual (cf. Ashkanasy et al., 2000; Klein & Kozlowski, 2000).

In the next section we review in more detail work that has recently been accomplished on attraction, selection, and attrition in organizations. The purpose of this review is to show how the outcomes from these processes can be used to infer that for any one organization the chances are good that the range of personalities there will be relatively narrow and constrained. It is this constrained or narrowed range of personalities that we argue serve as the base for organizational culture.

Since the ASA model was introduced there have been numerous studies of especially the attraction and selection portion of it. Although much of the research on these facets of the model has been summarized previously (Schneider, Goldstein, & Smith, 1995), we present here research for the most part done since about 1994 that is relevant to the model. In brief, what the research shows is that there is differential attraction, selection, and attrition into and out of organizations that can be predicted based on the degree to which the person fits (objectively, subjectively, or both) the attributes of the organization.

Attraction

Cable and Judge (1996) for example, in various combinations have produced a series of studies relevant to the ASA model. Cable and Judge (1996) conducted both a lab and field study and both revealed some interactions suggesting that particular kinds of organizational characteristics were more attractive to some job seekers than to others. For example, they showed that "Job seekers with an internal locus of control were more attracted to organizations offering flexible benefits than those with an external locus of control. Individualists were more attracted to individual-based pay plans than collectivists. Job seekers with high self-efficacy were more likely to pursue an organization with individual-based pay than were those with low self-efficacy" (p. 341).

Judge and Cable (1997) collected data on 182 students who were seeking jobs. They used the five-factor model (FFM) of personality (Costa

& McCrae, 1992) as the individual measure and the Organizational Culture Profile (OCP; O'Reilly, Chatman, & Caldwell, 1991) to assess applicants' perceptions of the organizational culture of companies with whom they interviewed. They proposed a series of hypotheses about relationships between FFM scores and OCP preferences and found support for a large proportion of them. In addition, they showed that both objective fit (fit of applicants' own OCP values to their OCP preferences) and subjective fit (how well applicants reported they fit the organizations after interviewing with them) predicted the attraction of the organization to them 3 months later.

In a similar study with a longer (6-month) time frame, Cable and Judge (1997) showed (with another sample of college student job seekers) that again positive fit perceptions were predicted by perceived organizational OCP values and the students' own OCP values and that fit itself predicted job-incumbent organizational commitment, job satisfaction, turnover intentions, and willingness to recommend their organization to others after they were on the job for 6 months.

A neat twist on this line of research on attraction was accomplished by Scott (2000). She assessed the moral values of 413 entering MBA students and then followed them to see which of 100 organizations they bid for as an organization in which to do their internship. She coded the 100 organizations for their moral values via content analysis of the materials they had left for potential applicant review in the school's career development office. Analyses revealed that both organizational values and the fit of individual values to organizational values predicted the bid students made to be interviewed by one or more of the 100 companies. Although not all hypotheses were supported in this study, Scott (p. 424) concluded that: "Values and values-fit seem to matter for applicants."

Note that, as with Holland's work, the criterion of interest in the work by Cable and Judge and Scott just reviewed concerns individual consequences—what they report at a later time, their turnover, and so forth. This approach has also been used for research that has been done on the selection portion of the ASA model.

Selection

Cable and Judge (1997), for example, studied 38 interviewers making hiring recommendations about 93 job applicants. Interviewers were asked to complete the OCP about their own organization's values and their perceptions of their interviewees' values. In addition, interviewers reported their subjective assessment of interviewee fit to the organization and their recommendation regarding the hiring of the interviewee. Interviewees completed the OCP to reveal their own values. Finally, information about the organization's actual hiring decisions regarding the applicants was gathered.

Results revealed the following: (1) Interviewer perceptions of applicant fit were predicted by objective fit, (2) interviewer subjective fit perceptions significantly influenced their hiring recommendations, and (3) interviewer hiring recommendations predicted the organizational decisions to hire or not to hire. Cable and Judge (1997, p. 556) commented: "This cumulative set of findings is consistent with past practitioner-oriented research (e.g., Bowen et al., 1991) and also confirms the selection component of Schneider's (1987) model." Not so incidentally, Rynes and Gerhart (1990) also showed that interviewers use their judgments of fit of the applicant to the organization when considering their hiring recommendations.

Van Vianen and Kmieciak (1998) studied the selection issue when they explored the relationship between recruiters' perceptions of their organization's climate and their image of the personality of the ideal candidate for the organization. Van Vianen and Kmieciak studied 124 recruiters for Dutch firms and asked them to report on the climate of their organization and then to complete a personality questionnaire describing the ideal applicant for their company. Some weak support was found for a fit or match of these two variables, and where the support existed it concerned the fact that the ideal candidate would be high on conscientiousness when the climate is perceived as having less emphasis on control.

Another study relevant to the selection—this time self-selection—portion of the ASA framework was accomplished by Ryan, Sacco, McFarland, and Kriska (2000). Ryan et al. studied self-selection in a multiple hurdle process designed for hiring police officers. On a sample of 3,500 police officer applicants they showed that, among other findings, lack of perceived person–organization fit was a major reason for people self-selecting out of the selection process.

Attrition

With regard to the attrition portion of the ASA model, the most frequently cited studies are those conducted by Chatman and her colleagues (Chatman, 1991; O'Reilly et al., 1991). This work explored the relationship between the fit of accounting firm applicants' values to the values of those accounting firms. Firm values (culture) were defined by incumbent reports on the values that characterized their firm. Applicants used the same values and sorted them according to the degree to which they accurately characterized themselves. The OCP was the measure used in this research. Results showed that good fit of applicant values to accounting firm values predicted job satisfaction, organizational commitment, performance, and turnover.

In addition to the work they did on the attraction portion of the ASA model, Cable and Parsons (2001) further extended the time involved in another study relevant to the attrition portion of the model. In this project they studied 101 graduate students (the final number on whom all data were collected) over a 2-year period beginning with when the students entered the job market. Initially they collected applicant OCP values. One year later the sample was again surveyed, this time regarding their perceived fit with their employing organization, the socialization tactics the organization used, and their perceptions of their employing organization's values. One year later (2 years after initial data collection) individuals' OCP values were again assessed and information was collected on whether they were still employed at the same organization. Results revealed the following: (1) Some socialization tactics are positively related to perceptions of fit, (2) the fit of preentry values to postentry perceptions of their organization's values predicted their fit perceptions, and (3) both fit of preentry values and organizational values (objective fit) and subjective fit predicted long-term tenure in the original organization. These results, of course, support the attrition portion of the ASA model, with those objectively and subjectively fitting least well being the ones most likely to leave the organization.

In summary, these studies strongly support the conclusion that there is differential attraction, selection, and attrition into and out of organizations. It is a small inferential leap from this conclusion to the notion that people who enter an organization as a result of attraction and selection (including self-selection) and who stay with it because they fit it better are more similar to each other than they are to those who are employed elsewhere. What evidence is there for this conclusion?

Tests of the Homogeneity Hypothesis in the ASA Model

There have been two major studies of the homogeneity hypothesis, one by Schneider, Smith, Taylor, and Fleenor (1998), and one by Schaubroeck, Ganster, and Jones (1998). Schneider et al. (1998) studied 13,000 managers from 130 public and private organizations and assessed the degree to which there was a main effect for organization on personality. All managers had been part of a leadership training program at the Center for Creative Leadership where they had completed the Myers-Briggs Type Indicator (MBTI). Using MANOVA, Schneider et al. (1998) showed both organization and industry effects on personality. In other words they showed that (a) the personality attributes of managers in different industries were significantly different and (b) that the personality attributes of managers in different organizations were significantly different. Schneider et al. (1998) collected no data on the organizations themselves so they were unable to explore the degree to which these aggregate personality differences were reflected in organizational culture.

Schaubroeck et al. (1998) collected both personality and culture data in their study. They studied 681 people (all levels, not just managers) employed in five organizations. They administered a series of measures of 10 facets of personality to the sample of employees several days prior to administration of the other surveys. The other surveys assessed organization and job structure (culture for our purposes) along six dimensions, occupation type (dichotomized as mental and social), and intentions to remain. In brief, their results revealed the following: (1) main effects for personality on organizational culture with 7 of 10 personality facets significantly reflected in organizational culture factors; (2) main effects for personality on occupation; (3) an occupation × organization interaction on personality; and (4) turnover intentions moderated all relationships with the results being significantly weaker for those most likely to leave. It should also be noted that organizational contrasts revealed significant between-organization differences; that is, within organizations there was sharedness in perceptions of the organizational culture. As Schaubroeck et al. (p. 884) noted, "The overall pattern of results is highly suggestive of B. Schneider's (1987) hypothesis that organizational and occupational factors are determinants of the types of persons who tend to join and remain in settings."

In a similar study Resick, Giberson, and Dickson (2002) investigated the relationship between aggregate employee personality and perceptions of organizational culture. They collected personality (individual values) and culture data from 467 individuals in 32 organizations. There results suggested that aggregate personality predicts organizational culture. For instance, aggregate values of benevolence and affiliation were related to group-oriented cultures. Their results provide one of the few direct linkages between aggregate personality chacteristics and organizational culture variables.

An intriguing study that is related to the Schaubroeck et al. research is one conducted by De Fruyt and Mervielde (1999). De Fruyt and Mervielde studied MBA graduates in Belgium who had taken both the NEO PI-R (Costa & McCrae, 1992) and Holland's Self-Directed Search, the latter yielding scores on Holland's six factors, the former yielding data representing the five-factor model. Though De Fruyt and Mervielde did not collect data on the kinds of organizations in which people were employed, they showed that the NEO PI-R predicted whether people were employed a year later whereas Holland's model predicted the kinds of jobs at which those who were employed were working. Our prediction is that, had they collected data on the kinds of organizations where people were employed, they would have found that the personality data predicted this affiliation and Holland's vocational types would have predicted which jobs they had.

Summary

In sum, these results on tests of the homogeneity hypothesis, supported by the fairly extensive research that now exists on the various components of the ASA model, suggest that there is now some reason to believe that Schneider is correct and that, over time, organizations as a function of the ASA cycle come to contain people with similar personalities.

EFFECTS OF INDIVIDUAL PERSONALITY ON ORGANIZATIONAL CULTURE

The just-completed review focuses on research suggestive of the idea that aggregates of individuals of a similar personality likely end up in organizations with others like them. The results are further suggestive of the prediction (Resvick et al., 2000; Schaubroeck et al., 1998) that these aggregate personality differences are reflected in organizational culture. In this section we turn to another important potential linkage, that of the relationship of the individual personality to organizational culture.

The genesis of this idea rests on the early work of Lewin (e.g., Lewin, Lippitt, & White, 1939) and the later writings of Argyris (1957) and McGregor (1960). Lewin et al. proposed that the behavior of leaders creates a social climate, such climate being defined by the reactions of followers to the leader and to each other and their general affective behavior displays. A somewhat later version of this research was conducted by Litwin and Stringer (1968) who showed that leaders who behave in achievement, power, and affiliation styles can actually create in followers the needs for achievement, power, and affiliation.

As noted earlier, Argyris proposed that the way managers/leaders behave toward their employees (to infantilize them) gets reflected in the way employees in turn behave, reinforcing manager behavior towards them. McGregor (1960) proposed that managers, by their behavior toward subordinates, create a managerial climate of trust and fairness (or lack of trust and lack of fairness) that is reflected in the way their followers in turn behave. The famous theory X and theory Y are tightly connected to this managerial climate.

Argyris and McGregor, in particular, implicitly seem to assume that the behavior of the leader is a function of the leaders' personality (broadly conceived). McGregor (1960, p. 35), for example, merely states that "At the core of any theory of the management of human resources are assumptions about human motivation. Here, then, assumptions become the individual differences variable of interest." In a somewhat later work, McGregor (1967, p. 58) is more expansive on this issue: "We have examined a number of variables that exert an important influence on the manager's behavior as a manager: his beliefs about the nature of man and about cause-effect in human behavior (his cosmology), his perceptions of the role pressures that he faces in performing his job, his personal values, his needs, his perception of his own capabilities."

Argyris (1957; 1960) was more explicit in his perspective regarding the cultural consequences of management though the issue of individual differences in the personality of managers is difficult to find. Argyris focused more on the nature of formal organizations and the consequences of the way formal organizations are run for the way employees behave. Thus, his vantage point was that many (though not all) formal organizations make requirements on workers that are inconsistent with a mature adult personality (dependence, subordination, passivity, etc.) and several negative consequences follow. These consequences include employee frustration, feelings of failure, short time perspective, and the experience of conflict "... because as healthy agents they will dislike frustration, failure, and short time perspective which is characteristic of the present job" (Argyris, 1960, p. 15).

Although the role of manager or leader personality in the works just reviewed is difficult to see, we make the assumption that not all managers behave similarly and that the resultant differences in organizations are a function of these differences in managers. Argyris explicitly notes that he is not addressing all organizations or all managers but, for purposes of exposition, has chosen to focus on a narrow range of organizations and managers. What evidence is there for the assumption that individual differences in leaders and managers produce differences in culture?

Miller et al.

An early conceptualization and study of the relationship between manager/leader personality and organizational culture was presented by Miller, Kets de Vries, and Toulouse (1982). Early in the paper they note that "... the psychological approach [to understanding organizational phenomena] views behavior in and around organizations as a function of the personalities and capacities of specific individuals" (Miller et al., p. 237). Miller et al. conceptualized the effects of the personality of the CEO of organizations based on the internal–external locus of control proposals of Rotter (1966). They proposed that the more internal the CEO, the more innovative, risky, and future oriented the firm would be. In addition, they proposed that the more internal the CEO, the more the firm was likely a leader rather than a follower and that the firm would actually function in a more dynamic and heterogeneous environment.

To test the propositions, Miller et al. (1982) administered Rotter's (1966) measure of locus of control to the CEOs of 33 business firms of various sizes and in different industries. The strategy and organizational attributes (culture) data were collected via survey items administered through personal interviews with the CEOs and at least one other member of the top management team of the firms.

Results revealed strong support for the idea that CEO locus of control is reflected in organizational cultural variables. Organizational innovation, risk taking, proactiveness, and future orientation were significantly correlated with internal locus of control. In addition, internals operated firms that were in more dynamic and heterogeneous environments, and the firms themselves were seen as engaging in more environmental scanning and were more differentiated. The consistency and level of these relationships (*r*s in the .25 to .70 range) were quite striking.

Even more striking, given the ASA model as a potentially useful organizing scheme, were post hoc analyses Miller et al. ran in an attempt to provide some preliminary evidence on the issue of causality. Thus they, like Schneider et al. (1998), proceeded under the hypothesis that it was the CEO personality that eventuated in the cultural issues assessed. But they, like Schaubroeck et al. (1998), explored the role of tenure in the observed relationships. That is, they hypothesized that the relationships between CEO locus of control and the culture variables would be stronger for longer-tenured CEOs than for shorter-tenured CEOs and that is what they found. In addition, arguing that if CEO personality is the cause, then the effects should be more dramatic in smaller than larger firms—that is, it takes a shorter time in a smaller firm for a CEO to have an effect. In fact, the split on large versus small firms revealed significant differences in the relationship between CEO personality and the culture variables in the expected directions—in smaller firms the relationships were more consistent and consistently stronger.

In a later similar study, Miller and Droge (1986) focused on the relationship between personality and organizational structure, with the personality variable this time being need for achievement. Miller and Droge proposed that CEO need for achievement would be positively reflected in firm centralization of authority, formalization, complexity, and integration. As control variables, they assessed not only CEO need for achievement but the structural issues of size and technology so they could explore the relative contribution of CEO need for achievement and these structural issues as correlates of the four structural variables of interest. Finally they, like Miller et al. (1982), explored the hypothesized relationships in large versus small firms.

The sample consisted of 93 privately and publicly held firms in diverse industries. CEOs completed the need for achievement measure and the structure questionnaire; the most senior vice president or the general manager also completed the structure questionnaire, and all questionnaires were administered via individual interviews. Results revealed that, especially in small and young firms, CEO need for achievement is an important predictor of organizational structure: "In these kinds of firms [small and young], the more achievement-oriented the CEO, the more he or she centralizes power and employs instruments of formalization such as written policies and procedures, financial, performance, and quality controls and functional specialization. High achievers appear to favor rather centralized, highly structured, and well-integrated organizations that allow them to take the major credit for, and to carefully monitor and control, corporate performance" (Miller & Droge, 1986, p. 554).

Frese

It is interesting to frame this early work in the light of a very interesting research program being conducted by Frese and his colleagues in the former East Germany (Frese, Kring, Soose, & Zempel, 1996; Utsch, Rauch, Rothfuss, & Frese, undated). This research program conceptualized the issues of motivation and firm performance in East Germany in terms of personal initiative and asked questions about the status of personal initiative in a country that had been dominated by a communistic ethos. In one study, Utsch et al. asked the question: Who becomes a small scale entrepreneur in a post-Socialist environment? They contrasted the personalities of small-scale entrepreneurs and the managers of small-scale companies in the former East Germany ($N = 162$ entrepreneurs and $N = 75$ managers) and found that entrepreneurs were more achievement oriented, autonomous, innovative, and aggressive than were their counterpart managers. Using discriminant analysis, Utsch et al. were able to classify 79 percent of the sample correctly based on their personality data on these four issues. Of course, based on the results of Miller and his colleagues (1982), we might further predict that these entrepreneurs would structure their firms and adopt specific strategies as a function of how high they scored on these achievement-oriented personality measures.

Furnham and Stringfield

In a similar venture, Furnham and Stringfield (1993) conducted what could have been a potentially interesting study of the relationship between managerial personality and organizational climate (culture). In this project the sample had both Chinese and Western managers and employed the MBTI as the personality predictor. Data on climate were gathered from subordinates who also rated the performance of their manager. Rating both performance and climate may have yielded unknown confounds in the data, and in addition, there were strong cultural differences in the findings. So, although Furnham and Stringfield found some significant relationships between MBTI scales and climate, the results need to be interpreted with caution. On the other hand, given that there is such little research of this kind, it is useful to know about their project.

We should note that there is evidence in the literature that caution is the appropriate position with regard to the relationship between MBTI and organizational culture. Walck (1997) reviewed five studies accomplished over a 35-year period, none of which substantiated the implied link between MBTI type and climate or culture. In addition, Gardner and Martinko (1996) in their very extensive review of the literature on the MBTI report no studies of the link between MBTI type and culture, perhaps because all of their focus was on the individual level of analysis. But Gardner and Martinko make one methodological point in particular with regard to the MBTI that is worth noting here: Use continuous scale scores rather than type as the operationalization of the personality preferences. It is possible, as they note, that continuous scale scores have superior measurement properties than do types and this difference might be one (among numerous) reasons for lack of validity evidence for the MBTI as expected.

Lastly, Giberson, Resick, and Dickson (2003), conducted similar research on the relationship between leader personality and organizational culture. Examining personality data from leaders of 32 organizations and organizational culture data from 467 subordinates in those 32 organizations revealed specific linkages between leader personality and organization culture. For instance, leader agreeableness predicted group-oriented cultures, leader emotional stability predicted developmental cultures, and leader extroversion predicted hierarchical cultures.

Summary

The research on the relationship between the personality of an individual leader, manager, or CEO and organizational couture, as the reader can see, is scant. What literature does exist, however, suggests that differences in leader personality yield differences in organizational attributes. In the next section we further explore the conceptual issues surrounding this cross-level hypothesis.

APPLICATION OF THE PERSONALITY–ORGANIZATIONAL CULTURE LOGIC

The logic in the work by Miller and his colleagues (1982) reviewed earlier is that (a) leaders/managers have an effect and, further, that (b) leaders with different personality characteristics have different effects. There is a vast literature on the former and as we have recently demonstrated a scant literature on the latter. In fact, by this point in the chapter we have pretty much exhausted the works we have found relevant to the issue at hand. What is surprising to us, of course, is the paucity of research on the effects of leader personality on the vast domain of issues we have called here *organizational culture*.

This lack is surprising to us because there is such a vast literature that exhorts leaders to do this and that and the other thing to be an effective leader as if by knowing this advice leaders would be more effective! Psychologists interested in personality, on the other hand, have studied leader traits and related those trait attributes only to individual-level achievements (like salary or level achieved compared to cohort, or some performance-appraisal rating, or even 360° feedback ratings of the individual). Rarely, as we have shown, are relationships explored between personality and the creation of context—between personality and the creation of culture.

One of the more creative attempts to conceptualize this issue is found in a chapter by Born and Jansen (1997). They asked the question of the kinds of personality attributes required in leaders who can effectively manage an organizational turnaround. By even asking this question, they separated themselves from what we have come to call the *myth of infinite flexibility*. This myth is one that means that if you tell them what to do, anyone can do it. Born and Jansen (p. 255) clearly state the issue: "In the preceding section we argued that, in general, a turnaround implies that leaders are required to be effective in another way. That implies that other competencies, maybe even another style of leadership, are needed."

Born and Jansen (1997) do a very nice job of pulling together diverse studies relevant to their criterion of interest, that criterion ultimately being organizational change. Although we could quibble with the inclusion of some studies that focus on purely individual levels of analysis, they conclude as follows: "Turnaround managers often will have to deal with re-interpretation of reality. Transformational leadership is suggested as an effective way of leading turnaround. Environmental awareness, persuasiveness, internal locus of control and prudent risk-taking, among other things, have been found to be important personality factors of leaders of organizational change" (p. 263).

There are more applications of the notion that organizations require specific personalities for organizational-level goal accomplishment, though few of them are stated explicitly as personality requirements. The current theme in the practice literature is *competencies* defined as sets of attributes the organization requires in its employees for organizational effectiveness. The broad competencies are less detailed than the classical KSAOs of the job analysis tradition, but they permit macro specification of organizational requirements across jobs. For example, Higgs, Papper, and Carr (2000) note that Ford has 12 leadership behaviors on which they focus human resources (HR) processes including selection, and that Sears has 9 such leadership competencies on which they focus HR processes. Higgs et al. go on to note that the companies they spoke with as a base for their chapter tended to use these competency models as a base for selection and perhaps performance management, especially for selection of leaders, but that they tended not to be fully integrated across the broad range of HR processes. They further note that organizations could use selection to optimize such processes as belief in the mission of the organization, common attitudes or values, comfort with or preference for the work environment offered, and so forth. However, they were unable to find examples of organizations actively using selection in this way. As we have shown, of course, organizations actually do seem to be using selection as a basis for making hiring decisions but they are doing so informally and/or implicitly through recruiters and interviewers.

Silzer (1998) reports similar findings. He looked at what organizations are doing to integrate their strategy with the identification of the future leaders who might be required to carry out those strategies. Silzer makes a persuasive argument that organizations have typically done a poor job of integrating strategy with selection of leaders and, he argues, this yields haphazard hiring, a failure to plan effectively for the future needs of the organization, and so forth.

A very attractive feature of the paper by Silzer (1998) is its focus on the individual assessment of higher-level executives as leaders (as compared, for example, to the selection of managers; see Fogli & Whitney, 1998). Thus, much of what we have discussed to this point in the chapter concerns the use of personality questionnaires, but it is probably true that more executives are hired on the basis of individual assessment strategies than personality data collected with paper-and-pencil personality instruments.

Silzer (1998) makes the point that management and executives who go through an individual assessment process as part of their recruitment are being hired to produce organizational effects. Typically, then, the issue is one in which the company confronts some need for change or need to implement a new strategy, and the goal is to hire people who can make this happen. The goal of such hiring procedures is organizational performance. This goal holds true for all of the examples we have presented in this section of the chapter.

Our logic tells us (see Fig. 13.1) that organizations need to be more sophisticated than they apparently are in making such hiring decisions. They must focus ultimately, of course, on achieving the goal of organizational performance. But our loigic indicates that this is a disatal issue, one that will be achievable through the organizational culture created by the leaders hired. Thus, the reason that culture is important is that focusing only on outcome can yield a host of long-term negative consequences. As a simple example, it has long been known that autocratic leadership can yield equivalent levels of performance to democratic leadership (Lewin et al., 1939) but the consequences in morale and attitudes can be severe for the long term.

We also want to note that the focus on bringing in change agents through management and executive selection is a healthy one. Thus, in keeping with the ASA model, we recommend that organizations define their future needs and bring people into leadership positions that are at least somewhat different from those who have been in leadership positions in the past. The alternate perspectives such people can bring to the needs of the organization for the future can be salutary, and, although this strategy can create some tension and discomfort for those already there, such tension may be beneficial in the long run. Silzer (1998, p. 437) puts it this way: "Often organizations drift into habits that encourage the proliferation of certain types of individuals, and are not fully aware of the extent to which a skewed distribution of skills may exist in the organization. ... Leadership diversity is often critical if the organization must adapt to a variety of business situations."

SUMMARY AND CONCLUSION

Our goal in writing this chapter was to review some of the linkages in a cross-level model of individual personality and organizational culture. We showed (a) that there is evidence indicating that organizations seem to attract, select, and retain people with common personality attributes and that those personality attributes define organizations and are related to organizational culture, (b) that the personality of a single leader, manager, or CEO can influence organizational culture and structure, and (c) that the literature on organizational change presents some insightful indicants of the importance of certain personality attributes in leaders if change is to occur (including turnarounds). Finally, we expressed some dismay at the paucity of research on the organizational consequences for both personality in the aggregate and the personality of individual leaders.

ACKNOWLEGMENT

We benefited greatly from comments on an earlier version by Jonathan Ziegert and Beng-Chong Lim.

REFERENCES

Argyris, C. (1957). Some problems in conceptualizing organizational clime: A case study of a bank. *Administrative Science Quarterly, 2*, 501–520.

Argyris, C. (1960). *Understanding organizational behavior.* Homewood, IL: Dorsey.

Ashkanasy, N. M., Wilderom, C. P. M., & Peterson, M. F. (2000). Introduction. In N. M. Ashkanasy, C. P. M. Wilderom, & M. F. Peterson (Eds.), *Handbook of organizational culture and climate* (pp. 1–20). Thousand Oaks, CA: Sage.

Astin, A. W. (1965). Classroom environments in different fields of study. *Journal of Educational Psychology, 56*, 275–282.

Astin, A. W., & Holland, J. L. (1961). The Environmental Assessment Technique: A new way to measure college environments. *Journal of Educational Psychology, 52*, 308–316.

Betz, M., & Judkins, B. B. (1975). The impact of voluntary association characteristics on selective attraction and socialization. *The Sociological Quarterly, 16*, 228–240.

Born, M. Ph., & Jansen, P. G. W. (1997). Selection and assessment during organizational turnaround. In N. Anderson, & P. Herriot (Eds.), *International handbook of selection & assessment* (pp. 247–265). New York: Wiley.

Bowen, D. E., Ledford Jr., G. E., & Nathan, B. R. (1991) Hiring for the organization, not the job. *Academy of Management Executive, 5*, 35–52.

Cable, D. M., & Judge, T. A. (1996). Person-organization fit, job choice decisions, and organizational entry. *Organizational Behavior and Human Decision Processes, 67*, 294–311.

Cable, D. M., & Judge, T. A. (1997). Interviewers' perceptions of person-organization fit and organizational selection decisions. *Journal of Applied Psychology, 82*, 546–561.

Cable, D. M., & Parsons, C. K. (2001). Socialization tactics and person-organization fit. *Personnel Psychology, 54*, 1–24.

Chatman, J. (1991). Matching people and organizations: Selection and socialization in public accounting firms. *Administrative Science Quarterly, 36*, 459–484.

Costa, P. T., Jr., & McCrae, R. P. (1992). *NEO PI-R professional manual.* Odessa, FL: Psychological Assessment Resources.

Costa, P. T., Jr., McCrae, R. P., Zonderman, A. B., Barbano, H. E., Leibowitz, B., & Larson, D. M. (1986). Cross-sectional stability studies of personality in a national sample: 2. Stability in neuroticism, extraversion, and openness. *Psychology and Aging, 1*, 144–149.

De Fruyt, F., & Mervielde, I. (1999). RIASEC types and Big Five traits as predictors of employment status and nature of employment. *Personnel Psychology, 52*, 701–727.

Etzioni, A. (1975). *A comparative analysis of complex organizations (Rev. ed.).* New York: Free Press.

Fogli, L. & Whitney, K. (1998). Assessing and changing managers for new organizational roles. In R. Jeanneret & R. Silzer (Eds.), *Individual psychological assessment: Predicting behavior in organizational settings* (pp. 285–329). San Francisco: Jossey-Bass.

Frese, M., Kring, W., Soose, A., & Zemple, J. (1996). Personal initiative at work: Difference between East and West Germany. *Academy of Management Journal, 39*, 37–63

Furnham, A. (2001). Vocational preferences and P-O fit: Reflections on Holland's theory of vocational choice. *International Review of Applied Psychology, 50*, 5–29.

Furnham, A., & Stringfield, P. (1993). Personality and occupational behavior: Myers-Briggs Type Indicator correlates of managerial practices in two cultures. *Human Relations, 46*, 827–848.

Gardner, W. L., & Martinko, M. J. (1996). Using the Myers-Briggs Type Indicator to study managers: A literature review and research agenda. *Journal of Management, 22*, 45–83.

Giberson, T., Resick, C., & Dickson, M. W. (2003). *The effects of leader personality and values on follower characteristics, organizational demographics, and organizational culture.* Unpublished manuscript.

Higgs, A. C., Papper, E. M., & Carr, L. S. (2000). Integrating selection with other organizational processes and systems. In J. F. Kehoe (Ed.), *Managing selection in changing organizations: Human resource strategies* (pp. 73–122). San Francisco: Jossey-Bass.

Holland, J. L. (1966). *The psychology of vocational choice*. Waltham, MA: Blaisdell.

Holland, J. L. (1973). *Making vocational choices*. Englewood Cliffs, NJ: Prentice Hall.

Holland, J. L. (1997). *Making vocational choices: A theory of vocational personalities and work environments (3rd ed)*. Odessa, FL: Psychological Assessment Resources.

House, R. J., Rousseau, D. M., & Thomas-Hunt, M. (1995). The meso paradigm: A framework for the integration of micro and macro organizational behavior. In L. L. Cummings & B. M. Staw (Eds.), *Research in organizational behavior* (Vol. 17, pp. 71–114). Greenwich, CT: JAI.

Judge, T. A., & Cable, D. M. (1997). Applicant personality, organizational culture, and organization attraction. *Personnel Psychology, 50*, 359–394.

Klein, K. J., & Kozlowski, S. W. J. (Eds.). (2000). *Multilevel theory, research, and methods in organizations: Foundations, extensions, and new directions*. San Francisco, CA: Jossey-Bass.

Lewin, K., Lippitt, R., & White, R. K. (1939). Patterns of aggressive behavior in experimentally created social climates. *Journal of Social Psychology, 10*, 271–301.

Linton, R. (1945). *The cultural background of personality*. New York: Century.

Litwin, G. H., & Stringer, R. A., Jr. (1968). *Motivation and organizational climate*. Boston: Harvard Business School.

Maslow, A. (1954). *Motivation and personality*. New York: Harper.

McCaulley, M. H. (1990). The Myers-Briggs Type Indicator and leadership. In K. E. Clark & M. B. Clark (Eds.), *Measures of leadership* (pp. 381–418). Greensboro, NC: Center for Creative Leadership.

McGregor, D. (1960). *The human side of enterprise*. New York: McGraw-Hill.

McGregor, D. (1967). *The professional manager*. New York: McGraw-Hill.

Miller, D., & Droge, C. (1986). Psychological and traditional determinants of structure. *Administrative Science Quarterly, 31*, 539–560.

Miller, D., Kets de Vries, M. F. R., & Toulouse, J-M (1982). Top executive locus of control and its relationship to strategy-making, structure, and environment. *Academy of Management Journal, 25*, 237–253.

Muchinsky, P. (1999). Applications of Holland's theory in industrial and organizational settings. *Journal of Vocational Behavior, 55*, 127–135.

O'Reilly, C. A., Chatman, J., & Caldwell, D. F. (1991). People and organizational culture: A profile comparison approach to assessing person-organization fit. *Academy of Management Journal, 34*, 487–516.

Resick, C. J., Giberson, T. R., & Dickson, M. W. (2002, April). Linking shared personality and values to organizational culture. Poster presented at the annual conference of the Society of Industrial and Organizational Psychology. Toronto, Canada.

Rotter, Julian B. (1966). Generalized expectancies for internal versus external control of reinforcement. *Psychological Monographs, 80*(1, Whole No. 609).

Ryan, A. M., Sacco, J. M., McFarland, L. A., & Kriska, S. D. (2000). Applicant self-selection: Correlates of withdrawal from a multiple hurdle process. *Journal of Applied Psychology, 85*, 163–179.

Rynes, S., & Gerhart, B. (1990). Interviewer assessments of applicant "fit": An exploratory investigation. *Personnel Psychology, 43*, 13–22.

Schaubroeck, J., Ganster, D. C., & Jones, J. R. (1998). Organization and occupation influences in the attraction-selection-attrition process. *Journal of Applied Psychology, 83*, 869–891.

Schein, E. A. (1992). *Organizational culture and leadership, (2nd ed.)*. San Francisco: Jossey-Bass.

Schneider, B. (1987). The people make the place. *Personnel Psychology, 40*, 437–453.

Schneider, B. (1990). The climate for service: An application of the climate construct. In B. Schneider (Ed.), *Organizational climate and culture* (pp. 393–412). San Francisco, CA: Jossey-Bass.

Schneider, B., Goldstein, H. W., & Smith, D. B. (1995). The attraction-selection-attrition framework: An update. *Personnel Psychology, 48,* 747–773.

Schneider, B., Smith, D. B., & Sipe, W. P. (2000). Personnel selection psychology: Multilevel considerations. In K. J. Klein & S. W. J. Kozlowski (Eds.), *Multilevel theory, research, and methods in organizations: Foundations, extensions, and new directions.* San Francisco: Jossey-Bass.

Schneider, B., Smith, D. B., Taylor, S., & Fleenor, J. (1998). Personality and organization: A test of the homogeneity of personality hypothesis. *Journal of Applied Psychology, 83,* 462–470.

Schwartz, R. (1992). Is Holland's theory worthy of so much attention or should vocational psychology move on? *Journal of Vocational Behavior, 40,* 179–187.

Scott, E. D. (2000). Moral values fit: Do applicants really care? *Teaching Business Ethics, 4,* 405–435.

Silzer, R. (1998). Shaping organizational leadership: The ripple effect of assessment. In R. Jeanneret & R. Silzer (Eds.), *Individual psychological assessment: Predicting behavior in organizational setting* (pp. 391–441). San Francisco: Jossey-Bass.

Trice, H. M., & Beyer, J. M. (1993). *The cultures of work organizations.* Englewood Cliffs, NJ: Prentice Hall.

Utsch, A., Rauch, A., Rothfuss, R., & Frese, M. (Undated). *Who becomes a small-scale entrepreneur in a post-socialist environment: On the differences between entrepreneurs and managers in East Germany.* Germany: Department of Psychology, University of Giessen.

Van Vianen, A. E. M., & Kmieciak, Y. M. (1998). The match between recruiters' perceptions of organizational climate and personality of the ideal applicant for a management position. *International Journal of Selection and Assessment, 6,* 153–163.

Walck, C. L. (1997). Using the MBTI in management and leadership: A review of the literature. In C. Fitzgerald & L. K. Kirby (Eds.), *Developing leaders: Research and applications in psychological type and leadership development.* Palo Alto, CA: Davies-Black.

Williams, L. K. (1968). Personality and organizational behavior studies. In B. P. Indik & F. K. Berrien (Eds.), *People, groups, and organizations* (pp. 154–171). New York: Teachers College Press.

Reflections on Personality and Organization

Chris Argyris
Harvard University

The editors have asked that I reflect on the context of organizational research in the early 1950s and 1960s and then use the context to frame my own views of the relationship between the individual and the organization. Some have called this period the golden age of organizational research (Schneider, Smith, & Sipe, 2000).

The first feature of this age was that World War II had just ended. Many of us returned with an unabashed commitment to use social science theories and methodologies to help produce a better world. We knew that the first step would be to describe the world as it was, to document its inconsistencies in the service of developing a better fit between individuals and organizations. For example, McGregor stated (Heil, Bennis, & Stephens, 2000):

> We will succeed in increasing our utilization of human potential in organizational settings only as we succeed in creating conditions that generate a meaningful way of life... (p. 3)
>
> Perhaps the greatest disparity between reality and managerial perceptions is an underestimation of the potentialities of human beings for contribution to organizational effectiveness... (p. 19)
>
> I see a genuine potential for linkage of self-actualization with organizational goals... (p. 33)

These quotes illustrate two normative assumptions that many of the researchers held during this era. First, the world could be made into a better place. Second, it was the responsibility of social scientists to specify how to achieve this goal.

A third assumption was that this world did not exist and therefore it had to be created. The task of social science research was to create rare events that would persevere. A fourth assumption was that in order to create rare events, theories about what the universe looks like are required. But equally important are theories about what the new universe might be. It was important to specify causally how to get from here to there. The reason that causal specification was necessary was that in the interest of validity, the new domain that had to be created had to be tested empirically.

It follows that the primary methodology had to be one that could be used to actually create phenomena, not simply describe them. Intervention was the primary methodology to fulfill these requirements. Recalling the activities of some of the early founders, we note that Likert and his colleagues conducted field experiments where they attempted changes in the organizations. I conducted interventions at the upper levels of organizations in order to alter managerial values and behavior. McGregor became an interventionist when he accepted the presidency of Antioch College in order to try to change universities. William F. Whyte conducted interventions, not only in business organizations, but within trade unions with the intention to enhance the members' power and the unions' performance.

The emphasis on intervention to create rare events implied a major addition to the ideas in good currency about establishing validity of research findings. As always, it was important for researchers to establish internal and external validities for their findings. Internal validity had to do with the internal logical and conceptual consistency of theory as well as its operationability. External validity had to do with the claim that whatever findings were produced in the context of discovery were relevant to similar conditions external to those that produced the results.

The aspirations of the early organizational researchers included these criteria and went beyond because they had doubts that this approach was enough. If, for example, the task of social scientists was to describe the universe as it existed, how could these findings be relevant to a universe that admittedly did not exist? Moreover, if rare events were to be produced, it was necessary not only to describe them, it was also necessary to specify causal statements about how to get from here to there. Without such causal statements it would be difficult to test the claims of research based on intervention.

All these requirements led many of us to believe that what I call *implementable validity* should be viewed as equal to internal and external validities in establishing the validity of the findings. This belief ran counter to the ideas in good currency at the time. One could not find a written description about implementable validity. Indeed, where we would strive to hold such discussions many of our colleagues demurred, claiming that such research implied producing prescriptive generalizations that were not part of the responsibility of social scientists conducting research. I will return to the consequences of such a position after some reflections on *Personality and Organization*.

THE ORIGINS OF PERSONALITY AND ORGANIZATION

At the request of the Social Science Research Council, I had just finished a report on the empirical research being conducted at many of the main university centers in human problems of organization, industrial relations, and labor economics (Argyris, 1954). The good news was that the research was interesting and rich. The bad news was that most of the scholars did not know what the other scholars were doing. This situation seemed to me to be sad for two reasons. First, organizing and combining the research might make important scientific contributions hitherto not seen, no less acknowledged. Second, these new contributions could also make important contributions to practice.

I do remember during the conference that whenever I suggested these possibilities, in all cases the scholars thought the ideas were worth following up. Also, in all cases, none expressed interest in working toward developing a more comprehensive framework or theory. They were focused on their own disciplinary challenges.

As a beginning young scholar I was somewhat surprised and bewildered. My feelings were partially caused by the reading that I was doing at that time, on the philosophy of science. Kurt Lewin (1935) was especially advising scholars that disciplines progressed as they conducted empirical research that was guided by sound theory.

After some thought and discussion, I took it upon myself to try to begin to develop such as theory. The question arose how to begin. The question was not an easy one to answer for several reasons. First, it was interdisciplinary in focus and intent. At that time there were almost no books available on how to conduct interdisciplinary research. Second, research that was designed to be interdisciplinary partially in order to be implementable was not an idea in good currency among scholars. *Implementable* was interpreted by scholars to mean practical and vocational. These attributes were not seen as important and as a source for making scientific contributions. Third, Lewin's idea that sound theory could be practical was not embraced particularly because the theories available at that time were not, according to Lewin's views, sound. Lewin took seriously that the most robust test of theory was to be empirically shown not to be disconfirmed in the domain of practice (Argyris, 1997; Lewin, 1935).

Finally, even though my focus was on real problems that scholars had identified, the same scholars paid almost no attention to solving them. The most frequent explanation that I heard was that social science was based on empirical research that was cumulative and additive. Attention therefore had to be paid to conducting sound research, and implementability would follow. I believed in this claim. However, an analysis of the literature of this domain, some three decades later, indicated that the claim was disconfirmed. Indeed, one could make the case that the claim was part of a defensive routine in the scientific community to remain insular (Argyris, 1980).

THE CONCEPT OF FIT

How could I develop a theory that would organize the many diverse and multilevel variables that I described in my report? I developed a strategy as a result of reading some of the research being conducted by physical scientists who wanted to form an explanation of how the universe was created and developed into the organized complexity that we observe today. As I understood their strategy, it was based on a concept of fit. They hypothesized that certain physical–chemical entities existed and then inferred the likely consequences when these entities interacted. By knowing the properties of the original components, they were able to develop an explanatory theory of how the universe began and developed.

I followed the same strategy. My two original components were the individual (personality) and the organization. I chose these two components because I believed that "in the beginning there were people and organizations" was a claim that could be a legitimate premise for the entire exercise.

The first step was to define the features of each component. I developed a view of the organizational properties or components by drawing on the existing organizational theory. There was, for example, a wide range of agreement that organizations were composed of hierarchical pyramidal structures, of jobs that defined the molecularized tasks that had to be accomplished, and of control and reward systems that were required to make all these features work if human beings were to be the agents of organizations.

Finding a comparable description for personality was not as easy. I analyzed the existing theories and found that they differed importantly in the components they defined as the core of personality. The different views would lead to different consequences whenever each view interacted with organizations.

The strategy that I selected to overcome this challenge was to borrow an obvious property of organizational theories. The theories were primarily normative; that is, the theories of organizations were concerned about effective performance. This led me to inquire what the various theories of personality had to say about effectiveness. Many did not because the scholars believed much more research was necessary. Those who did concern themselves with effectiveness developed criteria that were primarily internal to the respective theory of personality. It was difficult to select one view over the others because each presented little advice on the problems of interaction with organizations.

I chose the literature on social–human development for two reasons. First, the scholars paid attention to the human beings interacting with their environment. Second, those that I found especially helpful focused heavily on observing human development. Therefore they developed dimensions whose existence could be observed and tested in everyday life. For example, the literature suggested that the growth of human beings could be conceptualized as children developing into adults, characterized as developing from a few abilities to many abilities and from skin-surface abilities to fewer that were deeper. Moreover, children developed from being dependent on their parents to adults who integrated dependency with relative independence (interdependency).

What would happen if human beings with such developmental trends became members of organizations? The answer was that the fit between personality and organizations would be problematic. The reasons were that organizations would require individuals to acquiesce to the requirements of hierarchy (dependence on people with power); to the requirements of Taylor-like jobs (use a few of their abilities and their more skin-surface ones at that); and to the requirements of unilateral control systems such as budgets and quality control (employees respect what management inspects).

The conflict just described would be problematic for those human beings who aspired to have work conditions that encouraged their adultlike potentials. It would also be problematic for employees who preferred the childlike working conditions but the organization pressed for the adultlike conditions (at that time there were very few known examples of this fit).

I focused, at the outset, on the first conflict because the existing literature suggested that many employees did prefer the adultlike work conditions. I wanted to see what would be the second, third, and so forth, order consequences of this problematic fit. For example, the conflict should lead to employees experiencing frustration. This should lead to frustration (Barker, Dembo, & Lewin, 1941), which in turn could produce regression. Regression could lead to win–lose counterproductive actions such as goldbricking, rate setting, and apathy. These, it could be shown, could lead employees to attack the basic causes of the frustration, namely unilateral managerial power. One result would be the creation of trade unions or another informal work system that fought managerial policies and practices.

There was another consequence that produced counterproductive results. The personality literature indicated that human beings could be said to have psychological energy (in addition to the physical energy). The psychological energy tended to be strong if individuals worked under conditions of psychological success (Festinger, 1953) and internal commitment (Lewin, 1935). The demands of the traditional organizational structures and leadership were the opposite. Human beings were asked to engage in work that combined being productive with psychological failure and external commitment. These conditions reinforced the counterproductive ones described previously.

FIT AND THE IMPORTANCE OF CAUSALITY

The concept of fit between the individual and the organization was the foundation for developing a theory that could account for a wide range of phenomena already documented by scholars (e.g., ranging from satisfaction, turnover, commitment, informal group norms, accounting, and financial systems for control to the development of trade unions). The logic was relatively straightforward. The basic properties of each component (personality and organization) were defined. Next, the interdependence of these units was made explicit. Interdependence meant specifying what each component needed and gave to others if its own needs were to be fulfilled.

The specification was in the form of causal claims. These claims specified the actions that occurred while implementing the interdependence. For example, individuals who sought work conditions consistent with maturelike features but were offered work conditions consistent with childlike conditions should report dissatisfaction, frustration, and so forth. Second-order causal consequences were then specified. For example, the frustration could lead to regression, which, in turn, could lead to withdrawal or involvement by fighting management. Third-order consequences were then specified. For example, if management considered the second-order actions as disloyal, they were likely to reinforce their control mechanisms, which, in turn, would feed back to upset the employees, who, in turn, would increase their adaptive actions. Because these actions were consistent with their views of how to deal with a problematic fit, they led to management reacting defensively.

Another consequence that flowed from such causal hypothesizing was to surface the tendency of organizations to create behavior worlds that were characterized by self-fulfilling, self-fueling, counterproductive consequences. Although these conditions were, and still are, characteristics of organizational defensive behavioral worlds, one could not find them in the literature about the nature of formal organizations. Nor could one find, in the personality literature, predictions about how human beings, in the name of self-actualization, helped to create a work world that inhibited their actualization. Not surprisingly, the employees and managers increasingly felt that the situation was hopeless and they felt helpless about taking constructive action (Argyris, 1990).

FIT AND THE STATUS QUO

The empirical consequences of the fit model also reinforced the responsibility of the employees and managers to maintain the status quo. As long as the fit research remained descriptive of the universe as it was then social scientists could be accused of being servants of the status quo. Social scientists dedicated to the description of reality necessarily produced propositions whose validity depended on accepting the status quo.

However, some changes were made in the status quo. If my memory serves me correctly, these changes grew out of actions taken primarily by practitioners. For example, job enlargement grew out of an incident where Thomas Watson, Sr., gave permission to employees, in the interests of not waiting around, to make changes in their work that normally were delegated to industrial engineers. Perhaps a more powerful example was the creation, at Michigan University, of the Center for Change (CRUSK). Again, if my recollection is correct, the charge stated that practitioners were conducting all sorts of experiments. CRUSK scientists were to describe them in order to document rigorously what was occurring. With the exception of Likert (and a few close associates) most of the research was in the service of documenting the actions of thoughtful practitioners.

About the same time, social scientists were studying the impact of small-group participation on performance. Their results, especially as promulgated by National Training Laboratories (NTL), influenced the practitioners who attended the seminar to take initiatives to explore new conditions of fit. Again, the dominant role of social scientist was to describe these experiments.

I believe that it is fair to say that most of these experiments intended to create work conditions for employees that were consistent with the experience of maturelike work requirements, psychological success, and internal commitment. The causal theory that was embedded in *Personality and Organization* could be used to design new experiments and to help us understand those initiated by the practitioners.

As the trend toward employee participation enlarged and strengthened programs such as reengineering, quality management and high performance work groups developed. These programs had mixed results. But, so do most programs of this type (Argyris, 2000). The point that I should like to make is that if one described and analyzed them carefully, one would find that they became increasingly based on defining work reminiscent of a Taylor mentality, described previously. Thus below the surface, the trends were to create systems that were akin to the old fit problems described in *Personality and Organizaiton* (Argyris, 1957; Argyris, 2000; Argyris & Schön, 1996). It appeared that management, as in the old days, were willing to relax their controls but not the power to end or limit the relaxation. The result was programs that lacked credibility with the employees and middle-level management.

SUMMARY AND CONCLUSION

Many of the scholars leading what has been called the *golden era of organizational research* (Schneider et al., 2000) believed the following:

1. The task of social science researchers is to describe the universe as accurately as possible, to derive propositions that are generalizable, and to test them through the use of prediction. However, these scholars added an additional criterion. The description of the universe should be in the service of creating a better world. One criterion of a better world is a better fit between the self-actualizing needs of individuals and the requirements of organizational effectiveness.

2. The fundamental purpose was normative because it was about creating features of the organizational world that did not exist. The task therefore was to create rare events and to implement them in ways such that the events persisted. This approach not only required descriptions of the universe as was, it also required the development of theories that specified causally how to get from here to there.

3. Because *there* meant nontrivial changes in organizations, the task was to define changes in the status quo and to implement such changes in order to see if a better fit did lead to such consequences as those McGregor (Heil et al., 2000) stated at the outset. In order to create these changes, the most powerful research methodology would be interventions. *Interventions* were active experiments intended to change the status quo by creating features of a new order.

4. The criteria in good currency about conducting experiments were, and still are, internal and external validities. These criteria are necessary but inadequate if one has the just-mentioned purposes in mind. Implementable validity was equally important. It is possible to have high internal and external validity and low implementable validity (e.g., the concept of trust). It is also possible to have all three validities be high because the research focuses on remaining within the status quo.

Gaps and Inconsistencies in Present Research and Practice

I should like to illustrate gaps and inconsistencies that occur because the empirical research does not take seriously the concepts of fit and implementability. I will use performance reviews and tests of individual (personality) characteristics as examples. I will then turn to policies and practices in learning and transformational change, which are also limited by similar gaps and inconsistencies.

Performance Appraisal and Reviews

A dominant aspiration of researchers is to create performance appraisal instruments that exhibit high internal and external validity. They want their component of the fit (the formal organizational features) to provide a sound basis for integration. This stance is not dissimilar to the one taken by organizational design experts who, for years, seek to make the formal hierarchy, job description, and other such features as valid as possible. In *Personality and Organization* I asked, if this component were implemented according to these designs, what would be the impact upon the participants? Oversimplifying the answer given at the outset, the consequence is that it would create a fit where employees would be required to accept dependence and subordination to those in power. This condition, the argument continued, would produce employee frustration and lead to consequences such as absenteeism and/or informal activities such as performance restriction, manipulation of managers, and trade unionism. In effect, the consequences would be counterproductive to the management hopes and aspirations.

I suggest that research about performance appraisal instruments and activities be conducted guided by a similar logic. For example, the requirements embedded in the appraisal instruments are the equivalent of the formal organizational requirements. The reaction of the employees as they experience the implementation of the performance appraisal would have a status similar to the informal activities described earlier in organizations.

The research would focus on the actual behavior of the ratees and raters. To what extent is the relationship a top-down one mirroring the hierarchy? To what extent do the ratees report that they experience dependency and submissiveness? Can we observe activities by the ratees to counter the top-down impact of the raters? How, for example, do ratees fight the performance appraisal system that they experience?

Can the same data set be used to ascertain the degree to which the raters experience frustration with the ratees defensive maneuvers? Do they create their own defensive routines? If so, to what extent does this response result in mutual miscommunication and defensiveness?

In an unpublished study, I observed and interviewed raters and ratees during the evaluation process. I interviewed each individually after the appraisal process was completed. I asked how the individuals evaluated the effectiveness of the process. The managers responded that it went well until they came to the evaluation of the ratees' poor performance. In their views the ratees became defensive. The managers did not appreciate the ratee's defensive actions. I asked how long it took them (raters) to sense the ratees defensiveness. The answer was, in effect, almost immediately. I then asked if they chose to discuss their disappointments with the ratees. Again the answer was no. The reason was that such a cure would make the illness a worse disease and take much more time than was available.

The ratees responses were similar. They felt the session went fine until the however-but moment. The ratees reported that when they reacted by questioning the negative evaluation that followed the statement of the poor performance, the raters became defensive; that they saw the raters' defensiveness almost immediately; and that talking about it openly would be potentially dangerous for the ratees. In effect, the result was self-sealing nonlearning consequences that took up more time than either party wished to consume.

If these findings are supported by further research, then I suggest that we have an explanation for the following puzzle. Over the years, managers have expressed doubts about the effectiveness of performance reviews. These doubts continue even though the empirical research around designing performance appraisal systems increased in amount and in sophistication. (Murphy & Cleveland, 1995; Schuler, Farr, & Smith, 1993; Schuler, 1987).

The explanation may be related to the implementation processes. It may help the professionals to create performance appraisal instruments that exhibit better internal, external, and implementable validity if they would conduct empirical research in the many training programs where the attempt is to deal with these important consequences.

Such research could also provide insight into how the performance appraisal puzzle is reinforced by trainers who are typically not competent to create performance appraisal instruments. Moreover, even if they were competent, it is unlikely that they would have the freedom to make real changes. Again, if these speculations were confirmed, they would be evidence that the performance appraisal instruments and their present systems of implementation support the managerial status quo.

Tests of Individual Features

Similar questions may be worth exploring regarding the use of individual (personality) tests that are intended to assess such phenomena as styles of, for example, leadership, decision making, thinking, and reasoning.

I should like to use as an example the Myers-Briggs test. It is one of the most extensively researched instruments. It is also one of the most extensively used instruments in executive and MBA programs. The experience at the Harvard Business School in both settings is that the response of the students is positive. They report that they learn much about themselves and their colleagues. They also report that they expect to be more tolerant of differences that previously they questioned.

Research is needed to study the actual behaviors of the individuals to assess the degree to which they act consistently with their expectations. For example, my colleagues and I (1990) designed and executed a program on leadership and learning that was rolled out to nearly 1500 managers. The findings that I reported came from the first session that was composed of about 30 senior executives. In this organization the rule was that the top had to experience any workshop first. If they approved, it would then be given to the managers below them. The executive group had participated in a Myers-Briggs workshop. They reported that they developed important insights about themselves and their fellow officers. They also predicted that these insights would lead to greater tolerance and respect for the differences among themselves. Not surprisingly, they approved it to be rolled out to the managerial groups.

The same group was exposed to a workshop designed consistently with a theory of action perspective (Argyris, 1990, 1993; Argyris & Schön, 1996). The workshop was designed around cases that the executives wrote describing how they behaved in dealing with important and controversial issues. From an analysis they made from their own cases, they concluded that the respect, patience, and understanding that they predicted they would exhibit (after the Myers-Briggs workshop) had all but vanished.

A second inquiry that is recommended is that of the impact that the fundamental features of such tests have on the individuals and the organization. Tests assume that the individual (personality) features that are measured are systematic, patterned, and stable over time and under different conditions. The concept of fit is relevant in this case. The fundamental assumption is that the better the fit between the individual characteristics and the organizational requirements, especially as found in jobs, the more likely is performance to be productive and effective.

Tests of the type being described here also assumes that because the individuals' patterns are stable, it is not likely that they can be altered. There is therefore little likelihood of improving the fit when neither the job nor the individual requirements can be changed importantly. Testing therefore becomes a servant of the status quo.

One troubling consequence suggested in the literature is that if the fit is poor then the individuals may leave or should leave to find a better fit (Schneider, 1987). The likely validity of this advice is enhanced if it is true, as I reported earlier, that although individuals predict that they would become more respectful of differences, they do not do so when dealing with embarrassing or difficult organizational situations.

These are not trivial issues for human beings experiencing a poor fit. Is it not fair to ask the scholars who design and produce the instruments to conduct research to discover ways of helping individuals alter the characteristics that are considered stable? As a minimum we would then understand what causes stability. What would be the features of such educational interventions? How could they be integrated with the everyday actions that the individuals perform?

The Implementation of Change Programs

The problems described above are not limited to performance appraisals and tests of individuals features. In a recent review of the literature on leadership, learning, change, and internal commitment, I found gaps in describing the fit between the requirements of the change programs and the behavior of the change experts. These gaps is especially of interest because, in the examples reported, it was the change professionals and human resources professionals who activated the discrepancies (Argyris, 2000).

For example, I led three different workshops with senior practitioners (each seminar had at least 25 participants with 5 to over 15 years experience, about evenly divided between females and males). The participants were asked to solve a case faced by a change professional (CP). The CP had difficulty in building the trust and openness among line managers. A transcript of his conversation indicted that as he tried to overcome the resistance of the line managers, he created more mistrust and closeness. He agreed with this assessment but held the line managers responsible.

In each group, the participants role played how they would try to help the CP professional act more effectively. All sessions were tape-recorded. A review of the transcripts, as published, indicates that they did to the CP what they were advising him not to do with the line managers (Argyris, 2000).

SUMMARY AND CONCLUSION

In closing, it appears that the beliefs, values, and aspirations exhibited by the scholars of the golden age of organizational research and those exhibited by *Personality and Organization* (Argyris, 1957) have relevance for research and practice. It is suggested that a major research emphasis should be on what actually goes on during the implementation phases.

Such research could lead to important findings as to how to diminish the counterproductive consequences just described. It should also lead to knowledge that can strengthen emancipatory opportunities for individuals and a deeper respect for organizations if they are to be effective and in control over their own destiny.

REFERENCES

Argyris, C. (1954). *The present state of human relation research.* New Haven, CT: Labor and Management Center, Yale University.
Argyris, C. (1957). *Personality and organization torch book.* New York: Harper & Brothers.
Argyris, C. (1980). *Inner contradictions of rigorous research.* San Diego, CA: Academic.
Argyris, C. (1990). *Overcoming organizational defenses.* Needham, MA: Allyn & Bacon.
Argyris, C. (1993). *Knowledge for action.* San Francisco: Jossey-Bass.
Argyris, C. (1996). Unrecognized defenses of Scholars: Impact on theory and research. *Organizational Science, 7*(1), 79–87.
Argyris, C. (1997). Field theory as a basis for scholarly consulting. *Journal of Social Issues, 53*(4), 811–827.
Argyris, C. (2000). *Flawed advice.* New York: Oxford University Press.
Argyris, C., & Schön, D. (1974). *Theory in practice.* San Francisco: Jossey-Bass.
Argyris, C., and Schön, D. (1996). *Organizational learning II.* Reading, MA: Addison-Wesley.
Barker, R. G., Dembo, T., & Lewin, K. (1941). *Frustration and regression* (University of Iowa Studies of Child Welfare I, pp. 1–43). Ames: University of Iowa Press.
Festinger, L. (1953). Laboratory experiments. In L. Festinger and D. Katz (Eds.), *Research methods in the behavioral sciences.* New York: Holt, Rinehart & Winston.
Heil, G., Bennis, W., & Stephens, D. C. (2000). *Douglas McGregor revisited.* New York: Wiley.
Lewin, K. (1935). *A dynamic theory of personality.* New York: McGraw-Hill.
Murphy, K. R., & Cleveland, J. H. (1995). *Understanding performance appraisal.* Thousand Oaks, CA: Sage.
Schneider, B. (1987). The people make the place. *Personnel Psychology, 40,* 437–454.
Schneider, B., Smith, B. D., & Sipe, W. P. (2000). Personal selection psychology: Multilevel considerations. In K. J. Klein & S. W. J. Kozlowski (Eds.), *Multilevel theory, research and methods in organizations* (pp. 91–120). San Francisco: Jossey-Bass.
Schuler, H., Farr, J. L., & Smith, M. (1993). *Personal selection and assessment: Individual and organizational perspectives.* Hillsdale, NJ: Lawrence Erlbaum Associates, Inc.
Schuler, R. D. (1987). *Personal and human resources management.* New York: West.

VI

Conclusions

Chapter 15   **Where We've Been and Where We're Going: Some Conclusions Regarding Personality and Organization**
D. Brent Smith and Benjamin Schneider

This chapter serves as an overview of where we have been, where we are now, and what the future might hold for the role of personality in organizations.

Where We've Been and Where We're Going: Some Conclusions Regarding Personality and Organizations

D. Brent Smith
Rice University

Benjamin Schneider
University of Maryland and Personnel Research Associates, Inc.

We began working on the idea for this book in the late 1990s, after spending some time reflecting on the previous decade of research on personality in organizations. We noted, as many have, that research on personality proliferated during this decade. If the 1980s had been characterized by the cognitive revolution, the 1990s were characterized by the rebirth of personality research. Many factors played a significant role in this rebirth (particularly the rebirth of organizationally focused personality research). These factors included the tentative resolution of the person–situation debate, the rise of the five-factor model as an organizing and descriptive taxonomy, meta-analyses demonstrating the validity of various personality dimensions for the prediction of important work-related behaviors and outcomes, and a zeitgeist that seemed once again to accept dispositional explanations for individual and organizational phenomena. We thought it was time to take stock of what we know, what we have learned, where progress has been made, and where the future of organizational personality research lies. This was the purpose of this volume, and the authors of the various chapters have provided an excellent overview of the research on personality in many of the primary topical areas in OB/HR and I–O psychology.

It is not our intention to review the contributions of each chapter here. Rather, we would like to offer a brief commentary on some of the themes that arose as we thought about personality in organizations and read the chapters. In a few cases our comments are reflections on the field, in some cases they are directions for future research, and in still others, they are criticisms of the way we have been going about things. Clearly, we have made substantial progress in our understanding of personality and its effects on individual behavior and have even made some progress at understanding the role of personality at group and organizational levels of analyses, too. But, as the authors in this volume unmistakably acknowledged, there is work yet to be done.

In what follows, we provide a brief commentary on the past, present, and future of organizational personality research. We stop far short of proposing an all-encompassing agenda for the future. However, we hope some of the ideas we present will help shape that future. The issues we discuss evolved chiefly from two somewhat different perspectives on personality. First, of course, the ideas emerged from an analysis of the perspectives of the authors who wrote the chapters in this volume. Second, we considered the fact that, in our pursuit of the prediction of performance criteria, applied psychologists have not always remained true to the theoretical richness of personality constructs. So, while the practitioner side of the house has perhaps worked with the end goal of predicting performance, the academic side of the house has worked more on understanding process issues that might eventuate in understanding performance. Our goal here will be to tie together these two sides of the coin and suggest some avenues for research that will shed light on both the prediction and the understanding of behavior and performance in organizations.

Although a few of the issues we raise may be viewed as an indictment of the way we have been doing things, they are intended to direct future research on personality. Without the solid foundation of research conducted over the past decade, we certainly would not be in the enviable situation of calling for additional research that builds on that base. Please note that these issues are presented in no particular order of importance.

LIMITATIONS OF THE FIVE-FACTOR MODEL (FFM)

These days if one mentions *personality*, it is assumed he or she is referring to the five-factor model. Our intent in the book was to have authors explore the relationship between personality and specific other constructs of interest (e.g., attitudes, leadership, performance). As we expected, many authors chose to focus on or at least refer to research conducted using the FFM. Other books on personality and work (e.g., Barrick & Ryan, 2002) have attended more to personality measurement itself than ours, yet it is important for us to stand back and ask whether the dominance of the FFM in work on personality and organizations is healthy.

It is hard to criticize that which is primarily responsible for the renaissance in personality research. Without the FFM, we would surely not be where we are today. It provided a simple, unifying framework that allowed research to flourish and contributed substantially to the accumulation of knowledge on the correlates of personality variables. Many saw the emerging consensus regarding a personality framework (if not THE personality framework) as a critical moment in the development of personality psychology (McAdams, 1992). However, in looking back at the past decade of research, we can see both strengths and limitations to the FFM. For many, the FFM was intended to be a descriptive taxonomy that allowed personality researchers to use a common language to describe their research findings. In this sense, it was a response to what has been referred to as the tower of babble problem (Wiggins, 1992)—a reference to a time when there were so many different (yet often overlapping) languages used to describe personality that progress in the field was hindered. However, we fear the consequence, perhaps unexpected, of the FFM was much more than this. In effect, it became (or has become) a constraint on personality research by narrowly defining what was (is) acceptable to measure, perhaps limiting research on theoretically interesting personality constructs not clearly linked to the FFM (Briggs, 1992). In other words, we fear the effect of this consensual model has been to limit the very definition of personality in applied studies. One of us recently submitted an article for possible publication in an esteemed journal in the field, and the article was summarily rejected simply because the personality measure used was not of the FFM persuasion. The fact that there was validity for the measure, that it mapped conceptually to the outcome of interest, and that previous research had demonstrated its relationship to the FFM seemed to be irrelevant.

But fortunately in reality the often referred to consensus of support for the FFM is anything but a true consensus (see Block, 1995, 2001; Hough, 1992; Paunonen & Jackson, 2000). Noteworthy criticisms have always been present and several critics are quite impassioned in their opposition to the FFM (e.g., Eysenck, 1990). We do not wish the reader to construe the comments to follow as a condemnation of the FFM or a call for continued research on the dimensionality of the personality sphere. Rather, given its influence, we believe it is time to reexamine the role of the FFM in applied personality research.

With regard to the limitations of the FFM, we believe there are four primary concerns: (1) its comprehensiveness, (2) its heterogeneity, (3) the lack of consensus regarding the facet structure, and (4) its atheoretical origins. In many ways, the first three concerns are intertwined and may reflect competing criteria used to evaluate the adequacy of a personality model. It is probably too much to ask for a model to be comprehensive in covering the personality sphere, replicable across time, raters, situations, and cultures, and be homogeneous at the broad domain level. We may very well have to relax one of these criteria to achieve the others. The latter concern, regarding the atheoretical origins of the model, has received less attention by applied psychologists, although it remains a significant and persistent concern among personality psychologists. Fortunately, many thoughtful FFM advocates have made progress in providing theoretical justifications for the five factors, albeit post hoc (Wiggins, 1996).

Comprehensiveness

Perhaps the earliest and most persistent criticism of the FFM relates to the claim of comprehensiveness, which is not surprising given that the model claims the complete personality construct space can be reduced to five and only five broad factors. Several authors have suggested that in our endeavor to achieve parsimony we have crafted a replicable model that excludes important individual differences (see Block, 1995; Hough, 1992; Paunonen & Jackson, 2000). This concern is clearly significant. If the FFM excludes important personality constructs, its utility as an organizing taxonomy is limited.

As a case in point, Hough (1992) examined the comprehensiveness of the FFM and argued that if prediction is a concern, the FFM excludes important variables. As the foundation for developing a personality taxonomy for the Army's Project Alpha, Hough and colleagues categorized existing personality scales and then summarized personality-criterion relationships for each category. Hough's results suggested the possibility of important (from a prediction standpoint) personality characteristics that fall outside of the Big Five. For instance, she argued that the FFM excludes the construct of rugged individualism reflecting traditionally masculine characteristics, a construct correlated with military combat performance.

Similarly, Saucier and Goldberg (1998) found preliminary evidence of extra-FFM constructs. In a provocatively entitled article, "What is Beyond the Big Five," Saucier and Goldberg examined 53 clusters of person-descriptive characteristics generated through an exhaustive search for Big Five–independent constructs in an effort to demarcate the FFM. Although their results largely supported the comprehensiveness of the FFM, they did find constructs that likely fall outside of the FFM including negative valence (feelings of untrustworthiness and evil), cunning, folksiness, masculinity, frugality, humor, and prejudice. Paunonen and Jackson (2000) reanalyzed the Saucier and Goldberg data, suggesting their criteria for inclusion in the FFM was too liberal. Their results suggest nine clusters they argue are relatively independent of the FFM, including reverence, manipulativeness, honesty/integrity, conservativeness, masculinity, frugality, humor/witty, and egotistical, among others.

Block (1995, 2001) has argued quite convincingly that the peculiar history of the FFM (including its origins in the natural language or lexical model of personality) explains its noncomprehensiveness. Through reliance on factor-analytic methods and a belief in the supremacy of the lexical hypothesis (that important individual differences get encoded in the natural language and that an analysis of natural language can uncover the critical dimensions of personality), Block argues that we have been lulled into the belief that the FFM is comprehensive. Why, Block argued, should we place a priority on laypersons' descriptions of personality or a statistical technique so dependent on so many extraneous factors? In reality, Block suggests, the mountain of evidence supporting the validity of the FFM is based on a limited set of original studies of person-descriptive trait terms that prestructured later studies in ways that may have unduly influenced the interpretation of subsequent factor-analytic solutions. As Block (1995, p. 189) notes, "If so [early studies prestructured later studies], then the 'recurrence' and 'robustness' [of the FFM] over diverse samples of factor structures may be attributable more to the sameness of the variable sets used than to the intrinsic structure of the personality-descriptive domain."

Finally, there are clearly important individual differences that are related to the FFM, but cannot be captured well by the FFM. For instance, the construct of self-monitoring (Snyder, 1987) has received considerable attention in applied contexts (see Kilduff & Day, 1994). Although self-monitoring is related to extraversion, agreeableness, and neuroticism, it is not possible to recapture the quintessence of self-monitoring with knowledge of a person's scores on these three characteristics (Funder, 2001).

Our own noncomprehensive sampling of studies examining the FFM suggests that we may be somewhat premature in our conclusion that the FFM comprehensively surveys the entirety of the personality domain. Again, our purpose here is to express caution, not to deny the usefulness of the FFM. Given the enthusiastic proclamations made by the ardent supporters and advocates of the FFM,[1] it is not surprising that so many researchers default to a measure of these five characteristics as their operational definition of *personality*. Doing so runs the risk of excluding potentially important individual differences. The FFM, "like the results of meta-analysis, should not halt the search for additional explanatory constructs—or the latest and newest fad will, as night follows day, emerge" (Schneider, 1996, p. 295).

Domain Heterogeneity

A second and related concern regarding the FFM is domain heterogeneity. A focus on the broad domains often obscures the finer detail associated

---

[1]For instance, John (1989, p. 269) has argued that the FFM represents the "accumulated knowledge about personality as it has been laid down over the ages in natural language."

with more specific personality constructs. Recently, there have been several important demonstrations of the heterogeneity of the FFM domain scales (see Moon, 2001). These studies have demonstrated the significance of considering this heterogeneity when proposing theoretical linkages between the FFM domains and various outcomes. For example, Moon examined the relationship between conscientiousness and the propensity to escalate commitment to a failing course of action. His results demonstrated that when conscientiousness is separated into the components of duty (responsibility) and achievement striving, the components were both significantly correlated with the propensity to escalate but in opposite directions. When the components were pooled, conscientiousness was unrelated to escalation. Moon's findings suggest it is important to consider domain heterogeneity in the theoretical specification of models including the Big Five as potential antecedents and/or predictors. Failure to do so can lead to masking potentially important relationships.

When considering the hierarchical ordering of the FFM, this approach makes intuitive sense. Each of the five domains comprises many more specific facets. When you examine the facet structure of each domain, it is difficult not to see the breadth of the constructs represented. The duty and achievement-striving facets of conscientiousness are just one example. Hogan and Hogan's (1999) conceptualization of extroversion as containing an ambition (surgency) facet and a sociability facet and openness to experience containing an intellectaence (culture) facet and a school-success (academic focus) facet are additional examples. If you examine the neuroticism domain, you see facets related to both depression and anxiety. As Briggs (1992) noted, these facets are likely to relate very differently to important external criteria especially but not exclusively in clinical settings.

The recognition that there is substantial heterogeneity represented in the five domains has led many to suggest that the proper level of measurement of personality is the facet level (Briggs, 1992), something we have noted is an uncommon occurrence in most applied studies. There is disagreement, of course, and these arguments fueled the bandwidth-fidelity debate. This debate centered on the appropriate level of specificity in personality measurement. Paunonen and Ashton (2001) among others have demonstrated that a focus on the facet level can dramatically improve prediction of (particularly behavioral) criteria beyond the domain level. The debate has fizzled, with most parties now recognizing the importance of allowing theory to drive specification of the personality model and the appropriate level of description. However, it is still true that few studies actively specify their personality models at the facet level. This approach ignores the inevitable loss of specific variance as facets are aggregated into domain scales.

Proper Specification of the Facet Structure

A third related concern is the lack of consensus regarding the facet-level structure of each of the five personality domains. If we accept that personality traits are hierarchically organized (as opposed to horizontally organized, as in a circumplex) and we believe it is important to richly describe the heterogeneity of the five domains, we must also recognize the importance of proper specification of the facet structure. Although there may be some agreement regarding the existence and meaning of the five factors (although this view remains debatable—consider the various interpretations of openness to experience), there is virtually no consistency or systematic evaluation of the facet-level structure of each of the five factors. This lack becomes quite obvious if you compare different measures of the FFM. Disagreements and inconsistencies at the facet level appear to be the norm rather than the exception. Consider, for instance, Hogan and Hogan's (1999) conceptualization of intellectance versus Costa and McCrae's (1992) construct of openness to experience. Both reflect the somewhat elusive factor V of the FFM and both contain remarkably different facet-level specifications. On the one hand openness includes the facets of feelings, aesthetics, and values, whereas intellectance includes the facets of science, intellectual games, and culture. At this stage of the development of the FFM, we might consider the fact that we haven't turned our attention to facets to be something of an intellectual embarrassment. Certainly, this oversight may be one explanation for the lack of applied studies utilizing facet-level personality specifications. An important next step for FFM theorists is to dive into the facet-level structure of the various domains and provide empirical support for the appropriate content.

The Atheoretical Nature of the FFM

Finally, many have criticized the FFM for its atheoretical origins. In fact, Block (1995) objects to the use of the term *model* implying a theoretically determined personality system. It is certainly true that the FFM is not a theory of personality nor are there existing theories of personality that can neatly explain the five factors (see Wiggins, 1996, for several theoretical perspectives on the FFM). Although this criticism has been less of a concern for applied psychologists, we include it here because it is our purely subjective opinion that much of the dissatisfaction with applied personality research can be subsumed under this concern. Much of the 1990s was spent examining the correlates of the Big Five, with little attempt made to understand the theoretical linkages between constructs, much less the origins of the constructs themselves. We believe this approach has led to the perception of applied personality research as being a purely empirical enterprise. Yet, there is very little theoretical depth to the FFM; so, what should we have expected? There certainly are alternatives and most specify the choice of personality variables that are consistent with particular theoretical models of individual differences or provide greater depth to the explanation of why various personality scales are predictive. We will address these issues shortly.

We mentioned that our intent was not to cast a dark shadow over the FFM nor are we calling for continued research on the dimensionality of personality lest we return to a time when the study of personality was "seen as the domain of a little group of rational technicians who specialize in criticizing each other's measure of the insignificant, then conclude that the existence of the obvious is doubtful, then doubt whether the study of personality is worthwhile" (Helson & Mitchell, 1978, pp. 579–580). Rather, we believe it is time to evaluate what the FFM has done for us, and perhaps to us. We believe it is time to give the FFM a more circumscribed role in future applied personality research. It is certainly time to examine personality constructs that may be only loosely tied to the FFM or from domains not succinctly summarized by the FFM (e.g., interests, identity, values, motive, etc; see Hogan, chapter 1 for a review). In other words, open our eyes a bit to the broader landscape of personality characteristics. In this regard, we are quite heartened by the fact that several authors in this volume moved beyond the FFM in their conceptualizations of personality. Notable examples include George and Brief in chapter 8 on work-related stress, James and Rentsch in chapter 9 on motivation, Spangler, House, and Palrecha in chapter 10 on leadership, and Walsh in chapter 6 who shows that, at least for understanding vocational choice, the FFM is not very useful when compared to more vocationally relevant personality (interest) constructs.

LACK OF PROCESS MODELS

Schneider (1996) noted, "we have focused on outcomes of behaviour as correlates of personality (and other predictors) and have relatively little insight into the *behaviour* that intervenes between the personality and the outcome. In the absence of such information, we have no understanding of the processes by which personality becomes reflected in outcomes" (p. 291). We would expand Schneider's admonition by suggesting that we have very little insight into the processes that mediate personality–outcome relationships, be those mediators behavioral, cognitive, or affective. In effect, we pay very little attention to the processes that underlie personality–outcome relationships. In fact, the complexity of most dependent variables we study in OB and HR management suggests that there are likely many such intermediate mechanisms. Organizational research on personality rarely takes a process-oriented view of explaining how and why personality predicts various individual and organizational criteria. There are certainly notable exceptions;[2] however, the field is at a point where these studies should be the rule and not the exception.

Take, for instance, the research on the relationship between personality and job performance. Much of this research has attempted to find FFM correlates of performance appraisal data without thought to the various intermediate stages that fall between someone's dispositions and the expression of behaviors that leads to a rater's perception of performance. Are we honestly surprised by the often unimpressive criterion-related validities we find for personality constructs? Or consider the more extreme (and perhaps unfortunately more usual) case where personality data from a generic measure of the FFM is correlated with sales or promotion or group effectiveness without considering the processes that mediate such relationships.

In this volume Stewart and Barrick begin to break ground on the mediating mechanisms that underlie the personality–job performance relationship by examining motivational mediators of the FFM. They argue that traits (the FFM) affect performance through their effects on communion-striving (cooperation), accomplishment-striving (recognition), and agency-striving (dominance) behaviors. We believe that such models are necessary to specify more fully the complex nature of the relationship between personality and outcomes.

Additionally, Schneider's original admonition remains true. We rarely attempt to identify the specific behaviors that mediate personality–outcome relationships, when it is specific behavior and not broad, distal personality characteristics that directly cause variability in outcomes. Furthermore, the failure to specify behavior leaves us impotent with regard to potential interventions, if we wish to transfer our knowledge to practice. Consider the chapter by Schneider and Smith on organizational culture. In that chapter, they explicitly note that personality does not lead to culture but leads to the behaviors that result in culture. An example they might have used there concerns Schein's (1992) idea that leaders embed culture in organizations through their actions. More specifically, Schein (1992, p. 231) argues that, leaders send the message of what is important in the organization and to what ends they wish to work by what leaders pay attention to, measure, and control; by how leaders react to crises; by what they teach and coach; and for what they allocate rewards and status, among others.

---

[2]A good example is M. Barrick, G. Stewart, & M. Piotrowski (2002). Personality and job performance: Test of the mediating effects of motivation among sales representatives. *Journal of Applied Psychology, 87,* 43–51.

Schein (1992) does not address the likely antecedents of the differences in the ways leaders might carry out these culture-embedding mechanisms, but clearly there is a role for personality—and it is these cultural factors that likely produce the effectiveness differences we observe in organizations. Our conclusion is that personality researchers must focus on the proximal behaviors and activities that are the likely mediators of the personality–performance relationship in which we appropriately have applied interest. These mediators will have more causes than personality—like the nature of the industry (Hambrick & Finkelstein, 1987), the status of the economy (Tushman & Romanelli, 1985), and the size of the organization (Huber, Sutcliffe, Miller, & Glick, 1993)—but it is precisely this logic that suggests why it is important to find personality correlates of the mediators.

AWARENESS OF ALTERNATIVES TO TRAIT APPROACHES

Within personality psychology there are multiple paradigms that seek to explain human behavior. Two of these paradigms seem to have different agendas—trait theory and social-cognitive theory. The first of these approaches to personality seeks to identify consistencies in individual behavior as evidence of the existence of transcontextual traits. Applied psychologists have naturally drifted to trait conceptualization and sought evidence of behavioral consistency to predict work behavior, satisfaction, or productivity. The agenda of trait theory fits very well with the typical agenda of applied psychology—reliable prediction. Social–cognitive theory, on the other hand, grew out of behaviorist and social learning approaches in psychology (Funder, 2001) and seeks to explain inconsistencies in behavior. That is, for them the question is, what explains variability in behavior across situations? In reality, social–cognitive theory represents a rather loose collection of perspectives that focus on uncovering the mechanisms that explain the contextual dependence of behavior (Cantor, 1990). At first glance, these perspectives may appear to be antithetical. In fact, we believe they are not at all antithetical. Rather, integration of the social–cognitive and trait approaches could represent one of the most promising future directions for personality psychology. In short, it just may be that the reliable prediction of how people respond to contextual differences is where we need to be. Block (1977) called this phenomenon *coherence*, but it has received almost no research in applications of personality-based research in organizations.

Unfortunately, even among more basic personality researchers, there appears to be a rather substantial divide between advocates of the trait and the social–cognitive approaches. Many do not see ground for integration. For example, Cervone (1999) suggested that the integration of the two approaches was "conceptually problematic and empirically unnecessary" (p. 329). This is an unfortunate perspective given that both paradigms have much to learn from each other and perhaps only through both perspectives can we achieve an adequate explanation for transsituational individual behavior. This divide was likely a function of what were once considered to be opposing agendas—explaining consistency versus change in behavior across situations. However, recently, many have come to recognize that, as Funder (2001) put it, "behavioral consistency and change are orthogonal phenomenon" (p. 199). Although it is widely recognized that experimental (situational) manipulations can cause dramatic mean differences in behavior, this fact has virtually no bearing on the consistency of individual differences (or, barring ceiling or floor effects, on the correlation that indexes consistency). The two quests are, therefore, complementary and not competing. If the ultimate task of personality psychology is to explain individual behavior, either perspective, alone, is incomplete. Trait conceptualization may help explain consistencies, whereas social–cognitive explanations can help explain deviations from the expected and the mechanisms that explain those deviations.

In general, social–cognitive models seek to identify the contextual factors that affect behavior and uncover the cognitive and emotional mechanisms that explain behavioral variability (for a nice review of social–cognitive models see Cervone & Shoda, 1999). Cantor (1990) refers to the Allportian distinction between the having and doing sides of personality in describing social–cognitive approaches. Behavioral consistency and trait approaches are represented by the *having* aspect of personality, which does not negate the fact that the expression of behavior can have powerful contextual antecedents—the *doing* side. Social–cognitive approaches explore the individual as an active agent in perceiving and interpreting the environment. In addition, social–cognitive theorists have sought *middle-level* units as the basis of personality description—units that are necessarily contextual in nature and provide greater fidelity in the expression of personality characteristics (Buss & Cantor, 1989). Examples of social–cognitive models and middle-level units include Cantor's life tasks, Emmon's (1986) personal strivings, Dweck's (1991) goal orientation and Palys and Littles' (1983) personal projects. In each case, these middle-level units pay much greater attention to context than does the FFM and, subsequently, can explain deviations from trait-based expectations of behavior based on differences in people's perception of the context.

It is interesting that Mischel, who in 1968 inveighed against trait perspectives, over time has developed (e.g., Mischel, 1977) and now has offered (Mischel, 1999) a theoretically broad social–cognitive model with the capacity to incorporate traits—the cognitive affective personality system or CAPS model. CAPS portrays behavioral consistency as the outcome of stable or cross-situationally consistent if–then profiles (i.e., if this situation, then this behavior). In Mischel's personality system there is a place for both traits and context and a substantial theoretical model grounded in both biology and cognitive psychology.

We mention social–cognitive models here because we believe applied theorists have become all too comfortable with trait approaches because they fit neatly with the applied agenda and the traditional individual differences approach to prediction. However, if we learned anything from the person–situation debate, it was that both traits and context matter, and Stewart and Barrick in chapter 3 show us this viewpoint again for personality and work. Unfortunately, the focus on the FFM and most standardized personality measures means that our prediction attempts are inherently decontextual (Murtha, Kanfer, & Ackerman, 1996). Again, are we surprised by the size of our validity coefficients? It is interesting that recent research suggests that as you add context to standardized personality items, you improve their validity (Cellar, Miller, Doverspike, & Klawsky, 1996).

In this volume, James and Rentsch (chapter 9) provide an outstanding example of the benefits of blending social–cognitive models and trait models. James' (1998; James & Mazerolle, 2002) conditional reasoning approach to measuring personality is predicated on research from the domain of social cognition, and, as he has shown, can dramatically improve the prediction of behavior by overcoming some of the limitations of decontextualized trait measures. James and Rentsch also provide an interesting process view of behavior as the conditioned expression of motive–trait relationships.

On a final note, this discussion of social–cognitive models forces us to take seriously the prescriptions of interactional psychology—context matters! There is a broad array of research on person–environment fit (see Judge and Kristof-Brown in chapter 4); however, we are still quite nascent in our understanding of the characteristics of the situation or environment that affect behavior. Unlike personality, there are no well-accepted taxonomies we can use to describe the critical dimensions of situational variability. This lack is one of the major difficulties and obstacles to integration in the social–cognitive arena. Future research needs to address this shortcoming.

The kind of research needed will track individuals of known personality characteristics (okay, use the FFM but use it with the facets) across different contexts. The expectation would not be for individuals to behave consistently across all contexts but to behave consistently in contexts of a similar type. Contexts could, for example, be defined by the modal personality of others there (as in Holland's, 1997, approach to assessing the career environment), by the nature of the strategies being pursued (as in Porter's, 1980, categorization of strategic goals), and/or by the nature of the organizational culture experienced by members (as in the O'Reilly, Chatman, & Caldwell, 1991, approach to assessing organizational culture).

The database for such a study might be placements made by recruiting firms who collect assessment data on possible placements and then follow them up for how they behave and perform in different settings. A simpler design might be to assess candidates for jobs as they go through assessment simulations that present them with different contexts. That literature (see Guion, 1998, for a review) reveals dismay over the fact that people are not consistent in their behavior across exercises, but our bet is that they are predictably consistent in their inconsistencies and that raters take these inconsistencies into account when making final ratings over the suitability of a candidate for a specific job. Our point is that context matters and it has not been incorporated into prediction studies using personality constructs and measures.

RESPONSE DISTORTION

Smith and Robie (chapter 5 on impression management) and Stewart and Barrick (chapter 3 on the person–situation debate) both address the age-old issue of response dynamics related to responses to personality questionnaires. This issue is, without question, the most enduring criticism of the applied use of personality assessments and, although there have been multiple attempts to resolve the debate, the critics—those who believe in response distortion—remain unconvinced. It seems fairly clear from existing research that social desirability, faking, or impression management does not adversely affect the construct or criterion-related validity of personality constructs (except in the limited domain of directed-faking studies). However, with that said, we really have very little information regarding the effect of impression management on rank-order changes in a distribution of applicants—so, the question of selection utility is somewhat unanswered. We agree with Smith and Robie that further explorations of impression management need to be grounded in a broader theoretical approach to understanding the construct. We are at the stage of ignoring theory and attempting either to prove or disprove the deleterious effects of an ambiguous construct. Attempts to understand impression management need to be grounded in the broader psychological, social–psychological, and sociological literature relevant for the topic. Furthermore, understanding impression management can only be achieved with reference to a particular theoretical model explaining what responses to a personality questionnaire mean (and there are several competing perspectives; see Hogan & Hogan, 1999). We are certainly not calling for a moratorium on response distortion research; however, we need to step back and reground ourselves in the theoretical history of the debate unless we are interested in repeating that history.

MOVING BEYOND SIMPLE LINEAR MODELS

One interesting avenue for future research on personality represents non-linear models (quadratic, interactive/multiplicative, etc.) of the relationships between personality and behavior and other distal outcomes of interest. It is interesting to note how often these models are implied or discussed yet never explicitly hypothesized or tested. In our own work, we frequently think of the potential interactive or nonlinear effects of personality characteristics. For instance, conscientiousness has negative characteristics at both the high end (rigid, inflexible) and the low end (undependable, lax). Similarly, neuroticism at the high end characterizes someone who experiences excessive stress and anxiety, yet at the very low end may be narcissistic. It may very well be that our performance measures do not provide sufficient detail for us to tease apart the positive and negative characteristics associated with the poles of personality constructs. Yet, it is interesting and intuitively appealing to suspect that there are likely negative consequences associated with the extremes of most personality dimensions. Additionally, there remains very little research that hypothesizes or examines trait interactions in the prediction of behavior. That is, personality constructs are most often treated in isolation or as multiple predictors in a regression, but certainly not as interactions or configurations. However, personality is an integrated system. Each characteristic conditions the interpretation of others. Yet, most of our models fail to consider or account for these conditional relationships. For instance, we might predict that a manager who is high on extroversion (ambitious, outgoing, assertive, and dominant) might run roughshod over others unless her agreeableness score was also high, meaning that she was also viewed as warm, trusting, and considerate; certainly Spangler et al. show in chapter 10 that the need for power must be conditioned by the need for affiliation or the trait results in negative consequences.

We recognize that finding interactions can be a challenging task. Furthermore, we have not yet developed sophisticated methods of creating configural profiles usable in our analysis. However, this task would appear to be a fruitful next step in applied personality research.

Of a similar ilk is the idea that relationships between personality attributes and behavior may be nonlinear (curvilinear) such that low levels and high levels each deviate from the optimum level of the personality construct. The classic example of such a nonlinear relationship is the one between stress and task performance but we have suggested others previously for conscientiousness, for example. The problem is that the Pearson product–moment correlation coefficient is so robust as to not frequently permit the identification of statistically significant differences between, for example, eta and r. When we plot data it clearly looks to us like there are these nonlinear effects, but it is going to be tough to publish such results if statistically they are not significantly better than those when r is calculated.

LEVELS OF ANALYSIS

One of the dominant themes in recent organizational research is the recognition that multiple levels of analysis are necessary to explain fully most interesting organizational phenomena (Kozlowski & Klein, 2000). Individuals are nested in groups, and groups are nested in organizations. Personality, we believe, plays a role at all of these levels. However, we are only just beginning to explore the personality construct across these various levels of analysis. Schneider and Smith (chapter 13) and Moynihan and Peterson (chapter 12) review research on the organizational and group (respectively) implications of the personality construct. Both chapters suggest that there is a role for personality across levels and both point to many of the difficulties in moving personality beyond the individual level of analysis. For instance, we have not yet explored the validity of various composition models as we transition personality from the individual to the group and organizational levels. Nonetheless, this study is another potentially fruitful avenue for future research.

We, of course, cannot leave the levels of analysis issue without noting the importance of Argyris' (see chapter 14) early contributions to jumping the level of analysis in personality thinking and research. His idea, that organizations can facilitate or inhibit the display of the usual or typical adult personality, still has not received the research attention it deserved. Most if not all researchers interested in personality in organizations still think about personality as something on which individuals differ rather than thinking about the usual or typical personality of a group of people or people in general. Unless we begin to think in terms of aggregates of people or an aggregate of people and the relationship of those people in the aggregate to the organizations in which they play out their collective work lives, we will not have made the leap to an organization-level conceptualization of human personality.

CONCLUSION

Our own research is characterized by both hopes and hypotheses, the former being the affective piece and the latter being the rational piece. In thinking about what we hoped to do with this book, we had a hypothesis that there was more going on in the realm of personality relevant to organizational behavior than met the eye. We looked through some I–O and

OB texts and reached the conclusion that if personality was relegated to its own chapter (as is true) then it would appear to students as if personality constructs are not important for understanding the broad range of issues thought to be important in understanding the behavior in and of work organizations. So, our plan was to take topics typical for study under the personality rubric and have people write about them but then to take the classic topics in OB and have authors take a personality perspective on those, too. Our hypothesis was correct—there is a lot more going on with regard to personality than one would guess by reading a textbook—and our hopes that our authors could make this fact come alive were met beyond even our wildest dreams.

Who would have thought that job satisfaction has such strong dispositional roots (Staw in chapter 7) if one read a chapter on job satisfaction in a text? And what about OCB—we know job satisfaction is important, but personality (Organ and Paine in chapter 11)? And, hey, if dispositions predict job satisfaction and job satisfaction predicts OCB, then satisfaction mediates the personality–OCB relationship? And who knew that people have characteristic modes by which they interpret the causes of events and that these, in turn, predict their behavior in specific situations? James and Rentsch (chapter 9) show us this view is true, and Spangler et al. (chapter 10) show that these characteristic modes of event interpretation also get manifested in the way leaders choose to behave.

Leadership, motivation, job satisfaction, OCB—core OB and I–O topics usually not associated with personality, and now they have been inextricably linked for us in comprehensive reviews. Our hopes have been met and we hope yours have been too.

REFERENCES

Barrick, M. R., & Ryan, A. M. (2002). *Personality and Work: Reconsidering the role of personality in organizations*. San Francisco: Jossey-Bass.

Barrick, M., Stewart, G., & Piotrowski, M. (2002). Personality and job performance: Test of the mediating effects of motivation among sales representatives. *Journal of Applied Psychology, 87*, 43–51.

Block, J. (1977). Advancing the psychology of personality: Paradigmatic shift or improving the quality of research? In D. Magnusson & N. S. Endler (Eds.), *Personality at the crossroads: Current issues in interactional psychology* (pp. 37–64). Hillsdale, NJ: Lawrence Erlbaum Associates, Inc.

Block, J. (1995). A contrarian view of the five-factor approach to personality description. *Psychological Bulletin, 117*, 187–215.

Block, J. (2001). Millenial contrarianism: The five factor approach to personality description 5 years later. *Journal of Research in Personality, 35*, 98–107.

Briggs, S. R. (1992). Assessing the five-factor model of personality description. *Journal of Personality, 60*, 253–293.

Buss, D. M., & Cantor, N. (1989). *Personality psychology: Recent trends and emerging directions.* New York: Guilford.

Cantor, N. (1990). From thought to behavior: "Having" and "Doing" in the study of personality and cognition. *American Psychologist, 45,* 735–750.

Cellar, D. F., Miller, M. L., Doverspike, D. D., & Klawsky, J. D. (1996). Comparison of factor structures and criterion-related validity coefficients of two measures of personality based on the Five Factor Model. *Journal of Applied Psychology, 81,* 694–704.

Cervone, D. (1999). Bottom-up explanation in personality psychology: The case of cross-situational coherence. In D. Cervone & Y. Shoda (Eds.), *The coherence of personality: Social-cognitive bases of consistency, variability, and organization* (pp. 303–341). New York: Guilford.

Cervone, D., & Shoda, Y. (Eds.) (1999). *The coherence of personality: Social-cognitive bases of consistency, variability, and organization.* New York: Guilford.

Costa P. T., Jr., & McCrae, R. R. (1992). *Revised NEO Personality Inventory (NEO-PI-R) and NEO Five-Factor Inventory (NEO-FFI) professional manual.* Odessa, FL: Psychological Assessment Resources.

Dweck, C. S. (1991). Self-theories and goals: Their role in motivation, personality, and development. In R. Dienstbier (Ed.), *Nebraska Symposium on Motivation* (pp. 199–235). Lincoln: University of Nebraska Press.

Emmons, R. A. (1986). Personal strivings: An approach to personality and subjective well-being. *Journal of Personality and Social Psychology, 51,* 1058–1068.

Eysenck, H. J. (1990). Genetic and environmental contributions to individual differences: The three major dimensions of personality. *Journal of Personality, 58,* 245–262.

Funder, D. (2001). Personality. *Annual Review of Psychology, 52,* 197–221.

Guion, R. M. (1998). *Assessment, measurement, and prediction for personnel decisions.* Hillsdale, NJ: Lawrence Erlbaum Associates, Inc.

Hambrick, D. C., & Finkelstein, S. (1987). Managerial discretion: A bridge between polar views.*Research in organizational behavior, 9,* 369–406.

Helson, R., & Mitchell, V. (1978). Personality. *Annual Review of Psychology, 29,* 555–586.

Hogan, R., & Hogan, J. (1999). *Manual for the Hogan Personality Inventory.* Tulsa, OK: Hogan Assessment Systems.

Holland, J. L. (1997). *Making vocational choices: A theory of vocational personalities and work environments (3rd ed.).* Odessa, FL: Psychological Assessment Resources.

Hough, L. M. (1992). The "Big Five" personality variables—construct confusion: Description versus prediction. *Human Performance, 5,* 139–155.

Huber, G. P., Sutcliffe, K. M., Miller, C. C., & Glick, W. H. (1993). Understanding and predicting organizational change. In G. P. Huber & W. H. Glick (Eds.), *Organizational change and redesign: Ideas and insights for improving performance.* New York: Oxford University Press.

James, L. R. (1998). Measurement of personality via conditional reasoning. *Organizational Research Methods, 1,* 131–163.

James, L. R., & Mazzerole, M. D. (2002). *Personality in work organizations.* Thousand Oaks, CA: Sage.

John, O. P. (1989). Toward a taxonomy of personality descriptors. In D. M. Buss and N. Cantor (Eds.), *Personality psychology: Recent trends and emerging directions* (pp. 66–100). New York: Guilford.

Kilduff, M., & Day, D. (1994). Do chameleons get ahead? The effects of self-monitoring on managerial careers. *Academy of Management Journal, 37,* 1047–1060.

Kozlowski, S. W. J., & Klein, K. J. (2000). A multilevel approach to theory and research in organizations: Contextual, temporal, and emergent processes. In K. J. Klein & S. W. J. Kozlowski (Eds.), *Multilevel theory, research, and methods in organizations: Foundations, extensions, and new directions* (pp. 3–90). San Francisco: Jossey-Bass.

McAdams, D. P. (1992). The five-factor model of personality: A critical appraisal. *Journal of Personality, 60,* 329–361.

Mischel, W. (1977). The interaction of person and situation. In D. Magnusson & N. S. Endler (Eds.), *Personality at the crossroads: Current issues in interactional psychology* (pp. 333–352). Hillsdale, NJ: Lawrence Erlbaum Associates, Inc.

Mischel, W. (1999). Personality coherence and dispositions in a cognitive-affective personality system (CAPS) approach. In D. Cervone & Y. Shoda (Eds.), *The coherence of personality: Social-cognitive bases of consistency, variability, and organization* (pp. 37–60). New York: Guilford.

Moon, H. (2001). The two faces of conscientiousness: Duty and achievement striving in escalation of commitment dilemmas. *Journal of Applied Psychology, 86,* 533–540.

Murtha, T., Kanfer, R., & Ackerman, P. (1996). Toward an interactionist taxonomy of personality and situations: An integrative situation-dispositional representation of personality traits. *Journal of Personality and Social Psychology, 71,* 913–207.

O'Reilly, C. A., Chatman, J., & Caldwell, D. F. (1991). People and organizational culture: A profile comparison approach to assessing person-organization fit. *Academy of Management Journal, 34,* 487–516.

Palys, T. S., & Little, B. R. (1983). Perceived life satisfaction and the organization of personal project systems. *Journal of Personality and Social Psychology, 44,* 1221–1230.

Paunonen, S., & Ashton, M. C. (2001). Big five factors and facets and the prediction of behavior. *Journal of Personality and Social Psychology, 81,* 524–539.

Paunonen, S. V., & Jackson, D. N. (2000). What is beyond the Big Five? Plenty! *Journal of Personality, 68,* 821–835.

Porter, M. E. (1980). *Competitive strategy: Techniques for analyzing industries and competitors.* New York: Free Press.

Saucier, G., & Goldberg, L. R. (1998). What is beyond the Big Five? *Journal of Personality, 66,* 495–524.

Schneider, B. (1996). Whither goest personality at work? *Applied Psychology: An International Review, 45,* 289–296.

Schein, E. (1992). *Organizational Culture and Leadership.* (2nd edition). San Francisco, CA: Jossey-Bass.

Snyder, M. (1987). *Public appearances, private realities: The psychology of self-monitoring.* New York: Freeman.

Tushman, M. L., & Romanelli, E. (1985). Organizational evolution: A metamorphosis model of convergence and reorientation. *Research in organizational behavior, 7,* 171–222.

Wiggins, J. S. (1992). Have model, will travel. *Journal of Personality, 60,* 527–532.

Wiggins, J. S. (Ed.) (1996). *The Five-Factor Model of personality: Theoretical perspectives.* New York: Guilford.

Author Index

Subject Index

V

W